Birding in the Northern Plains:

The Ornithological Writings of Herbert Krause

SONG TOMORROW

Before I thought to let the hazel bushes
Latch the woods behind me, I heard him,
Shuttered in a thorny plum-twist hedge:
A pertling robin not long graduated
From pinfeathers and gray down, piping
A raspy note or so of something April
Would remember in the breathing dusk.

He gave up trying for the afternoon;
No sense in learning all of it today:
Let something be to whet to-morrow's edge.

Herbert Krause, *Neighbor Boy, 1939*

Birding in the Northern Plains:

The Ornithological Writings of Herbert Krause

Edited by Ronald R. Nelson

THE CENTER FOR WESTERN STUDIES
AUGUSTANA COLLEGE   2008

Publication made possible by gifts from Ronald R. Nelson, L.M. Baylor, and Mark S. Anderson.

THE CENTER FOR WESTERN STUDIES
The Center for Western Studies (CWS) is an educational agency of Augustana College concerned principally with collecting, preserving, and interpreting prehistoric, historic, and contemporary materials that document native and immigrant cultures of the northern plains. The Center promotes understanding of the region through its archives, library, exhibits, publications, art shows, conferences, and forums. It is committed, ultimately, to defining the contribution of the northern plains to American civilization. Visit the Fantle Building for the Center for Western Studies, Augustana College, 2121 S. Summit Avenue, Sioux Falls, South Dakota, or contact CWS at 605-274-4007 / 605-274-4999 (fax) / cws@augie.edu / www.augie.edu/cws.

First Edition, First Printing

ISBN: 978-0-931170-87-4

LCCN: 2008932817

Number 12 in the Prairie Plains Series

Printed in the United States of America by
Pine Hill Press, Sioux Falls, South Dakota

TABLE OF CONTENTS

SECTION VI WRITINGS FOR THE SOUTH DAKOTA ORNITHOLOGISTS' UNION

Northern Cardinal

PUBLISHER'S FOREWORD

This publication of Herbert Krause's ornithological writings brings together for the first time a body of prose that spans a quarter of a century in the life of one of America's foremost Western writers. Professor Krause's contributions to our understanding and appreciation of the rich cultures of the Northern Plains began with his publication in 1939 of the tragic novel *Wind Without Rain*, the story of German immigrant life in western Minnesota at the turn of the century. It won the $1,000 Friends of American Writers Award that winter and by mid-March was listed as a best seller by both the *New York Herald Tribune* and the *Chicago Daily News*. In the thirty-seven years that followed, Krause published two more novels about the western frontier, a book of poetry called *Neighbor Boy*, and a remarkable array of essays, plays, lectures, ornithological studies, and—in the last years of his life—a co-edited collection of newspaper articles about Col. George Armstrong Custer's incursion into the Black Hills of South Dakota in 1874.

In all of his writing, Krause had as his home base the English Department at Augustana College, Sioux Falls, South Dakota, which he served first as chairman beginning in 1938 and then later as writer-in-residence. With the encouragement of faculty friends and a mandate from the Board of Regents, in 1970 he founded the Center for Western Studies as a division of the college and thus gave organizational shape to his belief that the American West should engage the college as a region rich in resources for study, and that in turn the college can serve the Northern Plains region, with its diverse populations, by encouraging students, scholars, and researchers of every discipline to seek to improve the quality of life for Americans here and elsewhere.

Following the publication of *Wind Without Rain*, Krause began research on yet another novel about the Germans of western Minnesota, in the region around Fergus Falls that he had come to call "Pockerbrush," a term describing the hilly land of timber and tangled brush that made up his home territory. The result after seven years of research, and despite a heavy teaching load, was *The Thresher* (1946), set in that period of transition on the American frontier when high-speed farm machinery, powered by steam and gasoline, rapidly replaced the horse- and oxen-powered equipment that had been the farmer's mainstay for centuries. This second novel was an even more critical and popular success, with critics comparing Krause to Hamlin Garland and Ole Rölvaag as an interpreter of life on the farming frontier.

Another long interval followed the appearance of *The Thresher*, while Krause read widely in the literature about western Minnesota, the Red River Valley of the North, and the trade in furs and manufactured goods that traveled the trail leading north and south, from the Upper Mississippi River at Minneapolis and on into Canada. The result was *The Oxcart Trail* (1954), his last novel, rich in the details of the frontier life of that era.

From his earliest days as a child in Pockerbrush, Krause had wanted to be a writer, or a teacher. After ten years of rural school, he labored for another five years at farming and construction work in order to continue his education. He enrolled in Park Region Lutheran Academy and College in nearby Fergus Falls. There and for three more years at St. Olaf College he wrote poetry, drama, and the first pages of the novel that would become *Wind Without Rain*. The drama that he completed at St. Olaf, *Bondsmen to the Hills*, turned out to be a prize winner, taking second place in playwriting two years later at the Midwest Folk Drama Tournament in Cape Girardeau, Missouri, on April 4, 1936. The previous spring he had earned an M.A. degree at Iowa with a collection of verse called *Pockerbrush*, and that summer he won a scholarship to the Bread Loaf School of English in Middlebury, Vermont. There he met the poet Robert Frost and other well-known writers—Dorothy Canfield Fisher, Theodore Morrison, and Stephen Vincent Benét—all of them supportive of his writing.

Through the next two years Krause studied for his doctorate, taught freshman composition, and in his spare time labored at *Wind Without Rain*, which Benét was to call "the work of a man who is going to be one of our essential writers." In the fall of 1938 there occurred a succession of events that were to change Krause's life forever. His first novel was accepted by Bobbs-Merrill for publication, he began his teaching career at Augustana College, and he was invited by President Clemens Granskou "to establish a division of creative writing by which means…young men and women of this region will be encouraged to preserve the history of their forefathers." That challenge was the start of a center for western studies, a challenge and a dream for Krause that would not be realized in full until 1970 and the creation by the Regents of Augustana College of the Center for Western Studies, a research agency whose mission would be to "preserve and interpret the history and cultures of the Northern Plains."

During his years at Augustana College, Krause earned a reputation as a brilliant lecturer, a scholar in history as well as in literature, and of course as an ornithologist. He wrote two short stories in the 1940s, wrote reviews, essays, and lectures throughout his career, the Minnesota Statehood Poem in 1958, and in 1960 completed a full-length pageant called *Crazy Horse*, about the Lakota warrior and nemesis of Custer. Produced only once, and then in an abbreviated form, the pageant remains unperformed, waiting, perhaps, for the right occasion to be produced in full.

The two crowning achievements of Krause's career were, of course, the creation of a center for western studies and a body of ornithological writing that is impressive. Krause had pursued both interests from his early years at the college until his last. His interest in birds was life-long, and his three novels are replete with bird-lore and natural history. His serious pursuit of the study of birds, however, can be traced to a course in ornithology that he engaged in in the winter of 1945. Writing from Fergus Falls to his landlady, Mrs. Henry Hahn, on June 21, 1945, he said: "Birds, birds, birds and a few fish. But Birds mostly. I never dreamed we had so many varieties in Pockerbrush. Am I glad now that we held a kind of course in ornithology this last winter. The information from talks and observation and reading is coming in mighty handy." It was a study that he pursued with increasing emphasis for the next thirty years. The present work brings together the fruit of his endeavors.

In 1970 Krause met Ronald R. Nelson, a history professor at Western Carolina University and a native South Dakotan. The two men became fast "birding" friends and after Krause's death in 1976, and when the Center determined to publish Krause's ornithological writings, Nelson appeared to this publisher to be the ideal editor. Born in 1941 on a farm near Sioux Falls and growing up with a love of nature, Nelson developed an early interest in bird watching upon reading Roger Tory Peterson's *Field Guide to the Birds*. This avocation continued through many continents. Although most of Nelson's adult life has passed outside the United States, his ties to Sioux Falls remain strong. He is a member of the National Advisory Council of the Center for Western Studies, a Trustee of the Foundation of the University of South Dakota, and a member of the South Dakota Nature Conservancy.

Dr. Nelson holds a B.A. from the University of South Dakota and an M.A. and Ph.D. from Duke University. After service in Vietnam, he taught history at Western Carolina University from 1969-1973. After additional years in the U.S. Army, he served on the staff of the Senate Foreign Relations Committee, and in the Departments of State and Defense in various positions in the field of arms control and disarmament. During his tenure as the Representative of the Secretary of Defense to the Conference on Disarmament, he participated in negotiating the Chemical Weapons Convention. Since 1993, he has spent most of the ensuing years as a staff member of the Organisation for the Prohibition of Chemical Weapons in The Hague, the Netherlands. He is currently Director of Administration.

– Arthur R. Huseboe

INTRODUCTION

Herbert Krause as Ornithologist

The title of this introduction "Herbert Krause as Ornithologist" I chose deliberately, as Herb *was* an ornithologist, even if not a scientist. I am a bird watcher, indeed for forty-five years, but I am not an ornithologist. Perhaps for that reason, I feel compelled to take these few pages to express my admiration for the self-discipline of someone who at about age 40 turned from writing novels and, except rarely, poems and began studies that made him a respected ornithologist, as well as a historian. Of course, throughout his life, Herb was foremost a teacher whether of literature or ornithology. Numbers of his students whom I have met described him as the best of this profession.

I first met Herb on August 26, 1970, through the good offices of Wesley Halbritter, who introduced us—certain that our mutual interest in bird watching would prove beneficial. It did indeed. My diary records that "Wes, his wife, Bev, Herb and I dined in Canton on "a disappointingly dry meal of pheasant. The conversation more than compensated. We stayed nearly three hours. Krause has a fascinating, active, inquiring mind." These characteristics also made him a good ornithologist, a careful observer, an inquiring one and a faithful recorder.

During many subsequent birding forays, I learned much from him. His skills were greatly superior to mine, but he patiently encouraged me by emphasizing the importance of identifying birds by field characteristics. I hope Herb derived some benefit from our friendship. At least I was driving the automobile when we both added a new bird to our life lists, the King Rail, at Grass Lake on August 21, 1971. Although not living in South Dakota, I returned frequently and invariably went with Herb on birding expeditions from 1970 to mid 1974, when the Army assigned me to duty in Germany. Usually just the two of us went but sometimes I was fortunate enough to join Herb and Gil Blankespoor, Augustana College's ornithologist, on one of their regular excursions.

Herb had keen vision and keen hearing. On a delightful trip on June 2, 1972, I drove on gravel roads all the way from Sioux Falls to Mobridge, where the South Dakota Ornithologists' Union was holdings its annual meeting that weekend. I recall the astonishment of several of us in the Mobridge area the following day when Herb spotted at a remarkable distance on the crown of a hill the head of a hawk, and correctly identified it as a Ferruginous Hawk. Shortly it flew to allow the near-blind amongst us to identify it with certainty. In his tribute to Krause in the March 1977 issue of *Bird Notes*, L.M. Baylor points out that "In Dr. Pettingill's 35 summers of teaching at the University of Michigan, Herb distinguished himself as one of the very few students among 850 to identify all bird songs during field quizzes."

I last saw him in April, 1976, when I returned on leave from Germany. Not long thereafter a stroke permanently incapacitated him. He died the last day of summer. It is with gratitude for his friendship that I offer this token of my regard—his collected writings on ornithology.

In August 2003, I began collecting Herb's works on ornithology, or bird watching. These extended from 1947 until his final contribution in 1973. I excluded from this effort references to birds in his novels and poems. I also did not include articles written by others, which included mention of Herb's participation in a bird-watching foray.

I'm grateful to a number of people for assistance in this project. Art Huseboe, Dean Schueler, and Harry Thompson all encouraged me. Art was generous in providing me his time and advice and most definitely the typescript by Raymond Dunmire with annotations of the bibliography of all Herb's works. Without this, the journey would have been far more difficult. Harry was most generous with time and patience during my completing the process early in 2006 in the Netherlands. He must have dreaded my emails, asking to double check references. I'm grateful to both of them. I must also mention Professor Les Baylor, whose tribute to Herb in the March 1977 *South Dakota Bird Notes* is a literary gem that I will not attempt to emulate. I have however drawn upon it for various observations that I am making here.

In short, then, my effort was a modest one—to collect the works, edit them where required, and make them available in a single document to the Center for Western Studies. Through the wonders of modern technology, the electronic files rest with lots of spare room on a memory stick, smaller than the end of one's thumb.

One can divide Herb's works on ornithology into seven broad categories:

1. Three historical works on ornithology in the Great Plains
2. Early writings: *Fergus Falls* [Minnesota] *Daily Journal*
3. Works written with or for Olin Sewell Pettingill, Jr.
4. Major works on individual species or area surveys
5. Book reviews
6. South Dakota Ornithologists' Union
7. Appendix. Editor of the Northern Great Plains region for *Audubon Field Notes*

Historical works on ornithology

In 1956, Herb published a five-page essay on "Ornithology in South Dakota Before Audubon." He traces the scant literature on this subject from 1794, when J.B. Truteau, a French fur trader, began a journal in the vicinity of where Fort Randall dam now sits. His observations were few—mostly about turkeys. Another French-Canadian, Pierre-Antoine Tabeau, began in 1803. Herb reminds the reader that Lewis and Clark entered South Dakota August 21, 1804. The journals of the two captains, from that time through their return trip across

South Dakota in August 1806, have added much to our understanding of bird life in the area. Herb mines the writings of another fur trader, John Luttig (1812); of Paul Wilhelm of Wuerteemberg (1823) and of Prince Maximilian of Wied (1833-1834) to rescue from obscurity the little that we know of bird life in South Dakota in the early 19th century.

Later that year he followed up his article on ornithology before Audubon with an account of the "Ornithology of the Major Long Expedition, 1823." He also wrote a companion piece on the mammals recorded by this expedition. Major Stephen H. Long (1784-1864) led an expedition in 1823 to explore the source of the Minnesota River and the boundary between the United States and Canada. Krause's careful reading of the existing records credited the men with identifying fifty-three species. Of these, he points out that one species is extinct–the passenger pigeon–and four no longer nest there: the sandhill crane, trumpeter swan, swallow-tailed kite, and whooping crane. He concludes that "True, with our indifference toward our natural resources, our calloused attitude toward the reduction in number of our wildlife, our ignorance of basic factors in wildlife, we have done a lot of damage in 130-odd years. The miracle is that we haven't done more damage. In this respect, the ornithology of the Long Expedition, meager as it is, is nevertheless a reminder of what we had and what we have lost."

In 1962, Herb produced a fifteen-page essay on "The Ornithology of the Great Plains." It begins with a geographical description of the region that extends from Texas to Canada, to include western sections of Oklahoma, Kansas, most of Nebraska, half of South Dakota, a small part of North Dakota, eastern New Mexico, Colorado, Wyoming and Montana; the eastern-most part of the Great Plains are the Great Prairies, which slant toward the Mississippi River. He then describes the vegetation that preceded the introduction of wide-spread agriculture. He recounts, on the basis of journals and descriptions of the early 19th century, the staggering abundance of wildlife.

In one sense, it is painful to read. Indeed, the second half of the essay catalogues the lost and depleted species:

Such was the optimistic situation historically; such was the rosy picture in the immediate past of our Great Plains record. What it is today is only too tragically well-known. It probably serves little purpose to mourn over the errors of the past. What is tragic is that man seems to learn so beggarly little from the experiences of the past. Only in the slow accretion of trial and error does one see an attempt to correct the faults of antecedent generations. Then it is usually late if not too late to benefit man or the object of his mistakes; then it is only because man himself feels the constricting consequence of his own stupidity. As he draws to a close, however, he sees the potential for hope:

However, if our words are sincere, if we really want to save what still remains, then it now behooves us to study the Great Plains, to become familiar with the habitat of the terrain and better acquainted with its avian inhabitants.

The final choice, however, lies with the people of the Great Plains and of South Dakota. Theirs is the choice. They can preserve what habitat remains; they can enlarge that habitat wherever it is possible. They can inform themselves and educate their neighbors. They can insist that official opinion be based on enlightened leadership and work in harmony with state and local conservation groups. They can do this, or they can watch the disappearance of species after species of bird and mammal as now they are watching the decline of the Whooping Crane, the Masked Quail in New Mexico, the Atwater's Prairie Chicken in Texas. All are being extirpated because their habitat is being changed.

In the final two lines, he reflects that "the Ornithology of the Great Plains once amazed the world. Today the ornithology of the Great Plains amazes few indeed. Tomorrow the ornithology of the Great Plains will amaze—whom?"

Herb received a grant in 1957 from the American Association for the Advancement of Science, and collected a great deal of material for an annotated bibliography of South Dakota ornithology 1794-1954, but it was never published. To date, I was unable to determine why.

Early Writings: *Fergus Falls Daily Journal*

"Sometime in the spring of 1945," writes Arthur Huseboe in *Herbert Krause Poems and Essays* (1990), "Herb developed a passion for ornithology that would later rule his life." Herb wrote four articles for the newspaper near the place where he was born in 1905. These appeared in the fall of 1947. The originals have no distinct titles, but Art Huseboe devised four perfect ones. "Brushpile Days" describes the fall migration of sparrows that "best of all, however, ... seem to like a pile of limbs and branches that someone has thrown together and forgotten. In these piles of twisted bareness they appear and disappear..." (p. 188).

The second, "The Peevish Bird Watcher," captures the bird watcher's frustration at identifying the fall warblers, which have cast off their distinct spring uniforms for camouflage ones: "But when he comes to the warbler, he is tempted to lug a gun along and bring them to a standstill" (p. 190).

The third, "Mighty Hunters Are Still Seen on the Ottertail," is by far the most amusing and biting—three young men with guns who have dispatched a luckless bird: "With a true hunter's flourish he held the quarry up—four and a half inches of sparrow, feather-ruffled and limp" (p. 193). By the way, Herb once told me that as a boy he had shot a rabbit that cried out piteously. That was his final experience as a hunter.

The last, "Don't Laugh at the Bird Watcher": "Up in Friberg last year in an Easter snowstorm that howled about my ears, I watched horned larks walking...about a neighbor's cornshocks until my hands were too numb to hold the glasses and my breath first fogged and then frosted the lenses and I had to give up. (Don't laugh at the bird watcher. He is no crazier than the duck hunter dripping in his blind or a deer hunter freezing while he's posting.)" (p. 194).

Works with Pettingill

One of the most distinguished of America's ornithologists, Olin Sewall Pettingill, Jr., (1907-2001) wrote in his 1965 publication *The Bird Watcher's America* this about Herb:

> Birds were common about his home on the bank of the Otter Tail River. He watched Purple Martins carrying green leaves to their nests and wondered why; he crawled stomach-fashion up a hillside to see a Ruffed Grouse drumming and was fascinated; but his slight interest was undirected and undeveloped. He only knew he wanted to write.
>
> In 1946, with borrowed binoculars, the Cornell Laboratory of Ornithology record, "American Bird Songs," and the suggestions of helpful friends, "birds and bird songs came together in exciting meaningfulness." He wanted to write about birds and realized that in order to do so he must know about birds—comprehensively and accurately. Since his education had included no formal work in biology, he spent one of the hottest summers on record at the University of Minnesota grinding away at a course in zoology. After this came two summers studying ornithology at the University of Michigan biological Station. It was there that I became closely acquainted with him. No student that I have ever had was more determined to absorb so much information and to pass every available moment in the field learning more about birds. For having spent a total of 207 hours in a blind watching the nesting habits of a pair of Canada Warblers, he has my greatest admiration (pp. 143-44).

Although Herb's friendship with Pettingill dated from 1957, Herb had contributed a description of places to watch birds in the Sioux Falls area for the 1953 publication *A Guide to Bird Finding West of the Mississippi*. Fifteen years later, Herb bemoaned the growth of Sioux Falls westward, as it eliminated some of these natural areas. Although he would now be horrified, one can happily report that some, such as Grass Lake and Wall Lake, remain.

Two essays appeared in Pettingill's *The Bird Watcher's America*. The first article sings the praises of "The Black Hills of South Dakota": "It is a mountain upthrust, a pine-covered island outpost in a sea of rolling grass." Krause emphasizes its uniqueness, blending not only mountain and prairie, but also the ranges of birds normally confined either east or west of the 100th meridian. Three sentences from different parts of the article reveal his writing style: "What brought me shock-still, listening, however, was a house wren in front of me, filling a thicket with domestic chatter while above me on the crag a rock wren bounced its wild *cher-wee, cher-wee* along the ledge rim. I have never forgotten that moment: two birds, as it were, voicing the dramatic difference between two ecological areas...." "My first violet-green swallow appeared in Deadwood, perched on a wire no more than a block from No. 10 Saloon where Wild Bill Hickok was pistoled to death...." "A drive through Spearfish Canyon is to see geology rolled out on the tapestries of cliffs." He ends his seven-page article by concluding that from Harney's peak "neither time nor change can quite dim the bright hue of adventure."

In the second piece, "Geese Along the Missouri," Herb begins: "From the edge of sleep I heard them—the call of the wild geese in the hour before midnight, bringing me to a sudden wakefulness." In a few sentences he describes the journey of the geese from the Gulf coast to Baffin Island. "But now comes a day in late February or early March when the gabble and the outcry sharpen, when restlessness apparently becomes an insistent prod." He writes that "such wheeling legions must be seen to be believed." This publication was meant both for the bird watcher and the general reader. One supposes that some of the latter became members of the former after reading this excellent prose. Reading this reminded me of one of my many fond memories of a trip with Herb–at Lake Thompson, near Brookings, on April 5, 1973. In my diary I wrote, "We saw magnificent lines of geese—perhaps 80,000—Snows, Blues, Canadas, and White-fronts. They had been resting and were rising in flocks of thousands, probably to resume migration."

Herb wrote a third piece as a guest contributor for Pettingill's column in *Audubon Magazine* in March-April, 1966. "Trailing Lewis and Clark" is also a masterly blending of birding, geography, and history, describing Route 50 from Elk Point to Chamberlain: "...the chapel of old Fort Randall reminds the birder of vespers held in the wilderness when the Sioux and Poncas lifted their battle cries. Today, barn swallows sweep through the ruins of the empty arches...." "Where Army bugles rang on the parade grounds 100 years ago, black-billed magpies lift the black and white of their wing patterns in flight."

His final work with Pettingill was *Seminars in Ornithology: A Home Study Course in Bird Biology*, published by the Laboratory of Ornithology at Cornell University in 1972. Unfortunately it is impossible to determine from the book what Herb contributed.

Major Works on Ornithology

Herb's first major work was with Sven G. Froiland in 1955, "Distribution of the Cardinal in South Dakota," in which they drew upon existing literature in the field to describe (with maps) the slow expansion northward of this species. Herb always took his work seriously. His novels, historical in genre, required meticulous research. Extending this to the field of ornithology was natural. Few if any reports about the cardinal escaped his search.

His first publication, based on his personal observation, was "Nesting of a Pair of Canada Warblers," researched from June 23–July 1, 1957, but published in *The Living Bird* in 1965. Like his other works, this combines meticulous attention to detail with literary excellence. "One moment she [the female Canada Warbler] was perched, motionless as the wood on which she sat. The next instant she was a bundle of restless activity, dashing up a branch to snatch something from a leaf or grab up an insect from a bud scar. Sometimes she tore a worm from the bark and, if it was wriggly, slammed it against the side of a limb" (p. 7). It was this publication that Pettingill praised.

During the summer of 1957 Herb prepared a report for Pettingill's course in advanced ornithology, "A Census of Breeding Bird Populations in an Aspen Plot," at the University of Michigan's Biological Station. His comments could be biting. He was using the accepted guide to birding census, May Thacher Cooke's 1927 "The Purposes of Bird Censuses and How to Take Them." Herb confessed that he had "serious misgivings about the accuracy or the validity of the figures in my compilation." He agreed with Cooke that these censuses provided useful information on breeding bird populations:

> But I am left helpless with wonder at the confident way Cooke (1927:1) defines a census of breeding birds. "A census of breeding birds means an exact and complete enumeration of the birds that actually nest within the boundaries of a selected tract of land." Her definition is precise but how precise is her application?
>
> True, she describes the mechanics of the process adequately. But I look in vain for methods to achieve exactitude and completeness. How can one be "exact and complete?" I remember the bird that darted away in the underbrush, only a dark form visible to the eye. And I recall a bird in a leafy treetop which inconsiderately permitted me no more than a glimpse of it. I have no doubt my crashing footsteps in the underbrush have sent more than one bird fluttering through the bracken ahead of me without a *chin* to indicate its presence or a moving fern leaf to announce its departure. After my experience with a pair of Canada Warblers, I have some familiarity with avian elusiveness.
>
> Miss Cooke writes (1927:2), "Count the singing males very early in the morning" and with charming intrepidity continues, "At this time every male bird is usually in full song near the nest site." But suppose he isn't? May not wind velocity and weather conditions be limiting factors? And what about a male that is uncooperative enough to sing his heart out on every other day but the one on which you happen to stumble through the deadfalls of the area? And how about the unattached male which, with small consideration for propriety or population indices, will come into a study plot and sing, sans mate and sans nest?
>
> And those transients which stop long enough to deliver an aria but have set up domestic facilities elsewhere? How can one determine by song alone, except in obvious instances, which is a citizen and which a foreigner of the area? Miss Cooke is very firm about this. Birds that merely visit are to be cast out of the count, "no matter how close to

the line their nests may be." But how can one determine by song alone, except perhaps in obvious instances, which is a citizen and which a foreigner? And how about the unattached male, the avian wolf, which with small consideration for propriety or population indices, will come into study plot and sing (pages 2-3)?

In 1968, the final volume in the *Life Histories of North American Birds*, edited by Arthur Cleveland Bent, contained Herb's chapter on the McCown's Longspur. He had expected to write the one on the Chestnut-collared Longspur, a bird with which he was quite familiar. Despite having seen the McCown's Longspur only once, he doggedly reviewed the range of literature on this species, now much reduced in numbers due to the spread of agriculture. In sixty-two pages he recounted the habits, spring, territory, courtship, nesting, eggs, incubation, plumages, food, behavior, voice, field marks, enemies, fall, winter, distribution, and literature cited. Although based only marginally on personal observation, this work was doubtless his most important. As Les Baylor pointed out in his tribute, Herb's own description of the birds in a 1958 April snow squall "exemplifies the facility with descriptive language that Herb carried into his scientific writing from his skills as a poet, novelist, and dramatist. His fortunate writing style added reading flavor not often found in the technical communications of science, but at the same time Herb avoided the pitfall of blatant anthropomorphism in science and maintained the scientist's dedication to objectivity."

In 1963 or 1964, Herb prepared a compilation of the" Nesting Sites of the Bird of the Audubon Center of Greenwich, Connecticut." Although the compilation is simply a brief description species by species of typical nesting sites, the introduction is sage:

> Why a bird selects a certain shrub or a particular branch for its nesting site is probably governed by psychological and physical requirements no more mysterious than those which guide the human being in the amazing choice of some of his dwelling places. The motivation, both avian and human, is obscure: which should encourage the bird student to observe carefully, to record accurately, and to try to understand objectively every instance of avian behavior or activity which comes to his notice. Human behavior too might profit from such scrutiny. Puzzling bits and pieces put together often make something like a comprehensible whole.

In 1964 Herb spoke to an environmental group on the decline of the Bald Eagle in the United States. It was a clear warning about the dangers of pesticides, a subject that greatly troubled him, and one that he highlighted while president of the South Dakota Ornithologists' Union. Herb originally intended to write a book on the subject, but wide-spread legislation limiting pesticides followed the 1962 publication of Rachel Carson's *Silent Spring*. He then set aside the project on the Bald Eagle.

Book Reviews

Herb wrote three book reviews in 1954, 1965, and 1966. The first briefly reviews Chester Reed's *Bird Guide: Land Birds East of the Rockies* (1951). "While the new edition is fresh and crisp in make-up, I wish the plates had the sharp clarity of the earlier editions. The illustrations on the glazed paper of the tattered, dog-eared copy of the 1915 issue before me have a sharpness of color and detail which the present edition lacks on its unglazed pages." "Nevertheless, this is, as always, a handy little pocket book on any field trip."

His review of Helen Cruickshank's *Thoreau on Birds* (1964) manages in less than two pages to recall the errors of the earlier critics of Thoreau's scientific writings, provide a correction that restores Thoreau's reputation in this area, and review Mrs. Cruickshank's book: "Pretty close to being the definitive of Thoreau's observations on birds." "It is a pity to mention typographical errors, those skulkers in the blindspots of the proofreader's eye...."

The final review is of Kenneth Allsop's popular *Adventure Lit Their Star* (1964 reprint of 1939 edition). This book tells of the successful nesting over years of the Little Ringed Plover in Great Britain. The reviewer commends Allsop for his objectivity, and only gently raps him on the knuckles when he drifts into anthropomorphism (of which there is no trace in Herb's writings on ornithology).

One regrets that Herb did not review more books.

South Dakota Ornithologists' Union (SDOU)

Herb was amongst the charter members of the South Dakota Ornithologists' Union, founded in 1949. In respect to SDOU, Herb made a major and lasting contribution. His account of the life of Herman F. Chapman (1888-1974), one of the founders of the Union, records Chapman's contributions. Herb spent many hours bird watching with Herman and his wife Lois (1884-1978). In his dedication to "The McCown's Longspur," Herb credits them with introducing him to the art of recognizing identification marks in the field. "Even without a Union, however, Chapman's enthusiasm for South Dakota birds would have been an inspiring stimulation to state bird study. There are scores of individuals, eager bird observers now, who will testify that the Chapmans first aroused their interest by showing them how much fun birding really is—how much of sky and season-changing hillside, of stream and prairie out-of-doors there is in birding beside the excitement of identifying a new bird or discovering unexpected facts about an old." "This writer is one of them, gratefully acknowledging his debt to the persuasive encouragement" (p. 63). One could also say the same for Herbert Krause.

During his two terms as president of the South Dakota Ornithologists' Union (1957-1958, 1964-1965), he wrote eight "President's Pages." In these he stressed the importance of habitat and the dangers to it. He underscored the importance of accurate data: "SDOU was founded eight years ago on the firm idea that the gathering and dissemination of information about state birds was an important contribution not only to the natural history of South Dakota but also to the conservation of natural resources of the state" (June 1957). The theme of two president's pages (September and December 1957) was the importance of the annotated checklist of birds of South Dakota. It is a tribute to the efforts of those who were instrumental in producing the checklist that its third edition is now available in a handsome volume. His final president's page for his first term (March 1958) reiterates the importance of data, but accurate data and proposes means of verifying it.

During his second term, Herb urged all SDOUers "to talk about wildlife and its dire predicament, discuss its problems, write to the officials. Above all, express your feelings" (June 1964). He excoriated the destruction of much of the natural habitat on Farm Island southeast of Pierre (September 1964). "Can the economic advantages said to be derived from the destruction of these historical and ecological resources be justified?" The question remains as timely today as then. The final two presidential pages (December 1964 and March 1965) sounded the alarm about the dangers of pesticides.

In addition to serving twice as president, he served as a director from 1955 until his death, except for 1969 when he was in the Philippines. Herb prepared the index to the first five volumes of *South Dakota Bird Notes*. He contributed more than 50 articles to the publication from 1949 to 1960 (and one in 1973). *The Birds of South Dakota* still cites some of Herb's observations that remain of scientific interest.

Herb wrote 34 articles of varying length on 28 separate species, on five migrations, and one on "defensive flocking" of small birds as protection against a hawk. He reported sightings of many other species, particularly in the articles on migration. Of these articles 20 pertained to Sioux Falls. He regularly went on foot to Woodlawn Cemetery, which then, he told me, had far more bushes and other under story than is now the case. It is fitting that Woodlawn became his final resting place.

Except for two articles on species seen in the Black Hills and his final report from Fort Randall, the remaining twelve are sightings in eastern South Dakota, usually Minnehaha County. Except for the briefest accounts, most exemplify Herb's attention to detail, to the field marks that are diagnostic in identifying birds. He usually found fellow birders to corroborate the sightings of birds that are rare to the area, for example, the Sanderling at Grass Lake in September 1956. Both he and Augustana biology professor Willard Rosine (1926-1973) saw that "the plumage of the birds was in sharp contrast to the dark [muddy] shore. The pure white of the underparts, the white stripe in the wings and the mottled white of the upper parts were distinctively clear, set off against the yellowish water."

The discovery of a yellow-throated warbler in Sioux Falls on April 23, 1960, inspired a three-page report. He recounts that he summoned three of his colleagues from Augustana to bear witness: "When we arrived at the pine grove I had three Ph.D's but no bird. There wasn't a sound. Nothing. Any bird observer knows how these things go. Ten minutes of red-faced listening and looking—not a feather." Fortunately for Herb, the bird took pity, materialized and saved his reputation.*

In the cases of rare or uncommon birds, Herb frequently consulted the historical literature on the species in South Dakota, and summarized the records. He was both an active birder and a thorough researcher.

Many of these 34 articles contain a sentence or more that charms the eye and ear. Les Baylor has cited some, including this one, the September 24, 1955, account of the winter wren, of which there had been no recorded sightings since 1908 in Minnehaha County:

> The midget-size (smaller than a House Wren), the brownish back and dark brown bars on the belly, the whitish line over the eye, and many small flecks of white on the throat and breast, the stubby tail held at a pert, ridiculous upright angle–all indicated this species. It bobbed its whole body rather than its head only, appearing to bend at the knees like a Dipper. While we watched, it darted in and out of sight among the rocks and debris, moving with astonishing rapidity. We saw it pull what looked like insect larvae from the rocks and swallow them. It had a way of leaping suddenly, jack-in-the-box like, into sight and of disappearing abruptly. About every 30 seconds it popped up and surveyed us, bobbing and crying 'Kip-kip, kip-kip' with a metallic quality. Finally it hopped from rock to root and vanished.

For much of 1961 to 1969, Herb lived mostly outside the United States, particularly in South Africa and the Philippines. His interest in birds continued abroad. He told me of his purchasing captured rails at the market in the Philippines and then having someone drive him to the rice fields where he released them. He added 470 birds to his South African life list (O.S. Pettingil, *The Bird Watcher's America.* 1965, p. 144).

Upon returning to the United States, his interest in birding continued unabated. In 1982, Gil Blankespoor, citing Herb as co-author, published "Breeding Birds of Minnehaha County" in *American Birds,* vol. XXXVI (1) January 1982, pp. 22-27. The article describes the nearly weekly trips May through August 1971-1975 that provided data on breeding birds. Herb's handwritten notes on other bird sightings also provided valuable data.

Fortunately for us, Herb has not, like the winter wren, vanished. Those of us fortunate to have known him will recall him as a special person for the rest of our days. His writings are for posterity. The Center for Western Studies is a fitting memorial.

—————

*This amusing story was featured by Jim Johnson, "Bird Talk: Bird Watcher's Stories Will Outlast the Years," *Public Opinion* [Watertown, South Dakota], February 2, 1958.

– Ronald R. Nelson

SECTION I

THE LAND

CHAPTER 1

The Ornithology of the Great Plains, with Special Reference to South Dakota

One does not have to read far in trans-Mississippi literature to realize how important the Great Plains are, not only ornithologically but geographically and topographically.

Geographically, the Great Plains lie in a mighty belt extending from Texas to the Canadian border in the United States and beyond the Saskatchewan River in Canada. On their eastern side they include western sections of Oklahoma, Kansas, most of Nebraska, about half of South Dakota and a corner of North Dakota. On their western border they include eastern portions of New Mexico, Colorado, Wyoming and Montana. This is the area properly called the Great Plains.

East of the Plains lie the Great Prairies which encompass eastern areas of Kansas, Nebraska and South Dakota, and nearly all of North Dakota. This vast land region slants toward the Mississippi River generally and spills over into Illinois, Indiana and the western part of Ohio to form the Great Plains environment or complex.

The term Great Plains, as used in this paper, follows the monumental studies of Walter Prescott Webb of the University of Texas, and considers both the Great Plains proper with their northward extensions and the Great Prairies as one great environmental unit. However, for practical purposes, only that portion lying west of the Mississippi will be considered in detail. The two land regions form a terrace sloping from the Rocky Mountains to the Mississippi.

In South Dakota, this long lean to the eastward is dramatically illustrated. Thus, Moran, Wyo., on the edge of the Tetons, lies 6,742 feet above sea level; Cody declines to 5,016 feet, Buffalo 4,645 and Gillett 4,544. In South Dakota, Rapid City's 3,231 feet above the ocean slants to Pierre's 1,490 feet and Sioux Falls' 1,440 feet.

Since the terrace of the Great Plains slopes gently eastward, the rivers drain their watersheds by taking a generally easterly direction to merge at last in the southward flowing Mississippi River. This is important in any study of the ornithology of the Great Plains. In South Dakota the rivers to the west of the Missouri flow eastward, following the slope of the Great Plains themselves. East of the Missouri, however, they flow southward—the James, the Vermillion, the Big Sioux; an ancient geographical upthrust in the northeast, providing the state with its morainic complex of potholes and sloughs, also provides a share of the height of land with its southerly inclination.

Ornithologically, the vegetation of the Great Plains is important, for in a large measure it determines the kind of bird life found there. Instead of tall trees, abundant understory and extensive brushy edges, as is characteristic of the Forested area, the Plains are, for the most part, treeless. Only in the valleys of the rivers and their tributaries does one find timber of any consequence. Woody plants, shrubby and small in size, are found in valleys or in low-lying areas. Over all the region spreads the endlessness of grass, the dominant growth of the Plains. It too, however, reflects the variegated character of this land region. From east to west there are first the grasses of the Prairie Plains—the blue-stem sod, the blue-stem bunch grass, the needle and the thin-stemmed wheat grasses. The very names—sod, bunch grass, needle grass—dramatize the soil and climatic conditions in which they flourish. Blue-stem bunch grass is characteristic of central Kansas and Oklahoma while blue-stem sod, needle and wheat grasses cover vast stretches in the northern states. All three appear in eastern South Dakota; their range extends apparently no farther west, however, than the James River.

West of the Prairie grasses rise the short or Plains grasses—gramma, galleta, buffalo and mesquite. Thanks to the movie and the novel, "mesquite" is almost a symbol of the desert or desert-like environment. It is found in western Texas, in southern New Mexico and in Arizona. But the gramma and buffalo grasses extend in a wide belt from Texas and Oklahoma northward, touching eastern Colorado and Wyoming, western Nebraska and fanning out widely into South Dakota where generally it merges with the Prairie grasses in a line drawn roughly north and south through Mitchell.

Thus, South Dakota participates in a great measure in the types and changes of vegetation from east to west which one finds in the Great Plains generally. The state is largely treeless except in valleys and ravines where flourish cottonwood, scrub oak, box elder and willow. In moist draws and hollows grow such plants as wolfberry, silverberry, buffaloberry, sumacs and wildrose. Prairie grasses—blue-stem sod, needle and wheat—merge with the Plains grasses—gramma and buffalo grasses—beyond the James River.

The effect of such a vegetative environment upon bird-life can be seen immediately although its total effect is probably less readily recognizable. Birds dependent upon forests or the edges of woods, such as the greater number of Passerine forms—warblers, vireos, tanagers, kinglets, thrushes, and the like—are at once ruled out for lack of suitable habitat except that minority group as to species and number which inhabits valleys and low-lying sheltered places. Deep water birds will be absent; so will certain of the duck family. And those birds which find large trees indispensable will naturally be excluded. Thus the habitat—the kind of vegetation flourishing here—will have important determinations upon both species and numbers of birds.

Species which have adapted themselves to a habitat of grass, long, short or intermittent; to a habitat of bushy growths in draws and valleys; to trees along the streams; to cat-tail and wide-grass islands on the prairie landscape— such species will be found as resident populations. One example of this habitat would be the so-called pothole country, extending from eastern Kansas northward through eastern Nebraska into South Dakota where sloughs and small bodies of water increase in number until they seem to reach a kind of maximum number in northeastern South Dakota and well into North Dakota. This is one of the Prairie segments of the Great Plains, a prime and almost unparalleled example of habitat for waterfowl and wading birds. South Dakota is famous nation-wide for just such habitat. In such Prairie environment are found large waders such as Sandhill Crane, Whooping Crane, American Bittern; waterfowl such as Trumpeter Swan, Canada Geese and a great variety of ducks—Mallard, Pintail, Blue-winged Teal, Shoveler, Gadwall and the like; smaller waders such as Willet, Marbled Godwit, Avocet and Wilson's Phalarope. The dryer areas support abundantly such upland birds as Greater and Lesser Prairie Chicken, Sharp-tailed Grouse, Bob-white Quail, Long-billed Curlew, Upland Plover. In various transitional niches are found Savannah Sparrow, Grasshopper Sparrow and their relatives–Chestnut-collared Longspur and Lark Bunting.

Such is an inadequate description of the Great Plains; such are the avifaunal forms which are found in this habitat. That it was a productive habitat, one conducive of great populations, is indicated by the reports of the earliest explorers to this area—reports of abundance that filled the first beholders with amazement and brought charges of downright falsehood from listeners who heard or read the first reports.

I think one cannot emphasize too strongly the role of habitat in the abundance of the avifauna during the early history of the Plains; one cannot repeat too often, I believe, the fact that habitat played a most conspicuous part in the maintainance of the level of bird and mammal populations, described by the pioneers upon the Plains as teeming in myriads upon the wide spaces. Official reports, semi-official records, the narratives of adventurers, the accounts of journalists and magazine writers and the letters sent back home—all agree that the areas beyond the Mississippi were indeed a paradise of game, for in those days few animals indeed were non-game. Robins, bobolinks, bunting, curlews, killdeer, as well as song birds—all were considered delicacies for the well developed gourmet tastes of the time.

The Great Plains are important not only for the bird-life of the immediate historical past but also for bird forms of the remote geologic ages. One such geological species is *Hesperoranis*, "western-bird," a name given to what is apparently the third oldest avian fossil known. This large bird, some five feet in length, resembling a loon or a cormorant, is from Upper Cretacious geological period and lived perhaps 100-million years ago. According to Wetmore's *Check List of Fossil and Prehistoric Birds of North America* (1956), it was found in the shale beds of Logan County in western Kansas. Another fossil bird from the

Upper Cretacious is *Ichthyornis*—"fish-bird" so-called—which apparently was gull-like in size and habits. This too was found in the shale beds of western Kansas. Of modern forms the Great Plains has contributed such fossil species as an Eared Grebe from Sherman Country, Kans., a vulturine and a kite-like form from Sioux Country, Nebr., to mention several among many.

South Dakota too is well known for its paleontological findings. (See *Bird Notes* 14:14). Eleven bird fossils from the western part of the state are listed in Wetmore's *Check List*, including a tree duck and several teal-like forms, Old World vulture forms, buzzard and eagle forms, a grouse of the Genus *Tympanuchus* from which apparently also descended our present-day Prairie Chicken or Pinnated Grouse; and an owl form of the Genus *Stryx* in which we find at least one contemporary species, the Barred Owl, once common in the state but now seen with ever decreasing frequency.

It is a long step from the prehistoric imprints in the Pleistocene, less than a million years ago, to the historical record of yesterday; or to be factual, to 1794, when the historical record begins for South Dakota, as I tried to point out in an article, "Ornithology in South Dakota Before Audubon," in *Proceedings*, The South Dakota Academy of Sciences (1956). That year, 1794, may very well be one of the first dates in ornithological recording for the Plains area. From that year onward as hardy men pushed up the rivers—the Missouri, the Arkansas, the Platte—and extended their exploratory efforts more and more from the rivers out onto the plains, the accounts from the western country abound in reports of the bird life on the Great Plains: Trudeau in 1794, Tabeau in 1803, Lewis and Clark in 1804–1806, Pike in 1806 on the Osage River in Missouri, Long in 1820 up the Platte, Washington Irving, the famous writer, in 1832 on the Kansas and the Canadian Rivers. After 1832 there are dozens of journals including Parkman's travels in 1846 which enriched American literature when they were incorporated in his *The Oregon Trail* in 1849.

Tabeau, the narrator of the Loisel Expedition to the Arikaree Nation, was one of the first to describe the fauna of the Upper Missouri region. In 1803 he found "plovers in abundance in spring" and "the pheasants (grouse) in every season abundant. The hawk, the merlin (Pigeon Hawk), the crow, the owl and other similar birds are very common." In 1820 Capt. John Long wrote, "The country along the Platte is enlivened by great numbers of deer, badger, hares, eagles, buzzards, ravens and owls." On the headwaters of the Arkansas, Washington Irving in 1832 saw "flights of Carolina Parakeets,"…"flocks of turkeys and ducks"…"herds of elk." Parkman in 1846 describes a "multitude of quail plaintively whistling" at Westport, Kans., the jumping-off place for western regions at the time, a part of west Kansas City now. At St. Louis, he notes, "The country overflows with game." Near Brule, Nebr. on the South Fork of the Platte, June 6 he saw Burrowing Owls and wild geese. In western Kansas on the Arkansas River on September 4 he recorded "clouds of buzzards."

Keen-eyed men like John Bradbury, traveling up the Missouri in 1811; naturalists like Audubon, ascending the same river in 1843, all exclaimed in amazement at what they saw: "acres of wild geese rising from sandbars to form soldier-like lines in the sky;" "herons, cranes, geese, swans, ducks and all other kinds of water-fowl abounding in the greatest quantities." Prairies swarmed with Prairie Chicken and quail; in certain areas, particularly where there was considerable brush and timber, wild turkeys were so numerous that their gobble was continuous; great sections of the timber along small creeks served as gigantic turkey-roosts. "Migrations of Passenger Pigeons were so heavy that the continual flight darkened the sky and when they alighted on the ground they covered whole acres;" "Swallow-tailed Kites sailed like great Swallows." In the tall trees Carolina Parakeets were flashes of green and yellow, flocks of them. Such were the panegyrics about the abundance of game.

In the 1850's Col. Richard Dodge found the deer in Texas as abundant as jackrabbits in North Carolina. "Turkeys appeared in such flocks that I used occasionally to kill them with a stick from horseback," he writes. In the sixties he found the Plains well supplied with Sharp-tailed Grouse; they were plentiful as far east as the Missouri River, he advised his hunting friends in New York. He told of a soldier in his command who "bagged 26 turkeys from one tree without changing his position." Plovers, that is, Upland Plovers, he notes, "collected in flocks almost innumerable."

In 1868 Mrs. Elizabeth Custer, wife of the commandant of the ill-fated Little Big Horn expedition, who spent a winter on Big Creek, Kans., writes that in the Antelope Hills "the trees were black with wild turkeys;" "trees were weighed down to the end of the branches" with the birds. One can scarcely find a narrative of the period between 1820 and 1870 without finding equally startling illustrations of the immense swarms of game populations teeming upon the Plains. Everyone is familiar with the reports of vast herds of buffalo, sometimes so huge as to halt railroad trains; herds of antelope and elk; bears leaving their tracks on the muddy edges of every stream, it seemed.

As South Dakota is a part of the environment of the Great Plains complex, so it is a participant in the profusion of its faunal life. The state was one of the great buffalo pastures of the west. Red River hunters came as far as Mobridge—the Mandan and Arikaree villages—in 1804 to stock their winter larders. In 1845, Lieut. Allen, exploring the country westward from the Des Moines River to the Big Sioux River, found that buffalo were in sight from the moment he struck the river. He found "more than 100 buffaloes" at his encampment near the Sioux Falls and shot three. But "we might have killed hundreds by delaying for that purpose," he continued. On the lower Big Sioux he found elk, some herds numbering a hundred or more. Col. Dodge found the Ruffed Grouse so plentiful in the Black Hills in 1874 that his command killed a large number without difficulty, although the cover was brushy and exceedingly thick, he writes in *The Black Hills* (1876). In September 1843, Audubon on the Missouri saw Passenger Pigeons on the Little Missouri River in North Dakota and flocks of them on the Moreau in South Dakota, as well as numbers all the way down stream to St. Louis. In 1856-1857 Lieut. Warren's expedition found them at the mouth of the Big Sioux. In the fall of 1877 Dr. Charles McChesney, the post surgeon, saw Passenger Pigeons "taken in numbers" at Fort Sisseton in northeastern South Dakota. As late as 1885 G.S. Agersborg, writing in the *Auk*, reported them in the Missouri River bottom lands in Clay County.

Carolina Parakeets, as Audubon painted them, were green-bodied birds with yellow heads over which ran a broad red band well down below the eye. They ranged widely along the Mississippi, chattering wildly as they flew; like the Passenger Pigeon they found the wooded river valleys attractive. In 1832 Irving found them as far out on the Great Plains as the Cimaroon River in eastern Oklahoma. They were still seen in flocks in Decatur County, Iowa, in 1872, and in eastern Kansas in 1873. Travel accounts abound in reports of the "little parrots," as they were called, and the numbers seen on the Missouri. Like all members of the family, they had shrill, high-pitched, squeaky calls which once heard are not likely ever to be forgotten. I shall never forget the shrieky cries of the Meyers' Parrot which I heard on the Crocodile River in South Africa. In 1843 Audubon saw flocks of the parakeets at Council Bluffs; he noted them in South Dakota near the mouth of the White River. Swallow-tailed Kites ranged widely over the Great Plains, especially along rivers like the Arkansas; their white heads and underparts, their black wings and long black forked tails, their buoyant swallow-like flight were an unforgettable sight. They were common along the Missouri. During the entire winter of 1875–1876, Dr. McChesney saw them at Fort Sisseton. They were seen on the James River in 1885. Agersborg reported that "a few spend the summer here (in Clay County), have no doubt that they breed across the Missouri River in Nebraska." And Visher, writing in the Auk, reports that as recently as 1910 one was shot near Vermillion, a specimen now in the Over Museum at the University of South Dakota.

According to all available evidence, the Whooping Crane nested as far south as Iowa and Nebraska, including South Dakota. The moist and watery places of the pothole country were ideal for its breeding. In South Dakota Dr. McChesney reported it only in spring and fall migration for the Coteau area but Trippe recorded it as nesting in Minnesota in 1871 and in Iowa in 1872. Adrian Larson's article on the birds of Sioux Falls in *Wilson Bulletin* recounts the shooting of a Whooper a few miles northwest of the city "a few years before 1916."

The Sandhill Crane, a prolific breeder, nested well into Nebraska and Iowa. Its flocks in thousands in spring and fall migration, its dancing courtship were a common sight on the breeding grounds. In South Dakota it nested in the Coteau area near Fort Sisseton during 1875–1876, writes Dr. McChesney; in 1885 Agersborg reported it breeding in Clay County; in 1910 Tullsen reported it visiting at LaCreek in Martin County in huge numbers; in 1915 Visher found nests in Sanborn County and called it "a tolerably common breeder."

Smaller birds, less dramatic, but just as important in the whole picture, nested over the prairie swales—Bobolink, Lark Bunting, Lark Sparrow, Swamp Sparrow, Chestnut-Collared Longspur, Sprague's Pipit, to mention only a few. A great many of the birds found on the Great Plains are found in South Dakota as residents in suitable habitat, as migrants, or as individuals in post-nuptial dispersion. Exceptions are the large number of southern species such as Verdin and its relatives, Scissor-tailed Flycatcher and its southern allies, Elf Owl and other *strigid* forms, Gambel's Quail and its *phasianid* relatives—a sizable list which is restricted to the southern reaches of the Great Plains.

Again one must stress habitat as one of the dominant features absolutely necessary for nesting as it is for migratory stop-overs or post-nesting expansion or winter ranging. Habitat is basic to all other considerations in any study of the birdlife of an area, large or small.

Such was the optimistic situation historically; such was the rosy picture in the immediate past of our Great Plains record. What it is today is only too tragically well-known. It probably serves little purpose to mourn over the errors of the past. What is tragic is that man seems to learn so beggarly little from the experiences of the past. Only in the slow accretion of trial and error does one see an attempt to correct the faults of antecedent generations. Then it is usually late if not too late to benefit man or the object of his mistakes; then it is only because man himself feels the constricting consequence of his own stupidity.

If one is at all sensitive to what Christians call God's creatures, the wild animals, one can hardly feel comfortable at the thought that buffalo roam no more, that the elk on the prairies trumpet their silver bugles no longer, that the antelope on a thousand prairie rises will never flash their white rumps again.

Buffalo as wild animals can be counted among the extirpated species on the North American continent. They were slaughtered out of a wantonness that makes one wonder whether savages or the descendants of civilized Europeans marched against them. Ruthlessly were they mowed down, shot even from coach windows of trains by pleasure-loving sportsmen. They were taken by professional hide hunters who ripped off the skins and left the carcass. Near Wood River, Nebr., in 1860 "rotting buffalo dotted the prairie so that the whole area stank." And many sections along the South Platte River in 1873 were "rank with odor of decaying buffalo."

Nor can the blame be laid entirely upon the hunter whether professional or not. The plain truth is that it was allegedly government policy to destroy the buffalo in order to bring the Indian under control. The testimony of Representative Garfield of Illinois was inserted in the *Congressional Record* in 1874, when a bill was reported out by the Committee on Territories "to prevent the useless slaughter of buffaloes within the Territories of the U.S." Said Garfield, "The very best thing that could occur for the solution of the difficulties of that (the Indian) question…would be that the last remaining buffalo should perish…so long as the Indian can hope to subsist by hunting buffalo, so long will he resist all efforts to put him forward in the work of civilization…; he will never take a step toward civilization until his savage means of support were cut off…. The Secretary of the Interior would rejoice so far as the Indian question is concerned, when the last buffalo was gone."

What the Secretary of the Interior really said is included in his *Annual Report for 1873*: "I would not seriously regret the total disappearance of the buffalo from our western prairies, in its effect upon the Indians, regarding it rather as a means of hastening their sense of dependence upon the products of the soil and their own labors."

However, misgiving must have filled several Congressional hearts. Representative Ford said, "I am not in favor of civilizing the Indian by starving him to death." Said Representative Eldridge: "The Argument, Mr. Speaker, is a disgrace to anybody who makes it." The bill to prevent the slaughter was passed. It was sent to President Grant for his signature. But the President pigeon-holed it—and the slaughter went on.

Apparently the army was not wholly uninterested in this question. In 1874, after the southern buffalo herd had been virtually exterminated, the Texas legislature met to pass a bill outlawing the hide hunter. At once the legislature met the opposition of General Philip Sheridan, General of the Army, then in command of the southwest division. "You ought to thank the hide hunters," he told the legislators. "Their men have done more in the last two years, and will do more in the next year, to settle the vexed Indian question than the entire regular army has done in the last thirty years…; let them kill, skin and sell until the buffaloes are exterminated." The Texas legislature did not pass the bill.

Not only the hunter but official opinion must also face the consequences of unenlightened attitudes toward wildlife conservation. Official opinion, almost always selfish in its desire to achieve its own ends rather than to consider ultimate goals, certainly leaves the average citizen often in a state of complete bewilderment.

In 1949, when the South Dakota Ornithologists' Union held its formative meeting in Sioux Falls, a representative of a government agency concerned with proposed impoundments on the Missouri River, addressed the meeting. At that time there was concern about the Missouri reservoirs and the destruction of habitat along that stream. The representative of official opinion, himself not the author of the speech but merely the speaker, read the official opinion to the members: "It will certainly be a new day for ducks in this region when the thousands of acres of new water are a reality…. River improvement work in the State will increase the total square miles of water by about 71 percent (551 square miles). This increase will certainly have a beneficial effect upon waterfowl populations of the region…. Large reservoirs with indented shore lines are ideally suited for duck mating…. The South Dakota reservoirs will offer duck and goose environment with shelving flats and bars, sloping shores, shallow and deeper areas, and wind protected bays and coves…; it will be a veritable haven for ducks and geese;…large bars and shallow water cut-offs and ponds will be used by resting water fowl. Aquatic food in sufficient quantities will be available."

When individuals who had made some study of habitat pointed out that it might take a long time before the bars and resting places would provide those organisms which make such places attractive, the question was brushed aside as unimportant. When it was pointed out that in other reservoirs, the shelving flats would remain mud bars for years, with scarcely a sign of aquatic life on them, and that it might take a hundred years or more to build up such places with that animal and vegetative life which the goose desires, the subject was allowed to die of inertia.

That was in 1949. Now, in 1963, anyone who wishes to know how accurate alleged official opinion was, need only consult the tabulations of goose and duck populations, compiled from official sources, which appear in the newspapers.

A study of the ornithology of the Great Plains shows clearly that while we can rejoice in the species and numbers which still remain with us, the optimism must be tempered with the cold fact that we have lost many species and that population numbers have been drastically reduced. Some species have declined so much that they are extirpated from areas where they were common forty years ago. What is true of the Plains in general is true of South Dakota also. To bring the matter closely home, Lark Bunting, Grasshopper Sparrow, Burrowing Owl, Bob-White, Chestnut-collared Longspur and Wood Thrush, to mention only a few, used to nest in the Sioux Falls area. There has been no report of actual nesting of any of these species since 1949, at least.

Today some species are already completely lost to us as residents. Once all nesters in South Dakota, the following must now be considered as extirpated as wild birds from the state: Whooping Crane, Sandhill Crane, Canada Goose (except captive and semi-captive birds on refuges), Trumpeter Swan, Swallow-tailed Kite, Passenger Pigeon, Wild Turkey (except those introduced in the Black Hills for sporting purposes), Raven, McCown's Sparrow, Osprey, Sprague's Pipit. All were reported nesters at or just before the turn of the century. All are gone as nesters today.

Migratory species lost to us must include the Hudsonian and Eskimo Curlews, once reported on the prairies in large numbers. Birds drastically reduced in number and in range are Burrowing Owl, Chestnut-collared Longspur, Swamp Sparrow, the Golden and Black-bellied Plovers in migration, the Long-billed Curlew and the Sage Grouse.

However, the Cardinal has steadily advanced both as a migrant and as a nester. In South Dakota it now breeds as far north as Madison and is seen at various seasons of the year in nearly all parts of the area east of the Missouri and occasionally west to the Black Hills. However, Beddall's study in the *Auk* (June 1963) indicates its decline again, possibly because of the destruction of winter habitat along the Missouri River. The Wood Thrush, whose song is one of the most inspiring one can hear in the forest, nested until recently in the Sioux Falls area. In 1916 it still nested in the Big Sioux bottoms near Newton Hills. I heard it sing there in June of 1956, but found no evidence of nesting. Extensive road improvements some four or five years ago cleared away the understory in which it likes to nest. The song of the nesting Wood Thrush will probably be heard no more in South Dakota.

The loss is irreparable, if we still are human beings. The consequences, however intangible, may be greater than we are willing to admit. "Can society," asked the editor of the *Christian Science Monitor*, commenting on the near-extinction of the Whooping Crane, "can society, whether through sheer wantonness or callous neglect, permit the extinction of something beautiful or grand in its own character?" The answer to this query may lie in the search each man makes of his own soul—if he has the integrity to face reality. The answer may also lie in the uneasy probing now being made into the national conscience and character and the reluctance many feel about evaluating the exposure.

However, if our words are sincere, if we really want to save what still remains, then it now behooves us to study the Great Plains, to become familiar with the habitat of the terrain and better acquainted with its avian inhabitants.

The final choice, however, lies with the people of the Great Plains and of South Dakota. Theirs is the choice. They can preserve what habitat remains; they can enlarge that habitat wherever it is possible. They can inform themselves and educate their neighbors. They can insist that official opinion be based on enlightened leadership and work in harmony with state and local conservation groups. They can do this, or they can watch the disappearance of species after species of bird and mammal as now they are watching the decline of the Whooping Crane, the Masked Quail in New Mexico, the Atwater's Prairie Chicken in Texas. All are being extirpated because their habitat is being changed.

A re-thinking of our hunting practices too seems in order. We have been hunting on the premise of abundance. But the abundance is already gone, tragically, irrecoverably gone. Hunters must adapt themselves to hunting on the premise of scarcity, of making a little go a long way. At the very time when hunters are increasing year by year, game birds and other species are decreasing year by year, available habitat is decreasing year by year. It is not likely that ducks and geese will nest on the asphalt pavements or in the concrete highway cloverleafs.

Where is our courage, our initiative, our inspired leadership?

The ornithology of the Great Plains once amazed the world. Today the ornithology of the Great Plains amazes few indeed. Tomorrow the ornithology of the Great Plains will amaze–whom?

(*South Dakota Bird Notes*, March 1964)

CHAPTER 2

The Ornithology of the Major Long Expedition, 1823

Apparently there were very good reasons, that April, why Major Stephen Long was sent into that remote and unknown wilderness, the so-called Unorganized Territory, so far north of the teacups and boudoirs of urbane Philadelphia. Once known as the Old Missouri Territory, that untracked region included the western and the greater portion of Minnesota in the spring of 1823. There were reasons, apparently, but none of them seem to have been ornithological.

For now that Mr. Lewis and Mr. Clark had examined a portion of that domain, breath-takingly vast, which Mr. Jefferson had acquired from France, now that Major Pike had during the years 1805–1806 explored the northern reaches of the Upper Mississippi, now that the war with Great Britain was over though still in vivid memory, now that the boundary line had been drawn, at least on a map, between His British Majesty's territories and the realms of the United States–now that all these events had transpired, it behooved Mr. Monroe's administration to hurry the business of probing the untracked vastness between the Mississippi on the east and the Missouri on the west, especially that area above a line drawn from Fort St. Anthony (Fort Snelling) west to the Missouri.

With the burning of the White House and the Capitol in Washington and the British threat from the north militarily and politically still fresh in mind, Mr. Calhoun, the Secretary of War, had for some time contemplated a series of forts reaching westward to hold the frontier against the restless Indians—or against anybody else, for that matter. Besides that, there was the question of the Indians collaborating with the British during the recent hostilities; and there were the fur traders to the north, who, despite the Licensing Act of 1816, caused no end of trouble, trading with Indians on American soil, and without licenses, at that—or so it was charged. The traders, however, might very well ask the embarrassing question, "Where does the United States begin?"

Was it to ascertain the boundary line in the northwest that the Major left Philadelphia in such haste, bent on this expedition? Or was he fishing in potentially more troubled waters?

With such pressing matters at hand, Major Stephen Long, that early summer of 1823, came somewhat hastily up the Mississippi, his mind no doubt bristling with arms and bastions and men, with small room for ornithology except of course as it might assist his larder and keep his men from short rations. He disembarked at Fort St. Anthony on July 3rd, where almost at once that irrepressible Italian, Count Giacomo Beltrami, attached himself to the party, apparently willy-nilly. There is no record that the flamboyant nobleman was dissuaded from this attachment, not by the Major nor by anybody else—not by Mr. Keating, the geologist and historiographer of the expedition, nor by Mr. Say, the zoologist, nor by Mr. Colhoun, the astronomer. The Count went along, dreaming of Marco Polo and Columbus and his own heroic search for the sources of the Mississippi. There seems to have been little that was ornithological about the Italian. He despised the Americans and said so succinctly. For the time being, however, he accepted their protection and assistance, if he didn't command their respect. The Major dismisses him with the remark, "Amateur traveller."

One can hardly read Keating's *Narrative* without being aware of the sense of urgency which pervades the writing as it may very well have pervaded the expedition. This appears in the formal orders. Not until April, Keating writes, did the Executive determine "that an expedition be immediately fitted out." Immediately. But this was late in the season for such an undertaking, Keating concedes as much. "The advanced state of the season admitted of no delay." He goes on: "The necessary preparations were hastily made." Hastily. The expedition didn't leave Philadelphia until April 30. Late indeed. But the annual migration of birds up the Mississippi flyway would be in full swing.

As it turned out, once at Prairie du Chien, the expedition followed the Mississippi to Fort St. Anthony, went partly up the St. Peters, Minn. river, crossed the prairies past Lac qui Parle to Lake Traverse, up the Bois de Sioux and Red Rivers to Lake Winnipeg, then eastward to Lake of the Woods and along the Rainy River canoe route to Fort William.

This urgency also appears in the preparation for the expedition. Apparently, Long hoped to live off the land. He employed an "excellent hunter," but game, except for the Passenger Pigeon, appeared to have dwindled sadly. Even as the party was entering the Minnesota wilderness, not many days out of Prairie du Chien, Keating was beginning to grumble. "Game will be judged to be very scarce when two parties, traveling by land and by water, can kill but two or three dozens of birds upon a distance of two hundred miles." The men found turtles' eggs and appeared "to be very fond of them." Colhoun notes that the party traveled the 211 miles from Prairie du Chien to the Fort in eight days—26 3/8 miles per day.

Previous to the arrival at St. Anthony, Keating mentions only the passenger pigeon, of which a good many were shot as variation of a scanty menu—biscuit and salt pork. At the Fort itself he found that game was scarce indeed. With the building of wall and bastion, with the forays of hunting parties, species that once were familiar sights now had retreated to less molested areas.

While biscuits for the next stage of the journey were baking in the ovens at the Fort, Keating and Say visited the famous falls that Hennepin had named. They saw Brown's Falls which fifty years later was to be celebrated in a poem as Minnehaha Falls. Among the birds observed by Mr. Say were the woodcock, the house wren, the hairy woodpecker, the towhee bunting (which today we know as the rufous-sided towhee); the flecker, as Keating called the yellow-shafted flicker. But this list seems almost an afterthought, hastily flung together and ending with "and so forth and so forth."

The party left the Fort on July 9th and followed the valley of the St. Peter's River. Six days out, Keating notes regretfully that he sees "no birds interrupting the solemn stillness which uniformly reigns over the country—no living object of any kind." The Minnesota valley is wooded, its shorelines brushy. One wonders where the warblers were, the edge birds and the shrub. Or was the party too preoccupied with state affairs to note the occurrence of a *tyrannid* form or a *parulid*?

On the same route Beltrami noticed with remarkable ornithological terseness whole "lakes covered with swans and other aquatic birds," but contributed little that is descriptive. When the party arrived at Swan Lake, near Mankato, he observed swans on the water and recorded the only remark on wild life history in the annals of the expedition. "It was the season at which these beautiful birds cannot fly," he writes. "The old ones, because they are changing their feathers; the young because they have yet only a soft down."

Then he added what may be a significant comment: "We might have had some good shooting and the savans among us might have gained new and valuable ornithological information, but the Major was intent on making an expedition, and consulted nothing but his compass." More than anything else, this may suggest the mood of the expedition.

As for the swans on Swan Lake, Keating said only and rather scornfully that he saw a "group of ponds dignified with the appellation of the Swan Lakes, on account of the abundance of these birds said to exist in the neighborhoods." Although Beltrami does not name the species and Keating does not indicate actual observations of swans, Dr. Roberts has identified these birds as trumpeter swans. Dr. Suckley saw trumpeters farther north at Pike Lake twenty years later.

Ten days beyond Fort St. Anthony Keating had to admit that game simply didn't exist and that "our stores were wasting away too fast to permit delay" for hunting along the stream. The party left the bends of the river, therefore, and went overland, Beltrami growling at their haste. Was there more in this journey than the determination of a boundary line? Was Long's hurry motivated by the Secretary of War's desire to learn how vulnerable the frontier really was, what the resources of the region were, what the attitudes of the Indians were and whether the fur traders were anti-American? And what about the sympathies of the Selkirkers at Red River Settlements? Keating devotes much space to descriptions of the Indians, their number, their folklore, their legends. Much time is devoted to the mineral and geological lore of the country. The forests and their possibilities, even the bushes, especially the fruitbearing varieties, are carefully examined, for this was included in the Major's interests. Rivers, lakes and portages are almost minutely observed. There is information aplenty but it is information which one might gather to allay the secret fears of leaders in high places, far from the scene of events. Keating's *Narrative* is packed with something like vital statistics which could, if necessary, have immediate utility. No wonder then that, even with as eminent a zoologist as Mr. Thomas Say in the party, there were only a few scraps of information tossed in regarding the ornithology of the expedition. The avifauna of the country, for obvious reasons, was apparently less important than its other resources. Lists of birds are hastened over and ended with a couple of "and so forth's"—indifferent ampersands. Again and again, in enumerating the species of an area or at a fur trading post, Keating begins the list with "Among the birds observed by Mr. Say," as if to suggest many more, if only time and space permitted the listing. Although the Appendix to the volumes carries Say's catalog of the zoology and botany of the expedition, a descriptive list of birds is wanting. Meteorological observations are there, astronomical data, even an Indian vocabulary, but nothing about the avifauna, references to which appear only in the text.

Once on the prairie, members of the party found that distance played havoc with accuracy. For instance, sandhill cranes looked like elk. Generally, however, birds were scarce. In addition to the sandhill cranes, they saw only "the reed-bird" (bobolink), what Keating calls a "blackbird" and identifies as *Oriolus phoenicens* (red-winged blackbird), the yellow-headed blackbird and the black-breasted tern, which seems to have been the black tern. On the route Mr. Say shot a female hooded merganser and a blue-winged teal. Mosquitoes drove the party frantic.

Between the Redwood and the Yellow Medicine Rivers, Colhoun notes in his diary the appearance of sparrows, cow buntings (certainly the cowbird), curlews (probably the long-billed) and the Bartram sandpiper (upland plover). Near Lac qui Parle the young of the whip-poor-will was found, "nearly strong enough to fly." And Colhoun writes, "Two swallow-tailed kites soared over our heads." Later the party saw an Indian with a live sparrowhawk on his head by way of ornament. It is strange that Keating does not include Colhoun's observation of the plover and the swallow-tailed kite.

At the fur post at Lake Traverse, Keating examined the Columbia Fur Company's trade list of skins and noted the swan (trumpeter, very likely) numbered among the pelts. Two packs of 60 skins were worth 120 Spanish dollars. In those days apparently swans were regarded in the same way that beaver and mink were. They served as ornaments and decorations as well as food. If there were other birds near the post at Lake Traverse, nobody mentions them unless one counts the owls' feathers which decorated an Indian's mantle, the turkey feathers of a fan and the feathers of a war-eagle adorning a head-dress. They can only suggest that these birds were found in the area.

After Lake Traverse, "among the birds, there were only seen the bald eagle and the hooping [sic] crane." Passenger pigeons they saw everywhere. A pigeon hawk was shot. Where the Otter Tail River joins the Red River, Colhoun saw a bald eagle flying overhead and alighting on a nest not far away.

After many rivers to cross and no birds to add to the *Narrative* (except the geese, probably a form of the Canada, which Beltrami mentions on Bustard's or Goose River) the expedition arrived at Pembina, where Mr. Colhoun fixed the boundary line, the Major made a speech, the party saw an oak post driven down with the letters G.B. on the north side and U.S. on the south, and Mr. Beltrami sneered at the whole foolish proceedings.

Thus was the fur post safely corralled into the territory of the United States along with most of the buffalo–so, Keating admitted, the colonists themselves averred. Apparently, then, the purpose of the expedition was at least partly fulfilled here, although the *Narrative* is terse. Keating says, "The main object of the party in visiting this place was the determination of the 49th degree of latitude." But Thomas Say, the zoologist, once safely back home in Philadelphia, wrote his friend, John Melsheimer, November 30, 1823: "There [at Pembina] we established the north boundary line of the U.S., and took possession of that part of the country with customary military ceremonies." A kind of show of force perhaps for those inimical to the interests of the United States?

At Pembina, Mr. Say reported the turkey vulture, red-headed woodpecker, flicker, hemp-bird (which must be the common goldfinch, for Keating designates it as *Fringilla tristis*), the kingbird (which appears in a footnote as *Tyrannus pipiri*, the eastern kingbird), the sparrow hawk, robin, chimney-bird (the chimney swift), barn swallow, nighthawk, whip-poor-will, bald eagle, hairy woodpecker, great blue heron, grackle (probably the common grackle), killdeer, blue-winged teal, ruddy duck, rose-breasted grosbeak, crow, raven and passenger pigeon, "the last of which is very abundant in the woods," concluded Keating. Here, as at Lake Taverse, he found the swan, probably again the trumpeter, in the list of pelts collected at the post. Mr. Say could count 22 species for the area.

At Pembina Beltrami sniffed and sneered and left in a huff to search for the sources of the Mississippi, sure that the eyes of heroic explorers were upon him. Troubled by less expansive if more realistic problems, the Long party also left the little settlement–this was on August 9–and headed down the Red River Valley. At Saline River, they found a salt spring, watched an antelope and shot a redstart and a lesser yellowlegs. Ducks and geese were abundant, "of which we might have killed many, had we been able to spare the time," mourns Keating: a remark which strengthens Beltrami's rather testy judgment. Apparently the Major was still consulting only his compass and, in the Italian's scornful phrase, "making an expedition." Instead of shooting wild game, says Keating, "the men caught a great many fish in the evenings" to vary the diet.

The expedition stopped at the Selkirk colony long enough to learn something of its history and perhaps more about the attitude of the colonists (was Long ascertaining whether the settlers were anti- or pro-American?) before the Major secured provisions and hired Canadians and Bois Brule canoe men. The party set out in three bark canoes—long freighters called *canot du nord*. Down the Red River the explorers went. Entering Lake Winnipeg, they paddled up the eastern shoreline to the mouth of the Winnipeg River, apparently never sighting as much as a gull or a tern, although somewhere on those choppy waters they heard the notes of the whip-poor-will: a fact which apparently nobody records and which Keating remembers and notes down only at Bonnet Lake, miles up the Winnipeg River. In fact, not until they reached Bonnet Lake did Mr. Say pause in his botanical duties—for trees and bushes are described in detail—long enough to note "among the birds" the cedar-bird (cedar waxwing), the fish-hawk or osprey, the belted kingfisher, killdeer, black-headed tern and "numberless ducks."

I have been unable to identify the tern. Keating does not indicate either generic or specific designation. Since this is August 21, the species might have been the black tern in molting stage. But this seems somewhat doubtful since Keating writes "the black-headed Tern, which apparently indicates a definite form.

At the Bonnet Falls he saw eagles and hawks soaring over the tumbling waters where fish, killed or hurt among the rocks, offered easy prey. Beyond Jack's Falls, "a large loon flew by in the afternoon." Keating remembered that among the natives its scream is a sure sign of rain, but doubted the truth of the folklore until rain fell in torrents, whereupon he concluded that the verification of one instance does not prove universality.

He says little about the passage over the Lake of the Woods. Mr. Say was busy describing the botanical features of the landscape. At the end of the lake, however, he recorded "two kinds of gulls, one of which was probably the Herring-gull, *Larus argentus*, young" writes Keating. A number of white pelicans were sighted and "a few ducks." At Rainy Lake Fort Mr. Say "killed the ruby-throated hummingbird, the black-headed titmouse (which we know as the black-capped chickadee) and pileated woodpecker."

From this point on, one senses less urgency in the hurry of the expedition. Perhaps the Major had come to some conclusion about the defenses of this area and its resources. Perhaps he paid less attention to his compass, for Keating has time to describe the incredible numbers of an ephemera (insect) and to visit the famous John Tanner, kidnapped in childhood by Indians and brought to manhood among them. Mr. Say, very busy these days, jots down Tanner's story, speculates on the life of the ephemera, and notes the kinds and qualities of the trees in the endless forest. One wonders that he had time to observe birds at all or hear the notes of the whip-poor-will near Rainy Lake. Perhaps this bustling about his botanical duties explains why from Rainy Lake to Lake Superior, no birds are mentioned in the day-by-day account. They are left for a single summary paragraph, recorded after the party reached Fort William. There Keating writes, "From Rainy Lake to Lake Superior we did not meet with a single quadruped. The only animals we saw were thirty or forty birds, chiefly ducks": a statement so astonishing that one readily agrees with Dr. W.J. Breckenridge's observation, "Almost unbelievable." It is a statement so hastily unscientific and generalized that one is forced to the conclusion that the observations made were highly selective and that other matters lay heavy on the minds of the leaders.

"Among the birds" noted were Canada jay, blue jay, hairy woodpecker, Indian hen (probably the spruce grouse) and the woodcock. Keating also mentions the golden plover, which must have been on its return migration, for this is early September. However, there may be an error in designation here. In a footnote Keating states that the species is *Vanellus Helveticus*, which according to Coues and the American Ornithological Union Check List (1886) is the black-bellied plover.

On the trail the party killed five "pheasants," a common name for the ruffled grouse. And there Mr. Say and Mr. Keating end their ornithological labors except to note a rail seen somewhere on the way; but "it disappeared too soon to enable Mr. Say to determine the species," says Mr. Keating, almost as if washing his hands of the whole affair. No locality is attached to any one of the seven species numbered in the list, which was made after the party arrived at Fort William.

Before long the expedition left for the United States. The Major, apparently less hasty now, was satisfied. From a military point of view, the northern frontier, a region "the most dreary imaginable," guarded on the west by the Great American Desert, destined forever to remain almost unpopulated, was safe, quite safe, he wrote in his Topographical Report to the War Department. "We shall always remain secure from the inroads of any regular hostile force in that direction." Whatever palpitations agitated Washington military circles could now subside, it seemed. The Republic was safe, if avifauna was somewhat uncertain.

Whatever its purpose, whatever it may or may not have accomplished, the Long Expedition does open up a glimpse of the bird life of the Minnesota area in the 1820's. True, these are glimpses only: a list at Fort Snelling, another on the prairie, one at Pembina, another on Winnipeg River, a summary at Fort William. There are no running commentaries on the birds seen along the route as there are of the mineral and the forest resources and of the quadrupeds, especially buffalo, deer and elk. There are no descriptions. Nothing is said of life histories, of habitat, of relative populations (except the passenger pigeons), of behavior.

Nevertheless, one is glad to know that a hundred and thirty-odd years ago the hairy woodpecker and the blue-winged teal, the house wren and the red-eyed towhee were found in the Minnesota Valley as they are today; that the flicker, then as now, was as much at home in the southeast at Fort St. Anthony as it was at Pembina in the northwest.

The expedition noted fifty-three species, if one counts those in Colhoun's diary. There were four unspecified forms: a gull, a rail, curlews and sparrows. Of the fifty-three, four species are no longer found on their former nesting grounds: the sandhill crane, the trumpeter swan, the swallow-tailed kite and the whooping crane. Perhaps one should add the long-billed curlew. One, the passenger pigeon, is forever gone. And one, the whooping crane, is barely evading extinction. However, forty-eight of the species identified by Mr. Say are, in greater or lesser numbers, still with us, with perhaps no immediate alarm over their survival. True, with our indifference toward our natural resources, our calloused attitude toward the reduction in number of our wildlife, our ignorance of basic factors in wildlife, we have done a lot of damage in 130-odd years. The miracle is that we haven't done more damage. In this respect, the ornithology of the Long Expedition, meager as it is, is nevertheless a reminder of what we had and what we have lost.

Beltrami, J.C., 1828. *A Pilgrimage in Europe and America*, 2 vols, London.

Breckenridge, W.J. "A Century of Minnesota Wild Life," *Minnesota History*, 30:123-134, 220-231. *Entomological News*, February, 1902.

Colhoun, Edward. "Diary" and Long's "Papers," both unpublished, are in the possession of the Minn. Hist. Soc.; to Miss Lucile Kane, Curator of Manuscripts, and her associates, my thanks for permission to use both.

Keating, William. 1825. *Narrative of an Expedition to the Sources of St. Peter's River*, 2 vols., London.

Welsey, Edgar.1935. *Guarding the Frontier*, University of Minnesota Press.

(*Minnesota Naturalist*, September 1956)

CHAPTER 3

Ornithology in South Dakota Before Audubon

Ornithology in South Dakota is often regarded as beginning with John James Audubon (1900) who journeyed up the Missouri in 1843. Over and Thoms include Audubon in the bibliography of their *Birds of South Dakota* (41) but seem not to refer to previous writers. In Dr. T.C. Stephens' bibliographical listing (5), the earliest date for a report on birds is Audubon's for 1843. This would seem to neglect the narratives of previous travelers, including the reports of the doughty captains, Lewis and Clark, and the important work of Maximilian of Wied.

According to available sources, the first mention of birds in South Dakota appears in Trudeau's journal of 1794 (412–474). Trudeau, a schoolmaster of St. Louis, was sent up the Missouri River to scout the fur trade. In the fall of 1794 he built a log cabin on the river in what Will Robinson calls "the 2nd valley on the north side below Fort Randall Dam" (11). Here he and his men somewhat fearfully avoided the Indians and shot wild turkeys and other game. Trudeau himself wrote a narrative of events for his superiors. This was common practice. A log or journal was almost always required by a fur company of its clerks and traders; it mattered little whether the post was near or far, whether at Hudson Bay or in the Rockies, on the Great Lakes or in the farthest reaches of the Yukon. Once settled beside the Missouri, Trudeau writes almost complacently of his "scaffolds" hung with plenty of "deer, turkeys and other wild animals" against the winter's long cold. Zoology and economics are thus curiously associated and, in South Dakota at least, ornithology seems the reluctant partner of commerce. Trudeau's mention of turkeys, which had a practical, not a scientific purpose, is probably the first reference to this species on the Upper Missouri, certainly in South Dakota. It fixes one point in determining historically the range of this species.

The man who appears first to have described South Dakota avifauna in some detail is Pierre-Antoine Tabeau (88–91), an educated French-Canadian voyageur. Tabeau, narrator of the Loisel Expedition, came up the Missouri River in 1803 and lived among the Arikara Indians on Cedar Island near the extreme southeastern corner of Stanley county. He describes the magpie and its voracious habit of alighting on the backs of Indian ponies and picking at the living flesh where wooden saddles had worn the skin raw. He says that the kiliou, the golden eagle, "is not rare" and is prized among the Arikara who in autumn set special traps for the bird. Turkeyhens, he relates, are seldom found above the River qui Court (the Niobrara) but the hawk, the merlin (probably the pigeon hawk), the crow, the owl—these are "very common." Thus in the early part of the nineteenth century, even before the Lewis and Clark Expedition, we have at least some light thrown on the avifauna of the Missouri River region in South Dakota.

The exploits of Captains Lewis and Clark are too well known to be repeated here. Less well known perhaps is the ornithological list which they recorded. Arriving in the state on August 21, 1804, they saw their first South Dakota birds at Spirit Mound, not far from Vermillion in Clay county. Here they saw "the wren, the backbird and the Western Meadowlark." In Charles Mix county they shot geese and near what is now Fort Randall Dam they bagged three wild turkeys. This locality, interestingly enough, is not far from the place where Trudeau had built his cabin ten years before. They collected a white pelican somewhere in northern Charles Mix county; saw great numbers of "growse" (sharp-tailed grouse) not far from the Bijoux Hills in Brule county; killed a magpie below Chamberlain; and saw "hawks" on the plains. Of the magpie, Lewis wrote: "Killed a bird of the *Corvus* genus and order of the *pica*"–the only instance, as Coues notes, of the captains "venturing a technical Latin name in zoology." On the prairies of the Big Bend in Hughes county they saw more sharp-tailed grouse and western meadowlarks; below the Cheyenne River they came upon a "great abundance" of "the white gull," which may have been the ring-billed gull or possibly the Franklin's or even, considering the date, September 30, returning herring gulls. Just north of the Sully-Potter county line they beheld an Indian with a wild turkey on his back, which may or may not have some bearing on the penetration up the river of this species. In this area they saw also grayish "brant" with several "white brant" among "the dark colored ones." These must have been the now common snow and blue goose. Although in a note to the *History of the Expedition*, Coues calls the "dark colored" birds common brant (*Bernicla brenta*), it is very probable that they were either the blue goose (*Chen caerulescens*) or the white-fronted goose (*Anser albifrons*), for the brant is, in Roger Tory Peterson's words (32), "almost strictly coastal." In the Potter-Sully county region, the captains also saw swans but whether whistling or trumpeter, their records do not indicate. With this observation they travel out of South Dakota. In the hurry of the return journey in August 1806, they noted little that was new. While their account of the mammalian fauna of the area somewhat overshadows their avian reports, for there is nothing in the latter which is as startling as the prairie-dog, and the antelope in the former, nevertheless the captains' report adds materially to our knowledge by ascribing many species to this area, the range of which hitherto had been virtually if not completely unknown.

In 1811, the Astorians followed the Missouri River up to a point near the North Dakota-South Dakota border (perhaps north of Mobridge) and then westward overland to the Pacific. With them was Thomas Nuttal, the botanist, and

Henry Brackenridge, the novelist and statesman. If Nuttal kept a journal, it has not survived; and whatever notes he made are so generally incorporated in his *Manual of Ornithology* that specific references are difficult to locate with any accuracy. Brackenridge left a journal (27–166) and the opinion that settlement of any consequence on the Upper Missouri would necessarily not appear "for centuries, if ever." He saw a magpie at Chamberlain.

Near the mouth of the Cheyenne River he observed blackbirds, the thrush, and the wren; their species he did not indicate. Near there he noted the martin and what he calls the field lark (western meadowlark). Otherwise he has little to say about the avifauna of the region.

In 1812, John Luttig came to Fort Manuel on the Missouri River, just inside the South Dakota border (north of Mobridge), there to spend the late summer, autumn, and winter. His account may lack polish and new ornithological information, but it is a fascinating narrative of daily life at an early fur-trade post and the hunting necessary to keep the larder stocked. Thus, it indirectly indicates the species of birds present. Luttig tells about shooting quantities of ducks and numbers of "chickens" (probably the pinnated grouse) and many plover, bagging twenty-eight in one day. This might well be the upland plover, for the month is August; but early returning *charadriidae* such as the golden or the black-bellied should perhaps not be ruled out.

Up to this point, these accounts designate birds by their common names–the magpie, the grouse, the crow; or by even more general designations–ducks, geese, hawks. Except for Lewis's magpie, little or no attempt was made to employ scientific terminology. The man who apparently first applied scientific names to birds along the Missouri in South Dakota was Paul Wilhelm of Wuerttemberg. He came to the state during the last days of August 1823. Below the Bijoux Hills he saw the *Hirundo virdis* (tree swallow) and near the Bijoux Hills themselves he collected a *Falco mississippiensis* (Mississippi kite). Not far from the Vermillion River he saw pelican and swan.

Another man who, perhaps in a larger measure than Wuerttemberg, applied scientific terms to South Dakota birds was Maximilian of Wied (1906). Early in May of 1833, this soldier-naturalist entered the state. Near the James River he encountered pairs of "the great yellow-breasted lark (*Sturnella, Vieillot*)," (our meadowlark), and the "great long-billed curlews (*Numenius longirostris*)." Near Ponca Creek in Charles Mix county he saw turkey buzzards (probably turkey vultures), Carolina pigeon (mourning dove), and on the steep banks and cliffs the nests of swallows (probably cliff swallows). He notes that Cedar Island (near Wheeler, S. Dak.) is the limit of the wild turkey. In this area he saw the raven and the red-eyed finch (Eastern towhee). Sometimes he employs only the binomial. Thus, beyond Cedar Island he saw the *Sylvia aestiva* (yellow warbler) and the *Sylvia striata* (blackpoll warbler). Near the Bijoux Hills he came on the *Fringilla grammaca* (lark bunting) and not far from what is now Fort Pierre the *Lanius excubitoroides* (loggerhead or migrant shrike). On his return trip in April and May 1834, he saw at Fort Pierre what he calls a "starling" but which from his scientific designation (*Sturnella ludoviciana*) appears to be the western mead-owlark (*S. neglecta*). Near Cedar Island he found the titmouse (black-capped chickadee) and the *Sylvia coronata* (myrtle warbler). At the James River he saw the *Falco cyaneus* (marsh hawk) and above the Vermillion the *Fringilla pennsylvanica* (white-throated sparrow), the whip-poor-will which "flew round the fire within three paces of it," the avocet, the purple martin (*Hirundo purpurae*), the house wren (*Troglodytes aedon*), the *Fringilla caudacuta* (Leconte's sparrow), the double-crested cormorant (*Carbo*) and others.

Before 1794 our knowledge of the avifauna of South Dakota amounted to little or nothing, although the fur-traders had important geographical knowledge of the areas adjacent to the Missouri River. By 1834, forty years later, we had considerable information on at least thirty-one species of birds and some data on their distribution. Thus these early accounts, all antedating Audubon's journey, have added materially to our knowledge of the avian species of the state.

Bibliography

Audubon, Maria R. 1900. *Audubon and His Journals*, 2 vols. New York: Chas. Scribner's Sons.
Brackenridge, H.M. "Journal of a Voyage up the River Missouri," *Early Western Travels*, VI. Cleveland: Arthur H. Clark Co.
Lewis, M., and W. Clark. 1893. *History of the Expedition*, ed. by Elliott Coues, Vols. I and IV. New York: Francis Harper.
Luttig, J. 1920. *Journal of a Fur-trading Expedition to the Upper Missouri 1812–1813*, Missouri Hist. Soc.
Over, W., and Thoms, C.S. 1921. *Birds of South Dakota*, Nat. Hist. Stud., No. 1, University of South Dakota.
Peterson, R.T. 1947. *Field Guide to the Birds*. New York: Houghton Mifflin Co.
Robinson, W. 1954. "Fur Trade." *Wi-iyohi*, 7, 11:1–12.
Stephens, T.C. 1944. *An Annotated Bibliography of South Dakota Ornithology*. Sioux City, Iowa.
Tabeau, P. 1939. *Narrative of Loisel's Expedition to the Upper Missouri*, University of Oklahoma.
Trudeau, J.B. 1914. *Journal*, S.D. Hist. Coll., 6. Pierre, S.D.
Wied, Maximilian of. 1906. "Travels in the Interior of North America," *Early Western Travels*, Vols. XXII and XXIV. Cleveland: Arthur Clark Co.
Wuerttemberg, Paul W. of. 1938. *First Journey to North America*, S.D. Hist. Coll., 19, South Dakota Historical Society.

(South Dakota Academy of Science, *Proceedings*, 1956)

SECTION II
EARLY AFIELD

CHAPTER 1

Song Sparrows

These are the "brushpile" days for any watcher of birds, especially of so-called "song" sparrows. They are down from Canada in full but leisurely flight now. Every plum hedge and hazel thicket is full of their flutterings. Best of all, however, they seem to like a pile of limbs and branches that someone has thrown together and forgotten. In these piles of twisted bareness they appear and disappear–Harris sparrows, white crowns, white throats, tree and sava-nahs cavorting with occasional fox sparrows and those sparrows that nest in Otter Tail County–the chipping, field, vesper, song, and clay-colored sparrows.

Recently one morning I came on such a colony in a pasture belonging to my good friend George Duenow. It was one of those mornings, bright and early, when every sound is as clear as if struck just outside the ear. Not far away I could hear the Duenow boys at their fall work, Harold's tractor roaring beyond a hill, Eddie's maul clanging iron on iron as he drove posts for a temporary fence across a cornfield. From where I stood I could see the maul-head lift above his shoulder with each stroke.

Sharply, through these sounds I heard a loud "weenk, weenk" from a near-by brushpile–the call of the Harris sparrow. As I watched quietly, that sagging heap of brush came to life. A pair of Harris sparrows, their black napkins plain to see, chased each other in the upper branches. A white throat, hopping down the twigs as if they were steps, sang the first notes of its spring song, "Pee, pee," and gave it up for the year. From behind leaves caught in a fork, a white crown examined me cautiously.

There was a quick flutter, and a tumble of birds wheeled around the pile–song sparrows, chippies and clay-colored sparrows scattering over the leaves, twittering, chirping, breaking into whistles. Even a grasshopper spar-row, which is as much mouse as bird, poked a striped crown out of the under-brush to join the restlessness that moved the flock. Over the brush they went, ribbons of vague grayness in flight; up into sight again as if the pile were a play-ground and this a game of flying tag: down into the grass and leaves. Then, just as suddenly as they appeared, they vanished. Into crevice and hole they flung themselves, and were gone.

For several minutes there was Eddie's clanging maul in the early morning silence and the tractor roar. From the brushheap not a squeak or the lift of a feather. Then I heard a faint "weenk, weenk" from the heart of the pile. In a minute or so the game would be in full round again.

(*Fergus Falls Daily Journal*, October 18, 1947)

CHAPTER 2

Autumn Plumage

In autumn Nature is of no help to the bird watcher. In fact, Nature hinders the watcher and goes out of her way to aid and abet in an amazing degree the birds that go skittering south through our boldly painted woods in September and October and sometimes early November. Or so it seems to anyone who on a brisk fall morning sharp with frost and the smell of wild grape has slung the strap of his field glasses over his head, stuck his notebook into his hip pocket, and pushed through a hazel thicket into shadow-hung woods.

He soon learns that by the time the oaks are in dark-red flame and the maples a light-yellow butter tinged with crimson, the plumage of many of the birds he recognized instantly in the spring is no longer vivid with spots or streaks of color but has taken on a washed out and neutral hue only faintly reminiscent of an earlier brightness.

Usually he doesn't have much trouble with the song sparrows although even the snowy stripe back of a white-crown's eye is smudgy and the Harris sparrow has a ragged dark blotch instead of a black napkin at its throat–that is, it does if it is of this year's brood. The towhee he finds is as rusty-sided and white-breasted as ever, the indigo bunting as indigo as before and the rose-breasted grosbeak (Thoreau's most beautiful bird) as crimson-fronted as in spring. Generally, however, he finds that the sharp edges of color, red or blue or yellow, are shaded, into nondescript merging hues.

But when he comes to the warbler, he is tempted to lug a gun along and bring them to a standstill. Here is the bay-breasted, in spring a strikingly-colored bird with chestnut sides and throat and a pale buff spot on its neck. Now in autumn it is a very pale shadow of itself. Gone is the chestnut. In its place is an olive-green color like the back of a red-eyed vireo; the buff is powdered with dusty gray. And the chestnut-sided warbler–you'd never guess the plain-feathered bird hiding behind a faded elm leaf, its color something like a lemon that is still green, is the same bird which in spring has a shining golden crown, a large white spot on its neck, and sides of rich chestnut. As for the myrtle and the magnolia, gone are their vivid streaks. The one has a white bar across his tail and the other a yellow rump. Otherwise both have plain olive greens and whitish or yellowish breasts. The blackburnian, aptly called the fire throat, has in spring a flaming orange head and breast, and black and white markings on sides and back. Now as it sidles along a branch it is hardly noticeable among the turning ash leaves, its feathers greenish and ordinary, its brightness gone for the year.

And so it is with a good many of those birds whose plumage in April brings one to a pause for a moment in sheer admiration. Several have unforgettable changes. The Wilson warbler has lost his little black cap, the yellow-throated vireo wears yellow spectacles, the black-throated green warbler has discarded his black neckerchief.

Add to these confusing changes the stripling brood from this season's nesting, all soberly garbed and shying away from loud colors for a half year's trial of plain beginnings (in which they are wiser than the offspring of man, which dotes on screaming colors in youth); add also those birds which in the second year have a plumage different from that of the fully matured adult, like the tanager and the orchard oriole; add these up and it is little wonder that the bird watcher comes out of the woods with a sense of frustration and a stiff neck, peevish over the way Nature turns bright feathers to dullness and dull greenness into vivid hues while the autumn migrations filter through the trees.

(*Fergus Falls Daily Journal*, November 12, 1947)

CHAPTER 3

Mighty Hunters are Still Seen on the Ottertail

A couple of Sundays ago I was walking along the Ottertail river not too far from town. I was thinking that few people know and fewer seem to care that this stream has a history and a story that in its way stands beside the historic rivers of our country. The late song sparrows, the white-throats and the Harris sparrows that now "weenk-weenked" at me–these had fluttered in and out of the bushes when the Indians pushed their birch bark canoes up this stream centuries ago, when Hallet led his surveying party here, when Owen in June of 1848 came downstream and upset his canoe, presumably in what is now the heart of Fergus Falls; when Densmore in 1856 platted Echota at the foot of that lake (called Truth lake then) which today is divided by Schmidt's bridge: platted it on the farther shore of the lake which is west of the bridge on what was, so far as I can tell, my father's farm. The years that have flowed away with this stream; and during these years, voyageurs, black-robed priests, missionaries, traders, merchants, not to mention the painted war-parties of Objibwa and Dacotah, paddled up and down this river. And all this on the Ottertail, all this remembered by few.

I was walking along, sorry over the way we neglect our past, when I saw them, three hunters, not young enough to be called "kids," but I soon found not old enough to be called men either–at least, not *real* men. Whether they were city people or country folk, I couldn't tell. It used to be said that you could tell a city man by his shoulder-stoop, slight but noticeable, got from bending over ledgers, account-books and the counter. But today, what with country clubs, recreational centers, cottages at the lakes, paid vacations, and the forty-hour week, the only stoop noticeable in a city man is the one he gets bending over a golf tee or crouching in a duck blind.

And it used to be said that you could tell a farmer by the way he dragged his feet along the street, as if he were still steadying himself against the plow. But nowadays, what with combines, enclosed-cab tractors (with radio), mechanical devices of all kinds–well, whatever a farmer drags, it's not his feet.

I couldn't say whether these three were city or country. But they were mighty hunters. You could tell by the red-and-green-and-black of their shirts that they were after big game. There was something purposeful in the way they strode along, their guns huge and glinting in the sun, making you think that an elk or a buffalo would break into sight any minute. Sometimes they crouched, and you felt the sting of danger; you had visions of tigers on the Ottertail, or wild cats, at least. I felt my blood tingle at their bravery. Not once did they pause. Not all the sporting blood of the pioneer had piddled away then; some was left in these three anyway.

And when the one shouted, "Look out, there he is!" I automatically dropped down. Courageously the hunter threw his gun to his shoulder. I saw the flash. Boldly he rushed into the brush, came forth valiantly with the quarry, wide-shouldered in triumph. "Got him," he yelled in excitment. The others crowded around him admiringly.

With a true hunter's flourish he held the quarry up–four and a half inches of sparrow, feather-ruffled and limp. (I found the body afterward.) For a moment the hunter stood, head thrown back, in the sweep of his shoulders the daring of Buffalo Bill, of Byrd the explorer, of Roosevelt (the hunter, not the armchair strategist), of countless heroic frontiersmen. Then he carelessly threw the limp body back into the brush, all passion sated, the instinct to conquer satisfied. Carefully he wiped his hands on his trousers, as if the smell of blood were over-powering. The three went on to more desperate game. I stayed behind to watch the river. I thought it was good that the backbone of our indomitable pioneers had not entirely changed to spinach.

(*Fergus Falls Daily Journal*, November 26, 1947)

CHAPTER 4

Don't Laugh at the Bird Watcher

Let the first frost strike down and blacken the gardens and put a white dusting on fields and pastures, and the freshman bird watcher is ready to pack his field glasses and notebook away with his sport shirt and tennis shoes. After the first snow fall, he gives up entirely, prepared to watch birds from the safety of a shoveled walk or through a window, a pipe or an apple in one hand and Roberts' *Bird Guide* in the other.

Not quite so ready to give up is the more toughened watcher who is hardened by rain and sleet and long hours lying belly-length in the wet leaves on a hillside. He won't let a drift or two interfere with his curiosity about birds. Up in Friberg last year in an Easter snowstorm that howled about my ears, I watched horned larks walking (they don't hop) about a neighbor's cornshocks until my hands were too numb to hold the glasses and my breath first fogged and then frosted the lenses and I had to give up. (Don't laugh at the bird watcher. He is no crazier than the duck hunter dripping in his blind or a deer hunter freezing while he's posting.) The seasoned naturalist knows that neither snow nor rain will end his studies. Birds may be few in number but this very scarceness adds zest to his kind of hunting. It is the few, not the many, that after all is the spur to zeal.

Some birds spend the winter in Ottertail County—at least they do in Friberg township: chickadees, blue jays, woodpeckers, both downy and hairy; occasionally the American three-toed and the yellow-bellied sapsucker; nuthatches, both rosy-breasted and white-breasted, ordinary residents, and now and then a brown creeper. They are as familiar as our names.

A glimpse of some others requires more than a little alertness. The purple finches are here already, although they may winter rather erratically in Ottertail County. I saw a flock in the woods just east of the Friberg dam early in November. They were cracking the brown seeds of the ash tree for lunch, with nearby ripe viburnam berries for dessert. They really aren't purple-colored at all; dark cranberry would be more like it. They are the rosiest thing to be seen in the leaden-hued late autumn or early winter. Against a snow-covered oak tree they are like fistsful of fire.

The redpolls, wintering here as erratically as the purple finches, will come later, their red foreheads showy, their pink breasts rosy. I see them frequently at my brother Julius's house in Friberg. They flutter in the spirea bushes just outside the window. Great is the excitement among my nephews when the redpolls come to peek in at their unfeathered friends.

Any day now the snow buntings will arrive, if they haven't already, to stay for the winter. From fields and pastures they fly up in swirling dozens. As they run over the snow-covered lumps on the ground, they may look brownish, but once in the air, they turn whitish. The way they burst up in flocks and then drift over the fields, no wonder they are called "snow flakes."

Once in a while the watcher hears the red crossbills "chip-chip-chipping" from an ash tree or an ironwood. They'd probably stay oftener if there were more evergreen trees here, on which they pick at the cones, upside down more often than not. And in many a weedy patch along a road or field the watcher will find the pine siskins, small, heavy-streaked birds with a darkish color: as if a goldfinch had dusted in a coal-bin. He won't be surprised if, some winter's day, he finds a couple of golden-crowned kinglets fluttering restlessly in a thicket, eyeing him as curiously as he them. The ruby-crowned kinglet, cousin of the golden-crowned, appears by the half dozens in spring but rarely here in winter. Prairie horned larks sometimes remain, not often during December, January, or February; they return in March. I have seen them paddling in the snow around Easter. Any time, then, is a good time to find out more about birds, even if in winter you need to put on mittens and ear-muffs and have to buck the drifts.

(*Fergus Falls Daily Journal*, December 1, 1947)

SECTION III

SOUTH DAKOTA BIRDS

CHAPTER 1

Birding in the Sioux Falls, South Dakota, Area

In the farming country west of Sioux Falls, the largest city in the state, lie marshy lakes and potholes, considered by members of the Sioux Falls Bird Club to be the most exciting areas for bird finding in the vicinity. They are readily accessible by car; in fact, many of the birds can easily be seen from the car windows.

Drive west from Sioux Falls on U.S. Route 16 for 11 miles to a crossroad; turn left (south) to Wall Lake, which will soon appear on the right. Follow the section-line roads around the Lake. At the Girl Scout Camp on the east shore, Baltimore and Orchard Orioles are summer residents in the grove of trees and bordering shrubs, Bobolinks in the near-by pastures and haylands. Just southeast of the lake, a section-line road crosses a marsh (no name) with cattails, quillreeds, and pickerelweeds, where, during the summer months, such birds may be observed as Pied-billed Grebes, Great Blue Herons, Black-crowned Night Herons, American Bitterns, Blue-winged Teal, Coots, Yellow-headed Blackbirds, and Red-wings.

Another marsh may be reached by turning right (north) from Route 16 at the aforementioned crossroad and taking the next road to the right, which crosses the marsh half a mile distant. Virginia Rails, Soras, Black Terns, and Short-billed Marsh Wrens are among the birds that nest commonly here.

Continue west on Route 16 for four miles beyond the crossroad that leads to Wall Lake, then turn north on a road to Grass Lake, on the left, three miles distant. At a point half a mile after turning north, the road passes (on the right) a shallow marsh with muddy shores and flats attractive to shorebirds in May, August, and September. Between this point and Grass Lake are big fields (on the right), where thousands of Snow and Blue Geese stop to feed during the northward migration in late March. Grass Lake itself, an extensive marsh with open water, is attractive to many transient waterbirds and waterfowl. Whistling Swans in late March and White Pelicans in fall are the Lake's outstanding ornithological features.

The Sioux Falls Bird Club, whose members may be contacted through the Pettigrew Museum at North Duluth and 8th Street, sponsors a series of lectures each year and conducts field trips in the spring and fall.

(A Guide to Bird Finding West of the Mississippi, 1953)

CHAPTER 2

The Black Hills of South Dakota

It is a mountain upthrust, a pine-covered island outpost in a sea of rolling grass. Viewed from almost any direction across the miles of plains in South Dakota and Wyoming, it towers darkly on the skyline. *Pa-Sapa*, the Indians called it–Black Hills, the Abode of Thunders. *Côtes Noires*, the voyageur French described them; *Costa Negra*, the fur-hungry Spanish. Jean Valle, meeting Lewis and Clark on the Missouri in 1804, told of his wintering camp "under the Black Mountains" where "roams a kind of anamale with large circular horns . . . the size of an Elk" and where is found "a white-booted turkey, an inhabitant," and where frequently "a great noise is heard." Mystery, mammology, and ornithology thus meet in this first appearance of bighorn sheep and sage grouse in the record; it may be the first mention of birds in the Black Hills.

And "Black Hills" James Clyman did call them in his narrative of Ashley's 1823 fur-trading expedition through the southern part of the region where a grizzly bear charged down and ripped off Jedediah Smith's ear and where Black Harris and Bill Sublette found a "putrified" forest with "putrified" trees on which "putrified" birds sang "putrified" songs. As late as 1876, Colonel Dodge, commanding the 1875 Jenney expedition, wrote that the area was regarded as "the wildest and most mysterious of the unknown regions" of the West. Today, ribboned with highways, a brooding duskiness still hangs over the sweeps of blue valley and dour peak.

Older than the Rockies themselves, an isolated yet geographically distinct area, this outlier manifests a complex of often puzzling floristic and faunistic relationships. Though the ponderosa or western yellow pine forest reaches its most eastern point here, it is as an outpost with vast stretches of plains, grasses, and shrubs between it and its duplicate in the Rockies. Northern white spruce, marooned in such cool retreats as Spearfish Canyon, find their counterparts miles to the northward in Canada. Bloodroot, downy violet, and bunchberry-probably never dry prairie inhabitants–grow here, though characteristic of eastern deciduous woods. Short-tailed weasels forage here, although their nearest kin seem to be found in the Laramie Range and the Big Horn Mountains; mountain goats, whitely statuesque on Harney's shoulders, occupying a southern outpost in their range, seem far from their kindred in the western Montana and northern Idaho Rockies.

Like the montane coniferous forms, many of the avian species of the Rockies reach the eastern edge of their breeding ranges in the hills. White-throated swift and Lewis' woodpecker nest here as do western wood pewee and western flycatcher, violet-green swallow, piñon jay, dipper, cañon and rock wrens, mountain bluebird, Townsend's solitaire, two warblers, MacGillivray's and Audubon's, and the spectacular western tanager.

Like the white spruce, two northern coniferous-forest birds apparently are isolated here–the black-backed and northern three-toed woodpeckers. More continent-wide boreal species nesting in this montane outpost include the kinglets, red-breasted nuthatch, gray jay, solitary vireo (the *Plumbeous* form), and red crossbill. Eastern species present are ovenbird, American redstart, house wren, and others.

One species, the white-winged junco, is closely confined to the hills and the immediately contiguous environs. It is actually the only species endemic to the hills and, according to Dr. N.R. Whitney, Jr., is readily observed the year around. I've seen it in early and late spring in the pines back of the Whitneys' Rapid City home, generally with a raucous chorus of Piñon Jays.

Intriguing aspects of biological relationships pop up when least expected. One June day in the southern hills near Hot Springs, I was following a creek up a draw whose steep sides terminated in a craggy rim a hundred feet up. Chokecherry, plum, pin cherry, box elder, and festoons of wild grape, bushy along the water's edge, are plants usually associated with eastern woods. Their shade cooled my face. On the rock rim a hundred feet up, yucca thrust its hedge of bayonets protectively about the light-green flowering stalk; prickly-pear cactus hid its pads of needles in the sage. These were plants usually associated with semi-arid or arid western situations. No "togetherness" here; each in its xeric environment maintained an unneighborly distance from the other. Heat rolled down in waves.

What brought me shock-still, listening, however, was a house wren in front of me, filling a thicket with domestic chatter while above me on the crag a rock wren bounced its wild *cher-wee, cher-wee* along the ledge rim. I have never forgotten that moment: two birds, as it were, voicing the dramatic difference between two ecological areas; a hundred feet apart in space, they were who knows how many hundred miles and years apart in ecological adaptation. Each in its favorable niche, they exchanged notes across the centuries of time and shift and change which brought their disparate perches within singing distance of each other.

The history-conscious bird observer will find legend and biological enigma side by side with the fabulous in the hills. Deadwood, for instance, symbolizing the hardy-spirited as well as the outlaw West; Rushmore, Shrine of Democracy; Custer State Park with its Sylvan Lake; Harney Peak, the Needles, and French Creek with "gold in its grass roots." Others the bird observer will discover for himself.

My first violet-green swallow appeared in Deadwood, perched on a wire no more than a block from No. 10 Saloon where Wild Bill Hickok was pistoled to death and not far from Old Town Hall where each summer *The Trial of Jack McCall* melodramatically recreates the wild 1870's. On a July day I stood in Mt. Moriah Cemetery high on a ridge overlooking the city. Calamity Jane lies there; so does Wild Bill–his second burial. When disinterred in the earlier Boot Hill graveyard, the diggers found him "solid, petrified stone." So the legend runs. But over the city violet-green swallows wheeled: red crossbills "kipped" loudly in the silence and a Clark's nutcracker unfolded the black-and-white of his flight pattern against the green of the opposite ridge. That was in 1957. In 1959 fire left the green ridges a bristle of charred and blackened spires: human carelessness and a trash fire escaping. But the Mt. Moriah overlook is still excellent; swallows and crossbills and an occasional white-throated swift still circle over indestructible Deadwood.

A drive through Spearfish Canyon is to see geology rolled out on the tapestries of cliffs. As the road drops and the walls rise, red shades of sandstone and pink-hued limestone contrast with the changing foliage, but the green-stained shales are almost lost in the green of trees–dark pine, lighter spruce, still lighter deciduous. I have found MacGillivray's warbler in the tangles along Spearfish Creek in June and July. The black-headed grosbeak haunts the thickets, his song deceptively like the rose-breasted's. Dippers bob on the rocks or slip into the water, drawing what seems to be a white sheath of air about them. White-throated swifts (common in almost every canyon) dash along the precipices or swoop down with thin whining sounds. On the dizzy ledges, rock pigeons, long departed from the domestic cotes, are feral here.

The road to Deerfield, running northwest out of Hill City, strikes through the heart of the hills. As Lenord and Clara Yarger told me on the way, the road, though unmarked, is clearly shown on maps available in any Black Hills information center. My first Townsend's solitaire was perched on a fence rail at Deerfield. It was a nondescript grayish bird, I thought, until in flight overhead I saw the wing patches were buffy windows to the sky.

Deerfield looks over the wide meadows bordering Castle Creek. Down this valley from the west in July 1874, rode Custer, self-styled "General" of a thousand-man expedition. An invader of Indian land, clearly a violater of the Indian treaty of 1868, he brought with him 300 beefs for the larder, his brass band, and his bloodhounds. George Bird Grinnell was the zoologist-naturalist. Ludlow's "Report of 1875" pictures the command: riders in grass and flowers shoulder-high, picking bouquets to festoon their horses; the band at night, playing "Garry Owen" and "Artist's Life" to the echoing cliffs; Custer waxing lyrical while he participated in what was probably the first grab by vested interests of land set aside for specific purposes by federal legislation.

Somewhere in the valley or on the prairie above, Grinnell found sandhill cranes half-grown in late July. Today cranes no longer nest in the hills, although, Nat Whitney tells me, they can still be seen over Rapid City in a brief though spectacular flight in late September or early October. Instead of cranes on the prairie–called Reynold's prairie now the Yargers and I saw mountain bluebirds lining a wire fence.

Custer's men noted thousands of burnt-over acres in 1874. Today no hazard is as threatening in the hills as fire. The Hill City-Deerfield road skirts McVey Burn, a slash of green second growth with blackened snags like tombstones to mark the fire of 1939. Here as elsewhere in dry clearings Lewis' woodpecker can be found propped at an angle against a limb or stump–sometimes a fence post. Grinnell found it in the area in 1874. In flight the dark greenish body is unmistakable.

I remember a late afternoon at Rushmore. Shadows fell across the Four Faces. Near the museum, Audubon's warblers, two males, were determining some kind of superiority in swift lunges and evasions among the pines. Crowds, quiet for the most part, gazed at the monolithic symbol, this figured past, framed by ponderosa slants and the arching sky. In a nearby ravine an ovenbird lifted its "teacher" song. Shadows deepened on Lincoln's face. In the tall pines near the parking lot, I heard a western tanager, his note as burry as a scarlet tanager's but uttered more hurriedly, emphatically accentuated. For a moment the fiery scarlet of his head almost illuminated the green spray of needles back of him. A bird of the upper boughs, it can be found almost anywhere in the open pine woods of the middle elevations. A car roared past; a pop bottle exploded against a rock. The tanager flew, a wondrous blur of yellow, red and black. A day to remember–birds, the tired face of Lincoln, and a pop bottle thrown from a raucous car.

To visit Custer State Park is to encounter the past of buffalo herds roaming the virgin prairie and miles of grass. It means ranging through almost 4,000 feet of altitude. It means mountain meadows edging streams and massed bergamot in patches of pink lavender and coneflowers yellow as butter and sometimes a red-shafted flicker flashing in scarlet undulations across white acres of yarrow. It means western meadowlarks and vesper sparrows; rock and cañon wrens where ledges overhang; white-winged juncos, piñon jays, and western tanagers; Clark's nutcrackers, kinglets and red-breasted nuthatches on the shoulders of peaks. It means ranging from antelope and elk to mountain goat.

The Needles Highway–State Route 87–sweeps through northern Custer Park over ridges and down across valleys where the ovenbird sings and the veery's call is part of the shadows. As the road ascends, lifting one above valleys of pine, it worms through a maze of spires, campaniles, steeples of rock, chimneys with needle's-eye holes at the top, and stripes of blue sky seen as if hanging between split gray columns. One hardly notices a Clark's nutcracker darting past a dark monolith or a gray jay diving down on crumbs left by tourists in an overlook.

A hike up Harney Peak begins at Sylvan Lake. We set off, Lenord Yarger and I. The jeep track up Harney leads through ponderosa woods where occasionally, Lenord told me, ruffled grouse explode from the bushes. A quarter way up we looked down on a green meadow below Harney's ramparts. Beaver had flung four dams across the lushness. From a ledge a red-tailed hawk shrilled his warning. Back of us in an open space of deciduous growth a solitary vireo chirred softly.

Midway up the three-and-a-half mile climb, a drink of cold water from a spring heartened the midriff for the final spurt. Here golden-crowned kinglets' faint *seet, seet* made us stop to listen in an uproar of half a dozen red-breasted nuthatches and a colony of chickadees. A western flycatcher monotonously repeated his two-syllabled effort. Mariposa lilies with petals white inside and pale lavender outside dotted the open pine wood. In a moist place we came on deer sign, one pointed hoof track carefully laid on top of the other.

Then we were on the summit, wind in our faces. Below us, studded with blunt gray pinnacles of rock, lay mile on mile of green conifer forests rolling to the horizon; nearer, green blankets of meadows lay flung between mountains. Overhead a violet-green swallow drifted toward a crag.

I thought of Jean Valle's "white-booted turkey." The sage grouse, which Colonel Dodge saw in Red Valley in the southern hills, no longer dance anywhere in the hills. Gone are the cranes, the grizzly bear, and the Indian's penitential dancing floor. But swallows still wheel and bank; piñon jays call on lower levels; and white-winged juncos flash their white feathers like pale stars whirling through the thickets. To the initiate as to the initiated (on Harney's top assurance seems rock-rooted), neither time nor change can quite dim the bright hue of adventure in the Black Hills.

(*The Bird Watcher's America*, 1965)

CHAPTER 3

Geese Along the Missouri

From the edge of sleep I heard them–the call of the wild geese in the hour before midnight, bringing me to sudden wakefulness. The lights of Sioux Falls were pale on my half-opened window. The last snow scattered on the lawns in this South Dakota city reminded me that the retreat of winter was recent and by no means final.

For a week I had been lifting my eyes expectantly to the southeast and the Missouri River, sixty miles away at its nearest point, sharpening my ears for a sound that never failed to send a curious stir along my spine. Now, this evening in the last days of March, it came, the clamor of the first migrants, Canada geese probably, northward bound for their summer breeding grounds.

While winter locked with icy blasts the northern streams and potholes from Baffin Island southward across the Prairie Provinces in Canada to the middle reaches of Nebraska, Illinois, and Iowa in the United States, the congregations of the geese, especially those of the Mississippi Flyway blues, snows, white-fronts, Canadas—were concentrated generally along the gulf coasts of Louisiana, Texas, and northeastern Mexico. Excepting notable populations of blues and snows (which are largely coastal), they also sojourn inland from Arkansas to Illinois and northward, though sparingly, as far as South Dakota's southern marshes. Much less restricted to certain areas than the other species, Canada geese winter up the Mississippi and Missouri Rivers in a wide band. Huge flocks remain at Big Lake in Arkansas and in the Squaw Creek environs in Missouri. One of the largest concentrations of transient and wintering. Canadas in North America, writes Olin Sewall Pettingill in *Bird Finding West of the Mississippi* (1953), is to be found at Horseshoe Lake in the extreme southwest tip of Illinois. At all of these localities national or state wildlife refuges contain the bulk of the migrants. Sobering is the reflection that, in order to save these waterfowl numbers from their most dangerous predator, man himself, the greater share of the wintering flocks must find safety within these protected outposts—reserves pitifully small when compared with the land area of the nation.

Clear and resonant the honking rang in the night. Horseshoe Lake, Squaw Creek—the one more than 700, the other less than 400 miles from Sioux Falls. I wondered whether the flock beating its way over the city this night was an early splinter breaking from the aggregations in Arkansas or Illinois.

Standing at the window, shivering with a touch of something that was not entirely the late March chill, I thought that there is a moment when the loitering thews of winter become an irritation and the yearning for a season's change is overwhelming with the expectancy of a sign to say the ancient gods have not forgotten and the vernal quarter of the year is come again.

Since their arrival in the autumn, the flocks ranged over the wintering grounds. But now comes a day in late February or early March when the gabble and the outcry sharpen, when restlessness apparently becomes an insistent prod. As the sun mounts the zenith and the edge of winter creeps backward, this disturbance grows until, responding to stimuli that may be partly physiological, partly psychological, and partly meteorological, the geese clamor skyward. Those farthest south seem to be the first to respond. The excitement spreads like a contagion.

Northward they go, their twists and turns catching up, flock after flock rising to meet them. Threads become ropes, ropes become webs flung at the sky. At some point in their route, the flights destined to travel the Mississippi Flyway, disengaging themselves from the other flights, begin to converge. One such meeting place seems to be the Yazoo-Mississippi Delta strip, 190 miles of bottomland north of Vicksburg. Here the webs in the sky thicken to skeins as they surge northward, either following the Mississippi proper or paralleling the river in wide pathways overland.

The thousands become tens of thousands as the transients in Arkansas on the White River east of Stuttgart and the populations at Big Lake, northwest of Blytheville, are caught up in the whirl and surge of this contagious movement. They head straight into the broad flow of the Missouri River cutting across their paths eastward from Kansas City to St. Louis. Here the advancing contingents diverge. The greater portion of the blue, snow, and white-fronted geese and lesser numbers of Canadas bend to the west to follow the winding Missouri, while the greater share of the Canada geese with smaller numbers of blues and snows continue up the Mississippi.

Once along the Missouri the flocks become clouds drifting up the meanderings of the brushy bottomlands and over the unpredictable sand bars. By early March the circling thousands descend to the shallows of Sugar Lake near Kansas City and the Squaw Creek waters northwest of St. Joseph to mingle with the transients tarrying there. In dark billows flecked with white, about March 10, they enter Iowa in the Forney Lake environs near Thurman. By mid-March the peak of the flight sometimes reaches Kellogg and Green Bottom Sloughs near Glenwood and the river bottoms south of Council Bluffs. Adverse winds arrowed with icy rain may impede but do not stop their progress; dawns become vociferous with shrill cries as they swing out over the rich Iowa farms to feed in the cornrows. Daily the hills and bluffs, "the towers and castles and sheer cliff faces" farther upstream along the river (which delighted the Lewis and Clark chroniclers and the early travelers), the meander lakes and sloughs, re-echo with the late afternoon forays of the geese.

Not many days later they arrive in the cornfields in the Hornick, Owego, and Luton neighborhoods southeast of Sioux City, white patches of geese among the stalks along with occasional late-fallen snow.

Such wheeling legions must be seen to be believed. The highway paralleling the Missouri–U.S. Routes 275 and 75 across Iowa from Hamburg to Sioux City–offers hundreds of vantage points– ringside seats at one of the continent's great spectacles. Short drives on state and county roads often bring the observer "spitting close" to a cloud of blue and snow geese slanting down like rain upon a cornfield or a wheel of Canadas circling in wary indecision before settling down and almost vanishing into the camouflage of an autumn-plowed field.

By the first week in April the tens of thousands come swarming into South Dakota. Previous to the 1940's, Sioux City apparently was a forking place, a fairish number following up the Big Sioux River to the Red River into Canada. More recently, apparently since the development of a buzzy airport in Sioux Falls, few migrants seem to use this route. Now the flocks continue up the Missouri until they reach the Vermillion and the James Rivers. Usually they rest on what seems to have been traditional stopping places along the bottomlands between Elk Point and Yankton. The sand bars and cornfields here are no doubt safely out of reach of the airport's distraction. From this area they leave the river on a wide front as they point the way northward again.

Northward, as the flock now passing over the city was pointing. Tomorrow or the next day the sky would echo with the big flocks; not over these city streets, to be sure, as once they had, but farther west, twenty, thirty miles. And I would be there as for ten springs now, season after season, I had been, watching the passing of the geese.

Usually, the first sights were excitingly the same. I'd be in the Grass Lake area, west of Sioux Falls and near U.S. Route 16, or at Beaver Lake almost on the edge of the village of Humboldt on Star Route 38, or down on the Missouri bottoms. Sometimes I'd see the vanguards already stationed in a cornfield or resting, a mottled island, on the water. Often glancing afar, I had to squint and look again to see whether I was looking at a smudge of cloud or a drift of geese against the sky.

I remember a hill on a prairie with the sunset burning the skyline. From the zenith to the western horizon, the sky was marked with the black pencilings of the flights. As far as I could see, north was linked with south by the uncoiling tangles, the interlacing strings of the flocks; and the evening sang with a myriad of voices.

And I remember a Sunday in early April. On the banks of the Missouri near Elk Point I watched the geese drive in, rank on crescent rank. Sand bars and islands were a patchwork of gray and white concentrations. Above them more flights came in. As I looked across the river, I saw steps of geese slanting from the skyline of the hills down to the sand bars. Against the green of dwarf cedars on the Nebraska "breaks" opposite, they were clearly etched. Above them a crescent was beginning to break into segments of descending geese. Above these were strings and V's, their flight appearing slower with the deceptiveness of distance; higher above, moving even more slowly, tangles and broken curls of birds; higher still, imperfect M's and N's, broken letters moving across the sky; and black against a popcorn cloud, rows and chevrons in motion, orderly, precise, tiny at that great height; layer on layer they came in, each layer maintaining its direction. As I looked up, I was almost dizzied by the tracery of geese in motion, line moving against line, a flowing crisscross of birds. The highest often floated past and circled back before they began to break order, sideslipping, zigzagging, plummeting with rigid wings until they reached the lower flights when they seemed to check momentum and joined the sedately descending thousands.

Sometimes, as I remembered, winter in the backlash of fury hurled snow and sleet in a cold front upon the migration, grounding the flocks or pelting them into temporary retreat. I've seen them head south in a rain of snowflakes, but not often.

While on the river the flocks take to the country frequently before daybreak and settle to feed on waste grain in the fields, on new grasses, and such cereals as are sprouting. Sometimes the concentrations are so huge that, when disturbed, a whole cornfield seems to rise in a burst of wing-beats and wild clamor. By mid-morning the main groups are back at the river to rest and preen, to gather gravel and probe for aquatic organisms in the soil of the sand bars and mud flats, to maintain the mating ties, and, among the laggards, to complete the courtship rituals. By late afternoon they are in the fields again. Often the flocks, hidden in the cornstalks, are betrayed to the observer by the restless movements of small numbers passing from group to group. At dusk they rise to circle and wheel, some to return to the river, others to break off for more distant water. Hopping from lake to lake, they cross the state in a fairly wide belt to enter North Dakota. One morning the flocks are gray and white edges on marsh and shore and island; the next evening they are threads and skeins vanishing down the skyline's slant. Cornfield and shoreline are strangely empty.

It is disturbing to remember that even here in the Missouri Valley the traditional stopping places are threatened by man's egomaniac advances. Drainage programs now have the audacity of federal sanction. Despite twisty assurances of officialdom in 1949 that the Missouri impoundments in South Dakota would provide more shorelines and sand bars for more feeding geese, more shallows for greater concentrations of transient birds, a paradise for waterfowl, time and the records, on the contrary, dramatize the fact that each year fewer and fewer geese are counted along the impounded portions of the river and that the completed Eden for waterfowl is, as far as the geese are concerned apparently, a Hades of fluctuating, almost infertile mud-reaches.

By now the flock over the city this night was only a faint disturbance. I learned to listen. Tomorrow perhaps I would stand once more on a prairie hill or a Missouri bluff, enthralled by the crescent thousands passing. For a week or ten days I'd be aware of a queer sort of response to a stimulus—a stimulus common to those still sensitive to wild grape smell in autumn or bloodroots at the edge of snow: a strange sort of inner compulsion hard to describe in ordinary syllables and, in the gadgetry of our technological civilization, harder to explain. After that, with the last chevron fading like a wisp on the horizon, there would be quiet on the stopping places. Another year's migration would be over. But I'd remember this night and the silence after the flock's departure. Silence is a lonely sound—lonesome as the cry of the wild goose itself.

(*The Bird Watcher's America*, 1965)

CHAPTER 4

Trailing Lewis and Clark

A traveler on U.S. 16 (Interstate 90) going across southern Minnesota and South Dakota will be the richer ornithologically and historically for a side trip from Sioux Falls, S. Dak.

Take Interstate 29 south to Elk Point and then go west on State 50 to Chamberlain, generally following the Missouri River. In early spring and frequently in winter this route is rewarding.

At Elk Point, where Lewis and Clark hunted geese in 1804 and shot their first bison on a nearby prairie, a small but interesting sand dunes area borders the river. This is one of the few places in South Dakota where piping plovers, and sometimes the least tern, nest. Almost anyone in Elk Point will tell you how to find the dunes.

The plaintive notes of the plover, and possibly glimpses of the tiny, swallowlike tern, will be the reward for some difficulties of access. Make this trip soon, for river "improvements" now pending will certainly impair, if not destroy, this last natural sand dunes area on the Missouri.

Continuing along State 50 to Vermillion, you'll find, after April 20, migrating geese and ducks by the tens of thousands. Canada, blue, and snow geese, mallards, pintails and green-winged teal can be seen from the University of South Dakota campus or from the windows of Dr. Byron E. Harrell's "bird wing" house on the bluffs of the river. If you have any questions about birds of the area, write Dr. Harrell at the university's Department of Zoology.

In the bottomlands along the river, tall trees and jungle-type underbrush border small fields. The red-bellied woodpecker is seen here. Bobwhites, generally scarce, occasionally scuttle across the road. Yankton, on State 50, frequently offers an opportunity to view wintering eagles. In the spring the city's main streets offer excellent viewing sites for watching migrating waterfowl.

To reach the eagle roost, leave State 50 for County 52 and proceed westward toward Old Fort Yankton, Gavin's Point Dam and the eastern end of Lewis and Clark Lake. At the north end of the dam is a roost in cottonwoods where Al Grewe of the National Audubon Society's Continental Bald Eagle Research and Conservation Project has been conducting a three-year study. He has seen as many as eighty bald eagles here from about November 15 to April 1. With care, "one can approach relatively close to the perching birds," he writes.

At Springfield on County 52, Grewe says, there is a good chance of seeing double-crested cormorants nesting in dead trees along the widened river. These trunks once signaled the magnificence of the Missouri bottomlands, but now Lewis and Clark Lake rises and falls along an unstable shoreline.

A trip to Running Water on County 37 is a must, according to my hosts, Herman and Lois Chapman, residents of that area. At Running Water, a stern-wheel river boat evokes the old Missouri West by ferrying you and your car across the stream. The boat operates from April 1 to November 1. You may see cormorants either nesting or spreading their wings to dry on the dead tree stubs. To return to State 50, take County 37 and County 52 at Springfield.

Pickstown, where historic Fort Randall once stood, provides one of the best birding spots in the state. To reach Pickstown, leave State 50 at Wagner and follow County 40 west for 12 miles. From November until early April, you're likely to see bald and golden eagles, rough-legged and red-tailed hawks, and an occasional prairie falcon. Here, Al Grewe has seen upwards of 120 bald eagles in the trees of the picnic area below Fort Randall Dam.

Not far away, the chapel of old Fort Randall reminds the birder of vespers held in the wilderness when the Sioux and Poncas lifted their battle cries. Today, barn swallows sweep through the ruins of the empty arches, and Bell's vireo in nearby tangles is sure to call querulously, *cheedle-cheedle-chee* and answer without pause, *cheedle-cheedle-chew*. Where Army bugles rang on the parade grounds 100 years ago, black-billed magpies lift the white and black of their wing patterns in flight.

A mile or so downstream from Pickstown is the site where explorer Jean Baptiste Trudeau built his cabin in 1794 and shot turkeys for his winter larder. There are no turkeys here anymore, but rock wrens sing their *chee-ur, chee-ur* from the rimrocks. Blue grosbeaks nest in the bushy draws south of town. My brother John and his wife Hazel hear the birds singing on the family clothesline. During the first week in April they see long straggles of sandhill cranes bugling northward.

On the west edge of town prairie dogs bark thinly, flickering their tails. Prairie dog towns are fast disappearing from the scene under eradication pressures.

The spring dance of the greater prairie chicken is a reminder that mankind's delight in rhythmic movement may derive from observing the behavior of birds. At Burke, on U.S. 18 west of Pickstown, the Chapmans introduced me to this ritual and to the surprises of a prairie chicken dancing ground. Before you go there, write to Warren Jackson, District Game Manager, Chamberlain, S. Dak., for details.

Under the game manager's direction, you drive into the wondrous, undulating Missouri River breaks country before dawn. If you stop where Warren suggests, from your car you see prairie chicken cocks strutting out of the growing light, their feathers a maze of fluffed-out eagerness, their air sacs yellow or orange badges of male intensity.

Now and again the birds leap suddenly and impatiently into the air, as if propelled by superabundant but frustrated energy. In the reddening dawn you hear their hollow, booming woo-loo-oo calls, reminiscent of the sound made by blowing across the open end of an empty jug.

At Chamberlain on U.S. 16 (Interstate 90), where a new bridge spans the Missouri, cliff swallows dart among the girders. East of the city but within sight of the freeway lies Red Lake. In April and May, western grebes, arching their white necks, swim in pairs here. Horned and eared grebes ride the ripples, and white pelicans maneuver their formations gracefully out of and into the water. Resident ducks are common, and song sparrows warble from the shoreline bushes.

As we watch the waterfowl, it's worth remembering that the wetlands of the Dakotas must be preserved if our water birds, many of them game birds, are to survive in appreciable numbers.

(*Audubon Magazine*, March-April 1966)

SECTION IV
MAJOR WORKS

CHAPTER 1

Distribution of the Cardinal in South Dakota

By Herbert Krause and Sven G. Froiland

The extension of the range of the Cardinal (*Richmondena cardinalis*) and its seasonal status in the Upper Midwest apparently have received little attention in ornithological literature. This seems particularly true of the area bordering the Upper Mississippi River in Minnesota and the Missouri River in South Dakota. Roberts (1936:335) states that by 1936 this species was established in Minnesota but was "confined as a resident breeding bird to the southeastern portion of the state." However, he found that it was "extending its range northward and westward."

In South Dakota, Visher (1915:332) reported the Cardinal as "a tolerably common resident in the Missouri Valley near Vermillion" (Clay County) by 1913. Five years later, according to Stephens (1918:101) it had "become very well established as a permanent resident" in Union County. Both Clay and Union counties are located in the extreme southeastern part of the state. Few reports of the Cardinal in South Dakota appeared subsequently, and, as late as 1930, Stephens observed (pp. 365–366): "It would be very interesting to know how far up the Missouri River these birds have extended their range at the present time; and also how far up the tributaries in this region they have penetrated." This study has been undertaken in an effort to throw light on some of these queries.

In order to obtain as broad a presentation of data as possible, the historical background was searched and the items in Stephens' (1945) bibliography and in the available literature checked. In addition to notes and observations of some seven years of personal field work, the writers interviewed and corresponded with competent observers located in strategic positions in the state. These persons' generous reports and comments are gratefully acknowledged. Those of Art Lundquist, Alfred Peterson, Ruth Habeger and V.H. Gulp have been especially helpful.

The literature on the Cardinal in South Dakota is admittedly scanty. The scarcity of observers and collectors may be held responsible for many of the gaps in the information on this species. It was not listed in the journal of Audubon (1900), who was on the Missouri in 1843, nor was it included in Baird's (1858) list of the railroad survey made during the period 1853–1856. The first record seems to have been that of McChesney (1879:78), who observed a pair at Fort Sisseton in the extreme northeastern part of the state in the spring of

1877. During that summer he saw a male several times. Neither collection nor nesting data was reported, however.

McChesney (*op.cit.*) remarked that the Cardinal was "only of casual occurrence in this region." However, it is possible that these individuals were accidental rather than casual. It is not unusual for a Cardinal to appear far from its accustomed range. Roherls (1936:335) speaks of a male Cardinal reported in Minnesota in 1930 some 300 miles north of any previous record.

It may be significant that in the 75 years following McChesney's report of them, no further mention seems to be made of appearances of Cardinals in the vicinity of Fort Sisseton or in the northeast generally. Agersborg, whose list (1885) is the first important published record for the state by a resident, does not include it either for the state as a whole or for the southeastern part of the state. Larson (1925) did not list the Cardinal in his ten-year study (1906–1916) of the east-central area centering about Minnehaha County. Alfred Peterson, whose field work and publications began in the early 1920's, writes (letter, October 15, 1954) that he has never seen the Cardinal in the central northeastern region. Art Lundquist (letter, October 12, 1954), a veteran field man in the northeast area adjacent to the Fort Sisseton country, does not include occurrences until 1950 and does not report nesting data at this writing.

Though the Cardinal was noticed first in the 1870's, what seems to have been the first report of a Cardinal nest in South Dakota and perhaps the first indication of permanent residence in the state did not appear until after the turn of the century. In 1902 D.H. Talbot published a note regarding the breeding of this species in Union County, not far from Sioux City, Iowa (Fig. 1). Ten years later Visher (1915) noted it as "tolerably common in the Missouri Valley near Vermillion." This represents an advance upstream of some 40 miles. By the second decade, its nesting range seems to have included only the two counties in the extreme southeastern part of the state.

At the same time, as a winter bird, the Cardinal was appearing farther and farther up the Missouri. In the early 1920's it was found at Yankton, 50 miles upstream from Sioux City. In the 1930's it continued its march. In fact, during the period from 1930 to 1946, it apparently extended considerably its winter range in all the eastern part of the state. This species was making headway not only on the Missouri, but also on the James and the Big Sioux rivers, tributaries which drain a major share of the eastern half of the state. Reports of its appearances were noted from the Missouri on the south to the North Dakota border on the north. As early as the winter of 1929 Larrabee mentioned it as a December visitant in Minnehaha County, which is traversed by the Big Sioux. In the spring of 1937 Dr. J.F. Brenckle banded an individual in Spink County, 260 miles up the James River. In the years 1940–1942 it appeared as a winter bird in those northeastern counties bordering on North Dakota. This brought it again into the Fort Sisseton area where McChesney had seen it some 75 years before. In some forty-odd years, then, it had traversed the eastern portion of the state from south to north. What is more, apparently this area became familiar

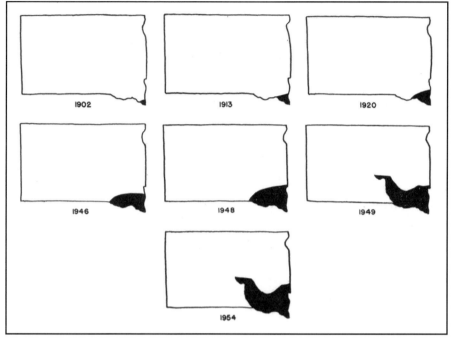

Fig. 1. Extension of the breeding range of the Cardinal in South Dakota based on available nesting records.

ground. In the years following the middle 1940's the Cardinal has been reported fairly regularly in the northeastern portion of South Dakota. In 1954 wintering individuals were reported at Mobridge in the Missouri bottoms, which brings this species to within 30 miles of the North Dakota border in the north-central portion of the state also.

However, all these northern occurrences were recorded in fall, winter and early spring, and most involved male birds only. No summer records are available in spite of search by field men such as Lundquist and Peterson.

Meanwhile the breeding range of the Cardinal was advancing northward also. Randall (1953) found nests and young in the Fort Randall (Pickstown) locality in 1946, a 72-mile advance up the Missouri and some 125 miles from Sioux City. In 1950 a nest was reported at Fort Thompson, 100 miles north of Fort Randall. At present (1954) the Cardinal is reported nesting in the river bottoms at Farm Island and at Pierre, some 260 miles upstream from the place in Union County where the first nest was found. This, according to present evidence, is its farthest penetration up the Missouri as a breeding bird.

In the eastern part of the state, Krause in 1948 found two nests and eggs at Sioux Falls, Minnehaha County, an advance of about 80 miles up the Big Sioux River. Since 1948 there have been many reports of nests, eggs, young and juveniles in this area (Froiland, Krause and others). The Cardinal is common the year around in Minnehaha County, and it is continuing to spread northward. According to Ruth Habeger (letter, October 29, 1954) it nests regularly in Lake and Moody counties just north of Minnehaha County, an advance in six years of some 40 miles northward along the Big Sioux River. On the basis of available data, this represents its farthest penetration northward as a breeding bird and perhaps as a permanent resident. Thus in half a century, the breeding range of the Cardinal has advanced some 100 miles northward in the eastern part of South Dakota.

Habitat Distribution

A study of the distribution map (Fig. 2) suggests that the main streams and their tributaries played a part in the widening range of the Cardinal in South Dakota. In almost every instance the reports come from localities on fairly large streams or their tributaries. There are no reports of Cardinals from areas of high land between watersheds. Neither is there information on appearances or nesting on the wide prairies or the hill counties or along the small prairie tributaries of larger streams with their somewhat less abundant vegetation. Few records come from counties which have intermittent streams and which therefore seem to offer less cover and fewer nesting possibilities.

It is perhaps significant that McChesney's sight record of the Cardinal occurs at Fort Sisseton, for this military post was in the lake country in that portion of the northeastern part of the state which is drained by the tributaries

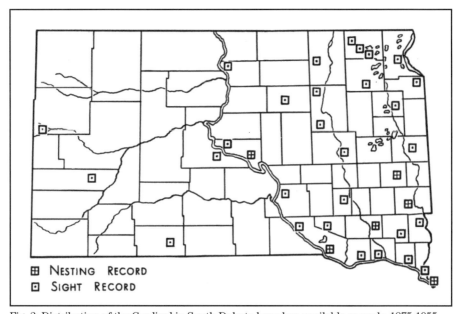

Fig. 2. Distribution of the Cardinal in South Dakota based on available records, 1875-1955.

of the Big Sioux River and which lies some 200 miles north—almost straight north—of the point where the Big Sioux empties into the Missouri.

Evidently the vegetation bordering these waterways offers the type of habitat suitable for nesting and cover. Generally, in the adjacent areas appear shrubby willow (*Salix*), plum-choke cherry (*Prunus*) and dogwood (*Cornus*) over which in many places tower cottonwood (*Populus deltoides*) and American elm (*Ulmus americana*), hackberry (*Celtis occidentalis*) and boxelder (*Acer negundo*), basswood (*Tilia americana*) and ash (*Fraxinus lanceolata*) trees. Vines, such as wild grape (*Vitis vulpina*) and Virginia creeper (*Parthenocissus quinquefolia*), occur in some localities. This kind of habitat provides not only shelter for the Cardinal but food as well.

Extension of the Cardinal's Range Westward

It is curious that appearances of the Cardinal have been singularly lacking in the area west of the Missouri River. At least available records fail to report them. Visher (1909) does not include this species in his comprehensive "List of the Birds of Western South Dakota" which takes into account the observations of Hayden on the Warren Expeditions in 1857 and 1869, and the Grinnell report on the Custer Expedition of 1874, as well as the reports of such competent observers and collectors as Lee, Sweet, and Behrens, whose collections are still available. The region covered by Visher's "List" includes the Bad Lands and the Black Hills with the adjacent areas. The Cardinal was not found on the Pine Ridge Reservation during Tullsen's (1911) stay there (1901–1908) nor was it seen by Visher (1912) during his survey (in 1908) of the area which also included a good portion of the White River drainage system.

Much of this region is semi-arid in character. The streams for the most part are intermittent and even those which persist during the greater part of the year are generally saline. While streams in the Black Hills are fresh-water, they too are frequently intermittent. Plants which produce bushy thickets or viny tangles are not as abundant as in the east nor do they appear as regularly. It may be that the area, including as it does both the Black Hills and the Bad Lands, offers a complex of factors which might be operative here—factors which involve unusual and often puzzling floral and faunal distribution patterns.

The first mention of the Cardinal in western South Dakota appeared in the literature in 1951, when Haight reported two Cardinals seen near Belle Fourche on the Cheyenne River in the northwestern part of the state. In the early spring of 1955 two occurrences were observed, one by Hyde (1955) in Rapid Canyon near Rapid City in the Black Hills and one by Krumm (1955) at La Creek Wildlife Refuge on the Nebraska border in the southwest. All three appearances were in winter and early spring and involved males. Considering the non-migratory behavior of this species and its sporadic appearances, one wonders whether these individuals came from the Missouri, following its tributaries, the Cheyenne in the north, the White in the south. There is also the possibility that the southern birds came from another tributary of the Missouri, the Niobrara River in Nebraska. At any rate, according to the data, the Cardinal has appeared west of the Missouri three times, all within the last five years. It will be interesting to see whether in the next 20 or 30 years it will increase in numbers as it did east of the Missouri with the possibility of finally establishing itself as a permanent resident in this western region.

Literature Cited

Acersborc, G.S. 1885. The birds of southeastern Dakota. *Auk*, 2:276–289.

Audubon, Maria R. 1990. Audubon and his journals, Vols. I and II. New York; Charles Scribner's Sons.

Baird, S.F. 1858. Birds. In: Explorations and surveys to ascertain the most practicable and economical route for a railroad from the Mississippi River to the Pacific Ocean, Vol. 9. *Senate Ex. Doc.* No. 78. Washington, D.C.

Haight, C. 1951. Birds of the hills. *South Dakota Bird Notes*, 3:52–54.

Hyde, Mrs. A.R. 1955. Cardinal at Rapid City. *South Dakota Bird Notes*, 7:29.

Krumm, K. 1955. Cardinal at LaCreek Federal Wildlife Refuge. *South Dakota Bird Notes*, 7:29–30.

Larrabee, A.P., and P.J. Larrabee. 1929. Christmas bird census. Yankton, S. Dakota. *Bird-Lore*, 31:58.

Larson, A. 1925. The birds of Sioux Falls, South Dakota, and vicinity. *Wilson Bull.* 37:18–38, 72–76.

McChesney, C.E. 1979. Notes on the birds of Fort Sisseton, Dakota Territory. *Bull., U.S. Geol. and Geogr. Surv. Terr.*, 5:71–103.

Randall, R. 1953. Birds of the Fort Randall reservoir area. *South Dakota Bird Notes*, 5:68.

Roberts, T.S. 1936. The birds of Minnesota, Vol. 2. Minneapolis; Univ. Minnesota Press.

Stephens, T.C. 1918. Notes on the birds of South Dakota, with a preliminary list for Union County. *Proc. Iowa Acad. Sci.*, 25:85–104.

Stephens, T.C. 1930. Bird records of two winters, 1920–1922, in the Upper Missouri Valley. *Proc. Iowa Acad. Sci.*, 37:357–366.

Stephens, T.C. 1945. An annotated bibliography of South Dakota ornithology. Privately printed, Sioux City, Iowa.

Talbot, D.H. 1902. The Cardinal breeding at Sioux City, Iowa. *Auk*, 19:86–87.

Tullsen, H. 1911. My avian visitors: notes from South Dakota. *Condor*, 13:89–104.

Visher, S.S. 1909. A list of the birds of western South Dakota. *Auk*, 26:144–153.

Visher, S.S. 1912. The biology of south-central South Dakota. *South Dakota State Geol. and Biol. Surv. Bull.*, 5:61–130.

Visher. S.S. 1915. A list of the birds of Clay County, south-eastern South Dakota. *Wilson Bull.*, 27:321–335.

(*The Wilson Bulletin*, June 1956)

CHAPTER 2

Nesting of a Pair of Canada Warblers

In the mid-afternoon of June 21, 1957, Dr. O.S. Pettingill, Jr. and I found a nest with eggs of a pair of Canada Warblers (*Wilsonia canadensis*) not far from the shore of North Fishtail Bay, an extension of Douglas Lake in Cheboygan County, northern Lower Michigan. The next day we set up a blind approximately ten feet from the nest-site. On the morning of June 23, I began daily observations.

A preliminary search of the literature revealed that the Canada Warbler is one of the *Parulidae* which has received little attention. To cite one instance, Bent (1953:649) says that it is not known "how long the young remain in the nest." Cordelia J. Stanwood (in Bent, 1953:648) seems to have been the first to put up a blind and study this species in some detail, though apparently only for a short time during the nestling period. Except for notes by Kendeigh (1945a, 1945b, and 1952), by Walkinshaw (1956), and by Middleton (1957), all of which provide excellent data, the literature does not include a comprehensive study of the Canada Warbler. Even reports on behavior during the nesting period are limited to brief notes.

From the morning of June 23 until August 9, I spent the major portion of each day, a total of 207 hours, in the blind or on the territory in the adjacent areas. The following remarks deal merely with the data recorded during the period of incubation from June 23 to July 1 in 39 hours and 39 minutes of observation.

The Nest-Site

The nest was in the middle of a small opening in a dry, mixed pine-maple-cedar community. White pine was the dominant growth; bracken grew rankly on the forest floor. A road, paralleling the lake shore, ran past the site, providing additional "edge effect" to that which was formed by the perimeter of the open space. According to the literature, the Canada Warbler seems inclined toward boggy or swampy situations, heavily shaded, but this nest was 400 feet or more from a spruce bog and an alder swale—places that would meet any such habitat requirements.

The nest itself was built under the fronds of dead bracken which had fallen about the foot of a small red maple. The fronds formed a projection over it.

Some 15 feet away grew a small white cedar, apparently the favorite resting haunt of this pair of Canada Warblers. The undergrowth surrounding the nest included wintergreen, wild lily-of-the-valley, blueberry, sarsaparilla, and the ever-present bracken. Above the bracken rose sapling red maple, aspen, beech, alder, pin cherry, and paper birch. And beyond the opening were mature white pine, aspen, birch, red maple, alder, and white cedar.

Forty-one species of birds were noted in the nesting area. The American Redstart (*Setophaga ruticilla*) and the Ovenbird (*Seiurus aurocapillus*) were the most common. Other birds regularly present included the Veery (*Hylocichla fuscescens*), Blue Jay (*Cyanocitta cristata*), Common Crow (*Corvus brachyrhynchos*), Yellow-shafted Flicker (*Colaptes auratus*), and Robin (*Turdus migratorius*). Occasional visitors were such birds as the Black-throated Green Warbler (*Dendroica virens*), Pileated Woodpecker (*Dryocopus pileatus*), and Wood Thrush (*Hylocichla mustelina*). The mammals included the red squirrel, gray squirrel, eastern chipmunk, short-tailed shrew, and white-tailed deer. A red fox was reported in the vicinity but I did not see it. The only reptile was a garter snake which I caught sight of sunning itself about 200 feet from the nest. However, I saw no activity which suggested any interaction between the Canada Warbler and these faunal forms.

The Nest

A statement that the Canada Warbler uses a variety of materials for nesting purposes but "appears not commonly to use any parts of evergreen trees" (Kendeigh 1945b:43I) met an exception here. The nest under observation was made of white pine needles mixed with the needles of red pine rounded into shape. Woven into these materials were bits of dead cedar leaves, rootlets, small plant stems, and several long strands of the dried inner bark of aspen. All the materials were brown in color so that in appearance the nest was dead-leaf brown. The forest floor, thickly strewn with layers of fallen white pine needles, was also brown, as ripe-acorn brown as the dead bracken that curled over the nest. There were four eggs, creamy-white and freckled rather heavily with reddish brown spots, especially at the large end.

Incubation Period

Though Kendeigh (1945a) considers 12 days to be the normal period for incubation in the *Parulidae* generally, Forbush's (1929:308) bleak words, "No data," seem to sum up what is known about the exact length of the incubation period of the Canada Warbler. Since the nest was found on June 21 and two eggs were found to be hatched by 7:35 a.m. on July 1, the portion of the incubation period under observation approximated nine days. If Kendeigh's 12-day period is used as a yardstick, the beginning of incubation must have occurred on June 18 or shortly before. The third egg hatched at 2:00 p.m. on July 1. The fourth egg unaccountably disappeared without a trace on the morning of June 26.

Female on the Nest

On the nest the female was often remarkably quiet. Frequently for periods of from ten to twenty minutes she would remain stone-still. Sometimes her eyes closed and she appeared to doze, though for short periods only. At such times she appeared to lose a certain alertness and to relax—the quiescence of sleep. But a noise or a distraction, so faint it escaped my eye and ear, brought her to instant and guarded wakefulness. After such a period her eyes seemed to glint with renewed intensity.

At other times, more restive, she would yawn, swallow repeatedly, stretch her neck, rise in the nest, poke at what I thought must be the eggs, push them closer to her, then, shifting her position, settle back and waggle down into sitting position. Sometimes watching her try to lift a wing slightly as if to stretch it I felt a sympathetic achy twinge in my own cramped legs—cramped from hours of being draped over a camp stool in my blind.

Female off the Nest

Seldom did I hear her voice except as *chep* often repeated. Once or twice, however, she uttered low *trep* notes as she left the nest. Once off she usually flew via an under-bracken route to the white cedar tree, apparently a favorite resting, loafing, and feeding place. Here, on a number of occasions especially during the early brooding period, I saw her come, hurrying in the rush of her wings. Once in the tree, she almost always raced up branches, darted from limb to limb, plunged from one elevation to another below, flipped her tail, fluttered her wings.

This violent activity finished, she sometimes rested, perched motionlessly perhaps for a minute or two, yawned, rubbed her mandibles against the branch on which she perched, defecated, ruffled her feathers and shook them. Sometimes she stretched wing and leg, one wing and one leg at a time. Sometimes she preened vigorously, especially on the breast, at other times lightly. She might nibble the bend of the wing, poke at the abdomen, pull at the base of the rectrices and prod at a spot under the wing.

Then for a space she fed. One moment she was perched, motionless as the wood on which she sat. The next instant she was a bundle of restless activity, dashing up a branch to snatch something from a leaf or grab up an insect from a bud scar. Sometimes she tore a worm from the bark and, if it was wriggly, slammed it against the side of a limb. Often she fluttered under a cluster of leaves or darted out to snap up a fly or mosquito or other insect with a *whirr* of the wings and a loud snap of the mandibles. This snapping of the bill, flycatcher-like, noted by Samuels as early as 1883, is probably responsible for the old names given this species—Canadian Flycatcher and Canadian Flycatching Warbler. In fact, the female's quick movements and unpredictableness while feeding remind one of the American Redstart, and the snapping of the bill of both the Redstart and many of the *tyrannids*.

Occasionally she went beyond the white cedar. Now and then she disappeared into the bracken and out of my view. At such times she may have gone some distance, perhaps out of sight of the nesting place, for often when I stepped out of the blind, no "cheps" of protest came from bush or tree. Perhaps she went to bathe or drink. One rainy morning I saw her beak lifted, nibbling the drops of moisture on the tip of a Juneberry leaf.

Frequently on her "off-the-nest" period the male would join the female in the white cedar. While she frisked animatedly among the branches or rested or fed, he was in attendance, sometimes only a few inches away but generally several feet. Now and again he seemed to be stimulated by her activity and preened or ran up a slanted branch when she did, but it seemed to be at a slower pace and was done as if he did this because she did and not because he was urged by necessity. At such times I half expected him to burst into a swelling aria, but beyond a few throaty "treeps," he remained silent. Several times after a resting period, there were chasing episodes, one bird following the other in quick flashes among the branches. It seemed to me that the male began the pursuit but at times I felt that the chase began with the female.

I noticed that when feeding or other activities took them out of the white cedar, the female usually led the way, the male immediately following and frequently entering into pursuit flight. Weaving and turning the two would disappear from view.

Female Attentive and Inattentiveness

During the nine days that I watched the nest, the female alone was involved in actually sitting on the eggs. Kendeigh (1952) believes this to be true of wood warblers in general, although he does not mention the Canada Warbler specifically. Her periods of attentiveness averaged 32 minutes and were longer than Kendeigh (1945a:163) found for the *Parulidae* generally—nine to twenty-eight minutes. During my observations she was on the nest 85 percent of the time. The longest period was 84 minutes on June 29 and the shortest, one minute on June 23.

Her inattentive periods averaged about seven minutes, well within the limits of from two to eleven minutes given by Kendeigh (1945a:163). Her longest period away from the nest was 17 minutes on June 23 and the shortest was one minute that same day. Most frequently she was gone for about four minutes.

The Female's Return to the Nest

The female's approach to the nest seemed to be on two different levels of elevation. If intruders had been about—crows, jays, or man—she perched on the aspen or maple sapling, "chepping" sometimes, silent other times, always peering about before she dived into the bracken and climbed into the nest. However, if the way seemed clear, she came in under the bracken and went directly to incubate or brood. Rarely did she perch on the nest or even near it.

She was either on it or off it. Sometimes, after a longer-than-usual rest stop, she fairly tumbled along the ground and up the little incline to the nest as if in a hurry to get back to the eggs.

She clung to the nest with remarkable tenacity. When I checked the eggs or young she would let me come to within three feet of her and once my hand was within twelve inches of her before she "exploded" into the bracken.

Male Attentiveness

During my observations, the male came to the nest-site only nine times. On many occasions though I caught him in attendance in the white cedar tree. And he may have been silently present more often than I know. Usually, however, I would hear a soft *trip* or *treep* or a series of such notes (like the buzz of a Cedar Waxwing, *Bombycilla cedrorum*, only lower in pitch and less musical). I would see him either in the white cedar or the white pine in back of the blind or across the road in a red maple or white pine. He was, as far as I know, in attendance about three percent of the time during incubation. His longest period of attentiveness was ten minutes on June 27 and the shortest one minute on June 26.

As far as I could see, the male never approached the nest as if he were about to join the female while she incubated the eggs, or to come close to her. Not once did I observe him perched on the edge of the nest while she was on the eggs. There was no sign of such behavior as touching of bills or even close proximity one with the other. Once, however, for a short period he sat under the bracken back of the nest-site.

As he approached the nest, the male uttered a rather sharp *threep* which seemed to be a kind of command. At any rate, on its utterance, the female left the nest immediately, almost as if in a hurry. On only one occasion did I see her remain on the nest at the appearance of the male. Usually she perched nearby among the bracken, although several times she flew as far as the white cedar. There she remained while the male came to the nest. Not once during incubation did I see her return to the nest while he was there.

Singing of the Male

Even when he was not in actual attendance either at the nest or in its immediate vicinity, the male presumably kept in communication with the female by a generous and full-throated amount of singing. I did not hear him singing at or near the nest-site until the nestling period began but always at some distance—anywhere from approximately 75 to 300 feet away. Although Kendeigh (1945a:159) reports that in the Canada Warbler the male sings "at a rate of six times per minute" and that "Soon after a mate is secured they [the males] usually become very quiet," I found no cessation of song in the white cedar male during that portion of the incubation which I observed. On June 23, he sang 13 times, each song period averaging nine minutes; on June 27 he sang eight times, each interval of song approximating 4.6 minutes per period; and on July 1, the day of the hatching and the inception of feeding, he sang seven times, lengthening the intervals of song to an average of 5.3 minutes.

So far as I could determine, the delivery of song was not confined to a selected perch or a particular locality or even a given area in the foraging range. I could not determine the extent of his territory. It seemed to me that when the desire to vocalize came on, the male sang where he happened to be.

Male Comes to Nest with Food

When the male did come, he came in the most striking fashion. I became aware of this remarkable behavior the first day in the blind. My notes for June 23 read: "3:32 p.m.. Female left the nest as male came in. Male appeared with green worm; approached the nest, hopped on the edge, and leaned forward as if offering food to young birds in nest; uttered 'run-together' series of Junco-like notes but duller with less carrying power; turned away from nest, still holding worm; returned to nest cavity, repeated his actions, stood on the nest edge, turning this way and that as if not sure what to do with the worm, flew to nearby aspen, swallowed the worm."

On this as well as on subsequent occasions I took careful note of his behavior. On four of the seven days of the incubation period I observed, in the forenoon as well as the afternoon and on one day (June 27) twice in the afternoon, I saw him repeat this. Each time he followed the same behavior as if it were a ritualized act—the approach to the nest with food in the mouth, the offering of the food to something in the nest which was here symbolized by the eggs, the *treep* call-notes, the turning about on the nest edge, the coming away from the nest, and the return to the cavity and finally the swallowing of the food.

At first I wondered whether this might be an example of "delayed" courtship feeding. Such display behavior akin to this has been reported in species of the genus *Dendroica* by Linsdale (1938), Harding (1931), and Mendall (1937). Lack (1940), summarizing the subject of courtship feeding in birds, has noted (p. 170) that "In many species in which courtship feeding occurs, the male also feeds the female on or near the nest during incubation."

The question needs further study but it would seem, in this instance at least, that the male's attempt to feed the eggs may have been a kind of "anticipatory feeding" of the young. Since food offering occurred on the first day of the observation—June 23 (probably the third day of incubation)—there is no reason to believe that the male did not exhibit the same behavior earlier. Perhaps there is a kind of anticipatory building up of tension, an innate drive to feed the young which grows in intensity during the incubation period. Perhaps there is present the instinctive urge to feed: there is at hand the nest but as yet there are no young to receive the food. Perhaps the urge is heightened by the deferments and failures to feed. It may be significant that the male offered food to the nest twice in the afternoon, June 27, near the end of the incubation period. It may also be significant that during the nestling period the male takes the dominant role in feeding the young. In fact, the female is relatively inactive as a provider until the end of the nestling period.

Although I watched with the utmost care to see if he would offer the food to the female and although the female was on several occasions perched on bracken nearby (once only five feet away), I did not see him bring or offer her the food. Instead after each failure to dispose of the morsel in the nest, he swallowed it himself. All told he swallowed the food eight times during the period under observation.

Only on one occasion, on June 23, did the female remain on the nest at the approach of the male and this time she was fed. When the male came flying in, uttering the usual *threep* notes, she fluttered her wings and replied with run-together "cheeps" but remained sitting. However, her behavior suggested some kind of tension. When the male in his customary way offered food (to her instead of to the eggs) she did not accept. He backed up slightly, then moved forward again, offering food. Still she did not take it. He withdrew to the edge of the nest, shifted about and returned. This time she ate the food.

The above instance occurred only once, at the end of a 43-minute period of attentiveness. I can only think that he offered food as before and that the female just happened to be there. She took the place of the "eggs-young," and was given the food. The occasion, I believe, was purely fortuitous, but may add weight to the idea that this behavior is anticipatory feeding of nestlings.

Literature Cited

Bent, A.C. 1953. Life histories of North American wood warblers. *U.S. Natl. Bull.*, 203.
Forbush, E.H. 1929. *Birds of Massachusetts and other New England States,* volume 3. Massachusetts Department of Agriculture, Boston.
Harding, K.C. 1931. Nesting habits of the Black-throated Blue Warbler. *Auk*, 48:512–522.
Kendeigh, S.C. 1945a. Nesting behavior of wood warblers. *Wilson Bull.*, 57:145–164.
Kendeigh, S.C. 1945b. Community selection by birds on the Helderberg Plateau of New York. *Auk*, 62:418–436.
Kendeigh, S.C. 1952. *Parental care and its evolution in birds. Illinois Biol. Mongr.*, 22.
Lack, D. 1940. Courtship feeding in birds. *Auk*, 57:169–178.
Linsdale, J.M. 1938. Vertebrates in the Great Basin. *Amer. Midland Nat.*, 19:1–206.
Mendall, H. L. 1937. Nesting of the Bay-breasted Warbler. *Auk*, 54:429–439.
Middleton, D.S. 1957. Notes on the summering warblers of Bruce Township, Macomb County, Michigan. *Jack-Pine Warbler*, 35:71–77.
Samuels, E.A. 1883. *Our Northern and Eastern birds.* R. Worthington, New York.
Walkinshaw, L. H. 1956. Some bird observations in the Northern Peninsula of Michigan. *Jack-Pine Warbler*, 34:107–117.

CHAPTER 3

A Census of Breeding Bird Populations in an Aspen Plot

The area selected for a study of bird populations lies within the confines of two townships in Cheboygan County. The north portion occupies the southwest corner of Section 3, Monroe Township, and the south portion the northwest corner of Section 3, Burt Township. The area, situated in the rolling hills country between Douglas Lake and Burt Lake, lies about a half a mile north of Burt Lake and about a mile south of the Biological Station at Douglas Lake.

The purpose of the study was to compile as accurately as possible a census of the birds of this mixed forest community, transients as well as breeding pairs. Though John Minot and I followed the grid lines on three mornings together, we assembled our information and arrived at conclusions independently. I have serious misgivings about the accuracy of my own data.

As the name, Aspen Plot, indicates, the area is dominated by the tree which natively is called the Popple. Two species are present, the Large-toothed Aspen (*Populus grandidentata*), the more abundant, and the Trembling or Quivering Aspen (*P. tremuloides*), the less abundant. Mixed with the Aspen in varying degrees depending somewhat upon the location are to be found other species of trees. Thus, the heaviest belt of vegetation, which runs from northwest to southeast, is composed of Aspen mixed with Maple (*Acer rubum*) and Birch (*Betula papyrifera*), some Red Oak (*Quercus borealis*) and an occasional pine, generally white Pine (*Pinus strobes*) but sometimes Red Pine (*P. resinosus*). In this region we found the Hermit Thrush (*Hylocichla guttata*), the Ovenbird (*Seiurus aurocapillus*) and the Red-eyed Virco (*Vireo olivaceas*), though the thrush and the vireo seemed to prefer stands of lighter timber than the warbler which song rang out in the densest wood.

The northeast area, which slants rather steeply to the top of what appears to be a "hogback," is largely covered with Red Oak intermixed with Maple, Aspen and Birch in that order. The extremest part opens into a space of Bracken Fern (*Pteridium aquilium*) and small Aspen with here and there a clump of Red Oak. In this area the Vesper Sparrow's song was loud.

The southeast corner, which includes portions of three units, is an open meadow with Bluegrass (*Poa pratensis*) the dominant vegetation. Islands of White Pine and Sumach (*Rhus glabrous*) dot this level glade, where the Vesper Sparrow sang each of the three mornings we came there.

A large section of the west central area, perhaps seven acres in extent, is a veritable jungle of fallen Aspens, the result apparently of a severe windstorm which must have swept over the county some years ago, to judge by the fragile condition of the wood. Where the terrain is depressed, the jumble is almost impenetrable. Growing up and around and where possible among these topsy-turvy heaps are clumps of Maple, Red Oak and Aspen, all providing thick leafy habitat. The area provides a semi-circle of edge for such birds as Robin (*Turdus migrattorius*), Cedar Waxwing (*Bombycilla cedrorum*), Baltimore Oriole (*Icterus galbula*) and Chipping Sparrow (*Spizzella passerine*), all of which we found in this windfall situation.

Of the herbaceous plants, the Bracken Fern grew almost everywhere except in the meadow. It appeared most profusely on the hill top, in the corridor and wherever possible among the windfalls. Other plants which I noted were Hawkweed (*Heiracium sp.*), Hairy Vetch (*Vicia villosa*), Blackberry (*Rubus sp.*), Poison Ivy (*Rhus radicans*) and in the meadow the Bluegrass (*Poa pratensis*).

At least three features ought perhaps to be mentioned. Two are topographical and natural, one industrial and man-made. The first is a small ravine that cuts across the middle of the south baseline. It is sparsely wooded, contains Maple, Birch and Aspen as under story and is accentuation of a clearing lying outside of the study plot. Here we found the Eastern Wood Pewee. The second feature, another lightly timbered place, is found on the lower slope of the hill in the northeast corner. It is much less heavily vegetated than the surroundings areas and is really the remains of the meadow of which this area is an extension. Both of these places provide environments different from either the open, thinly clad top of the hogback or the dense wood spread out from the base of the eminence. We heard the Eastern Wood Pewee, the Red-eyed Vireo and the Robin here. The third feature is man-made. Beginning at the meadow in the southeast corner and cutting a slightly diagonal corridor westward across the plot is a rectangular area, seven acres long by about an acre wide, where a power company has slashed a pathway for its high-power transmission lines. The swath is now growing up rankly with sapling Maple, Aspen and Birch Bushy, broad-leaved young growths. The edges of the corridor and the new "second" growth offer dense thickets as habitat for edge and shrub birds. The Indigo Bunting (Passerina cyanea) ranged almost the length of the corridor. Here were also the Chipping Sparrow and the Eastern Bluebird (*Sialia slalis*).

During the three days of the study, 26 species were recorded, of which 13 were presumably nesting. Somewhat hesitantly I estimated a total of 36 nesting pairs and 42 transients. Frankly, however, I have serious misgivings about the accuracy or the validity of the figures in my compilation. I am in agreement with Cooke (1927:1) that "these censuses furnish information concerning the numerical distribution of birds and their relative abundance;" that "they indicate whether birds as a whole or certain species are increasing or decreasing", and that "to obtain satisfactory results this work must continue for many years." Kendeigh (1944:90–91) found that the more often a survey was made, the greater the potential for accuracy.

I am sure that this is true. But I am left helpless with wonder at the confident way Cooke (1927:1) defines a census of breeding birds. "A census of breeding birds," she writes, "means an exact and complete enumeration of the birds that actually nest within the boundaries of a selected tract of land." Her definition is precise but how precise is her application?

True, she describes the mechanics of the process adequately. But I look in vain for methods to achieve exactitude and completeness. How can one be "exact and complete?" I remember the bird that darted away in the underbrush, only a dark form visible to the eye. And I recall a bird in a leafy treetop which inconsiderately permitted me no more than a glimpse of it. I have no doubt my crashing footsteps in the underbrush have sent more than one bird fluttering through the bracken ahead of me without a *chin* to indicate its presence or a moving fern leaf to announce its departure. After my experience with a pair of Canada Warblers, I have some familiarity with avian elusiveness.

Miss Cooke writes (1927:2), "Count the singing males very early in the morning" and with charming intrepidity continues, "At this time every male bird is usually in full song near the nest site." But suppose he isn't? May not wind velocity and weather conditions be limiting factors? And what about a male that is uncooperative enough to sing his heart out on every other day but the one on which you happen to stumble through the deadfalls of the area? And how about the unattached male which with small consideration for propriety or population indices, will come into a study plot and sing, sans mate and sans nest?

And those transients which stop long enough to deliver an aria but have set up domestic facilities elsewhere? How can one determine by song alone, except in obvious instances, which is a citizen and which a foreigner of the area? And those transients which stop long enough to deliver an aria but have set up domestic facilities elsewhere? Miss Cooke is very firm about this. Birds that merely visit are to be cast out of the count, "no matter how close to the line their nests may be." But how can one determine by song alone, except perhaps in obvious instances, which is a citizen and which a foreigner? And how about the unattached male, the avian wolf, which with small consideration for propriety or population indices, will come into study plot and sing?

Hickey (1940:256) found that in the American Redstart, for instance, there was an "indeter-minate number of unmated wandering males" in the area he canvassed. Kendeigh (1944:85–86) points out that "during any one breeding period this percentage of unmated males is high" and concludes that this "shows the potential degree of error when the population of breeding pairs is determined from counting only singing males." Because of this factor he finds that "there have been serious criticisms of counting singing males as representing nesting pairs in that a sizeable percentage, nine percent with the house wren, may be unmated." Nevertheless, he feels that the method is "essential" and probably "a reasonably reliable index of possible carrying power." (p. 90).

But I am still bothered by "exactitude and completeness." I remember the furtive glimpse I had of a bird I couldn't identify, an Ovenbird I may have counted twice and a crested Flycatcher that may have been a solid citizen of the area or an interloper. I remember this and have serious qualms about the data I am submitting, in spite of Kendeigh's (1944:90) assurances that this method "may be a reasonably reliable index of possible carrying capacity."

A Summary of the Population of an Aspen Plot

Breeding Pairs

Hairy Woodpecker	1
Crested Flycatcher	1
Eastern Wood Pewee	5
Black-capped Chickadee	3
Robin	2
Hermit Thrush	2
Eastern Bluebird	2
Cedar Waxwing	2
Red-eyed Vireo	1
Ovenbird	12
Baltimore Oriole	1
Indigo Bunting	1
Chipping Sparrow	3
	36

Transients

Mourning Dove	1
Yellow-shafted Flicker	3
Downy Woodpecker	1
Crested Flycatcher	4
Blue Jay	1
Black-capped Chickadee	2
White-breasted Nuthatch	1
Red-breasted Nuthatch	1
Robin	3
Hermit Thrush	1
Cedar Waxwing	1
Red-eyed Vireo	2
Black and White Warbler	2
Tennessee Warbler	1
Ovenbird	4
American Redstart	1
Brown-headed Cowbird	8
Scarlet tanager	2
Purple Finch	1
Chipping Sparrow	2
	42

Notes by the editor, January 2006:

May Thatcher Cooke, Member of the AOU since 1915 and Elective Member since 1926, died in Washington, D.C., on June 13, 1963. She was the daughter of Wells W. Cooke and followed in his footsteps as a leader in the bird distribution and migration recording program of the U.S. Biological Survey and its successor agency the U.S. Fish and Wildlife Service. This program of carding and filing data on occurrence of North American birds from the literature and a corps of volunteer observers pioneered by her father and now numbering about three million entries was supervised by Miss Cooke during much of her government

PLOT CENSUS OF BREEDING BIRD POPULATION			
General location of plot: In Section 34, Monroe Township and Section 3, Burt Township, Cheboygan County; about one mile south of the Biological Station, Douglas Lake.			
Size of plot:			
Classification of habitat: Mixed deciduous-coniferous forest			
General topography: Generally rolling hills			
DATE OF CENSUS TRIP	1st Trip July 9, 1957	2nd Trip July 14, 1957	3rd Trip July 15, 1957
TIME OF DAY INVOLVED:	5:30 AM	5:20 AM	5:10 AM
TEMPERATURE:	63	62	60
PRECIPITATION:	Trace	None	None
WIND:	Calm	N.E. 2	Calm
WEATHER RATING:	Clear	N.E. 2	Clear, Cool
SPECIES:			
Mourning Dove			1
Yellow shafted Flicker	1	1	1
Hairy Woodpecker		1	1
Downy Woodpecker		1	
Crested Flycatcher	3	1	2
Eastern Wood Pewee	3	5	3
Blue Jay	1		
Black capped Chickadee	4	4	
White-breasted Nuthatch	1		
Red-breasted Nuthatch	1		
Robin	3	3	1
Hermit Thrush	3	2	1
Eastern Bluebird	1	1	1
Cedar Waxwing	2	3	2
Red-eyed Vireo	1	2	1
Black and White Warbler	1		1
Tennessee Warbler	1		
Ovenbird	9	12	9
American Redstart	1		
Baltimore Oriole	1	1	
Brown-headed Cowbird	6	4	
Scarlet Tanager		2	

Indigo Bunting	2		1
Purple Finch		1	
Vesper Sparrow	2	2	3
Chipping Sparrow	4	2	2
TOTAL NUMBER OF PAIRS:	36	35	30
NUMBER OF PAIRS PER 100:	72	70	60

Estimated Total Number of Pairs (based on above censuses): 43

Final Total of Pairs per 100 Acres: 72

service from 1916 until her retirement in 1947. She also was very active in the administration of the bird banding program for many years after it became a function by the Biological Survey in 1920. May Cooke published many notes on long-distance movements and longevity of birds based on the recovery of banded individuals. She compiled information on distribution and migration for a number of volumes of the "Life histories of North American birds" by A.C. Bent. She also did a substantial amount of work in compiling distributional data for the 1957 edition of the AOU Check List of North American birds. Her most important publication was the "Birds of the Washington, D.C. region" (Proc. Biol. Soc. Washington, 42:1–80, 1929) –John W. Aldrich) *Auk* 82 4(1965), p. 685.

Bibliography

Cooke, May Thacher. 1927. The purpose of bird censuses and how to take them.
Hickey, Joseph J. (1907–1993), obituary. *Auk*, 111, 450–452.
Hickey, Joseph J. 1940. Territorial aspects of the American Redstart. *Auk*, 27, 255–256.
Kendeigh, Samuel Charles. 1944. Measurement of bird populations. *Ecological Monographs*, 14: 67–106.
Kendeigh, Samuel Charles. (1904–1986), obituary. *Auk*, 104, 508–509.

(University of Michigan Biological Station, 1957)

CHAPTER 4

The McCown's Longspur, A Life History

Habits

Whether on its winter range or summer breeding ground, McCown's long-spur *Rhynchopanes McCownii* (Lawrence) is a bird of the plains, of the "big sky" country where the land flattens to the blue haze of mesa or plateau; where distance is the hawk's flight from a line of craggy "breaks" to the horizon. Amid the features of such a vast landscape it was first collected about 1851. It happened apparently as much by accident as by design. "I fired at a flock of Shore Larks," writes Capt. John P. McCown, U.S.A. (1851), "and found this bird among the killed." For this, in the first published description of the bird, George N. Lawrence (1851) announced, "It gives me pleasure to bestow upon this species the name of my friend, Capt. J.P. McCown, U.S.A." He adds, "Two specimens were obtained…on the high prairies of Western Texas. When killed, they were feeding in company with Shore Larks. Although procured late in the spring, they still appear to be in their winter dress."

Very likely this is the bird that the fatigued Captain Meriwether Lewis saw on the Marias River (near Loma, Choteau County, Mont.). Had he been more explicit in his description he might have added McCown's longspur to the mag-pie and the prairie dog on the list of species new to science the Lewis and Clark Expedition was to bring out of the vast northwestern wilderness. As it happened, the company was footsore and weary, slightly rebellious, and nearly at the rope's end of its resources when on June 2, 1805, with its usual unpre-dictableness, the Missouri River divided in front of the explorers. One branch bore down on them from the right or north, the other seemed to come from the south or left, each flow about equally wicked in its rolling turbidity. Which was the Missouri and which it's affluent? An incorrect decision meant days of toil and pain spent for nothing, incalculable delay, the threat of spending winter in the mountains. On June 4, 1805, Lewis and six men, taking the righthand fork, the Marias River, explored upstream. A day's march brought him to extensive "plains" where prickly pear tore his feet through his "Mockersons," where rain soaked, and a windstorm chilled the party. What with haste, the fear of Indian attack, the distraction of bear, deer, elk, and "barking squirrels" continually un-der their gun sights, it is perhaps hardly surprising that when he encountered a new bird in the short grass, Lewis did not collect it and later was less precise in his report than was his custom. He listed (Thwaites, *Lewis and Clark Journals*, II:119–120) several sparrows and

> Also a small bird which in action resembles the lark, it is about the size of a large sparrow of a dark brown colour with some white feathers in the tail; this bird or that which I take to be the male rises into the air about 60 feet and supporting itself in the air with a brisk motion of the wings sings very sweetly, has several shrill soft notes reather of the plaintive order which it frequently repeats and varies, after remaining stationary about a minute in his aerial station he descends obliquely occasionally pausing and accompanying his descension with a note something like twit twit twit; on the ground he is silent. Thirty or forty of these birds will be stationed in the air at a time in view. These larks as I shall call them add much to the gayety and cheerfulness of the scene. All those birds are now setting and laying their eggs in the plains; their little nests are to be seen in great abundance as we pass. there are meriads of small grasshoppers in these plains which no doubt furnish the principal aliment of this numerous progeny of the feathered creation.

While Lewis' notation describes McCown's generally (though it lacks the precise detail necessary for positive identification), Elliott Coues in his annotation of the Biddle edition of the Lewis and Clark "Journals" in 1893 unhesitatingly identified the bird: "This is the black-breasted lark-bunting or longspur, *Centrophanes (Rhynchopanes) maccowni*, which abounds in Montana in the breeding season." Reuben G. Thwaites, the editor of the "Original Journals of Lewis and Clark" (1904–1905), accepts his conclusion. Between 1806, when Thomas Jefferson announced the news of the progress of the Expedition in a message to the Congress, and 1851, when George N. Lawrence published the discovery of the longspur, only the Biddle version of the "Journals" (published in 1814) appeared in print. The Biddle edition, however, is a paraphrase, a popular account of the most important events of the expedition. It omits the scientific data, including the zoological material, among which is the account of McCown's longspur. While the avian specimens collected on the Expedition were becoming well known, the scientific data remained in darkest obscurity.

For almost a hundred years Lewis' description of "a small bird" with a treasury of other ornithological information lay hidden in the unpublished portions of the "Journals" in the library vaults of the American Philosophical Society in Philadelphia. In 1892, Elliott Coues, his new Biddle edition largely completed, learned of the original papers, secured them, and from their largely untapped resources enriched his volume with pages of annotations. One of the notes pertains to the identification of Lewis' "small bird." But the actual text of Lewis' account of the discovery was not published until Thwaites brought out the original Lewis arid Clark "Journals," uncut and intact, in 1904–1905. By that time Captain McCown's discovery of the longspur was firmly established in the literature. With no specimen of McCown's from the expedition at hand, ornithologists since then seem indisposed to reopen the question whether the "small bird" Lewis saw on its breeding grounds really was, as Coues (1893) stoutly maintained, *Centrophanes (Rhynchopanes) maccowni*.

If his identification of the species lacks detail, Lewis' description of its habitat is certainly that of McCown's longspur. For McCown's is a bird of the land where mirages on miles of sage and salt flats deceive the eye with the illusion of gleaming tree-bordered lakes; where, as Lewis observed, "the whole country appears to be one continued plain to the foot of the mountains or as far as the eye can reach; the soil appears dark rich and fertile yet the grass...is short just sufficient to conceal the ground. Great abundance of prickly pears which are extremely troublesome; as the thorns very readily pierce the foot through the Mockerson; they are so numerous that it requires one half of the traveler's attention to avoid them;" a land where the temperature, as unpredictable as a cowboy's flapjacks, rises breathlessly high in summer and drops to icy lows in winter. In Custer County, Mont., in the late 1880s, Ewen S. Cameron (1907) watched McCown's long-spurs in the heat waves of a temperature standing at 114 degrees. In July 1911, near Choteau, Teton County, in the same state, Aretas A. Saunders (1912), caught in one of those thunderstorms which suddenly and commonly lash the plains, fled to cover under a sheep herder's shed to escape the rain which quickly changed to hail. Soon "a small flock" of McCown's longspurs joined him, "feeding on the ground under the shed as though they were out in the open in the best of weather."

I remember the flock of McCown's I saw in 1958 in a late April squall. According to my field notes:

> Mr. and Mrs. Herman Chapman, Dr. N.R. Whitney, Jr., and I drove near Casper, Wyo. With the unexpectedness characteristic of prairie weather, a spring storm hurled wind and snow upon us; the road ahead vanished. We no more than crawled along a road where side-banks, car high, were topped with sage.

> Suddenly we saw birds struggling into view over and into the road. Some came down no more than a car's length away. Chapman stopped altogether. We saw they were McCown's longspurs, the black caps and dark smudgy crescents on the breast marking the gray fronts of the males. Farther away were others, their bodies so light in color that frequently they were invisible, lost in the folds of snow. Several dozen swooped out of a gust. Through snow on the windshield and snow driven in windy sheets we watched. Perhaps as many as two hundred birds drifted into the road and up the side of the opposite bank.

> The wind ripped at the sage above them, but here in the lee of the bank in a sort of microclimate less severe than the white fury above, they fed, apparently on seeds; walked rather than hopped about, now in now out of view in the white spirals the wind flung down the roadway

Now and again two males squared off in what seemed to be threat postures, head down, beaks open, wings laid back and fluttering slightly. There was some chasing presumably of McCown's females by males. A male pursued a female across the road and back again; then both flew down the road; the white area in the tail and the black terminal band were sharply revealed in flight; both vanished in the obscurity of snow dust. A female faced an approaching male; male promptly veered aside, lifting his wings slightly but enough to show the white linings momentarily.

About five minutes passed. When the squall abated, the birds moved in short flights above the road and along the bank; appeared restless. As the road ahead cleared, the birds arose above the sage and met the hard push of the wind. For a moment they hung there, swinging sidewise, dark shapes moving at a cord's-end, without advancing. Then in a slacking wind or in an extra spurt of driving power, they swept over the sage and vanished. By the time we drove beyond the cutback, though the storm had lifted somewhat, the birds had become indistinguishable from the driven gusts.

It is a bird of a landscape dominated by rolling prairies where sage and buffalo grass are the characteristic floristic types, and chestnut-collared longspurs, horned larks and sage grouse are the characteristic birds. Saunders (1912), riding on horseback across the divide between the drainages of the Dearborn and Sun Rivers, gives an excellent account of the approach to prairie habitat for which McCown's seems to have a preference: "The rolling, round-topped hills changed to fantastically shaped, flat-topped, prairie buttes, the tall grass and blue lupine changed to short buffalo grass and prickly pear, and the bird voices changed from Vesper Sparrows and Meadowlarks, to Horned Larks and Mc-Cown Longspurs."

It has various names: McCown's bunting, rufous-winged lark bunting, black-breasted longspur, black-throated bunting. At Rush Lake in Saskatchewan "the natives" call it the "ground lark" (Raine, 1892). In southern Alberta it is often "one of the few common, widespread birds of the open country" (Rand, 1948). Sometimes "on flat-topped prairie benches, this is the only bird found" in Teton and Northern Lewis and Clark counties in Montana (Saunders, 1914).

The monotypic status of *Rhyncophanes mccownii* has been questioned several times. In his general discussion of the genus *Plectrophanes*, S.F. Baird (1858) suggested in 1858 a new genus, *Rhyncophanes*. In his description of the species, Baird says: "The *Plectrophanes Maccownii* is quite different from the other species of the genus in the enormously large bill and much shorter hind claw, so much so, in fact, that Bonaparte places it in an entirely different family. As, however, many of the characteristics are those of *Plectrophanes*, and the general coloration especially so, I see no objection to keeping it in this genus for the present."

Coues (1880) writes: "As Baird exhibited in 1858, there is a good deal of difference among the birds usually grouped with *Plectrophanes nivalis*, enough to separate them generically in the prevailing fashion. ...MacCown's Bunting has precisely the habits of *C. ornatus*, with which it is associated during the breeding season in Dakota and Montana."

When in 1946 Olin S. Pettingill, Jr., collected in Saskatchewan what proved to be a hybrid between the chestnut-collared and McCown's longspurs, the problem was discussed again. Enumerating similarities and differences, Sibley and Pettingill (1955) argue that, despite the difference in the size of the bill, the point of distinction between the two longspurs, "It is demonstrable that it merely represents the extreme development in a graded series." The authors conclude that "it seems doubtfully valid to separate the members of the genus *Calcarius*, including the Chestnut-collared, Lapland (*C. lapponicus*) and Smith's (*C. pictus*) longspurs from the monotypic genus *Rhyncophanes*." They recommend a return to the genus *Calcarius*.

Once the species ranged in the breeding season over the wide prairie interiors of the western United States and the southern expanses of the Canadian prairie provinces: Oklahoma (Nice, 1931), Colorado (Bergtold, 1928; Bailey and Niedrach, 1938), Wyoming (McCready, 1939; Mickey, 1943), Nebraska (Carriker, 1902), South Dakota (Visher, 1913, 1914), Minnesota (Brown, 1891; Currie, 1890), North Dakota (Allen, in Coues, 1874; Coues, 1878), Manitoba (Taverner, 1927), Saskatchewan (Raine, 1892; Macoun, 1909) and Alberta (Macoun, 1909).

If the foregoing is an indication of its former nesting grounds, then the breeding range of McCown's has been drastically reduced. It is no longer included among the breeding birds of Kansas (Johnston, 1964), if indeed it ever nested there, nor of Nebraska, where it is now designated a migrant and a winter resident (Rapp, Rapp, Baumgarten, and Moser, 1958).

In South Dakota it was last recorded by Visher (1914) in 1914; since 1949, no authenticated nesting has been reported (Krause, 1954; Holden and Hall, 1959). It vanished from the Minnesota scene after 1900 (Roberts, 1932) except for a single observation of two fall stragglers in October 1936 near Hassem (Peterson and Peterson, 1936). The first authentic specimen for Manitoba was not collected until May 1925 according to P.A. Taverner (1927); its status as a breeding bird in the province is at the moment unclear.

In North Dakota it has been reported from the southwest (J.A. Allen, in Coues, 1874), northeast (Peabody, in Roberts, 1932, at Pembina), and northwest (Coues, 1878). But Robert E. Stewart, wildlife research biologist of the Northern Prairie Wildlife Research Center at Jamestown, writes me (1964): "During the first quarter of this century, the species gradually disappeared over the greater portion of its former range, leaving only a small remnant population of scattered pairs in the extreme western part of the State near the Montana line."

It is sobering to reflect on his next statement: "At the present time, there is some doubt as to whether McCown's Longspurs breed anywhere in North Dakota, although spring and fall migrations are of regular occurrence in the western areas. If breeding populations are present they must be either very rare and local or irregular in occurrence. While searching for them during the past two summers, I have combed the native prairies in the northwest quarter of the State, but without success."

At this writing, Montana seems to be the last stronghold of McCown's longspur in the United States. Stewart (letter, 1964) says that it is "common and widespread over most of the short grass prairies" there; "in the northeast portion, considerable numbers may be found within 50 miles of the North Dakota boundary. On July 3, 1953, I made a detailed list count of breeding birds occurring in approximately 200 acres of lightly grazed short-grass prairie, located in Roosevelt County, about 18 miles northeast of Wolf Point."

How numerous McCown's was in the study area as compared with other emberizine forms can be seen in Stewart's list of relative abundance:

Savannah Sparrow 7
Clay-colored Sparrow 1
Chestnut-collared Longspur............. 44
McCown's Longspur.......................... 20

Is it significant that this area of comparative abundance is contiguous to the area in the Canadian Provinces where McCown's longspur still maintains itself with something of its former vigor? The center of population seems to be northeastern Montana westward to Gull Lake and Golden Prairie, and the southeastern portion of southern Alberta. Whether the density of population is contiguous or broken into widely distributed breeding colonies seems not to be known. C. Stuart Houston writes me (letter, 1964) that in Saskatchewan there appears to be additionally a wide area of lesser density which apparently runs from Estevan northward to Fort Qu'Appelle, northwest to Outlook and Rosetown, and westward to the Alberta border. This would include the "elbow" region of the South Saskatchewan River.

In this "fringe" area the bird seems to show considerable fluctuation in numbers and in appearances in a given locality. M. Ross Lein (letter, 1964) says that in the Estevan region during the period 1958–1962, "I never saw a McCown's Longspur," although he believes the bird may be resident but very much restricted. Writing about the South Saskatchewan River sector, Frank Roy (1958) comes to the conclusion that "longspurs, once the most common bird in the Coteau, are now a rare and local species." However, in a letter (1964) he adds, "I now believe that the fluctuations in numbers in the area north of the South Saskatchewan River are attributable to the birds being near the edge of their normal range."

Apparently McCown's is a bird that responds to not easily discernible environmental changes. Perhaps this is involved in the unpredictableness of its appearances at certain times and in certain places. Although not enough data seem to be at hand to draw conclusions, it appears to arrive in numbers more often in dry years than in wet. Roberts (1932) says that it visited western Minnesota "only in dry seasons–when very dry it was most abundant, and in wet seasons it was entirely absent."

In North Dakota Dr. and Mrs. Robert Gammel (letter, 1964), bird banders at Kenmare, are of the opinion that they secure McCown's "mostly during the dry years…. During the dry year of 1961 we caught six in July." This is contrasted with years of average or above average moisture when one bird was banded in June in 1959 and none in the years 1960, 1962, 1963, and 1964 until August; after the breeding season, that is, and at the beginning of the flocking and migration period. Frank Roy (1964) states that its abundance in the "elbow" region of Saskatchewan apparently depends on the year—an inference, I take it, to a wet or a dry year.

Another factor seems to complicate the problem. Writes Stewart (letter, 1964): "Certainly there seems to be ample habitat left, since large tracts of native prairie are still present in many areas, including the high, drier types that were preferred…. The reason for the gradual disappearance of this species in North Dakota is not apparent to me." He adds: "Possibly, some subtle climatic change may be involved."

Willard Rosine (MS) suggests that certain of the emberizine forms, such as lark bunting and grasshopper sparrow, may detect minute and subtle changes in the complex of soil and vegetation as well as of climate—changes too minute to be easily recognized—to which they respond. It may be that McCown's longspur is a member of this group.

I have been thinking about the effects of fire in the regeneration of the prairie environment and whether this may be one of the "changes" involved here. Early travelers on the plains have left many and vivid depictions of "oceans of flame" rolling over the prairie swales, from Kansas (Sage, 1846) to the Canadian Provinces where Henry Y. Hind (1860) describes one such holocaust which "extended for one thousand miles in length and several hundreds in breadth."

In the last 40 years at least, agricultural methods have largely prevented uncontrolled prairie fires or have contained them to the smallest area possible. One wonders if fire and its effect on the grasslands' environment, however minute and subtle, may be involved in the changing of the breeding range of McCown's longspur; whether fire is implicated in the environmental requirements of this species as there is the possibility that it may be in the requirements of Kirtland's warbler in Michigan (Van Tyne, 1953), although these have not yet been determined.

Nor can one ignore such factors as Frank Roy (1958) underscores in his query concerning the Coteau region of Saskatchewan: "Has cultivation brought about this rather sudden decline in the longspur population? Do newer methods of cultivation, and more frequent tilling to eradicate weeds, make it impossible for longspurs to rear their young in regions where they were abundant as recently as fifteen years ago?" Also the possible effects of aerial spraying pesticides, herbicides, and fertilizers upon the vast and still somewhat mysterious complex of soil composition and vegetational relationships have still to be assessed.

Once McCown's longspur apparently ranged a country where fences were farther apart than rivers or the far plateaus; today it nests where barbed and woven wire proclaim the domesticity of plowed acres. Once it bred on the plains where its associates included the antelope and the buffalo; today it is neighbor to the Hereford and the baby Angus.

Spring

Even while the blusters of spring are still raging on its summer range, Mc-Cown's longspur leaves its wintering grounds. In Texas watchers report that it usually leaves the San Antonio region late in March or early in April (Dresser, 1865; N.C. Brown, 1882, 1884) and the western areas, such as Tom Green and Concho counties, in March (Lloyd, 1887). An occasional straggler might be encountered as late as May (Cruickshank, 1950). In Arizona it apparently departs the southeast region late in February (Monson, 1942) and the central east in March (Swinburne, 1888). In New Mexico H.K. Coale (1894) collected a pair in March 1892 near Fort Union in the northwestern part of the state while A.W. Anthony (1892) writes that he saw them only until February in the southwestern region.

Apparently McCown's responds early to subtle environmental and physiological stimuli toward migration, for it arrives in numbers on "the Laramie Plains during the first week in April" (Mickey, 1943), in east and north central Montana from mid-April to the third week in the month (DuBois, 1937; Saunders, 1921), in southwestern North Dakota at Dickinson between April 9 and May 3 (nine years, Sorenson, letter, 1964), and in the Regina, Saskatchewan, environs during the last two weeks of the month (Belcher, 1961). The earliest data for spring arrivals in southern Alberta seem to be those of the Macouns (1909) who saw two individuals at Medicine Hat April 21, 1894. That same year Spreadborough (Rand, 1948) collected this species at the same place on April 26. These dates correspond pretty well with Margaret Belcher's (1961) observations in the Regina, Saskatchewan, region where she cites Ledingham's April 15 as an early date (letter, 1964).

In Saskatchewan dates recorded by Belcher (1961)—the last two weeks of April—presumably hold comparatively true for that part of the province west and south of Regina. W. Earl Godfrey (1950) lists two adult male specimens in the National Museum of Canada taken at Crane Lake near the Alberta border April 25, 1894.

In its usual penetration northward in spring McCown's apparently stays well south of Saskatoon (Bremner, letter, 1965). Houston and Street (1959) have no records for the Saskatchewan River between Carlton and Cumberland.

In the grasslands east and west of the "elbow" region of the South Saskatchewan River it still finds suitable habitat for breeding purposes, although Roy
(1964) finds that it ranges "from rare to fairly common depending on the area
and the year." I am greatly indebted to C. Stuart Houston of Saskatoon and his
indefatigable researches which include data on nearly all of my Saskatchewan
references. On a vegetation distribution map C.S. Houston laid out the range
of McCown's longspur in terms of greater and lesser densities of population.
In a note (1965) he reminds me: "Notice how well range corresponds to yellow
prairie area of enclosed map."

Cameron (1907) regards McCown's as "seemingly a most punctual migrant." Writing about its spring appearance in Dawson and Custer counties,
Mont., he adds, "My notes give April 26, 27, and 29, for 1897, 1898 and 1899 as
dates of first appearance." Davis (letter, 1964) collected a specimen near Judith
Gap on April 26.

In Montana McCown's is frequently in the vanguard of spring, arriving during the last harsh vestiges of winter. Perley M. Silloway (1902) in Fergus Country remembers that:

> It was on April 24, 1889, on a cloudy, raw afternoon, when I had
> gone out upon the neighboring bench to look for evidence of belated
> spring. In the bed of a miniature coulee that crossed my path was a bank
> of snow, sullenly giving way before the weak assaults of the advancing
> vernal season. Crouching under the lee of a small stone, and hugging
> the edge of the snowbank, a new bird caught my eye. The stranger was
> apparently as interested in the featherless biped as I was in him, for he
> allowed me to approach until I could observe every detail of his hand-
> some breeding plumage, so that there was no call for me to deprive him
> of the life he was supporting with so much hardihood along the line of
> melting snow. I can yet remember how the great tears crossed down
> my cheeks as I faced the raw south wind in my efforts to watch every
> movement of the longspur and to take in every detail of his dress. Pres-
> ently I observed a second McCown's longspur lurking near the first, the
> advance guards of the troops that were soon to throng the prairies to
> rear their broods.

> The following Sunday afternoon…while walking over the bench I
> suddenly found myself in the midst of a flock of McCown's Longspurs.
> They were crouching silently in the hollows of the road and in depres-
> sions of the ground, and I was not aware of their presence until I start-
> ed several near me. When flushed at my approach, after sitting undis-
> turbed until I was only five or six feet away from them, six or eight of
> them would flitter farther away, uttering a sharp chipping note as they
> flittered to stations beyond me.

> When I discovered myself among them, by looking carefully around
> me I could see them crouched upon the ground on all sides of me, their

gray attire assimilating them as closely with the background that only by their black crescentric breast markings could I detect them. Frequently, however, some of them would emit their chipping call in a gentle tone, and thus I could note their positions. In several instances there were fifty of the flock crouched around me, their black breasts showing as black spots on the dreary gray herbage and prairie soil.

E.S. Cameron (1907) who witnessed their arrival in Custer and Dawson counties in Montana says that "the birds scatter over the ground as they alight, hide in the horse and cattle prints, or other holes, and allow themselves to be almost trodden upon before rising."

Frances W. Mickey (1943), whose work on the breeding habits of McCown's is the most complete study to date, describes the arrival near Laramie, Wyo. "By the third week in April large flocks of male longspurs were common. These flocks spent most of their time feeding. However, those among them who were selecting territories sang a great deal, not only in characteristic flight song, but also from perches on the tops of rocks or shrubs within their chosen areas."

Mickey observes that at about the time flight song is initiated and territorial selection begins, "scattered groups of females made their appearance. By the last of April the females became numerous. Later than this, females were seldom seen in groups, for the transients had moved on and the resident females had separated and spread out over the areas defended by singing males."

Extremes for southern Wyoming are March 12 and April 24 (Mickey, 1943; McCreary, 1939). In Montana both sexes are common by the first week in May, with early arrivals between April 13 and 18 in Teton county (Dubois, 1937), on April 22 at Terry, and April 28 at Big Sandy in the north central part of the state (Saunders, 1921).

In Alberta John Macoun (1909) found them "in thousands at Medicine Hat and numbers of males were in full song" on May 2, 1894. In Saskatchewan C. G. Harrold (1933) found them "fairly common from May 20 to 26 in the Lake Johnston area south of Moose Jaw." Macoun (1909) reports them as "common at Crane Lake in June," presumably the first part of June. Crane Lake lies in the southwestern part of the Province north of Highway No. 1 at the village of Piapot. Early dates are April 7, 1947, and April 16, 1948, at Bladworth, some 50 miles southeast of Saskatoon; however, P.L. Beckie (1958), an observer there, writes, "Although I often see the McCown's in migration...I have no records of resident birds for this area."

In these northern latitudes there are intriguing records of McCown's wandering rather widely from its wonted purlieus. Macoun (1909) reports that "one was seen on the shore of an island in Lesser Slave Lake," and Salt and Wilk (1958) call attention to the fact that "wanderers have been taken...on an island in Lesser Slave Lake." This is nearly 500 miles from what seems to be its area of greatest density in southeastern Alberta. Other points where McCown's has been collected in the province are Beaverhill Lake and Sandy Creek near

Athabasca, the first east and the second about 100 miles north of Edmonton. In British Columbia Major Allan Brooks (1900) took a male and two females "on the lower Fraser River Valley at Chilliwack," the male on June 2, 1887, and the females on the same day, 1889. William Brewster (1893) acknowledged this unusual record in the *Auk*, adding Brooks' postscript to the observation: "I passed this place every day but saw no others, either there or elsewhere in British Columbia." Robert R. Taylor points out in a letter (1964) that during the summer of 1964 members of a party from the Saskatchewan Museum of Natural History at Regina collected a McCown's longspur on the Hanson Lake Road, in northern Saskatchewan."

In Alberta Salt and Wilk (1958) extend the range of McCown's as far north as "Youngstown on the east" and "Calgary on the west." The inclusion of Calgary brings up the matter of McCown's somewhat erratic appearances and disappearance. In 1897 Macoun (1909) "Observed a number at Calgary, Alta., on June 19"; and Salt and Wilk (1958) report "Eggs… (Calgary, May 28)." Whether these records are sporadic appearances, a trait that seems characteristic of this species, is intriguing in the light of an observation by Timothy Myres of the University of Alberta at Calgary. Dr. Myres writes in a letter (1965) that "there is nothing known on McCown's Longspur by local naturalists."

Territory

As F.W. Mickey (1943) observed on the Plains of Laramie, during the third week in April with large flocks of longspur males already present, the beginning of territorial selection soon became evident. Alert to their behavior on first arriving in Fergus County, Mont., Silloway (1903) writes:

> This longspur appears in this locality late in April. At first the birds keep in flocks, sitting on the ground so closely that an observer can get among them without detecting their presence until he startles one or more almost under his feet. On such occasions the startled birds will fly a few feet, while the remainder of the flock will continue to crouch upon the ground. As the days pass, the males utter a low, trilling song, not greatly different from that of the horned larks. Soon the longspurs scatter over the prairie and the peculiar flight-songs of the males begin. Rising with twittering hurried chant after an ascent of a few yards, they will drop downward with out-spread, unmoving wings, uttering their gush of song, thus descending parachute-like to earth.

From shrubs, rocks and piles of stone as well as from the air, those males early inclined toward the selection of territory fling their chiming notes across the benches, proclaiming their chosen plots of prairie habitat. Mickey (1943) describes the activity—I am indebted to her "Breeding Habits of McCown's Longspur," a paper meaty with information about this subject: "The male proclaimed his right to a territory chiefly by a characteristic flight-song. In the early spring he was a persistent and exuberant singer. He mounted into the air, spread his wings and floated downward, repeating over and over the phrases of his song, *see, see, see me, see me, hear me, hear me, see*. Sometimes the bird did not alight after descent, but rose immediately for another song. The first males to settle in a region claimed territories that were larger than necessary. As more and more resident males arrived, they tried to establish themselves on ground already claimed by others."

The result was increased tension among the males and a subsequent "squeezing" of available space into smaller units to accommodate the most recent arrivals. "The newcomers that I observed," Mickey continues, "succeeded in holding the territories that they appropriated. As their territories decreased in size the birds increased the vigor of their defense, in order to keep an area of sufficient size around the nest from which the adults could secure the large quantities of food needed by the young nestlings and still be able to brood them for long periods." Adjusted territories, in Mickey's judgment, were seldom less than 250 feet in diameter. But such close proximity, wing by beak, as it were, was enough to increase the possibility of tension and the necessity for defensive behavior.

"For the male longspurs, who held small territories in areas where more birds congregated, the conspicuous flight-song and occasional chasing of an intruder were not sufficient to hold their territories; they often had to fight neighboring males. The bird defending a territory challenged the trespasser by flying at him, singing and rapidly fluttering his wings. If the intruding bird was easily intimidated, he was chased off the territory; if not, the two males rose in the air fighting." Thus high above the grass and the blue lupine, where earlier the birds had performed in graceful solo, but now in fierce combativeness, "bill to bill, singing and fluttering their wings," they disputed the patch of prairie habitat which for each, holding dominantly a mate and a nest, was "his."

Mickey describes the progress of one of these conflicts:

> An interesting situation arose early in June 1938, when a new bird, M10, attempted to encroach upon the territory of an established bird, M2, at the same time and close to the same place that a nest was being constructed by M2's mate. M10 was an aggressive bird and finally succeeded in establishing himself in a small area.... When he secured a mate, it so happened that she chose a site for her nest close to the disputed boundary. On July 7, I watched these two pairs of birds for an hour or more. M10 was engaged in flight-song within his own territory when I arrived. After each descent, he hovered over the nest site, and then flew directly over into M2's territory, uttering a sharp *tweet-twur* on the way. M2 immediately flew toward M10, singing. They met head on and rose high in the air; then, bill to bill, singing lustily and with wings beating vigorously, they dropped to the ground, and each retired to his own territory. This performance was repeated eight times within twenty minutes.

Once boundaries were firmly laid out and apparently recognized by the adjoining claimants, an alert kind of truce apparently prevailed, broken only now and again by aerial encounters. Not that this put a stop to the singing. On the contrary. Writes Mickey, "After longspurs settled on their territories, they sang from or over these areas at intervals throughout the day and well into the evening." Thereafter apparently less and less energy was directed toward the maintenance of defensive attitudes and more and more toward the center of interest in the territory, the mate, and later the nest.

Courtship

In its own way, the courtship display of McCown's longspur, while it does not have the drama of the parachute descent, is in the terrestrial world of buffalo stems, blue lupine and sage, a spectacle in miniature. In early June, A.D. DuBois (1937b) came upon a "very pretty demonstration" of this amatory maneuvering: "On the ground…a male McCown longspur pranced around his mate in a circle about one foot radius, holding the nearer wing stretched vertically upward to its utmost, like the sail of a sloop, showing her its pure white lining, while he poured forth an ecstatic song."

It is the unexpectedness of the behavior that intrigues the beholder. The quick upraising of the dark wing and the sudden revelation of the white lining, shining silver in contrast to the darker body, is a rather astonishing performance, made all the more fanciful by the comparative diminutiveness of the actors. It reminds me of the courtship ballet of the buff-breasted sandpiper I saw in South Dakota where the male, with both wings elevated almost like an upland plover just alighting on the ground and the body held almost perpendicular, moved in a half-circle about the female, the white wing-linings satin shiny beside the buff of the body.

On another occasion DuBois (1937b) "saw a male standing at rest on a rock, holding one wing aloft and singing softly. Presumably his mate was in the grass nearby…. The same day I saw a female raise both wings and hold them quivering; and immediately her mate ran past her, singing, and hoisting his white sail toward her."

F.W. Mickey (1943) tells about a male that "was frequently seen singing softly from the top of a small rabbit brush, meanwhile making little bows to the female in the grass below. Occasionally, he would hold up one wing while he sang. At another time, while on the ground, he raised the wing nearest the female and held its silver lining before her. Then he ran over to the female; they both flew up and settled in the grass some ten feet away."

Sometimes what DuBois (1923) calls "a popular movie situation" develops where a second male intrudes upon the domesticity of a mated pair. One such incident occurred while nest building was still going forward; another took place so late in the season that the mated pair were brooding young. Mickey relates how on May 20 she encountered a pair of McCown's, apparently a mated pair. They were: "feeding side by side at the edge of the field. The female flushed and was followed by the male; as they settled in the grass, another male alighted beside them. Both males rose fighting; finally one was driven off. The victorious male returned to the female, which had remained on the ground, and started bowing to her. The other male returned; again they fought and chased each other about until the female flew a short distance into the field. One male followed and dropped close beside her; the other perched on the nearby fence. On May 24, the nest in this territory was practically finished, but the two males were still fighting each other." In this instance the affair ended somewhat inconclusively. Mickey says that "two weeks later, this nest was destroyed and one of the males disappeared."

DuBois (1923) has an account of a Don Juan among the McCown's which apparently was undismayed by an advanced season or a female attentive upon a nest of young. DuBois writes:

> This morning, while she stood in the garden with a grasshopper in her bill, an audacious stranger ran past her, making his bow with the wing nearer her. He quickly made another advance with the evident intention of bowing to her again, but she ran at him and drove him away. Her mate was on the nest, panting and sweltering in the hot sun while bravely shading the young. He seemed in a position to observe this attempted flirtation with his spouse, but he paid no attention to it. I afterward saw the stranger again.... This time [he] came marching into view ostensibly oblivious of the presence of the female which stood upon the rock at the edge of the garden. He made no advances toward her.... But she flew at him this time also, and he went away.

Nesting

The nest J.A. Allen (Coues, 1874) discovered in North Dakota, July 7, 1873, probably the first McCown's longspur nest to be described, "was built on the ground and is constructed of decomposing woody fibre and grasses, with a lining of finer grasses." Grinnell (1875), who encountered the species southwest of Fort Lincoln in North Dakota in 1874, found that the nest "resembles, both in position and construction," that of the Chestnut-collared longspur. In Minnesota Rolla P. Currie (1890) found two nests: "Composed of fine round grasses and fine dried weed stems, lined with very fine grasses and a few horse-hairs. One nest was on the ground in a clump of grass and the other in a small bush." Currie's observation is interesting; no where else have I found reference to McCown's building a nest above the ground.

In Nebraska M.A. Carriker (1902) located a nest in the dry hills of the northwest corner of the state near the Wyoming line. The nest was "sunken flush with the surface of the ground and made of dried prairie grass blades and rootlets." There was "no attempt whatever at concealment or protection by weed or tuft of grass." DuBois (1935) and Mickey (1943) also remark on nests where concealment was at a minimum. DuBois writes that one such nest was placed "in a grazed pasture" with "no standing grass about it—just three or four scant shoots. At another the growing tufts nearby had been cropped off by stock."

Of a nest in Fergus County, Mont., Silloway (1903) writes, "The site was a depression among grass-blades, open above. The nest was made of dried grass." And Barnes, quoted by Ferry (1910), took a nest on June 4 near Regina. "It was located in a depression near the road on the open prairie where there was practically no grass. It had been run over by a wagon, crushing the nest out of shape. The bird, however, was on the nest and the eggs were uninjured."

DuBois (1935) speaks of the oddity of nests "placed near old dried heaps of horse droppings; one was a foot away, one was quite close, one was at the edge of such a point of vantage, while another was in the midst of a scattered pile which had become very dry and weathered."

In Wyoming Mickey (1943) found that of a group of 40 nests, "nineteen were beside grass clumps, fifteen beside rabbit brush, five beside horse brush and one between rabbit-brush and horse brush." In Montana Silloway (1902, 1903) found nests in shallow depressions at the base of small Coronilla bushes. "A very common site," he adds, "and one most generally selected by this long-spur." In Colorado Bailey and Niedrach (1938) found them frequently "beauti-fully placed near prairie asters, phlox, or flowering cactus."

Where the advance of the plow has turned the short buffalo grass and blue-joint and sage into wheat and legumes, McCown's longspur clings somewhat precariously to the transitional areas or edges. DuBois (1935) found a nest "in a narrow strip of sod between two wheat fields, at the extreme edge of the grass, against the bare dirt turned over by the plow; another was found in a strip between a wheat field and new breaking, while another, though in the prairie grass, was near the edge of the wheat field. Even more notable was a nest on a narrow dead furrow of prairie sod, missed by the breaking plows, in the middle of a field of winter wheat." On the basis of such observations in Montana Du-Bois (1935) concludes, "no nests were found on cultivated ground." However, C.G. Harrold (1933), reporting his experiences in the Lake Johnston region south of Moose Jaw, Saskatchewan, during April and May, 1922, writes that the bird is "found chiefly in stubble fields on high ridges."

Roberts (1932) says that in the last reports of the species in western Min-nesota McCown's nested "only in the the high parts of wheat fields." He quotes a letter from A.D. Brown who writes that after 1899 "only a few were seen, even when quite numerous, as it hid most of the time in the growing grain." Margaret Belcher (1961), reviewing the opinions held by a number of writers that McCown's prefers "the drier and more sparse prairie vegetation," notes, "It is interesting that McCown's longspurs in the Regina area nest regularly in the cultivated fields." And in a letter (1964) she calls my attention to the re-port of George Fairfield on the breeding bird census conducted "in a 28-acre field of uncultivated prairie grassland at Moose Jaw." In this report, G. Fairfield (1963), in commenting on "the McCown's preferred nesting habitat," says that no horned larks "or McCown's were seen on the plowed (summer-fallow) fields close by."

Mickey (1943) found that "The majority of the nests were constructed entirely of grasses, the body consisting of coarse stems and blades, and the inner lining of finer grasses." As exceptions, however, occasional nests contained bits of lichen, "shredded bark of horse brush and rabbit-brush", down feathers and tag-ends of wool, with one nest "lined entirely with wool." Comments Mickey: "Very likely the nests constructed entirely of grass represented the primitive type of material used for nest before sheep, horses, and cattle were introduced into this region. However, when such materials as wool and hair became available, the birds made use of them." She notes too that the birds collected "bits of wool which clung to the barbed-wire fence bordering the territories in which these nests were located."

Not only does the female gather the nesting material within the territory but occasionally she helps to scrape out a shallow depression for the nest when such excavation seems necessary (Mickey, 1943; Silloway, 1902). "A new nest was constructed for each brood," writes Mickey, "usually at some distance from the old one, either within the previous boundaries of the territory or close enough to it so that, in uncrowded portions of the field, adjustments in the boundaries could easily be made."

Bailey and Niedrach (1938) found that "It is an easy matter to locate nests... after the song perches have been discovered, for the females are almost sure to be tucked away in the near vicinity, and it is only a matter of walking about until they flush from under foot." But, as they found, this is the beginning, not the end, of the problem. Nests are hard to locate, they learned. "Even when in the open, cut by only a few blades of wiry grass, they are difficult to see." To which Mr. Bent (1908) and DuBois (1937b) agree. In DuBois' opinion, "Typical nests are not effectively hidden by grasses; but...a nest may be effectively camouflaged by scant grass-clusters slanting over the top of it, or by dry blades of grass hanging loosely over it. It is surprising how few such blades are necessary to make an effective camouflage."

Parasitism of the nests by cowbirds does occur although apparently only a few instances have been recorded. Currie (1890) in Minnesota found a cowbird's egg in a nest from which he had removed four McCown's eggs the previous day. And John Macoun (1909) in Saskatchewan, in April 1894, discovered a cowbird egg in a nest of four longspur eggs.

Eggs

The usual number of eggs per clutch is three or four, occasionally five, though Sclater (1912) mentions six. Walter Raine (1892) says that in the nests he discovered at Rush Lake, southwest Saskatchewan, "the number of eggs to a clutch is usually five, sometimes only four. In my collection I have seven clutches of five eggs, and four clutches of four." Farther west at Crane Lake

Macoun (1904) found two nests with four eggs each. Brown (Roberts, 1932) reported 11 sets gathered in Minnesota between 1891 and 1899, of which six sets numbered three eggs each and five held four eggs each. Of 52 nests DuBois (1935) studied in Montana between 1915 and 1918, 24 had sets of three eggs, 26 had sets of four eggs and two contained sets of five eggs. In Oklahoma M.M. Nice (1931) found one nest with five eggs and one with six eggs.

Average size of eggs seems to vary from .80 by .65 inch, as reported by G.B. Grinnell (1875) from North Dakota, to .81 by .57 inch as measured by Brown (Roberts, 1932) of 11 sets in Minnesota. The 72 eggs Mickey (1943) recorded in Wyoming averaged .8089 by .6086 inch. Harris gives the average measurements of 100 eggs as 20.4 by 15.0 millimeters, with eggs showing the four extremes measuring 22.9 by 15.9, 18.8 by 14.6 and 19.8 by 13.7 millimeters.

Egg size and weight within a clutch may vary somewhat, according to Mickey (1943). At one nest she found that "one large egg was deposited the first day, followed on the second and third days by lighter, smaller eggs." Concerning the egg weight Mickey (1943) writes: "Fresh eggs varied in weight from 2.3 to 2.5 grams; the average of six was 2.4. Eggs weighed the day before hatching varied from 1.7 to 2.15 grams; the average of seven was 1.914 grams....The average total weight of a three-egg set was 7.21 grams as compared to 9.5 for a four-egg set and to 11.4 for the one five-egg set weighed."

There seems to be some geographical variation in the ground color of the eggs. Raine (1892) found that in the eggs near Rush Lake in Saskatchewan "the ground colour varies from white to greyish white, pinky white, clay and greyish olive, usually boldly spotted with umber and blackish brown; many of the eggs are clouded over with dark purple grey which almost conceals the ground colour, and many of the eggs have scratches and hair-like streaks of brown." The ground color of the eggs in the Brown (Roberts, 1932) collection from Minnesota is a "pale greenish-white of varying intensity, more or less obscured in three of the eleven sets by a buffy tinge." In Wyoming Mickey (1943) discovered that "The ground color...varied from white to pale olive. The markings consisted of various combinations of lines, scrawls, spots, and speckles of lilac, rusty-brown, mahogany, and in one case black." In general, Harris writes that "the ground may be grayish white or a very pale green such as 'tea green.' There is considerable variation in coloring and pattern." Raine (1892) found one set near Rush Lake in Saskatchewan which "is remarkable in having all the markings at the larger end of the egg where they form a zone."

The earliest date for full clutches of eggs is May 9 in a listing by DuBois (1935) for Montana, the latest being July 28. In the same state near Lewistown, Silloway (1903) reports a nest of three fresh eggs on May 29. In Wyoming, McCreary (1937) quotes Neilson as finding "full sets of four eggs near Wheatland by May 20." Near Laramie, Mickey (1943) came upon a nest with one egg on May 20 and a full complement of four on May 25. She reports the latest date for a full clutch as August 6. In Saskatchewan, Raine (1892) "flushed a McCown's longspur from its nest and five eggs" on June 10, 1891. Brown (Roberts, 1932) collected "five sets of eggs, all nearly fresh" in early June 1891 in Minnesota.

Apparently eggs are laid in the morning. In a nest DuBois (1937a) visited "both morning and evening, they were laid before 6:00 or 7:00 a.m." Mickey (1943) writes: "On July 8, 1939, at 7:00 a.m. I observed F18 flying about in small circles just above the top of the grass in the vicinity of her nest. When I came into territory, she flew away. Then her mate flew around me as if he were trying to drive me off; so I walked a short distance away and sat down. About five minutes later the pair returned to the nest site; the female dropped into the grass, the male perched on top of a nearby rabbitbrush. After a while he dropped down and fed. I walked over and flushed the female from her nest, which contained one warm egg."

Incubation

DuBois (1937a) states that "the eggs are deposited at the rate of one each day" and "incubation begins when the last egg is laid." There seems to be room for latitude here, for Mickey (1943) sees it differently. "It seemed to me that the birds were somewhat erratic in this respect; for I found that the eggs of a complement were not always deposited on successive days, nor did the female always wait for the completion of the clutch before starting to incubate."

Incubation seems to be the duty of the female. DuBois (1937a) writes, "I have never seen a male on the nest before hatching time," and Mickey (1943) concurs: "I did not at any time flush a male from a nest containing eggs."

Information on the length of the incubation period is confined to the detailed observations of Mickey (1943) who states, "I have data on two pairs that were successful in hatching more than one brood. Nests three and twenty-three were thought to be those of the same pair.... The length of the incubation period was twelve days. This was calculated from the laying of the last egg until the time of its hatching, from June 22 to July 4, at nest three." While the female incubates, "she turns around very often in the nest, and sometimes erects the feathers of her crown," writes DuBois (1923). He adds, "the female sometimes sings at her nest when the male is approaching."

During this period, writes Mickey, the male longspur spent a great deal of time (a) guarding the nest from some nearby rock or shrub, (b) engaging in flight-song, or (c) defending his territory, particularly if nests were close together.

Sometimes the male was seen guarding the nest during the female's absence; at other times neither bird was near the nest. M4 was never in the vicinity of the nest when the female was absent. M6 was usually on guard from a pile of stones close to the nest, not only while the female was off the nest, but also while she incubated. He often sang from this stone pile. Whenever I came near the nest...he either flew about over the nest or circled about in the grass nearby, making some pretense of collecting food.

Male longspurs sang during the incubation period, but with less intensity than prior to mating.

On one occasion DuBois (1923) watched while "a male came to the nest and presumably fed the female, for she was on the nest."

On the hatching of the eggs Mickey (1943) writes: "On July 5, 1938, at 6:30 a.m., after flushing the female from nest nine, I found that her eggs were in the process of hatching. One young bird had already emerged from the shell; its down was still wet and clinging to the body. There was a large hole in the side of a second egg, through which could be seen the bill and part of the head of its occupant. A small, circular, cracked area, not yet broken through, was observed in the side of a third egg. Sounds and faint tappings could be detected coming from the fourth egg. When I visited the nest the following morning, all four had successfully hatched."

DuBois (1923) observes that during the early stages of the second nesting young birds are sometimes seen near the nest. On June 28 he discovered "a young bird, fully grown and 'on the wing'" on the ground near an incubating female, "presumably her offspring, from an earlier nest, although no more definite evidence could be secured to prove this assumption." On June 29, at a second nest from which the female had been flushed, "Two birds, able to fly, were in the grass near her; the nest contains four eggs which are apparently incubated." These eggs hatched on July 5.

In her studies on the Laramie Plains, Mickey (1943) found that climatic conditions might affect hatching success to a considerable degree, as might an increase in the number of predators in the area. During a three-year period, 11 of 45 nests were completely successful, 16 were partially successful, and 18 were failures. "A total of 153 eggs were deposited in 45 nests, averaging 3.4 eggs per nest. Of these 92, or 60 percent of the total number laid, were hatched: 71 birds, representing 46.4 percent of the eggs laid, were fledged, giving an average of 1.58 birds per total nest, or 3.5 birds per successful nest."

Young

Details concerning the young have been chronicled discerningly by DuBois (1937a) and Mickey (1943), especially by the latter who writes:

The young were hatched blind but not entirely naked, for the dorsal feather tracts were covered with long, buffy down. The skin appeared dark where it was stretched over the body, yellowish where it lay in loose folds. The light, tan-colored egg-tooth was very prominent on the grayish bill. The egg-tooth was shed the fifth day....

The nestlings were blind for two days. Occasionally on the third day they momentarily opened their tiny, slit-like eyes. By the fourth day they could keep their eyes open for several minutes although, if undisturbed, they rested quietly in the bottom of the nest with eyes closed. On the fifth day they appeared much more alert for even though they sat quietly in the nest, they peered over the rim with bright, beady eyes.

When eight days old, the nestlings were no longer content to sit quietly in the nest, but moved about considerably, preening, stretching their necks, raising themselves up and fluttering their wings. By the ninth day, fear instinct was evident. Before this they had not been much disturbed at the weighing process but now they either crouched on the scale with neck drawn down between the scapulars, or fluttered about trying to escape, cheeping constantly. At this the adults became quite alarmed and circled low over the box containing the scales, uttering sharp alarm notes.

Regarding the progressive increase in the growth of feathers, DuBois (1937b) has this to say:

The newly hatched young, as soon as dry, are protected above by fluffy natal down, about one-fourth inch long, of a whitish buff or pale dead-grass color similar to that of young Desert Horned Larks. The invisibility afforded by this covering is truly marvelous. The skin is light-colored but reddish. The tongue and inside of the mouth are of a strong pink color, without spots or marks of any kind. This distinguishes them from young of Desert Horned Larks.

When the nestlings are four days old, the feathers of their under-parts become well sprouted, forming a longitudinal band along each side. When six days old, the natal down of the upper parts has been pushed out on the feather tips so that the covering is a combination of down and feathers. The young are well feathered at the age of eight or nine days.

Mickey adds:

By the sixth day, the feather tips had broken from all sheaths except those on the capital tract. Another day was needed for the head feathers to emerge, otherwise, on the seventh day the bird appeared well feathered. Down still clung to the head and occasionally to some of the back feathers on the eighth day....

The wing feathers developed at a slightly different rate from those on the body proper. The developing flight feathers, enclosed in their sheaths, appeared on the wings on the second day. These sheaths grew from one-sixteenth of an inch on the third day to one-fourth of an inch by the fifth day. On the sixth day, feather tips had broken from the sheaths of the primary coverts and on the inner margins of the secondaries.... By the time the bird was ready to leave the nest, the feathers of the secondaries protruded one-half an inch beyond the end of the sheaths and those of the primaries one-fourth of an inch. The primary feathers of a bird captured when eighteen days old measured two inches in length.

The caudal feathers were the slowest of all to grow. The nestlings were six days old before the tail feathers could be measured.... The tail of an eighteen-day-old bird measured one inch in length. At this time the characteristic color pattern of the tail was clearly indicated.

Early dates for the discovery of young in the nest appear in tabulation by DuBois (1935) for Teton County, Mont.. May 22 appears to be the earliest, other dates being May 26, 27, and 31. In the same state for Chouteau County, A.A. Saunders (1921) has May 23 as the first day on which young were found, but he adds, "the young were already half grown," which suggests a hatching date as early as May 18 or 19.

Care of the young is assumed by both male and female, especially during the nestling period. "The female brooded most of the first two days after the young hatched," observes Mickey (1943), "but she was relieved at intervals by the male. From the third day on, more and more time was spent by both adults gathering food for the young and less time brooding them. During showers the female brooded the nestlings even after they were well feathered. At nest 22, where the female had either deserted or been killed while away from the nest, the male fed the young, but apparently failed to brood them during a downpour, for the young were found wet and dead after the rain."

The young were shielded not only against the rain but against the heat of the July prairies also. DuBois (1923) has several notations regarding this behavior:

> July 8…The mother bird stood in the nest sheltering the young from the sun, but she left every few minutes to go for food for them….
>
> As the parent stands on the nest in the hot sun, she usually keeps her mouth open, panting. Her breathing is rapid, and when there is no wind her puffing is audible….
>
> The male, as well as the female, goes on the nest after feeding and stands with his wings partly spread, if the sun is hot, until his mate comes with more food to relieve him. She then takes his place and remains until he returns….
>
> July 12…This evening after supper I watched for a while from the tent-blind. Both parents were feeding hastily and in rapid succession. A thunder shower was brewing, night was coming on, and drops of rain, striking the nestlings, made them stretch up their heads and open their mouths when both parents were away. The female sat on the nest a few minutes between meals, and the thunder did not seem to startle or disturb her….
>
> The position of the male while brooding is to stand astride the nest with a foot on each side, at the rim, the young filling the cavity between. Once, while the female was brooding, the male came with food which he fed to the young at her side. At another time under similar circumstances he gave the food to his mate and she fed it to the young under her breast, the food being nearly always grasshoppers. On one occasion, after feeding, the female stood at the edge of the nest facing

the young, and, stooping over them, sang a little warble close to their heads while the male was approaching with another ration. She was obviously tired and sleepy, as she frequently yawned and dozed while brooding in the short intervals between feedings.

At another nest on July 8, DuBois (1923) found "at noon the male standing in the nest with his feathers all 'fluffed up,' shading the young from the hot, penetrating rays of the noonday sun." Mickey (1943) observed a similar position in the female which straddled "the nest while brooding. She placed one foot on either side of the rim of the nest."

For about half of their nestling life the young are brooded at night also, as Mickey learned:

> On the night of July 10, 1938, my husband and I visited the field at ten o'clock. We had previously marked the nests so that they could be found easily in the dark. When a nest was located, a flashlight was turned on it. The young birds in nest 9, which were five days old, were being brooded. The adult bird left the nest, but the young birds did not open their eyes. The seven-day-old nestlings in nest three were not being brooded. The adults were on the ground in the immediate vicinity. The male, evidently disturbed, sang a short snatch of song. From this night visit it seems that the young birds are brooded at night until they are well feathered, or until about six or seven days old.

Both DuBois (1923) and Mickey (1943) agree that the young are fed insects from the very start and that the food is not regurgitated. Both parents feed the young. "Moths and grasshoppers furnished the bulk of the food," says Mickey. In addition to this menu DuBois includes larval worms. On one occasion, he adds, "I thought I recognized a spider as it went into one of the throats." He declares the female gives as a food call "a brief twitter. The young, which must be less than twenty-four hours old, have a note which can be easily heard from the tent: it is a clear 'peep.' They frequently give utterance to it while their mother is standing in the nest shading them." As they grew, "the food call of the young longspurs," Mickey notes, "changed from the continuous chippering of the nestling to the shriller intermittent call of the fledgling."

Mickey (1943) weighed and tabulated the young from 13 nests. The minimum weight of nestlings at hatching was 1.6 grams, the maximum was 2.9 grams, while the average was 2.03 grams. Sometimes a nestling had to cope with the drawback of hatching out a day later than its nest mates. "A nestling never overcame such a handicap," states Mickey; "in fact, it often did not make normal daily gains in either weight or length.... The chances of the survival of these underlings were closely associated with the amount of food that they received. In cases where the adults did not respond readily to their weaker food calls, they died either before leaving the nest (as in the nests 24 and 28), or shortly afterward (as the one from nest three, which was found dead six inches from the nest)."

Sanitation of nests is maintained by both parents. "The nests are kept quite clean until the last two days of nest life," reports Mickey. "By this time the young so filled the nest cavity that an occasional excrement sac was often over-looked.... Ants were omnipresent. From the observation blind at nest 13, the female was seen picking them from the young and out of the nest." DuBois (1923) has these additional notes on sanitation: "The excrement is sometimes swallowed and sometimes carried away, the two methods in about equal pro-portions.... At this state of the development of the young (age six days) the parents begin carrying the excrement away from the nest, after one feeding the male being observed to fly away with it, but at the next trip he swallowed it as formerly.... The practice of swallowing excrement has been entirely dis-continued. It is being carried away and is usually dropped while the bird is on the wing."

The solicitude of the male and the female for the young increases as the nestlings become more and more feathered. DuBois (1937a) writes: "When I caught a fledgling near nest 59, on the day it left,...its father flew at my head, excitedly singing the trio of notes that is so characteristic. One day I managed to catch a youngster that was an excellent runner. Upon turning it loose I gave forth the most distressing squeaks of which I was capable. Quickly five adults appeared upon the scene and tried to lead me away. They alighted approxi-mately in a row, well deployed, as though for battle; and when I followed, they all ran through the grass ahead of me, in company front, in a manner that was very amusing."

Mickey (1943) found that "an incubating female would normally leave the nest and settle in the grass some distance from her nest during my visit to it. The brooding female would leave the nest if disturbed, but fed close by. By the time the nestlings were nine days old, both adults kept close to the nest during my visit, alternately feeding nearby and circling low over the nest, uttering sharp calls. On the day the young left the nest, both adults continually flew about me calling, *chip-pur-r-r-r chip-pur-r.* They were just as excited at my intrusion on the following day, although later than this I did not notice any anxiety on the part of the adults unless I accidentally flushed a young bird."

In their Montana and Wyoming observations, DuBois (1935) and Mickey determined that, with some exceptions, the normal period of nestling life was ten days. At that time the nestlings "can run at a lively rate, fluttering their wings if pursued," says DuBois. "Two days later (age 12 days), as observed at nest 59, they are able to fly for short distances." One bird in Mickey's study area, an 11-day-old fledgling, had a very weak flight but "in another day it could fly thirty feet or more." A fledgling DuBois (1923) caught six feet from the nest on the 10th day, when released scrambled "over the ground at a lively rate, fluttering its wings as it runs, although it is not very large." Two days later he concluded his notations with: "The young longspurs are now able to fly for short distances."

Plumages

The following descriptions appear in Ridgway (1901):

Tail (except middle pair of rectrices) white, broadly tipped with dusky.

Adult male in summer— Forehead and anterior portion of crown, more or less distinct rictal streak, and crescentic path across chest, black; posterior portion of pileum and hindneck pale brownish gray, streaked with dusky, especially the former; back and scapulars, pale wood brown, or pale buff'y brown, broadly streaked with dusky; rump and upper tail-coverts grayer (especially the latter), less distinctly streaked; more anterior lesser wing-coverts ash gray with dusky (mostly concealed) centers; posterior lesser coverts and middle coverts chestnut; rest of wing grayish dusky with pale brownish gray edgings, the primaries narrowly edged with white (outer web of first primary almost entirely white), the greater coverts and secondaries rather broadly (but not distinctly) tipped with white; middle pair of rectrices dusky grayish brown margined with paler; rest of tail white, broadly tipped with dull black, except outermost rectrices, where the blackish, if present, is very much reduced in extent; under parts (except chest) white, tinged with pale gray laterally, the plumage deep gray beneath the surface; bill brownish, dusky at tip; iris brown; tarsi brown; toes dusky.

Adult male in winter— Black areas concealed by broad tips to feathers, brown on pileum, buffy on chest; otherwise not essentially different from summer plumage.

Adult female in summer— Above, light buffy brown (pale wood brown or isabella color), streaked with blackish, the streaks broadest on back and scapulars; wings dusky, with light buffy brown edgings (broadest on greater coverts and tertials, narrower, paler and grayer on primaries, and primary coverts), the middle coverts broadly tipped with buffy, the lesser coverts pale brownish gray; tail as in adult male; sides of head (including broad superciliary stripe) light dull buffy, relieved by a rather broad post ocular streak of brownish; under parts pale buffy, passing into white on abdomen and under tail-coverts; a brown or dusky streak (submalar) along each side of throat.

Adult female in winter— Similar to summer plumage, but dusky streaks on back, etc., narrower and less distinct, and under parts rather more strongly tinged with buffy.

Young— Back, scapulars, and rump dusky, with distinct pale buffy margins to the feather; pileum and hindneck streaked with dusky and pale buffy; middle wing-coverts broadly margined, and greater coverts broadly tipped with pale buffy or buffy whitish; chest broadly streaked with dusky; otherwise much like adult female.

Food

The principal items in the diet of McCown's longspur, according to Roberts (1932), consist of weed seed: pigweed, ragweed, bindweed, goosefoot, wild sunflower, sedges; foxtail, and other grass seeds; grain; grasshoppers, beetles; and other insects. On their wintering grounds in New Mexico, A.L. Heermann (1859) says that the birds include berries in their diet. Richard H. Pough (1946) states that "Grasshoppers are generally their staple summer food, seeds of grasses and weeds at other seasons." DuBois (1937a) considers the food of the young to be principally grasshoppers "with now and then a moth or a caterpillar." Mickey (1943) lists the grasshoppers which seemed to predominate in the bulk of the food: *Arphia pseudonietanus, Gamnula pellucida, Melanoplus femurrubrum*, and *Trimerotropis*.

From such data one can only conclude that economically McCown's longspur is to be counted among the beneficial species of birds, despite the comment of Arthur L. Goodrich, Jr. (1946) on wintering birds in Kansas: "It is reported that this race and other longspurs may be responsible for the destruction of large quantities of winter wheat in some areas of the west." Perhaps the subject has not yet been sufficiently investigated.

Behavior

The following account by George Bird Grinnell (Ludlow, 1875) suggests the kind of mate attachment in McCown's attributed to the mated Canada goose and the bald eagle pair. He writes:

> The male and female manifest an unusual degree of attachment for one another. While watching them feeding in the early morning, for they were very unsuspicious and would allow me to approach within a few yards of them, I noticed that they kept close to one another, generally walking side by side. If one ran a few steps from the other to secure an insect or a seed, it returned to the side of its mate almost immediately.
>
> On one occasion, a pair were startled from the ground while thus occupied, and I shot the female. As she fell, the male which was a few feet in advance, turned about, and flew to the spot where she lay, and, alighting, called to her in emphatic tones, evidently urging her to follow him. He remained by her side until I shot him.

Nest tenacity, developed to a high degree in the female of this species, is described by Raine (Macoun, 1909), DuBois (1937a) and Mickey (1943). "The female is a close sitter, not leaving the nest until the intruder has stepped close up to it," declares Raine.

Mickey (1943) remarks on the bird's awareness of the human gaze. "I was standing less than a foot from the incubating bird when I saw her. Not until I looked directly at her did she fly."

DuBois (1937b) describes a female apparently employing pretended food hunting as a distraction display. "After I had flushed her from the eggs, and had been seated for some time at the nest, she approached and deported herself very much as do the larks, running in the grass and pretending to hunt food, while she watched me."

Both male and female sometimes display remarkable intrepidity. DuBois (1923), taking pictures and having his camera set up near the nest, was surprised at the male's lack of concern. "He now permits me to sit at the camera, which is only three or four feet from him, as he stands or sits on his brood."

At a pond in north central Montana in 1911 Saunders (1912) found horned larks and McCown's longspurs feeding about the edge, "the longspurs walking daintily over the green scum at the edge and eating the small insects that swarmed there. Several young longspurs, barely able to fly, were here with their parents, and one such had evidently come to grief in its efforts to imitate its parents' example, and was drowned in the midst of the scum."

In eastern Alberta, A.L. Rand (1948) saw McCown's longspurs fly in "commonly to drink at the irrigation reservoirs, along with horned larks and the chestnut-collared longspurs."

G.B. Grinnell (Ludlow, 1875) asserted that he "did not see these birds hop at all. Their mode of progression was a walk rather hurried, and not nearly so dignified as that of the cow-bunting [brown-headed cowbird]."

Where Grinnell in 1874 found this species "unsuspicious" and fairly easy to approach on the prairies of southwestern North Dakota, Bailey and Niedrach (1938) in 1936 and 1937 found them "extremely wild" in northeastern Colorado.

Voice

To the dweller on the north central Great Plains, few experiences after a long hard winter equal the pleasure and the promise of the song bursts of certain early spring birds. Chaucer had his "smale foules" which "maken melodie" but the prairie-dweller has his horned larks and Sprague's pipits with their spectacular singing flights high aloft, seemingly cloud-high, and their dizzy plummeting to earth. He has his lark buntings and chestnut-collared longspurs with their less spectacular but more graceful butterfly-like descent to earth, bubbling with sound. With them McCown's forms a trio in the grace and musical quality of the aerial performances.

Writes P.M. Silloway (1902) of Montana: "In a wagon trip across many miles of prairie in the last week of May 1899 I was regaled by the well-known flight-songs of the males of this species. Numbers of them were frequently seen in the air at one time, some of them mounting upward in irregular, undulating, star-like lines of movement, pouring forth their hurried bursts of song; others could be seen floating downward with out-spread, elevated wings, uttering their ecstatic measures as they slowly floated to earth without moving a feather."

E.S. Cameron (1907) recalls that near Terry, Mont., "On June 22, 1894, I had ample opportunity for observing this species, as, my horse having run away, I was compelled to walk home, ten miles across the prairie. My way was enlivened by the handsome males, which hung above me, before sinking into the grass with a burst of song."

One of the earliest to describe the song of McCown's longspur was George Bird Grinnell (Ludlow, 1875). Traveling as zoologist with the Custer Expedition into the Black Hills in 1874, on observing the bird near Fort Lincoln (present-day Bismarck) in North Dakota, he calls it "by far the most melodious songster" on "the high dry plains. It rises briskly from the ground, after the manner of *C. bicolor* until it attains a height of 20 or 30 feet, and then, with outstretched wings and expanded tail, glides slowly to earth, all the time singing with the utmost vigor."

In July of 1911, Aretas A. Saunders (1912) took a horseback ride "nearly across the State of Montana"—one of those adventures which the more sedentary only dream about. In the flat open prairie of Broadwater County where the "principal vegetation was buffalo-grass and prickly pear," he found McCown's longspur

> in full song, a charmingly sweet song, that tinkled across the prairie continually and from all sides. The song has been compared to that of the Horned Lark, but to my mind it is much better. The quality is sweeter and richer; the notes are louder and clearer, and above all, the manner in which it is rendered is so different from that of the lark or any other bird that the lark passes into insignificance in comparison. The song is nearly always rendered when in flight. The bird leaves the ground and flies upward on a long slant till fifteen or twenty feet high, then spreads both wings outward and upward, lifts and spreads its white tail feathers, erects the upper tail coverts and feathers of the lower back, and bursting into song, floats downward into the grass like an animated parachute, singing all the way.

In Teton County, Mont., DuBois (1937b) also noted the parachute-like descent as well as "the usual song," which he says,

> is a variety of warbles, clear and sweet. It is a joyous song. In the height of the nesting season it ripples through the air from many directions. It is usually delivered in course of a special flight.
>
> The song-flight is a charming feat of grace. The male bird flies from the ground, in gradual ascent, to a height of perhaps six or eight yards, then spreads his white-lined wings, stretching them outward and upward, and floats slowly down to earth like a fairy parachute made buoyant with music. He continues to pour forth his song all the way down into the grass, and seems to swell with the rapture of his performance. Sometimes the descent is perfectly vertical. The song is delivered both while fluttering the wings and while making the parachute descent.

The birds let their legs hang down beneath them while in flight. The floating descent was unique in my experience with birds, for though the Chestnut-collared Longspur also has a song flight, it lacks the parachute descent.

In two records DuBois (1923, 1937a) describes a characteristic feature of the song: "Occasionally, while the bird is in the air, he utters a trio of staccato notes, each of decidedly different pitch, and separated by equal time intervals. The three notes are louder than the usual song; they are so short and clear, and have so pronounced a pause between them that the effect is very striking."

In the Prairie Provinces of Canada Raine (1892) seems to be the first to mention the song of this longspur. In June of 1891 near a slough north of Moose Jaw, he found the song "very cheering...the male always sings as he descends to the ground with outstretched, motionless wings." Mr. Bent (1908), investigating the prairies in the vicinity of Maple Creek in southwestern Saskatchewan in 1905–1906, considered McCown's song similar to the chestnut-collared longspur's "but somewhat louder and richer." The male "rises slowly and silently to a height of 10 or 15 feet and then floats downward, on outstretched wings and widespread tail, pouring out a most delightful, rich, warbling, bubbling song." But Harrold (1933), while mentioning the "remarkable butterfly-like flight," says that the song "consists of only a few notes one of them having a peculiar squeaky sound quite unlike that of any other bird in tune."

Olin S. Pettingill, Jr., (Sibley and Pettingill, 1955), describes the mechanics of the flight, comparing it with the chestnut-collared longspur's: "The flight songs of typical McCown's and Chestnut-collared longspurs differ in movements and in song pattern. Both species fly gradually upward, their wings beating rapidly. From the peak of the ascent McCown's proceeds to sail downward abruptly with wings held stiffly outstretched and raised high above the back. The Chestnut-collared, after reaching the peak of the ascent, prolongs the flight by circling and undulating, finally descending with the wings beating as rapidly as before. Both species sing after the ascent, but the song of the McCown's is louder with the notes uttered more slowly."

During the peak of breeding intensity, as calculated by Mr. Bent (1908), "the male makes about three song flights per minute, of about eight or ten seconds duration, feeding quietly on the ground during the intervals of 10 or 12 seconds."

A.A. Saunders, remembering his days in Montana, writes in a note that the general quality of the song is "sweet and musical, and is a broken warble, that is a group of several rapid, connected notes, then a short pause and another group, and so on to the end of the song. In this the song differs from the Chestnut-collared Longspur, whose song is continuous, without a break. It also differs in that the general pitch is maintained at about the same level throughout the song where that of the Chestnut-collared grades downward in pitch."

DuBois (1923) seems to be the only observer to record singing in the female. In Teton County, Mont., from a tent which served as a blind, he kept a series of nests under surveillance. On July 2, 1917, watching a female incubating, he notes, "I was surprised to hear her begin to sing. She sang a very pleasing little song." On July 5, when the male approached, "she again sang a little twittering, musical song." DuBois takes into consideration that at each of these occurrences the male was near. In the first instance, at the close of the song he saw the male drop suddenly into view; "he walked up to her and gave her a large insect, apparently a grasshopper with amputated legs." In his detailed study of 61 nests over three seasons (1915, 1916, 1917) DuBois mentions the female singing only in this one instance.

Though Saunders' (1922) observations lead him to believe that this species "sings from a perch only rarely" and that "the Chestnut-collared Longspur... sings from a perch more frequently than McCown's, but still rarely," he writes in a later note that occasionally McCown's will sing from "a wire fence or a stone." Salt and Wilk (1958) note in Alberta, that in its choice of song sites McCown's is similar to the chestnut-collared longspur's. "Both prefer low perches either on the ground or on a fence but not on bushes." The last part of the observation is interesting in its difference from the experience of Mickey (1943) who found in her Wyoming study that perches included shrubs as well as rocks and in one instance the top of a stone pile. She mentions the rabbitbrush (*Chrysothamnus*) specifically.

In Montana, DuBois (1923) discovered that a favorite singing spot was often a rock. Apparently some individuals are more concerned about its actual location than in the kind of perch they choose. Thus DuBois noted that the male of one nest under observation "has an habitual perch on an old kettle which has lodged at the edge of the garden some twenty feet from the nest. The kettle and Longspur combination, although perhaps picturesque, struck me as rather incongruous and I replaced the kettle by a rock which pleased me better and seemed to suit the Longspur just as well. He came repeatedly to perch there after descending from his song flight or returning from an absence...."

In May 1899, in Montana, Silloway (1902) found the longspurs singing from the ground. A concentration remained hidden by the blending of their coloration with the background of bare gray ground and last year's dead vegetation:

> When...about sixty yards to one side of their position, I was attracted by a series of strange songs, uttered with unusual force. Walking in the direction of the unfamiliar music, I found that the Longspurs were the authors, and for many minutes I watched different songsters twittering their pretty little songs. The performance was a continuous chatter, having some resemblance to portions of Meadowlark music. It was quite similar to the continuous, hurried measures of the Horned Larks, though louder and clearer. In some instances the performer uttered the act of singing while pecking for seeds among the dead herb-

age, thus showing a further resemblance in habit to the Horned Larks. A noticeable feature of the performance was the movements of the white throats as the spirited measures bubbled forth.

Field Marks

Silloway (1903) describes the male longspur as: "Upper parts chiefly grayish brown, streaked with darker; top of head, and large crescent on breast, black; wing coverts reddish-brown; lower parts grayish white." DuBois (1937b) has this description of the female: "The upper surface of the head is uniformly covered with faint, fine, wavy streaks…. The face has a buffy appearance, with a line over the eye that is more whitish…. The throat is white. There is just a faint suggestion of darker gray on the breast where the black patch adorns the male. The wrist of her wing shows a little of the reddish brown "shoulder" patch worn by her mate…. When the bird takes flight, she shows, conspicuously, an almost black T-shaped design at the end of the white spread tail. The sexes are alike in this tail pattern, which constitutes the best field mark."

Enemies

Various plundering marauders play havoc with the nests and eggs of McCown's longspurs. DuBois (1937a) relates that in Montana "carcasses of [longspur] fledglings were seen at a Short-eared Owl's nest and at a nest of Swainson Hawks" but concludes that raptores were in general "almost negligible factors in the lives of the longspurs at this place." Among the mammals considered predatory, DuBois points his finger at the weasel and the skunk. He adds, "Punctured eggs or broken shells showing tooth marks, noted in several instances, were thought to be the work of the common ground squirrels [the thirteen-lined (*Citellus tridecemlineatus*) and Richardson's (*C. richardsonii*)], though I have never caught one of these rodents in the act of plundering a nest. Whenever a ground squirrel approached a nest, the longspurs drove him away by swooping at him repeatedly, sometimes actually striking his back." Adds Mickey (1943), "On several occasions the birds were seen hovering over a ground squirrel, chirping and darting at it in an effort to drive it away from the nest site," suggesting that the birds recognize these animals as predators.

While the elements and the animal predators undoubtedly take a yearly toll of McCown's longspurs, the species has been subject to their onslaughts for millennia with little evidence of any serious reduction of the population. The real threat, whether recognized, minimized, or ignored, as DuBois (1936), states, is man—"man whose poisoned baits set out for ground squirrels apparently kills more birds than spermophiles." Man with his plow and his agricultural achievements: "Many nests were of course plowed under by the breaking plows of pioneer farmers," DuBois remembers. "I have seen one or two go over with the turning sod, when it was too late to prevent it."

To DuBois' list of enemies Mickey (1943) adds the cat, the badger (*Taxidea taxus*), and among birds the prairie falcon and western crow. "A pair of Swainson's Hawks, *Buteo swainsoni*, and a pair of Marsh Hawks, *Circus hudsonius*, were frequent visitors to this field. They swooped over the field in search of rodents, quite indifferent to the smaller birds. A Prairie Falcon, *Falco mexicanus*, occasionally visited the field, but did not seem to bother the longspurs. Sometimes the longspurs ignored the hawks, but oftener a group of birds would rise and twitter noisily as they flew around the hawk.... Although I did not actually witness any depredations by the crows, it is my belief that they were responsible for the disappearance of some of the eggs and young of the smaller birds."

Frequently the forces of nature itself are antagonistic. Unseasonably cold rainstorms and late spring snows often bring disaster to the young of McCown's longspur. DuBois (1937a) describes a Montana storm that brought a deep fall of snow on May 25 and continued into the 26th:

> I had previously marked a nest in which the bird was known to have begun incubating her four eggs on the morning of the 19th. The snow covered everything so completely that I could not find my marker; but in the afternoon of the 26th the marker-rock showed through the melting snow, and I uncovered the nest. The eggs had been in cold storage all of one day and part of another; but an hour or two after the nest was uncovered the female was sitting on the eggs. She continued to incubate until the 8th of June. That day she was absent morning and evening, though in the nest at noon. Before my return early in the next morning the eggs and nest had been mysteriously destroyed. The bird had continued incubation about nine days beyond the normal period. Perhaps it was her first experience with eggs under snow.

Fall

No sooner are the fledglings on the wing, fortified against the ardors of the migration journey, than they begin the annual flocking. In the Canadian Provinces the gathering begins by the first of August; by the early part of the month, writes Mr. Bent (1908), in southwestern Saskatchewan "almost all of the Longspurs of both species, had disappeared from the plains."

As they continue their southerly movement, their ever-increasing numbers growing larger and larger, they string out over the prairies like tiny black pepper kernels flung across the sky, rising up high and thickening darkly into compact groups, masses twisting and turning, then slanting down, lightening as they thin out, sometimes so near the ground that an obstruction like a fence sends them bending upward to flow serpentlike over the obstacle; at other times they sweep tree-high from one seed-rich area to another. At last the groups swell into the hundreds, so that by the time they leave southern Montana in September they are seen in immense congregations like that which P.M. Thorne (1895) reports on the Little Missouri in 1889.

After August 10, Visher (1912) considered them numerous on the plains of south central South Dakota in the years from 1901 to 1911. In Montana, Saunders (1921) has a September 27 date for the north central portion. By September the birds have reached Oklahoma (Sutton, 1934) although W.W. Cooke (1914) during 1883–1884 dates the arrival there as January 19. By October 16 they have arrived in Arizona and by November 5 (Lloyd, 1887) in the western part of Texas. Here as well as in New Mexico and northern Old Mexico they await the stimulus that will send them north again.

Winter

A.L. Heermann (1859) who was with the topographical surveyors along the 32nd parallel of north latitude during the season of 1873–1874 declares: "I found this species congregated in large flocks...engaged in gleaning the seeds from the scanty grass on the vast arid plains of New Mexico. Insects and berries form also part of their food, in search of which they show great activity, running about with ease and celerity. From Dr. Henry, U.S.A., I learned that in spring large flocks are seen at Fort Thorne, having migrated hither from the north the fall previous."

George B. Sennett (1878), who was on the lower Rio Grande during the season of 1877, writes of McCown's longspur:

I found these only about Galveston. They were in large flocks, and associated with them were *Eremophila chrysoloema*, Southwestern Skylark, and *Neocorys spraguii*, Missouri Skylark. They frequented the sandy ridges adjoining the salt-marshes. In habits they reminded me of *P. lapponicus*, Lapland Longspur, as I saw them in Minnesota last year. When flushed, they dart from side to side, taking a swift, irregular course, never very high, and suddenly drop down among the grass-tussocks, with their heads towards you. They are so quiet and so much the color of their surroundings that they are seen with difficulty. They fly in such scattered flocks that a single discharge of the gun can seldom bring down more than one or two. That they extend farther south than the vicinity of Galveston I very much doubt, for we would, in all probability, have noticed them if they had been farther down the coast.

In winter its peregrinations must occasionally have been extensive, for Coale (1877) has a note about its appearance at Champaign and Chicago, Ill., which suggests a field of study as yet largely untouched:

While looking over a box of Snow-buntings and Shore Larks in the market, January 5, 1877, I found a specimen of *Piectrophanes maccowni*, shot at Champaign, Ill. January 17; another box containing Lapland Longspurs was sent from the same place, and among them was a second specimen of *P. maccowni*, which is now in the collection of C.N. Holden, Jr., Chicago. January 19 I obtained a third specimen from the same source, which has been sent to Mr. E.W. Nelson, of this city. They were all males, showing plainly the chestnut coloring on the bend of the wing and the peculiar white markings of the tail. This is, I think, the first record of the occurrence of this bird in Illinois, if not east of Kansas.

That some birds may overwinter within the breeding range or near its borders is indicated by the Christmas Bird Counts listing 200 birds from Huron, S. Dak., in 1953 and 15 from Billings, Mont., in 1956.

Distribution

Range— Southern portions of Prairie Provinces south to northeastern Sonora, northern Durango, and southern Texas.

Breeding range— McCown's Longspur breeds from southern Alberta (Calgary, Medicine Hat), southern Saskatchewan (Davidson), southwestern Manitoba (Whitewater Lake), and central northern North Dakota (Cando) south to southeastern Wyoming (Laramie), northeastern Colorado (Pawnee Buttes), northwestern Nebraska (Sioux County), and central North Dakota (Fort Lincoln); formerly east to southwestern Minnesota (Pipestone County).

Winter range— Winters from central Arizona (Camp Verde), southwestern, central, and northeastern Colorado (Durango, Fort Morgan), west-central Kansas (Hays), and central Oklahoma (Cleveland County) south to northeastern Sonora (Pozo de Luis), Chihuahua, northern Durango (Villa Ocampo), and southern Texas (Rio Grande City, Corpus Christi, Galveston).

Casual records— Casual in southern British Columbia (Chilliwack), Oregon (Malheur National Wildlife Refuge), Idaho (Birch Creek), northern Alberta (20 miles south of Athabaska Landing), and Illinois (Champaign).

Migration—

Early dates of spring arrival are: Wyoming: Cheyenne, March 12 (average of nine years, April 14); Laramie, April 6.

Late dates of spring departure are: Minnesota: Lac Qui Parle County, May 8. Texas: Amarillo, April 4; Austin, March 27. Oklahoma: Camp Supply, March 8. Kansas: northeastern Kansas, April 3 (median of five years, February 17). New Mexico: Fort Union, March 22. Arizona – Bowie, March 7.

Early dates of fall arrival are: New Mexico: Mescalero Indian Agency, September 12. Kansas: northeastern Kansas, October 29 (median of four years, November 7). Oklahoma: Comanche County, November 21. Texas: Amarillo, October 18; Austin, November 15.

Late dates of fall departure are: Wyoming: Laramie, October 27 (average of six years, October 12).

Egg dates— Montana: 10 records, May 9 to July 28; five records, May 9 to May 26; North Dakota: 17 records, May 17 to July 22; nine records, May 27 to June 10; Saskatchewan: seven records, May 28 to June 14; Wyoming: five records, May 17 to June 29.

Literature Cited

Agersborg, G.S. 1885. The birds of southeastern South Dakota. *Auk*, 2, 276–289.

Allen, Joel Asaph. 1874. In Coues' *Birds of the Northwest. U.S. Geol. Surv. Terr.*, Misc. Publ. No. 3.

Allen, Joel Asaph. 1884. Notes on the natural history of portions of Dakota and Montana Territories. *Proc. Boston Soc. Nat. Hist.*, 7.

Anthony, Alfred Webster. 1892. Birds of southwestern New Mexico. *Auk*, 9, 357–369.

Bailey, Alfred Marshall, and Niedrach, Robert J. 1938. The chestnut-collared longspur in Colorado. *Wilson Bull.*, 50, 243–246.

Baird, Spencer Fullerton, John Cassin, and George N. Lawrence. 1858. Birds. *In Reports of explorations and surveys... for a railroad from the Mississippi River to the Pacific Ocean*, 9, 515–516.

Beckie, P.L. 1958. Observations of longspurs at Bladworth. *Blue Jay*, 16, 55–56.

Belcher, Margaret. 1961. Birds of Regina. *Saskatchewan Nat. Hist. Soc.*, Spec. Publ. No. 3.

Bent, Arthur C. 1907–1908. Summer birds of southwestern Saskatchewan. *Auk*, 24, 407–430; 25, 25–35.

Brewster, William. 1893. On the occurrence of certain birds in British Columbia. *Auk*, 10, 236–237.

Brooks, Allan. 1900. Notes on some birds of British Columbia. *Auk*, 17, 104–107.

Brown, A.D. 1891. The first record of McCown's Longspur breeding in Minnesota. *Ornith. and Ool.*, 16, 142.

Brown, Nathan C. 1882. A reconnaissance in southwestern Texas. *Bull., Nuttall Ornith. Club*, 7, 33–42.

Brown, Nathan C. 1884. A second season in Texas. *Auk*, 1, 120–124.

Cameron, Ewen S. 1907. The birds of Custer and Dawson Counties, Montana. *Auk*, 24, 241–270, 389–406.

Cameron, Ewen S. 1908. The birds of Custer and Dawson Counties, Montana. *Auk*, 25, 39–56.

Carriker, Melbourne A., Jr. 1902. Notes on the nesting of some Sioux County birds. *Proc. Nebraska Ornith. Union*, 3, 75–89.

Coale, Henry K. 1877. McCown's longspur in Illinois. *Bull. Nuttall Ornith. Club*, 2, 52.

Coale, Henry K. 1894. Ornithological notes on a flying trip through Kansas, New Mexico, Arizona, and Texas. *Auk*, 11, 215–222.

Cooke, Wells W. 1914. The migration of North American Sparrows. *Bird-Lore*, 16, 21–22, 351.

Coues, Elliott. 1874. Birds of the Northwest. *U.S. Geol. Surv. Terr.*, Misc. Publ., No. 3.

Coues, Elliott. 1878. Field Notes on birds observed in Dakota and Montana along the forty-ninth parallel during the seasons of 1873 and 1874. *U.S. Geol. Georgr. Surv. Terr.*, 4, 545–661.

Coues, Elliott. 1880. Notes and queries concerning the nomenclature of North American birds. *Bull., Nuttall Ornith. Club*, 5, 96.

Coues, Elliott. 1893. History of the expedition under the command of Lewis and Clark...to The Pacific Ocean.... 1804–5–6, 3 vols.

Cruickshank, Allan D. 1950. Records from Brewster County, Texas. *Wilson Bull.*, 62, 217–219.

Currie, Rolla P. 1890. Notes from northern Minnesota. *Oologist*, 7, 206.

Dresser, H.E. 1865. Notes on the birds of southern Texas. *Ibis*, N.S., 1, 312–330, 466–495.

DuBois, Alexander D. 1923. Two nest studies of McCown's longspur. *Bird-Lore*, 25, 95–105.

DuBois, Alexander D. 1935. Nests of horned larks and longspurs on a Montana prairie. *Condor*, 37, 56–72.

DuBois, Alexander D. 1937a. Notes on coloration and habits of the chestnut-collared longspur. *Condor*, 39, 104–107.

DuBois, Alexander D. 1937b. The McCown longspurs of a Montana prairie. *Condor*, 39, 233–238.

Ferry, John F. 1910. Birds observed in Saskatchewan during the summer of 1909. *Auk*, 27, 185–204.

Godfrey, W. Earl. 1950. Birds of the Cyprus Hills and Flotten Lake regions, Saskatchewan. *Nat. Mus. Canada Bull.*, 120, 1–96.

Grinnell, George Bird. 1875. In Ludlow's Report of a reconnaissance of the Black Hills of Dakota, made in the summer of 1874. *Ornith. Tracts*, No. 52, 85–102.

Harrold, C.G. 1933. Notes on the birds found at Lake Johnston and Last Mountain Lake, Saskatchewan, during April and May, 1922. *Wilson Bull.*, 45, 16–26.

Heermann, A.L. 1859. Report upon birds collected on the survey. *Rep. Expl. Surv. Pacific Railroad*, 10, pt. 4, 29–80.

Hind, Henry Youle. 1860. *Narrative of the Canadian Red River exploring expedition of 1857.* 2 vols.

Holden, Nelda, and Willis Hall. 1959. An index to South Dakota. *Bird Notes*, vols. 6–10.

Houston, C. Stuart, and Maurice Street. 1959. The birds of the Saskatchewan River. *Saskatchewan Nat. Hist. Soc.* Spec. Publ. No. 2.

Johnston, Richard F. 1964. The breeding birds of Kansas. *Univ. Kansas Publ. Mus. Nat. Hist.*, 12, No. 14, 575–655.

Krause, Herbert. 1954. An index to South Dakota. *Bird Notes*, vols. 1–5.

Lawrence, George N. 1851. Descriptions of new species of birds of the genera *Toxostoma* Wagler, *Tyrannula* Swainson and *Plectrophanes* Meyer. *Ann. Lyc. Nat. Hist.* New York, 5, No. 4, 121, 123.

Lloyd, William. 1887. Birds of Tom Green and Concho Counties, Texas. *Auk*, 4, 289–299.

Ludlow, William. 1875. Report of a reconnaissance of the Black Hills of Dakota, made in the summer of 1874. *Ornith. Tracts*, 52, 85–102.

Macoun, John. 1900–1904. *Catalogue of Canadian Birds.*

Macoun, John, and James M. Macoun. 1909. *Catalogue of Canadian Birds*, ed. 2.

McCown, John P. 1851. In Lawrence's description of new species of birds. *Ann. Lyc. Nat. Hist.* New York, 5, 121–124.

McCreary, Otto. 1939. *Wyoming Bird Life*. Rev. ed., p. 97.

Mickey, Frances W. 1943. Breeding habits of McCown's longspur. *Auk*, 60, 181–209.

Monson, Gale W. 1942. Notes on some birds of southeastern Arizona. *Condor*, 44, 222–225.

Nice, Margaret M. 1931. The birds of Oklahoma, rev. ed, *Publ. Univ. Oklahoma, Biol. Surv.*, 3, No. 1.

Peterson, Theodore, and Mrs. Theodore Peterson. 1936. Smith's and McCown's longspurs seen in Minnesota. *Auk*, 53, 342.

Pough, Richard H. 1946. *Audubon Bird guide. Eastern land birds.*

Raine, Walter. 1892. *Bird-nesting in North-west Canada.*

Rand, A.L. 1948. Birds of southern Alberta. *Nat. Mus. Ottawa Bull.*, vol. 111.

Rapp. William F., Jr., L.C. Rapp, Henry E. Baumgarten, and R.A. Moser. 1958. Revised checklist of Nebraska Birds. *Nebraska Ornith. Union*, Occas. Pap. 5.

Ridgway, Robert. 1901. Birds of North and Middle America. *U.S. Nat. Mus. Bull.*, 50, pt. 2.

Roberts, Thomas S. 1932. *The birds of Minnesota.* vol. 2.

Roy, Frank. 1958. Resident longspurs in Lucky Lake area. *Blue Jay*, 16, 56–57.

Roy, Frank. 1959. Further information on resident longspurs in Saskatchewan. *Blue Jay*, 17, 52.

Sage, Rufus B. 1846. *Scenes in the Rocky Mountains, and in Oregon, California, New Mexico, Texas, and the grand prairies.*

Salt, W. Ray, and A. L. Wilk. 1958. *The birds of Alberta.*

Saunders, Aretas A. 1912a. Some birds of southwestern Montana. *Condor*, 14, 22–23.

Saunders, Aretas A. 1912b. Some changes and additions to the list of birds of southwestern Montana. *Condor*, 14, 107.

Saunders, Aretas A. 1912c. A horseback ride across Montana. *Condor*, 14, 215–220.

Saunders, Aretas A. 1914a. An ecological study of the breeding birds of an area near Choteau, Montana. *Auk*, 31, 200–210.

Saunders, Aretas A. 1914b. The birds of Teton and northern Lewis and Clark Counties, Montana. *Condor*, 16, 124–144.

Saunders, Aretas A. 1921. A distributional list of the birds of Montana. *Pacific Coast Avifauna*, No. 14.

Sclater, William L. 1912. *A history of the birds of Colorado.*

Sennett, George B. 1878. Notes on the ornithology of the lower Rio Grande of Texas. *U.S. Geol. Geogr. Surv. Bull.*, 4, No. 1, 21.

Seton, Ernest Thompson. 1886. The birds of Western Manitoba. *Auk*, 3, 320–329.

Seton, Ernest Thompson. 1891. The birds of Manitoba. *Proc. U.S. Nat. Mus.*, 13, 457–643.

Sibley, Charles G., and Olin Sewall Pettingill, Jr. 1955. A hybrid longspur from Saskatchewan. *Auk*, 72, 423–425.

Silloway, Perley M. 1902. Notes of McCown's longspur in Montana. *Osprey*, 6, 42–44.

Silloway, Perley M. 1903. Birds of Fergus County. *Fergus County Free High School, Bull.* No. 1.

Sutton, George Miksch. 1934. Notes on some birds of the western panhandle of Oklahoma. *Ann. Carnegie Mus.*, vol. 24.

Swinburne, John. 1888. Occurrance [sic] of the chestnut-collared longspur (*Calcarius ornatus*) and also of MacCown's longspur (*Rhyncophanes maccownii*) in Apache County, Arizona. *Auk*, 5, 321–322.

Taverner, Percy A. 1922. Birds of eastern Canada, 2nd. ed. *Geol. Surv. Canada Mem.* 104.

Taverner, Percy A. 1926. Birds of western Canada. *Victoria Mem. Mus. Bull.*, 41.

Taverner, Percy A. 1927. Some recent Canadian records. *Auk*, 44, 217–228.

Thorne, Platte M. 1895. List of birds observed in vicinity of Fort Keogh, Montana. *Auk*, 12, 211–219.

Thwaites, Reuben G. 1904–1905. *Original journals of Lewis and Clark.* 2, 19–120.

Van Tyne, Josselyn. 1953. In Bent, *Life histories of North American wood warblers. U.S. Nat. Mus. Bull.,* 203.

Visher, Stephen S. 1911. Annotated list of the birds of Harding County, northwestern South Dakota. *Auk,* 28, 15–16.

Visher, Stephen S. 1912. A list of the birds of Pine Ridge Reservation. In The biology of south-central South Dakota. *Vermillion Bull. Geol. Surv. South Dakota,* No. 5, 61–136.

Visher, Stephen S. 1913. An annotated list of the birds of Sanborn County, southeast-central South Dakota. *Auk,* 30, 561–573.

Visher, Stephen S. 1914. A preliminary report on the biology of Harding County, north-western South Dakota. *South Dakota Geol. Surv.,* Bull. 6.

(Life Histories, 1968)

CHAPTER 5

Nesting Sites of the Birds of the Audubon Center of Greenwich, Connecticut

Why a bird selects a certain shrub or a particular branch for its nesting site is probably governed by psychological and physical requirements no more mysterious than those which guide the human being in the amazing choice of some of his dwelling places. The motivation, both avian and human, is obscure: which should encourage the bird student to observe carefully, to record accurately, and to try to understand objectively every instance of avian behavior or activity which comes to his notice. Human behavior too might profit from such scrutiny. Puzzling bits and pieces put together often make something like a comprehensible whole.

Since birds apparently exercise a wide latitude in the selection of nesting sites, both as to species and as to individuals, the following descriptions must be regarded not as final designations but as guides to locations where such avian structures are to be found "generally" or "usually."

The following species list is based on Morton's *Birds of the Audubon Center of Greenwich* (1963 revision). Species marked with an asterisk (*) have nested on the Sanctuary.

STATUS ON THE SANCTUARY		
P – permanent resident S – summer resident	A – accidental	T – transient W – winter visitor
Nesters On or Over Water		
SPECIES	STATUS	USUSAL NEST SITE
Grebe, Pied-billed	T	floating raft of debris or reeds anchored to vegetation; old muskrat houses
Duck, Ring-necked	A	marshy border of open water, just above water
*Blackbird, Red-winged	S	woven cup in cattails; occasionally in dense weed stems or bushes near or over watery situations

Ground Nesters (including sites just above ground and burrow dwellers)		
SPECIES	STATUS	USUSAL NEST SITE
Loon, Common	T	flat mass of vegetation near water's edge
Bittern, American	S	dense cattail growths, sedges in marshes and edges of wet meadows
GEESE		
*Canada	S	flat mound on high ground near water; man-made platforms
Snow	A	in marshy grass near pond, in flat tundra country
DUCKS		
*Mallard	P	dense reeds or grass near water; also considerable distance from water
*Black	P	shrubby tangles or thick grass on high ground near marsh or open water
Teal, Green-winged	T	grass clumps at varying distances from water
Teal, Blue-winged	A	long grass, sedge tussocks near water
Vulture, Turkey	T	sheltered spots on cliff ledges; hollow stumps, caves, sometimes old buildings
Eagle, Golden	A	high on cliff ledges
HAWKS		
Marsh	T	in shrubs very near the ground or under tall weedy plants or dense vegetation near meadows or marshes
Duck (Peregrine Falcon)	T	cliff ledge nesters, preferably seacoasts or along river chasms; sometimes treetops or large old nests of birds
*Grouse, Ruffed	P	under logs or at bases of stumps or rocks, in low shrubs near roads, clearings, swamps
Bobwhite	A	dense grassy cover, tangles of vines, brushy woodland edges
*Pheasant, Ring-necked	P	dense grass, weedy fence rows, roadside ditches, hayland
*Killdeer	S	fields, shores, pastures, open locations
*Woodcock	S	moist thickets, brushy cover, mixed hardwoods, conifers
SANDPIPERS		
Upland Plover	A	tuft of grass, grassy clump in pastures and haylands

*Spotted	S	dense vegetation, under brush, logs in fields, wastelands
Yellowlegs, Greater	A	"scrape" on hummock of boggy tundra, muskeg or marsh
Gull, Herring	P	weed-grown or rocky islands, shores, headlands
Chuck-will's-widow	A	among dead leaves, on bare ground, usually in woods
Whip-poor-will	T	among dead leaves, borders of deciduous woods
Nighthawk	T	open barren gravel or outcrops; roofs of asphalted buildings
Kingfisher, Belted	S	4–5 foot burrows in banks near or over running water
FLYCATCHERS		
*Phoebe, Eastern	S	cliff ledges, rocky shelves near streams; bridges, buildings
Yellow-bellied	T	mossy mounds, sphagnum, fallen tree roots, northern coniferous forests
Lark, Horned	T	in the open, fields, pastures, wastelands, near clod or stone
SWALLOWS		
*Barn	S	originally in caves, crevices, niches under overhanging cliffs; now bridges, barns, buildings
Bank	T	colonial; 2–3 foot burrows in gravel or sand banks
*Rough-winged	S	solitary; burrows in sand banks, crevices in rock ledges, buildings, bridges
Cliff	T	colonial; overhanging cliffs, eaves of buildings
Wren, Winter	T	old roots or stumps; under banks of overhanging streams; generally in coniferous woodlands
THRUSHES		
Hermit	T	low knolls or humps; usually associated with conifers
Gray-cheeked	T	in boreal forests on and sometimes just above the ground; up to 20 feet high occasionally
*Veery	S	fern tussocks, thick vegetation, logs, stumps; shrubby woods

Pipit, Water	T	shelter of rock, mossy hummock in treeless tundra
WARBLERS		
*Black and White	S	upturned roots; underlog, stumps, rocks
*Worm-eating	S	in thick drifts of leaves on rocky hillsides
Golden-winged	S	dense growth of weedy stems just above ground, openings in woodlands
*Blue-winged	S	dense vegetation just above ground, sometimes near edges
Tennessee	T	in sphagnum moss or sedgy tussock, northern woods
Nashville	T	mossy hummock; base of shrub or stump in brushy areas with clumps of young trees
Palm	T	mossy hummock or in sedge under small tree; coniferous bogs
*Ovenbird	S	arched-over nest in the open, on forest floor of mature woodlands
Waterthrush, Northern	T	side of stump, upturned roots, sometimes cavities in banks in shrub-grown bogs, wooded swamps
*Waterthrush, Louisiana	S	tree roots, in or under overhang of streams, sometimes holes in banks, usually near swift-running water
Kentucky	A	leafy vegetation; in small bush on or just above ground; not a sunken nest; moist rich woodlands
Connecticut	T	sunk in mound or grass clump in open bogs or brushy openings in poplar-aspen growths
Mourning	T	always in tangles of briars, canes, dense brushy vegetation; sometimes as much as 2 feet up
*Yellowthroat	S	rank vegetation in moist situations
Wilson's	T	mossy hummock, sedge tussock, shrubby ponds, streams, bogs
*Canada	S	fern clumps, upturned roots, stumps, moist or wet areas in cool mature woodlands
Bobolink	S	heavy stand of hay, grass or similar vegetation
*Meadowlark	S	partly domed-over nest in dense grassy or weedy cover
Dickcissel	A	dense growths of hay and similar vegetation in open fields

SPARROWS		
Savannah	T	dense vegetation in low moist areas, meadows
Vesper	T	near grass clump or in depressions, short-grass, pastures
Junco, Slate-colored	W	dense vegetation, upturned roots, over-hanging banks in northern coniferous forests
Tree	W	low vegetation, in stunted trees and shrubs south of Arctic tundra
*Field	S	grass clump or low bush in brushy area, pastures, edges
White-crowned	T	low shrubs, brushy cover near lakes or streams
White-throated	T	sunk into hollows or mossy hummocks in forest openings
Fox	W	under bush or a few feet up in tangles, dense woods, streamsides
Lincoln's	T	in swamp tussocks or bushes; wet situations
*Swamp	S	dense tussock, marsh vegetation, fresh-water marshes rank with growth
*Song	S	grass clumps, dense weedy stems, sometimes in dense shrubs or conifers, near moist situations
Shrub and Tree Nesters		
SPECIES	STATUS	USUAL NEST SITE
Cormorant, Double-crested	T	high in trees, cliff ledges, rocky islets
HERONS		
Great Blue	TS	colonies; flat nests in tree tops, isolated woodland patches or islands
*Green	S	15–20 feet up, dense-foliaged tree, low shrubs
Egret, Common	A	in rookeries, 20–40 feet up, swamp woods
Night Heron, Black-crowned	A	colonies; 20–30 feet up in dense groves near water
HAWKS		
Goshawk	AW	heavy timber stands, 20–60 feet up, bulky nest on horizontal limb
*Sharp-shinned	S	10–60 feet up, on a branch against the trunk conifers
Cooper's	T	20–60 feet up, against trunk on horizontal limb; upright fork in deciduous trees

Red-tailed	T	tall trees near timber edge; sometimes cliff ledges
*Red-shouldered	S	20–60 feet up in crotch of main trunk, wet woodlands
*Broad-winged	S	15–20 feet up, crotch of main trunk, deciduous woods
Rough-legged	A	20–30 feet up in tallest tree of area; sometimes cliff ledges, high rocky points
Eagle, Bald	A	top crotches of living trees, cliff edges
Osprey	T	tree platforms, man-made structures at any heights
Pigeon	A	tree crotches high up, old crow's nests, cliff ledges
SANDPIPERS		
Solitary	T	old robin or grackle or rusty blackbirds' nests, 4–20 feet, northern coniferous woods
*Dove, Mourning	S	flimsy structures, old robin and grackle nests, 15–25 feet up
CUCKOOS		
*Yellow-billed	S	flimsy platform in dense shrubbery or tree, 4–8 feet up
*Black-billed	S	thick shrubby slumps, 2–4 feet up
OWLS		
*Great Horned	P	old nests of herons, eagles, hawks; hollow trees high up, sometimes cliff ledges
*Hummingbird, Ruby-throated	S	10–20 feet up, in open woodlands, saddled on downward-slanting branch
FLYCATCHERS		
*Kingbird, Eastern	S	20–25 feet up, in open woodlands, often near water
Traill's (Alder)	S	2–4 feet up, in upright fork; sometimes fern clumps
Acadian	A	suspended from forked branch, up to 10 feet, mature but rather dense woodlands
*Least	S	5–15 feet up in a crotch, open country scattered trees
*Peewee, Eastern Wood	S	saddled on horizontal limb, up to 20 feet, deep woods
Olive-sided	T	end of horizontal limb, tall coniferous trees
* Jay, Blue	P	in tree crotch, branches of main trunk, 10–15 feet up

Magpie, Black-billed	A	huge nest of sticks; streamside bushy trees and thickets in the western country
*Crow, Common	P	from 6 feet to fairly high, substantial nest
*Catbird	S	4–8 feet in dense shrubbery, often near west situations
*Thrasher, Brown	S	1–5 feet up, dense and thorny shrubs; sometimes on ground
THRUSHES		
*Robin	S	usually 5–15 feet; dense bushes, fold of main trunk, sheltered recess in building
*Wood	S	5–12 feet, dense shrubbery, crotch or fork of sapling, well-developed woodlands, especially near wet situations
Swainson's (Olive-b.)	T	3–15 feet up, small tree, shrub, usually evergreen, spruce-fir forests
Gnat-catcher, Blue-grey	S	saddled on horizontal limb or in crotch; well up
KINGLETS		
Golden-crowned	W	30–60 feet up in thick twigs of conifers
Ruby-crowned	T	in pendent twigs near spruce top, northern conifers
Waxwing, Cedar	P	6–35 feet, horizontal limb, deciduous or conifers
SHRIKES		
Northern	W	dense conifers, fairly high up
Migrant (Loggerhead)	A	2–20 feet, center of clumps of thorny or shrubby plants
VIREOS		
*White-eyed	S	3–6 feet, thick low growths, moist areas
*Yellow-throated	S	12–40 feet, in forked twig, suspended; deciduous woods often along streams
Solitary	T	5–10 feet on forked twig, center portion of small tree, in coniferous or mixed woods
*Red-eyed	S	5–25 feet, suspended in forked twig
Philadelphia	T	10–40 feet, forked twig of deciduous tree
WARBLERS		
Parula	T	up to 50 feet, in usnea lichen (North) or Spanish moss (South)
Magnolia	T	5–15 feet, conifers along swamps, shallow ponds

Cape May	T	30–60 feet, near top of spruce or fir, north
Black-throated Blue	T	from several inches to 3 feet, shrubs, lank weed stems, deciduous or mixed woodlands with shrubby undergrowth
Myrtle	T	5–50 feet, in evergreens, northern coniferous forests
*Black-throated Green	S	branches of a conifer or deciduous tree, from low to high; generally in coniferous forests
Blackburnian	T	6–60 feet, conifer, well out on branch; large hemlocks, spruces, pines
*Chestnut-sided	S	2–3 feet in shrub in thickets and dense edges of woods
Bay-breasted	T	4–40 feet, spruce woodlands, openings, scattered trees
Blackpoll	T	4–12 feet, in small conifer, dwarfed spruces and firs northern forests
Pine	T	in foliage out of horizontal limb, 10 feet to highest part of tree; associated with pines
*Prairie	S	2–5 feet, leafy vegetation in thickets in brushy land
Chat, Yellow-breasted	S	bulky nest, 3–5 feet, small tree, shrub in dense tangles
*Hooded	S	2–3 feet, fork of shrub or small tree, moist sites in mature woodland with well-developed shrubbery
*Redstart	S	6–25 feet, upright of tree or shrub, deciduous woods
*Oriole, Baltimore	S	woven bag about 6 inches, deep, middle high to high
Blackbird, Rusty	T	up to 10 feet in dense conifers; thick wet woods, swamps overgrown with trees, shallow pools
*Grackle, Common	S	high in tree or low on ground; bulky nests
*Tanager, Scarlet	S	flat nest 10–50 feet out on horizontal limb; mature woods
FINCHES		
*Cardinal	S	6–8 feet, loosely made, in bushy thickets or tangles
*Grosbeak, Rose-breasted	S	6–15 feet, low branch or crotch; usually not far from water; sometimes high in tree
*Indigo Bunting	S	cup in crotch not far from ground in dense vegetation

Grosbeak, Evening	W	20–30 feet, dense leaf cluster on branch end, conifers in coniferous zone
*Finch, Purple	P	5–60 feet, in evergreen or deciduous growths
Grosbeak, Pine	W	6–30 feet, lower branches, conifer or shrub; coniferous
Redpoll, Common	W	colonies; forked branches of willows or birch; Sometimes in tundra tussocks; northern spruce, barren lands
Sisken, Pine	W	saddled out on end of coniferous branch; 10–20 feet; always associated with conifers
*Goldfinch, Common	S	upright fork of bush or small tree, a few feet to 20 feet
Crossbill, Red	A	5–80 feet, saddled in conifer; always associated with conifers
Crossbill, White-winged	A	similar to Red Crossbill
*Towhee, Rufous-sided	S	up to five feet in bush or small tree, in dense brushy cover; also on ground in clump of grass, stump, brushpile
Sparrow, Chipping	S	3–5 feet, dense shrubbery, evergreens, vines
Cavity Nesters		
SPECIES	STATUS	USUAL NEST SITE
*Wood Duck	S	hollows in trees, boxes; may be some distance from water
Bufflehead	T	old flicker or woodpecker hole near water
MERGANSERS		
Hooded	T	cavity of any type in forested watery places though site may sometimes be some distance from water
Common	A	old hawk's nests, but usually any cavity in tree; Sometimes among rocks
*Sparrow Hawk (Kestrel)	P	cavities high up, woodpecker holes, holes in cliffs
OWLS		
Screech	P	old woodpecker holes, cavities, bird houses
*Barred	P	hollows in trees, sometimes birdboxes; swamps and deep woodlands
Saw-whet	W	old woodpecker holes, dense woodlands, prefers conifers
*Swift, Chimney	S	bracketlike up cemented to walls of hollow trees, chimneys

WOODPECKERS		
*Flicker	S	old cavities, birdhouses, hollow trees; to 90 feet up
*Pileated	P	15–70 feet, dense stand of trees
Red-bellied	A	about 40 feet up, in dead trees, woodland edges
Sapsucker, Common	T	small holed entrance in dead or living tree near water
*Hairy	P	in dead or living trees, frequently near moist situations
*Downy	P	low to 60 feet, in a dead stub
Black-backed, Three-toed	A	2–15 feet in dead or living tree, near opening in coniferous forests
*Flycatcher, Crested	S	natural cavities, woodpecker holes, bird boxes
SWALLOWS		
*Tree	S	natural cavities, woodpecker holes, bird boxes preferably near water
*Purple Martin	S	"Originally holes and cavities in trees, cliffs, and among loose rocks" (Pough); bird boxes 15–20 feet up
TITMICE		
*Chickadee, Black-capped	P	natural cavities, woodpecker holes, bird boxes 1–10 feet, cavities excavated by the birds themselves in rotten stumps or stubs
Boreal	A	similar to Black-capped Chickadee
*Titmouse, Tufted	S	natural cavities in trees, woodpecker holes, boxes
NUTHATCHES		
*White-breasted	P	old woodpecker holes, natural openings in trees
Red-breasted	W	hole excavated by birds themselves in dead stub; wood-pecker holes, natural cavities in trees
*Creeper, Brown		crevice or cavity under loose-hanging bark
WRENS		
*House	S	tree hollow, old woodpecker hole, bird box, cavity in buildings, any cavity
*Carolina	P	holes in trees, stumps; crannies in man-made structures; ball-like nest of sticks in thickets, tangles

*Bluebird	P	natural tree cavities, old woodpecker holes, bird boxes, from 2–30 feet
*Starling	P	10–25 feet, natural cavity, woodpecker hole, cavity or crevice about buildings
Prothonotary Warbler	AS	5–10 feet, decayed-out hole in dead willow stub over water; old woodpecker holes, bird houses, crannies about buildings; only eastern warbler nesting in tree cavity
*Sparrow, House	P	crevice or cavity in building, bird box, natural tree cavity; in forks or trees or in bushes
Finch, House	T	tree cavities; bird boxes; crannies in buildings; also dense shrubbery, tangles, vines

References

Bent, Arthur Cleveland. *Life Histories of North American Birds*; series published by U.S. National Museum.
Forbush, Edward Howe. 1955. *Birds of Massachusetts and Other New England States.*
Krause, Herbert. Unpublished field notes.
Morton, Duryea. 1963. *Birds of the Audubon Center of Greenwich.*
Peterson, Roger Tory. 1934. *Field Guide to the Birds.*
Pough, Richard. *1946. Audubon, Eastern Land Birds Guide.*
Pough, Richard. 1951. *Audubon, Water Bird Guide.*

(*Audubon Center of Greenwich*, 1964)

CHAPTER 6

The Bald Eagle

It is indeed a pleasure to speak to as understanding a group as conservationists always are. The very word itself suggests that something is wrong with an environment and that here is a group that wants to do something about its correction. I congratulate you in having a division in an organization as large as yours which devotes itself exclusively to conservation. For the thorough-going conservationist there is something almost dedicatory about study of a problem in a maladjusted environment, and, in terms of your work, I am sure that that is exactly what it is–a dedication.

As an educator, I have always thought that there ought to be introduced very early in our education, perhaps as early as the eighth grade but certainly in high school, a course dealing with the principles of ecology. For ecology is the study of the organism, the individual, and his environment, the world he lives in. It is a study of the inter-relationship of the individual and the forces which surround him. It is a study which deals with this relationship whether it be in the immediate context of his family, his neighborhood, his community, or in the larger context of his state or nation. It seeks to understand those forces which are basic to tensions or lack of tensions. It seeks knowledge about which of these tensions seem inimical to the best interests of the organism and which seem most advantageous to the further development of the organism. Without this kind of study, without this knowledge and understanding, most efforts in conservation seem doomed to vitiation, to say the least.

To illustrate my point. There seems little use in legislation to control the shooting of ducks if at the same time there is not attention paid to habitat. There is little wisdom in trying to save ducks by the limitation of the harvest if there is no thought given to the preservation of holes and marshes. Ducks will not build their nests on the asphalt pavement; they will not lay their eggs in a plowed field; they will not raise their young on the rich green of a golf course. They must have water, they must have rushes, they must have areas for gathering of food and for relaxing, loafing and resting even as human beings must have, to save themselves from ulcers and peptic disturbances, must have times and places for rest and relaxation. I don't know that ducks ever get peptic ulcers. I do know that without areas for resting and loafing, they will soon depart for areas where such luxuries are provided or they disappear completely.

Thus, you can see that all the legislation in the world is not going to save ducks if there isn't legislation to provide the place where ducks can multiply. All the best intentioned efforts to save ducks will not save one duck, if at the same time there is not an effort made to save the environment in which they can breed and raise their families: that is, provide the marshes, the water and aquatic plants upon which they feed. The best way to assure this is to study the relationships of the ducks and their environment to see what they need. And this is the study of ecology, one of the cornerstones of conservation.

Another example, this one having to do with the subject of my talk, is the bald eagle. In Alaska for some seventy years, the bald eagle has been shot and trapped as a predator upon the salmon. The case was simple. Here were the salmon in the river. There were the eagles pouncing on the fish, dragging them out of the water, gorging on them. Stories of wholesale destruction of fish waves, an entire season's catch, soon were circulated. One has a vision of hordes of bald eagles descending upon the hapless salmon and utterly decimating a whole year's population. Outraged fishery owners appealed to legislatures–they were facing ruin. Something had to be done to stop the dastardly attacks of the outlaw eagles.

In 1917, the first bounty law was passed which provided a $.50 payment for each pair of eagle feet. But no one bothered to ask whether the eagle was really guilty. Guilt by association, circumstantial evidence: that was all that was needed to convict the eagle. No one bothered to study the food habits of the eagle or the relationships between the bird and the demands of its food habits. The bounty law of 1917 in the next five years was eminently successful: 15,745 eagles were slaughtered. Yet no one bothered to see how effective this method was in saving the salmon industry.

Apparently it wasn't doing much good. In 1923 the bounty was raised to $1. From 1923 to 1940, such records as are available showed that another 79,746 bald eagles were killed. Yet no one asked how much damage the bald eagle was actually doing. No money was appropriated for bounty purposes during the years 1940 to 1943; we have no way of knowing how many birds were brought down. In 1945, the bounty law was repealed, not because more knowledge about the relationship between bald eagle and fish had been accumulated but because it apparently became too expensive for the legislature. But in 1949 the bounty law was re-enacted, this time payment being $2 for every pair of eagle feet brought in. Some men made their living killing eagles and bringing in the feet; when the law was repealed, they complained that their source of livelihood was being taken away and asked for compensation. The new bounty law of 1949 continued to sanction the killing; between 1949 and 1951, 7,455 bald eagles were brought in. Nobody pretends to guess how many unrecorded birds were killed.

Meantime, game biologists had been studying the ecology of the bird, its food habits, its behavior. And soon the truth came out. The bald eagle was predominantly a fish eater, true; but it was an eater of fish that were dead or nearly dead. The period when its young needed food most coincided with the run of the salmon after they had spawned and were floating or swimming about in a dying condition. For you know that the salmon, after spawning, has completed its life's work and dies. Upon these dying fish the bald eagle preys; its predation on living fish was found to be almost negligible.

All this was found in the years approximately 1949 to 1962, when the National Emblem Act finally protected the bald eagle. This Act was passed only when it became apparent that the bald eagle had little or nothing to do with the salmon population. It was only when the ecology of the bird was studied and the facts became known that something was done to show people what the relationship between the bird and its environment was. Yet because this study had not been made, because so little knowledge about its relationship existed, more than 100,000 bald eagles died: a tragic grisly monument to man's unwillingness to study a problem in relationships before he applies drastic measures of control—measures of control which do nothing to ameliorate the difficulty and actually are productive of more harm than good. While more than 100,000 bald eagles were being killed, no one knows how many more were shot down, poisoned or trapped; and no one knows how many birds which resemble eagles were also slaughtered: the golden eagle, the rough-legged hawk, the gyrfalcon, the osprey, red-tailed hawk and Swainson's hawk, all residents of Alaska and the coast of Washington.

The National Emblem Act protects the bald eagle in legal terms: it is a law on the statute books. But no law is effective unless the people are educated enough to know why they obey the law. Even our judges who mete out sentences on those arrested for breaking the law are often, even under the most favorable circumstances, so unfamiliar with the principles of ecology that their judgments, while strictly legalitarian, are hardly compatible with the principles of true conservation.

Not all judges are so inadequately qualified as the one in Rockledge, Fla., about whom Helen Cruickshank told at the National Convention of the Audubon Society in Tucson last November. Helen Cruickshank is the author of a number of books, including the recent *Thoreau on Birds* (1964), which I urge all members of this group to read. Mrs. Cruickshank is the wife of Alan Cruickshank, Audubon lecturer, whose films have been shown here in Sioux Falls and who has at least twice appeared here in person. Helen Cruickshank tells of the judge in her home town who presided over the case of an armed guard in charge of a prison work crew. Gun on his arm, he stood boredly watching his prisoners labor. Finally, so restless he didn't know what to do, he noticed two hawks flying nearby. Up went the gun; down came the two birds. Now, Florida has a law protecting hawks and owls. So has South Dakota. The prison guard was arrested for shooting hawks–for breaking the law. But the judge who presided freed the prison guard who shot the hawks. Why? Because the guard testified that he shot in self defense and in defense of the prisoners he was guarding. The prisoners were being "threatened" by the hawks; he had to shoot them to save them. And the judge accepted his testimony and exonerated him. What would a judge in South Dakota under similar circumstances have done? Would he have exercised the law, or would he have legally slapped the wrist of the accused. I leave the answer to your own conscience.

Says Dr. Roland Clement, biologist for the National Audubon Society, "An important cause of continuing attrition of birds of prey is the failure of law enforcement even in states with good laws." The wisest of judges may be most conversant with the intricacies of legal argument and yet, unaware of the fundamentals of good ecological practice, actually be unable to mete out a sentence commensurate with the misdeed committed. Therefore, I feel that a knowledge of ecology is absolutely essential these days, not only in the field of wild life but in the wider aspects of our human relationships also. There must be conservation not only of our wildlife resources but of our human resources also.

How many bald eagles there are in Alaska isn't known. But to our sorrow, we know only too well approximately how many bald eagles we have in the United States. Once the bald eagle nested in almost every state in the Union. Now the total population of the bald eagle in the United States is only some 5,000 individuals. Once the bald eagle nested in South Dakota. It was reported along the big Sioux; Lewis and Clark saw it along the Missouri; it was recorded on many of the rivers which are tributary to the Missouri. Today not one bald eagle has been found nesting in South Dakota. Once it nested as close to Sioux Falls as Clay and Union Counties. Now the length and the breadth of the state contains not a single nest. In fact only a few states can point to an active nest. I visited with several Montana ornithologists last summer. Except for Yellowstone Park where one may find five or six active eyries, there probably is not an eagle nesting between here and the streams of the Rocky Mountains. Most of the 5,000 birds nesting in the U.S. are found in Florida. On the nesting census nationwide made in 1963, it was found that only 21 of the 48 states had breeding birds. Of these Florida had 190, Michigan had 81, Wisconsin had 64, Minnesota had 40, and Maine had 35. The rest of the 21 states had from one to eleven. That is the status of the bald eagle today—the bald eagle, our national emblem, the bird on our national seal, the bird that is described in the Federal Hall Memorial Museum in Washington as bearing on its breast an escutcheon without any other supporters, to denote that the United States of America ought to rely on its own virtue.

It is a proud-looking bird, as anyone who has seen it flying can testify. Its snow-white head and tail, its brownish dark body, its mighty spread of wing, the ease with which it circles the cloudy steps of heaven these befit a bird that is the seal and symbol of these states called the United. Once it truly denoted all the states of the Union, for by its nesting in all, it was a symbolic thread which drew all together. Now the thread is broken–broken by the citizens of those states themselves, who by their lack of understanding of ecological principles, have violated the laws of nature to the point where to return is difficult. The bald eagle is indeed protected by federal statute. Yet it declines at a frightening rate so that zoologists and conservationists are becoming increasingly alarmed lest the warning recently uttered by Prince Phillip of England come true. For the husband of the present queen said bluntly not long ago that "unless drastic action is taken the United States' bald eagle will become extinct and exist only on American coins and medals."

The eyrie of the bald eagle is the largest nest structure of any American bird. One in Ohio weighed more than a ton. One in Florida weighed more than eleven hundred pounds. Usually they are found in tops of large trees where huge solid branches offer secure supports for these structures. Sometimes they are found on the ledges of cliffs. Almost always they are found near rivers or lakes, for the most important part of the bald eagle's diet is fish.

One curious aspect of these nests and the habits of the bald eagle is that often one finds a spray of oak leaves or a branch of spruce or pine or as in the East a stalk of corn. Sometimes this stalk is one of last year's with the ear still on it. Into the nest it is placed, sometimes near the edge where the yellow ear hangs over the dark side.

But the number of these nests is yearly growing smaller thanks to industrialization, lumbering, the growth of cities, the spread of housing developments, the disturbance of recreational facilities which are destroying the sequestered nature of its wilderness nesting sites. Here again there is the same story of a disregard for ecology. The seal and the symbol of the United States cannot find house room in a land which makes no provision for it.

True, in Florida, far-seeing Floridians have set aside over a million-and-a-half acres of sanctuaries. Even that isn't enough today. For with the increase of pesticides, rivers and estuaries in Florida have become contaminated. Again ecological study is necessary. Pesticides contaminate the water; the fish in the waters eat smaller fish which eat smaller organisms which feed on plankton which are contaminated with pesticides. The bald eagle is a fish eater and eagerly takes the contaminated fish, and so ingests the toxins. The unfortunate part is that the eagle is at the end of the food chain. One of the characteristics of some pesticides is that they have an accumulative quality which increases their toxicity as they pass from organism to organism. The toxic materials are picked up by the smallest organism and passed on to the largest predator, each time increasing in concentration. The last to feed upon the organism in the chain naturally receives the largest concentration of DDT. In this instance, the bald eagle is the bird at the end of the chain.

Grossman and Hamlet write in *Birds of Prey of the World* (1964, p. 183): "Recent biological investigation strongly suggests that there is a link between DDT, DDE, and other derivatives which become highly concentrated in fish, and the bald eagle's lack of nesting success in certain places." The 1963 Progress Report on Pesticide-Bald Eagle Relationships concludes with the significant but cautious statement: "To sum up, we know that DDT in sufficient quantity will kill eagles. We know that wild eagles carry body burdens of DDT, and that some of this is transferred to the egg by the females.... We have no evidence that the levels we find in eggs and birds are innocuous." This is the 1963 report of the U.S. Bureau of Sport and Fisheries. At a meeting in Miami, Fla., in the fall of 1963, a meeting which I attended, Secretary of the Interior Udall said: "Research has told us that incredibly small quantities of some chemicals can destroy shrimp grounds, or reduce the reproductive capacity of oysters. Uncounted thousands of birds and other wildlife have suffered or died from the widespread use of chemical pesticides, as you know all too well." Anyone who doubts there is a linkage between pesticides and declining populations in some birds has not read such reports as Wildlife Studies, 1963, Fish and Wildlife Service Circular No. 199; the articles by Ratcliffe, More, and Lockie in the British periodicals *British Birds* and *Bird Study*; nor the monumental compilation by Dr. Timothy Myres of the University of Alberta, called *The Widespread Pollution of Soil, Water and Living Things by Toxic Materials Used in Insect Control Programs.*

Again, this is a matter of study; this is a matter of ecological relationships. For instance, why should an individual or a company be permitted to use a toxic material without first studying the relationships between the material and the organisms to which it is applied, and the consequential effects upon such organisms?

In the developing of such studies the conservation department or division of this organization can take a leading part. Films, studies, investigations are available. Urge a thorough study of immediate as well as long-range effects of such activities as widespread spraying for insects or for the destruction of herbs. Study the effect of chlorinated hydrocarbons and the possibility that they may affect children as yet unborn, as they might genetically; or those about to be born as thalidomide apparently does, and as America remembers in a recent scare. Tell your friends and neighbors about the possible harm of lethal insecticides and urge the greatest understanding in their application. A dedicated group such as this is can do much to promote that understanding which is the basis of conservation and the only way in which our wildlife can be saved. It is the only wise course to pursue if the seal and symbolic emblem of our country, the bald eagle, is to be preserved for generations yet to come.

(*Manuscript,* 1964)

SECTION V

BOOK REVIEWS

CHAPTER 1

Bird Guide: Land Birds East of the Rockies
By Chester Reed, Doubleday and Company, Garden City, New York. 1951.

It is good to see that old standby, *Reed's Bird Guide* in a new format, with revised descriptions, new plates and a new introduction. Included is a portion of the original preface but such appendages as subspecies are omitted. Instead, family designation is included for each species.

As the publishers point out, the "common and scientific bird names used" are those "currently favored by the AOU committee," and I find that the Short-billed Marsh Wren is now the Sedge Wren; the Canada Jay is the Gray Jay; and Wilson's Warbler is now the Black-capped Warbler.

While the new edition is fresh and crisp in make-up, I wish the plates had the sharp clarity of the earlier editions. The illustrations on the glazed paper of the tattered, dog-eared copy of the 1915 issue before me, have a sharpness of color and detail which the present edition lacks on its unglazed pages. In some instances the colors are exaggerated beyond any usefulness as marks of identification. The Bay-breasted Warbler in the 1915 edition is a remarkable likeness; the same bird in the new edition does not represent either diagnostically or realistically the colors of that species.

Nevertheless, this is, as always, a handy little pocket book on any field trip.

(The Wilson Bulletin, 1966)

CHAPTER 2

Thoreau on Birds
By Helen Cruickshank, McGraw-Hill Book Company,
New York, New York, 1964.

Surely the time is past when a serious critic, be he scientist or nonscientist, can dismiss Henry Thoreau's nature writings as lightly as John Burroughs did in *Century Magazine* (1882): "To the last his ornithology was not quite sure, not quite trustworthy." Or disparage him as Havelock Ellis did in *The New Spirit* (1890) where he maintains that Thoreau's science "is that of a fairly intelligent school boy–a counting of birds' eggs and a running after squirrels." Charles D. Stewart answered Burroughs' charges in *Atlantic* (1935): "Thoreau had a faculty, which Burroughs does not seem to admire or understand, of the modern research worker." And Mark Van Doren in "Thoreau" (1916) remarked that "Mr. Burroughs has never been quite able to understand what he was doing."

After the publication in 1904 of Bradford Torrey's edition of Thoreau's "Journal," critical opinion underwent a significant change. McAtee in *Scientific Monthly* (1939), for all his reservations, found that, in ideas of protective adaptation, Thoreau preceded Belt, Wallace, and Darwin. Deevey in *Quarterly Review of Biology* (1942) suggests that Thoreau is "the first American limnologist." Adams in *Scientific Monthly* (1945) regards him as an ecologist, Leopold and Jones in *Ecological Monographs* (1947) call him the "father of phenology," and Oehser in *Nature Magazine* (1945), recalling that, along with George Catlin, Thoreau was one of the first to suggest the establishment of a wilderness area as we think of it today, is convinced that "perhaps Thoreau was America's first real conservationist." What is noteworthy is that the recognition of these broad horizons of Thoreau's thinking appears not in the literary journals but in the scientific.

One of the early accounts of Thoreau and birds was Francis H. Allen's edition of Thoreau's "Notes on New England Birds" (1910); the latest to appear and perhaps the best is Helen Cruickshank's "Thoreau on Birds." It is a most attractive volume, illustrated with facsimiles from Wilson's "American Ornithology" and Nuttall's "Manual." The major portion of the volume, "Some Species of Birds from Thoreau's Journal," deals with Thoreau's notes on 103 species in the Concord vicinity. For each species there is an introductory section and excerpts from the Journal arranged in diary fashion as to month, day, and year. The selections are annotated with transitional passages set off in brackets. By and large, the transitions are judiciously executed. Occasionally they contain images which have their own integrity. Many of the Journal entries are put into the context of what seems to be Thoreau's knowledge of the species–an important addition. Useful too are the cross-references to many species in volumes other than the Journal. Nevertheless, these transitional commentaries sometimes lean toward the cumbersome, impeding the reader's progress and encouraging him to leap over the transitions to rejoin Thoreau's own lively flow of observation. Perhaps such information as range, distribution, and certain descriptive features might be left to the handbooks. Along with Journal excerpts are descriptions of birds in such volumes as "Walden" and "A Week on the Concord." A list of Thoreau's birds with the most recent designations clarifies such popular names as "Yorrick," "Belcher-squelcher" (for the American Bittern), and "Election-bird." This is by far the most comprehensive annotated compilation of Thoreau's birds available today. It naturally does not consider Thoreau's writing on birds in terms of zoological significance or contributions to ornithology as Deevey does for Thoreau's notes on limnology, Leopold and Jones for his phenological observations, or Adams for his ecological notations. Such a study would appear to be in order. As Roger Tory Peterson observes in a perceptive Foreword, "The measure of a man is his durability."

Mrs. Cruickshank has chosen the selections with a sure and discriminative taste. They illustrate Thoreau's careful recording of the behavior of birds. More than that, they underscore his passion for collecting and journalizing his data, his endless quest for facts. It is a pity to mention typographical errors, those skulkers in the blindspots of the proof-reader's eye: "*orysivorous*" (p. 170), "*gentillis*" (p. 315), "*Progna*" (p. 316), "*Toxostroma*" and "*pyrrhonta*" (p. 320), "*Philchela*," and "*cictotherus*" (p. 321).

This compilation seems to derive entirely from Torrey's edition of the Journal. It might have been useful to examine the original manuscript notebooks. Excellent as Torrey's edition is, the Journal now probably requires a more scrupulous and definitive treatment with the variant revisions. As Philip and Kathryn Whitford pointed out in *Scientific Monthly* (1951), Torrey omitted important sections, such as the physiography of the Concord River. And Perry Miller in "Consciousness in Concord" (1958) adds that Torrey did not always use the most felicitous revisions found in Thoreau's notebooks for the 14-volume edition of the Journal. In fact, Miller calls some of Torrey's choices "a bit capricious."

All in all, Mrs. Cruickshank's book comes pretty close to being the definitive gathering of Thoreau's observations on birds. One puts it down with a sense of agreement with the Whitfords (*Ibid.*) that "modern scientists have gradually come to claim Thoreau as one of themselves."

(*The Wilson Bulletin*, 1965)

CHAPTER 3

Adventure Lit Their Star
By Kenneth Allsop. Crown Publishers, New York, New York, 1964.

Kenneth Allsop's book, a reprint of the 1939 edition, may be regarded as a piece of fiction but it has the ring of authenticity. What he writes about a pair of Little Ringed Plovers (*Charadrius dubius*) in Great Britain, their migrations, their searches for secluded spots in which to build a nest, their behavior when confronted with the destruction of their previous nesting grounds, their reactions to such innovations of man as radar may not always be found in the literature as phenomena described or demonstrable. But it is so persuasively depicted the reader feels that, if the events described did not occur exactly as the author puts them down, they must have transpired in some such fashion in order to have happened at all. No one has been an active participant among the tens of thousands of birds in spring migration winging over the English Channel (or up the Atlantic or Mississippi Flyways). But the author's depiction of the event, the sense of peril and struggle, is so objectively yet intimately told that the reader catches the urgency of the participants themselves—the insistent drive to reach land becomes a part of the reader's experience. The cold, hard odds that not all will reach safety are implied with a minimum of the anthropomorphic.

The book is divided into three parts of which the first division (except chapters six and seven) and the first five chapters of the third division deal with the plovers without much intrusion of the human actors. The rest of the book, a comparatively small portion actually, deals with the struggle of Richard Locke to recover from tuberculosis and to find the nest of the Little Ringed Plover. The bouts with illness are the accessories of the novelist but no one interested in the outdoors will fail to respond to the obstacles, the excitement, and the frustrations which beset Locke in his quest. Allsop writes with economic imagery. A heron comes in "slanting down on its great cloaks of wings, stilt-like legs jammed out for the landing" (p. 60). London gulls each evening "oared across the sky like flotillas of white skiffs" (p. 100). His observations of the plovers, their mating, nesting, and resting behavior, their reactions to other animals in the area, are set down with a keen and discriminating eye for fresh and salient metaphor and image.

In a foreword to this welcome reprint, the recipient of the John Llewellyn Rhys Memorial Prize, Allsop writes that the work is "a combination of personal observation, recorded facts and imagination. Imagination was sparingly used, for I wanted the story to be truthful and factual, wildlife seen through binoculars' lenses" (p. vii). In the main he has hewn to this line. Actually, so objective is his writing generally that when he permits human connotations to enter a description of an avian reaction, the reader feels the bump of unreality. For instance, when in a description of the female's response to the male's courtship display, the reader finds this human interpretation: "She watched him fixedly, acutely conscious of the flow of excitement that the insistent song aroused in her" and further along learns that the female is "enchanted by the glimmering stream of his flight," he—this reader at least—cannot help wishing Mr. Allsop would not do this when he can do objectivity with such precision.

The fate of Allsop's plovers in this book ends on a happier note than Fred Bodsworth's curlews in "The Last of the Curlews" (1954). As Allsop points out in his Foreword, the first nest of the Little Ringed Plover in Great Britain was discovered in 1938. But the 1956 survey indicated 70 pairs and the 1959 survey nearly a hundred pairs. Latest returns, those of 1963, total at least 175 pairs (pp. vii, viii). "Birds can easily be overlooked," he concludes (p. viii). If that is true for "the London area's two hundred gravel pits" (p. vii), may it not be even truer of certain species of North American birds in such large areas in the United States as Texas or Alaska or, in Canada, such areas as the Prairie Provinces?

(*The Wilson Bulletin,* 1966)

WRITINGS FOR THE SOUTH DAKOTA ORNITHOLOGISTS' UNION

CHAPTER 1

H.F. Chapman–A Tribute

It may have been curiosity and youthful acquisitiveness which sent the boy, Herman Chapman, into the drought-stunted timber claims and onto the prairies surrounding his father's farm to collect birds' eggs and trade the blown shells to the kids in town. But it was more than that, much more, which stopped him at his work in the farm yard sometimes, head up and listening, and backed him into the barn's shadow where, hand shielding his eyes against the bright April sun, he "scanned the high sky for the makers of the faintly-ringing notes from afar; then, finding them, stood transfixed as he watched the slow spiraling of hundreds of tiny specks shining in the very depths of the great blue bowl, listening to the trilling bugle calls of the Sandhill Cranes which drifted down to him on the warm spring air."

The man Herman Chapman remembered the boy growing up on the farm near Alexandria, South Dakota, when years later, as editor of *South Dakota Bird Notes*, he wrote those nostalgic words. And he remembered those mornings when the new farm house was being built and he, the boy, slept outdoors on the newly laid floor, roofless to the sky, waking to the smell of new lumber, the dawn red beyond the studdings and the morning loud with the twitter-chatter of the Eastern Kingbird–"White Kingbirds," he called them then. And who will say such memories–kingbird-cry and crane-bugle–laid strongly upon the boy's mind, were not guidons to the man, years later, when strong compulsion urged him to organize the resources of bird enthusiasts to study, record and preserve the avifauna of the state? And no doubt he remembered the young clerk to the Register of the Land office at Gregory, S.Dak., in 1909 went into Tripp county with a homesteader while late winter leaned toward spring, and saw from a shanty door, pink sunlight on the snow and heard meadowlarks lifting the morning with the flagolets of song. "I can hear those meadowlarks yet," he recalls, yesterday's gleam in his eyes as he makes today's plans to arouse people to the peril of their diminishing wildlife resources.

He began hunting early, he remembers, carrying a shotgun with the boys, his friends in town. On one of these forays, he stalked a flock of Mallards in a pothole and blasted away; but he raised a horse-laugh among his buddies—the Mallards were nothing more than coots—mudhens, he might have called them. It probably was a lesson for the boy, one that smarted deeply. But the man recalls, "I was a hunter all those years." And so he was, training himself to launch the clean shot that kills rather than cripples. Even then no doubt the external desire to enjoy the out-of-doors and hunting was tempered by the inner awareness of the need for conserving the species.

Statistics are vital but skeletal. Herman Chapman was born on February 9, 1888, at Alexandria, then Dakota Territory, attended country school; graduated from the local high school; studied law and business; taught school; was deputy U.S. Marshal; became first Secretary of the South Dakota Tax Commission; and U.S. District court reporter; had time and energy to engage in a dozen activities.

These are overt statistics. They say little about shattering, deep-touching events, one of which was the shining awareness that he was not to be alone in his intense appreciation of wildlife. For in Miss Lois Nichols he found a wife who encouraged the direction of his interest in South Dakota avifauna.

Birding became mixed up with precedents, torts and cases. While studying at the Law School of the University of South Dakota (from which he graduated magna cum laude), he went with Dr. William Over to gather owls' nests along the Missouri River bottoms near Vermillion. With him he dragged ropes over the waving meadow grasses to flush out Marsh Hawks and collect their nests. Perhaps it was here that he acquired the habit of recording the observations which he later made on the miles he traveled about the state.

For a time as editor of *Sunshine Magazine* he published articles on birds as a part of his new determination to bring wildlife to the attention of his South Dakota readers. He was one of four lawyers who drafted the non-political bipartisan Game Commission law now operating in the state.

In May 1948, the Chapmans attended a joint meeting of the Iowa and Nebraska Ornithologists' Unions at Sioux City, Iowa, and a wonderful mischief was begun. Previously, their bird observations while intense had been personal and uncoordinated. Now began the desire to join with others to describe the state's rich wildlife, especially its birds.

Whatever catalyst was needed to precipitate action they undoubtedly found at this joint convention. Reporting the Sioux City bird meeting for the *Sturgis Times*, H.F. Foster wrote about the Chapmans: "They became very enthusiastic over identification of South Dakota birds and are trying to form a union in their state." A meeting of the National Union in Omaha in October, which they attended, apparently was the final impetus.

Writing to Victor Webster, State College, Brookings, Chapman confessed: "We felt a similar organization like that in Iowa and Nebraska should be functioning in South Dakota." Plans for organization included questionnaires sent to biologists and zoologists at colleges and high schools, but, wrote Chapman to Webster, "I am a little discouraged by the limited number of returns." Despite these disappointments, plans went ahead. In December, a circular informed interested wildlife people that at Sioux Falls on January 15, 1949, would be held an organizational meeting dedicated to "the early creation of a South Dakota Ornithologists' Union."

On that snow-stormy day in January, one of Herman Chapman's treasured visions took shape and form. Other individuals there were who nurtured the dream and assisted in its formation, no doubt. But his was the intense, unselfish devotion which insisted on a statewide unified study and recording of avian species in the state. His determination to preserve for future students the records of South Dakota bird life constituted the cornerstone of the organization. When apathy and lack of dedication threatened the fledgling Union, his enthusiasm and faith frequently seemed to be its only shield and bolster. He was its first president; and when the elected editor of the proposed quarterly became too busy, Chapman became the Union's first editor also, a position he held for the first five years. Although the records indicate that E.R. Lamster was chosen Editor-Librarian, actually Chapman launched *South Dakota Bird Notes*. In the first three issues he set high editorial standards which challenged succeeding editors. "The die is cast," Chapman wrote to Dr. O.A. Stevens, State College, Fargo, N. Dak.; "the bridge is crossed." SDOU was on its way.

In the following ten years Chapman saw the Union take root and settle down to assured permanence. He saw the inauguration of spring annual meetings; the excitement of first field trips; the initial appearance of a state Christmas Bird Count enumerating according to species, locality and numbers; the compilation of the first "five-year" index of *Bird Notes*; the assembling of a checklist of the state's birds and the formulation of plans for the writing of a volume on the state's ornithological resources.

Time and again the haul was long and the pull hard for the growing Union. Without Chapman's unflagging, enthusiastic often stubborn determination, without his sagacious forth-right-ness, single-gauged where SDOU was concerned, the Union probably would not be the sturdy organization it is today. In truth, there may never have been a Union, at all.

Even without a Union, however, Chapman's enthusiasm for South Dakota birds would have been an inspiring stimulation to state bird study. There are scores of individuals, eager bird observers now, who will testify that the Chapmans first aroused their interest by showing them how much fun birding really is—how much of sky and season-changing hillside, of stream and prairie out-of-doors there is in birding beside the excitement of identifying a new bird or discovering unexpected facts about an old. This writer is one of them, gratefully acknowledging his debt to their persuasive encouragement.

In this light there is much significance in what Chapman wrote after that memorable Sioux City meeting. "If we, Mrs. C. and I," he wrote, "could do a little to broaden the horizons of South Dakotans as to bird study as we have had ours widened, we might justify our existence to some extent." In such justification does history enshrine its formulaters.

(*South Dakota Bird Notes*, 1961)

CHAPTER 2

President's Pages in *Bird Notes*

President's Page–Purpose of SDOU, June 1957

SDOU is more than a roster of officers and directors. It is even more than the sum total of its membership. SDOU is that portion of the thinking in South Dakota which devotes its energies as an organization to state-wide studies of birds of all species, from the largest to the smallest, from the hummingbird to the Whooping Crane. SDOU does not distinguish between "game birds" and "non-game birds," between shorebirds and singing birds. It encompasses the study of all. SDOU was founded eight years ago on the firm idea that the gathering and dissemination of information about state birds was an important contribution not only to the natural history of South Dakota but also to the conservation of natural resources of the state. The past presidents of SDOU and the editors of *Bird Notes*, in maintaining this goal, have laid well the foundation stones of the organization.

SDOU has always insisted upon the preservation of an ample stock of all avian species. It has, however, maintained general open-mindedness on the harvest of populations in generous supply and under proper legal regulation. Many members, themselves avid fishermen and hunters, feel that the aims and purposes of SDOU are not in any sense inimical to those of other outdoor and conservation groups in the state. The goal is ultimately the same—the conservation in all its forms of South Dakota's varied natural resources, which includes the preservation of all avian species.

But in the face of condition such as the drainage of marshes and potholes, the inundation of river bottom-lands, the transformation of prairie land into cultivated fields, all of which threaten drastically to reduce native cover and habitat and diminish our wildlife, it is imperative that SDOUers report all information about the range and relative abundance, or scarcity, of South Dakota species. This is particularly true of the Sparrow family. We have little reliable information about the nesting areas and populations of Baird's, Henslow's, Leconte's, Sharp-tail and Grasshopper Sparrows. Does Baird's, reported from the northwest, actually nest? Who has recently seen or found nests of Leconte's, Henslow's or Grasshopper Sparrows? Or observed Sprague's Pipit or the Chestnut-collared Longspur? Is Brewer's Sparrow, listed for northwestern portions of Nebraska, possibly moving across our southern border? To report any or all of these birds would be a noteworthy contribution to SDOU and to South Dakota ornithology.

President's Page–SDOU Membership Duties, September 1957

Discussions at the annual convention of SDOU last spring underscored clearly the imperative need for an annotated checklist of South Dakota birds. Excellent as the present list (*Bird Notes*, 1956:13–19) is it does not include migration dates or relative abundance. However, the task of gathering information for a checklist and assembling it is tremendous. It will require the cooperation not only of every member of SDOU but of everyone interested in the bird life of the state. And it will take time.

Specifically, it means the assembling of items in important published historical reports, such as Baird's; published state .and county lists, such as Visher's; literature in ornithological and other periodicals; unpublished state lists and private records as yet inaccessible to workers. Information is needed about all collections of specimens within the state and the records of all collections or individual items outside the state, such as specimens in the National Museum. Data on waterfowl and upland game birds, efficiently kept by state and federal wildlife managers, by Department of Fish, Game and Parks and by personnel of the Pittman-Robinson office should be a part of the material. Bird banding records, too, must be included.

This mass of material must be recorded on file cards or in some organized fashion so all reported information about a given species is readily available. It must be maintained somewhere and kept up to date. Such a species file system has been initiated this year in Department of Biology, Augustana College, Sioux Falls. Intended primarily for departmental use, it naturally has much wider implications.

Once completed, this file should throw much new light on such problems as range, relative abundance, nesting, and dates of arrival and departure of all resident species. It should suggest answers to questions about migratory species, especially their ranges, about which too little is known. For instance, how far westward in South Dakota does the flyway of eastern wood warblers extend? How often do Cinnamon Teal and Black Duck occur? Do sparrows of the Genus *Zonotrichia* (Harris', White-crowned and White-throated) migrate in broad or narrow lanes across the state? What are the arrival and departure dates in spring and fall of non-resident birds?

Right now, please jot down the arrival of fall birds and their departure with resident birds. Next spring, note the first appearance of all species and the last sight of non-residents. During the winter, list any northern species. By sending these reports to SDOU, you will be contributing immeasurably to the forthcoming annotated checklist.

President's Page–The AOU Check List, December 1957

The new AOU Check List containing the latest information on breeding ranges of North American birds, is required reading for every one concerned about South Dakota bird life. Our interest naturally lies mainly in nesters in the state, and here the checklist offers real surprises. Thus we find that the Prairie Warbler breeds in the southeast, the Black-and-White Warbler is a summer resident in the Black Hills, and Sandhill Cranes still nest in Sanborn county. Available published literature, at least since 1931, the date of the previous AOU Check List, scarcely supports such optimism. Without a doubt the AOU Check List Committee utilized the most up-to-date and reliable published reports from South Dakota. However, since 1930, Stephens and Youngworth's Missouri River lists (1930–1947), Youngworth's Fort Sisseton area account (1935), the revised Over and Thoms list (1946), South Dakota *Bird Notes* (1949), Stephens, Youngworth and Felton's Union county list (1954) and the new state checklist (1956) probably sum up the formal literature. Important as they are, they reflect the state's bird life only scatteredly and thus inadequately, since few of the reports are based on such essential data as migration dates, nesting records, populations and ranges based on actual investigations. Yet this material probably represented the total amount of information available to the AOU Committee. On this it apparently based its findings, and, under the circumstances, rightly so. Otherwise it would have been remiss in its considerations. The blame, if blame there is for the misinformation, rests not on the Committee but on the lack of information available about the birds of the state. The responsibility comes back to South Dakota. It highlights dramatically Vice-president Whitney's unwearied and often-heard plea for an annotated state checklist, a list that tells us what birds are present, where and when; what birds are migrants, when they arrive and depart, and where. Had such a list been in the Committee's hands, the errors in the new AOU volume could scarcely have occurred.

I am glad to report that work is well underway on the collection of material for such an annotated checklist. In the Department of Biology, Augustana College, Dr. S.G. Froiland, Dr. Willard Rosine and I are pushing this project, originally departmental, which will record permanently in a Species File System all information available on South Dakota birds. After some consultation, Dr. Whitney, Chairman of the checklist Committee, and I believe that this project merits the consideration and sponsorship of SDOU and suggest that, in "Whitney's words, "all efforts, of the checklist committee be directed toward the completion of the species file as the next step toward the preparation of the checklist revision." In this proposal I feel sure that every member of SDOU will heartily concur.

President's Page–Accuracy in Birding Observations, March 1958

In this, my last "page," I should like to congratulate the membership of SDOU on its increasing awareness of the need for the greatest possible care in making observations and in recording them. Along with our enthusiasm for bird watching and reporting must go a virile respect for accuracy, not only in what we see but also in how we record what we do see. Time, locality, weather conditions, behavior, habitat in which the species is observed…these should be as carefully listed as the exact identification of the bird itself.

Of all activities, the accurate and unquestionable identification of the species, especially during periods of migration, cannot be over-emphasized. In addition to noting exactly what one sees, one must check his observation with those of others, such as Peterson or Pough; and SDOU Check List in Bird Notes ought not to be neglected. It is wiser perhaps to withhold a vague or uncertain recognition than to rush into print with a doubtful report. Where uncommon varieties, winter visitants and migrants are concerned, the utmost vigilance must be exercised. For instance, apparently rather dull-colored wintering Tree Sparrows without a breast-spot are often reported without reservation as Chipping Sparrows.

True, sometimes the observer is sure of his identification even when the species is uncommon or far from its usual haunts or out of season. Such a report can be valuable indeed, especially if the observer describes exactly what he saw, suggests that this is what the bird seems to have been and permits the reader or researcher to draw his own conclusion. If the reporter, whether individual or group, has a reputation for accuracy in reporting, such a record will go far toward gaining acceptance in future studies. On the other hand, if the reporter, group or individual, is suspected of lack of objectivity or accuracy, or if the report is written in positive or absolute terms, the report will probably fail to gain recognition and the journal publishing it may suffer in consequence.

Personally, before I report an uncommon species, I feel I must have the corroboration of at least one other individual. I'd like to suggest that any group or organization which regularly reports data to national organizations or publishes data in its own journal appoint a committee of at least three competent observers to assist the compiler or editor in deciding the status of rarities, uncommon species, unusual migrants and such matters as wintering birds out of their ranges.

I am grateful for the cooperation and consideration of many people in and out of SDOU for keeping me and the record straight.

President's Page–The Check List of South Dakota Birds, June 1964

To be chosen president a second time by SDOU is indeed a high honor and a privilege, one I shall labor to deserve.

Actually an executive functions ably and vitally only when the membership of an organization supporting him is vital, energetic, imaginative, forward-looking and dedicated to its cause. And over the wide earth is there a better, a more desperately necessary cause to support than that of disappearing wild life—wild life which is threatened not only in South Dakota, our immediate concern, but the world over, a global problem of which South Dakota too is inevitably a part?

Nationally or locally your executive functions at his best only when he reflects the wishes and desires of the membership—your needs and wants, your disturbances over the encroachments of inimical forces; your demands for changes in existing conditions, if changes need to be made; your constant vigilance over the activities and accomplishments of the people you put into office; your duty to write letters and send wires of protest when your elected officials thwart the desires of the electorate; your insistence that elected and delegated officials represent *you*, the people state-wide, nationwide, who elected them, and not the power interests of the few, the lobbyists of the encroachers, whether they be local, state or federal, whose motives may be suspected as selfish rather than accepted as altruistic.

If such awareness and alertness is necessary in regard to other aspects of our national life, as it most certainly is, it is desperately, tragically necessary in regard to the plight of wildlife, the perils which threaten nearly all species in nearly all sections of the globe. Destruction of habitat, no room to live—that is the crux over which officialdom stumbles, whether it be habitat for upland, water or "other" birds in South Dakota or flamingoes in South Africa. But our dismay over the plight of flamingoes in Southern Africa or the disappearance of the White Stork in Europe must not blind us to the danger which darkly shadows the existence of all species of birds in our own country, in our state.

Only when the alert, dedicated membership of an organization is aware of these dire problems, supports its executive, and urges necessary action can that executive function at his best in terms of leadership and of lasting achievement.

I urge all SDOUers—talk about wildlife and its dire predicament, discuss its problems, write to the officials. Above all, express your feelings. Talk, or one day all of us may listen yearningly for the spring call of the Canada Goose—and listen in vain for a wild cry that never again will echo over the prairies to gladden our hearts and lift our eyes. That lonely desperate hour is nearer than we know.

President's Page–Farm Island, September 1964

From the questions I heard asked and the remarks that were made, I feel that almost every member of SDOU who attended the May meeting at Pierre was profoundly impressed by what happened to Farm Island. Any person at all interested in the future of our wildlife habitat and our natural scenic and historical resources must be deeply concerned at the disturbance he finds on this Missouri River island, this wooded island where the early explorers up the river probably stopped as early as the 1790s and which we know Lewis and Clark observed on their expedition September 24, 1804. The words I heard over and over were: I didn't know they were going to do this. Why did it happen?

The road the SDOUers followed from north to south on the island traversed almost tragic contrasts in ecological potentials. The northern portion, the smaller, was all green lushness and cool leafiness with birdsong weaving a tapestry of sound. Time and again I heard SDOUers say, "I've never heard so much singing in my life." Among other birds there were Yellowthroat, Chat, Redstart, Ovenbird, Bell's and Red-eyed Vireo, Robin, Wild Turkey, a Black-and-White Warbler, a Bullock's Oriole, two Turkey Vultures, three Great Horned Owls, a Wood Thrush, White-tailed Deer and squirrels were seen. Varied habitats are there: the edges of shoreline and meadow-like places, open areas under trees, bushy areas, the understories and the high trees dominated by cottonwood. Floral communities flourish here which are seldom if ever encountered elsewhere in prairie country. From one end to the other this is the Farm Island SDOUers remember from past field trips. And again the questions: Can the economic advantages said to be derived from the destruction of these historical and ecological resources be justified? Were the consequences of these changes presented clearly to the people of South Dakota and the neighboring states?

Abruptly leaf shade and birdsong ended. We stepped into sun glare. Before us lay the rest of the island, the larger part, denuded all its length, skinned of grass, bulldozed into sandy emptiness, pitted with bomb craters where trees had been ripped from the soil. A few Rough-winged Swallows moved toward the mainland; a Marsh Hawk winged along the shore, then flew back where open areas were willow-lined; a Killdeer called from a sandy flat. The dust-whipped wind rattled in our ears. Back of us was cool shade, moisture and birdsong. Ahead of us was the area, now cleared almost completely of its trees and bushes, birds and mammals, soon to be flooded by the impounded waters of the Big Bend Reservoir.

What of the vegetation-covered area back of us? Soon, we understood, bush and tree, bird song and deer's snort, turkey gobble and owl hoot too would vanish under the bulldozer's blade. Fallow as if salt-strewn, it would wait for the flooding waters. Or if left un-flooded, it now would offer few habitats suitable for bird or mammal. Again the queries: did our elected representatives objectively, disinterestedly consider whether the advantages of impoundments overweighed the advantages of having these floral and faunal resources last? Were the best interests of all people in the state considered? How were the final decisions made—by democratic processes or perhaps by bureaucratic, demagogic manipulation? And South Dakotans themselves—did they care enough to ask for clarification, to demand objective presentation of facts, to inquire about possible consequences? Back of these questions apparently lay an ominous query: must we have the case of Farm Island on every stream in South Dakota?

President's Page–Pesticide and Pheasants, December 1964

Where are the Wild Pigeons? wrote L.H. Smith from Strathway, Ontario, to the editor of *Forest and Stream.* "Twenty or twenty-five years ago, they were in countless thousands over the Eastern states and Canada, where they are known no more…. Is it possible that the beautiful Passenger Pigeon is becoming extinct? Let us hear from Michigan, Wisconsin, Arkansas, the Indian Territory and from anywhere this bird may still be staying."

The year was 1888; the date May 31. It might have been 1964, and the question contemporary: "Where are the pheasants in South Dakota which numbered millions in forties and fifties?"

In 1941 appeared a booklet with the enthusiastic title: "Fifty Million Pheasants." It was sponsored and published by the South Dakota Department of Game and Fish, Pierre. "In 1945," wrote Allen in *Our Wildlife Legacy,* "state biologists estimated the pre-hunting population (in South Dakota) at between 30 and 40 million" (1954:31). In 1946 Nelson reported to the Midwest Wildlife Conference, "The 1945 population was probably half that of 1944." Conservatively then, 60 million pheasants in 1944.

Now in 1964 the Department of Game and Fish estimates the population at about five million; hunters and bird students can indeed paraphrase Mr. Smith's question: "Where have the pheasants gone?" They might add, "The Mallards and Pintails, not many years ago two of our most abundant prairie ducks—where have they gone?" Where indeed? Fifty or more million pheasants in 1941–1945; five million in 1964. Has anyone compared the duck populations for these two periods?

All sorts of reasons have been offered for what seems a strange population crash, not one of which bears much scrutiny. One avenue of investigation apparently has been avoided, except in casual reference: the effects of pesticides. Why? Secretary of the Interior Udell said publicly at Miami in December 1963: "The unnerving fact is that pesticide residues have been found in virtually every type of warm-blooded animal across our land…. Research has told us that incredibly small quantities of some chemicals can destroy shrimp grounds or reduce the reproductive capacity of oysters."

Evidence in the pesticide-bird relationship is piling up, both in the U.S. and in Europe, particularly in discoveries of significant amounts of pesticide residues in eggs and flesh of birds. Even the carefully worded conclusion of the Progress Report for 1963 of the Bureau of Sport Fisheries and Wildlife has an ominous undertone: "Certainly, we have no evidence that the levels (of DDT) we find in eggs and birds are innocuous."

Since pesticide residues are involved in the reduction of "reproductive capacity" of some animals, why have not the proper authorities investigated this aspect of the pheasant reduction in South Dakota? Flesh and eggs of pheasants are surely not hard to procure for analysis for residues of chlorinated hydrocarbons, if such exist. Why hasn't this been done? Or if it has, why haven't the results been made available? Or is it possible that powerful commercial interests would rather have the truth about the disappearances of our wildlife left under the rug? Not only hunters, ornithologists and wildlife students but the public at large has a right to know.

President's Page–Pesticide Menace, March 1965

In this, my last President's Page, I end where I began, first in believing that the membership is the voice of SDOU and the president the agent of its expression; second, that the most urgent problem for SDOU bird observers as well as anyone interested in preserving the state's wildlife and the beauty of its out-of-doors, is the relationship between the effect of wide-spread use of chemicals and the well-being of living things, whether plant, or animal or human being. From any point of view beyond the immediate, there seems to be less danger of our being blown into oblivion then there is in our eating ourselves into extinction.

I urge SDOUers and anyone interested to read Dr. Timothy Myres' monumental compilation, *The Widespread Pollution of Soil, Water and Living Things by Toxic Materials Used in Insect Control Programs*. A work in progress in Canada, produced at the University of Alberta, it at once suggests the question, "Why hasn't a work like this been done in the United States, a country that is proud of its scientific progress?" Can it be that dedicated scientists in this field are persuaded to enter other activities, if not intellectually muzzled by interests which might find such studies economically embarrassing?

I urge you to read the articles in the British periodicals *British Birds* and *Bird Study*, by Ratcliffe, Moore and Lockie on chlorinated hydrocarbon residues in the eggs and tissues of Peregrine Falcon, Golden Eagle and other avian forms. And I urge you to read U.S. Fish and Wildlife Service Circular 199, *Pesticide–Wildlife Studies*, 1963. Reading the American and the British accounts, one is impressed by the caution, the reticence of the American investigators. One senses a caution which suggests fear of speaking out. Fear of what? Of whom? Is it possible that there is a deliberate attempt to keep vital information from the public? The public has a right to know. Elected and appointed officials are the servants, not the masters, of the people. And SDOUers must acquaint themselves with the whole body of the facts, and demand that they be made known.

Cancel all other engagements and come to the Black Hills to meet with the Wilson Ornithological Society folks in June. Not again for a long time will you see so many great figures in ornithology gathered in our state: Roger Tory Peterson, Olin Sewall Pettingill, Jr., P.B. Hofslund and a host of other star bird observers. See them in action and meet them in person.

CHAPTER 3

Guest Editorial – "SDOU...Tomorrow"

This year, 1959, is a good time in the history of SDOU to look backward—pridefully—and forward—optimistically. The first decade was one of beginnings, reporting steady development; of realizing an objective attitude toward the subject. The foundation was well laid yesterday; it is firm today. What of tomorrow?

It is high time we made ourselves known, associated more widely with neighboring societies and accepted a wider responsibility among the state organizations devoted to the study of our plant and animal life, particularly birds. I suggest that we see what benefits may be derived from closer ties with the South Dakota Academy of Science, especially the Junior Academy with its host of coming young scientists; with the various biological and zoological societies at the colleges and universities in the state; above all with the biological and zoological classes in our academic institutions, for when the enlarging varicose veins and arthritic joints of the present membership no longer permit field trips and attendance at SDOU conventions, it is from our young people that strength and interest must come.

I suggest an awareness of the possibilities in such organizations as the State Game and Fish Department and the officials of the U.S. Fish and Wildlife Service, the game technicians and managers at our state and federal wildlife refuges, with their huge backlog of data on waterfowl, upland game birds and frequently many other species; the field technicians and the local game wardens; the department of forestry, its technicians and field men. Many a significant observation may have been lost or buried in the files because no one encouraged its publication.

Scientific expeditions into South Dakota dating from at least 1843 (though many were earlier) have collected and removed from the state a significant amount of avian material in the form of bird skins, eggs and nests as well as information about species, locations, behavior and habitat. Most of these data were placed in museums, public and private, both here and abroad. As much as possible the data contained in these materials, especially as to species, localities, habitat and behavior, ought to be procured, assembled and placed on file for bird study in the state.

I suggest we examine the potentialities in such organizations as the National Wildlife Federation, with its state chapter, the South Dakota Wildlife Federation; the state and local Izaak Walton Leagues, and other kindred groups.

Other projects have been frequently discussed. Last but not least, I suggest a bigger SDOU. Let every member consider himself or herself a director. Talk to neighbors and friends about SDOU. Spread the news. Show that SDOU is vitally concerned about waterfowl and upland game programs. Take folks on trips; let them see the wonder of a green-winged teal or a scarlet tanager through a binocular. Encourage them into membership. The next decade rings with promise.

CHAPTER 4

Forty-four Articles

Audubon Warblers Breeding in the Black Hills (*Dendroica*)

On July 5, 1958, my brothers John and Julius, their families and I watched adult Audubon Warblers feeding two young at the campsite in a branch of Castle Canyon south of Deerfield. We heard the "cheeping" sounds of the young long before we discovered the fledglings in a spruce tree. The young were generally very graying in color with streakings of darker gray on breasts, sides and heads. Fledglings followed adults, hopping from limb to limb, begging with fluttering wings and insistent "cheep" calls. These calls became excited run-together sounds when the adults approached with food. The male was still in full song, although some authorities write that the song in male warblers diminishes as the feeding duties increase. Here, however, the male sang repeatedly. I observed the same phenomenon in the Canada Warbler, which sings in full tone far beyond the post-nesting period. (June 1958)

Bewick's Wren at Sioux Falls

A wren has been a visitor at our feeding tray in Sioux Falls this winter. Our earliest sight was on December 3, 1950, our latest February 26, 1951. My record lists 12 appearances at the feeding tray and seven in the hedges, vines and tree-tops. Three others were "ear" records. On February 20 it sang in a nearby pine for at least twenty minutes. We have noticed three song patterns: something like "clee-eeya, clee-eeya, clee-eeya" (uttered deliberately); "tell-reecher, tell-reecher, tell-rot" (accent on the second syllable, with the "rot" on a downward note); and "till-ya, till-ya, till-ya" (uttered rapidly). These phrases usually came in a series of three, although occasionally only two were sounded. Of the appearances recorded, 14 were accompanied with song, usually before feeding and usually from a treetop between 8 and 10 a.m. This specimen ate hugely of peanut butter, spaghetti strings, suet and scraps of meat (did it consider these worms?) but did not feed on grain or sunflower seeds. Identification of the specimen as a Bewick's Wren was almost complete. The feeding tray is at a window. We watched at a distance of about four feet. The white checks on the edge and at the end of the tail, the white mark over the eye, the very brown upper parts, the grayish breast, the lighter grayish throat, the slightly down curved bill–all were clearly observable. The shortest visit was a couple of seconds, the longest about 1.5 minutes (November 30, 1951). Occasionally, as it sat on the rim of the tray, it bobbed very much like a Water Ouzel. Over does not list Bewick's Wren as a South Dakota species but Roberts cites a number of appearances in southern Minnesota, although evidence of nesting there remains inconclusive. Mr. and Mrs. Henry Hahn, Sr., corroborate my observations. (March, 1951)

Black-Crowned Night Heron Comes to Town (*Nycticorax nycticorax*)

On April 15, 1958, I was walking through McKennan Park, Sioux Falls, past spruce trees which border one edge of the park, when I saw a large bird among the branches of a spruce. As I watched, it lifted its wings as if to fly but settled back again. I identified it as a Black-crowned Night Heron. This was a somewhat early date for the species, April 18 being the average date for Minnehaha County. (Larson, *Wilson Bull.*, 1925:24)

Except for a certain wariness, this bird seemed to pay little attention to cars and trucks passing in the street or to pedestrians on the walk. It looked weary with drooping head and wings. After several minutes it arose, flapping slowly, lifting its head and letting its legs hang as if ready to perch in the next tree. But perhaps the cars and the pedestrians were encouraging. It continued its flight though it seemed barely able to clear the tree tops as it passed out of sight.

This is my earliest record of the species in nine years of observing spring migrants. (March 1958)

The Black-Throated Blue Warbler in South Dakota (*Dendroica caerulescens*)

The Black-throated Blue Warbler (*Dendroica caerulescens*) was not reported for South Dakota by such early observers as Audubon, Baird, Hayden, Coues, or McChesney (1843–1879) nor by Agersborg (1885) for Clay County and southeastern South Dakota. Visher, apparently the first to re port this species for the state, lists it as "A fairly common migrant" in both Sanborn County (1898–1915) and Clay County (1909–1915), especially during 1910 to 1913, although neither specific dates nor localities are included. However, Stephens, Anderson, Youngworth, Felton, and others, reporting for the southeastern portion of the state generally and for Union County particularly during the period from 1910 to 1955, do not list it. Moreover, Over and Thoms fail to mention it in *Birds of South Dakota* (1921). Since this bird is conspicuously marked and unmistakable, there seems to be no question here of the validity or authenticity of the records. Perhaps a kind of "hiatus," similar to the phenomenon observed along the Gulf Coast, was operative here. Or perhaps a narrow but concentrated band of migration moved through Sanborn and Clay Counties during 1910 to 1913. In 1916 Larson called this species a "rare transient" in Minnehaha County, listing one observation, May 1909. In the autumn of 1931, Brenckle banded two individuals at Northville, Spink County. The revised Over and Thoms 1946 includes a banding record at Aberdeen, without dates. In September 1955, I identified two individuals at Sioux Falls, Minnehaha County. Perhaps the scarcity of observers rather than the rarity of this species accounts for the lack of data on this strikingly marked bird—throat and sides black; breast and belly white; upper parts blue-black; a white spot on the wings. It should be watched for and unfailingly reported. (*Proceedings*, 1958)

Blue-Winged Warbler (*Vermivora pinus*)

On May 15, 1954, I was in Woodlawn Cemetery observing the warbler wave, then nearing its peak. I noted two male Wilson's and many Yellow Warblers. Among them was a yellowish bird which, unlike the quick-moving Wilson's and Yellow Warblers, seemed to move leisurely from leaf-cluster to leaf-cluster. A black line through the eye caught my attention. It reminded me of the heavier, more mask-like line through the Cedar Waxwing's eye. Then I saw the whitish wing-bars suggesting those of the White-winged Junco. The wings themselves were darkish suggesting blue. The breast and under parts were bright yellow. The rump had a greenish-yellow tinge. I had a five-minute view of the bird and couldn't come to any other conclusion than that it was a Blue-winged Warbler. It fed slowly and seemed to examine twigs and leaves more thoroughly than the Wilson's or the Yellow Warblers. Its movements seemed to have the deliberateness of the vireos. Over says the Blue-winged Warbler is a rare migrant in the state. But Dr. Roberts found it in southern Minnesota and Dr. J.F. Brenckle banded one at Mellette, S. Dak., in 1931. (June 1954)

Bohemian Waxwings in Sioux Falls (*Bombycilla garrulous*)

On February 16, 1955, about 15 Bohemian Waxwings dropped into the Duchess and Hopi apple trees here at the Hahn residence. They made short work of the apples left shrivelled on the twigs. Eight of the birds fed in a Hopi tree near a window, often fluttering against the pane so close I could see plainly the reddish-brown under tail coverts and the whitish blotches on the wings. The blotches on these individuals were not in a geometric pattern as in the Peterson plate, but appeared irregular in shape and size. The under tail covers seemed more reddish than brown, although this may have been an individual difference. The song was much buzzier than the Cedar's; it seemed to be lower in pitch and coarser, and lacked the Cedar's throbbing double-noted quality.

On February 19, Sven Gordon Froiland, Chairman, Biology Department, Augustana College, saw what may have been the same flock near the Veteran's Hospital. A snow storm was blowing and the birds were feeding out of the wind in low-growing cedars.

On February 27, I saw 13 perched in American Elms at Woodlawn Cemetery, possibly the same flock again. (March 1955)

Broad-Winged Hawks in Eastern South Dakota
By H.F. Chapman and Herbert Krause

Of this one, Over and Thoms (1946) say: "This bird is only fairly common in South Dakota. Its range is farther east. Size 15 to 18 inches, the female larger. Upper parts dark brown; feathers on nape white at base, under parts irregularly barred with white and buff; under tail with two white bands and white tip. The young are usually much darker both above and below. The belly is not barred, but is streaked with blackish brown and tawny. On September 25, 1915, a young specimen was sent to the University Museum, and, upon examination, the crop and stomach showed the following contents: 13 large grasshoppers, two field mice, and one frog."

My first recognition of this species came a few years ago. I was driving with Roger Tory Peterson from Sioux Falls to Sioux City and we stopped at Union County Park, south of Beresford, for a quick "look-see." We were only well within the timber when RTP exclaimed, "There's a Broad-winged Hawk!" and, as it flew, "See the broad white bands in the tail!" Since that time we have seen individuals at various points throughout eastern South Dakota, and always in a tree.

During the last few days of April 1953, there were several of these scarcely crow-sized Buteos in Woodlawn Cemetery at Sioux Falls, where there are many large trees. Herbert Krause relates his observations there on April 28, 1953, in this informal fashion: "Yesterday evening I went out to Woodlawn. By the time I got there it must have been seven or so. Anyway, I got a good look at the Broad-winged Hawks. The light was excellent and the white bars in the tail could be clearly seen. Also, I was rather surprised to find how lacking in shyness they were. When I roused them in one part of the cemetery, they up and settled in another part. I laid this to the fact that they had seen the cemetery custodian so much they no longer minded an individual walking about the grounds. But Roberts says they are the most sluggish of the hawks, and seem to be the least afraid; that they can easily be approached, which has led to some ghastly hawk massacres in the past. I found that I could actually walk up to and under a pine tree in which one was perched before it finally took off. The result was that several times I saw the wide tail bands without the aid of glasses. There were three there last evening. I was surprised at the calmness with which other birds tolerated them. The Robins went on singing, the Mourning Doves cooing and a Chipping Sparrow twittering. I saw one Crow 'take a pass' at a hawk. Otherwise crows, hawks and smaller birds seem to be getting along more neighborly than many human communities." (September 1953)

Common Grackles on College Campus (*Quiscalus quiscula*)

For the second year in succession, Common Crackles nested on the Augustana College campus. Sutton (1928. *Birds of Pennsylvania*, 103) speaks of their preference for "parks, cemeteries and college campuses." One pair came perilously close to education, bringing off a brood at the very doorstep of the Administration Building.

I first noticed the nesting pairs on May 3 when I saw a grackle carrying a stick into a red cedar, one of six trees, three on a side, bordering the walk in front of the Ad Building. I found three nests in three of the trees. Two were completed, one nearly so. One completed nest was close to the entrance of the building where each day at the end of class hours hundreds of students and faculty members rush out in the chatter of hurry to the next class session. Yet here this pair built a nest and brooded eggs. They fed young through the pin-feather stages to fledgling growth and brought at least three young out of the cedar to the bushes on the lawn and then up and away, despite the commotion, academic and non-academic, of the pedants and professors, Phi Beta Kappas and unabashed "D's," entering and departing the building and passing the nest tree. Left alone, birds are not nearly as intolerant of the human species as the human species chooses to believe.

It was in this same cedar that a pair nested last year, although I have little information about their fortunes except that I heard young in the nest and saw adults bring food.

On May 23, I first heard the young giving their softly-uttered hard cries in the nest nearest the building. The incubation period is about 14 days (1958. Gross in Bent, *Life Histories of North American Blackbirds,* 401). This means that I probably noticed the birds about the time the last of the eggs was being laid. Four to five eggs seemed to be the average-sized clutch (Bent. *Ibid*).

After the 23rd the sounds of the growing birds increased in volume. I heard the young in the second and third cedar trees on the 25th and the 27th. The adults paid little attention to the usual passing fair. But if anyone stopped to peer up at the nest or brushed the tree, at once their loud scoldings descended on the intruder. Soon the rest of the colony joined in with noisy chatter and some downward swoopings.

On June 13, I found three young, fully feathered, on the lawn, their bodies slaty gray, their breasts darkly streaked. They flew readily if awkwardly, bumbling into the branches rather than alighting skillfully. Later I found two more on the ground about a block from the campus. Presumably these were from the cedar tree colony.

On June 27th, I heard harsh cheeping sounds from the tree nearest the Ad Building and saw an adult grackle alight there, carrying food. I found only one nest in this tree, apparently the same one that had housed the first brood, and can only conclude that this pair was solving the housing problem by re-using the old homestead. Second broodings apparently do occur (Bent, *Ibid.*) but whether this was a second brood by the original couple or a brood by another pair, I have no way of knowing. But another brood was certainly clamoring for food. (December 1960)

Defensive Flocking

On October 15, 1951, a Buteo was observed flying low over a cornfield a few miles southwest of Sioux Falls. Above, behind, but fairly close to the hawk there followed a compact flock of perhaps 100 small dark birds. The hawk paid no attention to them, apparently, and when it alighted the flock flew away. While this behavior, sometimes called "defensive flocking," is occasionally described in published reports, this was our first opportunity to observe it. We identified the hawk as an immature Red-tail, and believe the others were Redwings. (December 1951)

Gyrfalcon

On the rainy forenoon of April 23, 1955, Scout Leader George Goebel, Scouts Bob Hahn, Bob Rishois, Jeff Thisson and Jerry Vorpahl, and I were driving through a wooded spot on the south shore of Wall lake, Minnehaha County, when we saw a hawk-shaped bird perched on a dry limb. We stopped and all members of the party had a fairly good look at it.

Through 9x50 binocular, I saw a bird larger than a crow, of uniform dark slate color–salt and pepper gray with more pepper than salt giving the effect of dark gray sprinkled on light gray. The bird faced us. There were not distinctive marks. The head appeared small and of a shade a little lighter than the body. It seemed powerfully built, but not chunky like a Buteo, instead rather slender like an Accipiter.

When it flushed we saw pointed wings and a tightly folded, slightly pointed tail that appeared longer than a Butero's. No white showed although there was a suggestion of lightness near the rump. Small barrings were on the back and especially on the forepart of the wings. The wing beats were rapid but since it very soon perched on a tree near the water edge we did not see it sail. We had another good look at it before it again took wing and disappeared among the trees.

We believe we saw a Gyrfalcon in the gray phase. Over and Thoms (1946, *Birds of South Dakota*) call it "a rare winter visitor." However, the Gyrfalcon has occurred in the vicinity at least four times in recent years (1949, 1950. Chapman, Mallory, Donohoe, *South Dakota Bird Notes*, II:14. 1952. Dahlgren, *Bird Notes* IV:27). (September 1955)

Hermit Thrushes at Sioux Falls (*Catharus guttatus*)

On the morning of April 29, 1953, a chilly rainy day, five Hermit Thrushes appeared in the Henry Hahn backyard and on the adjacent lawns. I stay with the Hahns and so had a good chance to observe the birds. They remained all day and part of the next, feeding in the garden and hopping along the walks so close to the house that one could see clearly the rufous tail and the generally reddish-brown diffusion over the back. One hardly needed to see the habit of cocking the tail and then dropping it slowly to identify this species. With them was a solitary Gray-cheeked Thrush, looking almost dried-earth colored beside the Hermits. It too hopped close enough for identification without glasses. Perhaps the rainy chilly weather had something to do with the lack of shyness. Mrs. Hahn corroborates my observations. Over in *Birds of South Dakota* says the Hermit Thrush is "seen only as a straggler in migration." In 1948 I listed only two; likewise in 1951 and 52. In 1950 I observed nine single individuals between April 4 and 30. The 1953 observation seems a bit unusual—five birds in one habitat, remaining for a day and a half. (September 1953)

Hudsonian Godwits in Minnehaha County (*Limosa haemastica*)

Ordinarily in South Dakota, we see the Hudsonian Godwit sparingly, usually with Marbled Godwits, or at best in small flocks of eight or ten. But on May 19, 1957, Mr. and Mrs. Herman Chapman, Alfred Peterson and I had the pleasure of coming upon a flock of 40 of these comparatively scarce birds. We found them in a spring-flooded grassy pasture no more than two good stone's throw from the main street of Humboldt, Minnehaha county. They were feeding on a small grassy island, their dark reddish breasts and dark wings indicating clearly their identity. But it took us a moment to realize that we were fortunate enough to see before us two score of these birds, all in one flock. When, apparently alarmed at something, they took wing and made several circles, we had a good look at the deep black tail and the conspicuous band of white on the upper tail coverts, which flashed in and out of view as the birds turned and wheeled as one in their flight. As they flew, they uttered softly-voiced calls which sounded like "ga-witt, ga-wit." Finally, as they came in for a landing, they seemed to drift easily along the shore edge, their tail bars shining white and, after their feet touched the ground, their wings held aloft momentarily before they folded them unhurriedly back. The flight and the landing were thrilling both to the eye and the ear. In the shallow water where they fed, the birds used their longish bills to probe with quick thrusting movements. It was certainly good to know that this bird, once thought to be following the luckless Eskimo Curlew to utter extinction, is now apparently returning and increasing in some numbers. (September 1957)

Juncos!! (*Junco hyemalis*)

What I am sure was an Oregon Junco came to the feeding tray on a Sunday morning, February 12, 1950. We (Mr. and Mrs. Henry Hahn, Sr., and I) had a good view of this bird feeding in the tray, on the snow-covered ground, and at the suet cage. We saw the black hood, the rich reddish-brown back and the lighter brownish sides, distinctly–marks which suggest the adult of this species rather than an immature Slate-colored, or what Peterson calls a "mongrel between *oreganos* and the Slate-colored." What was apparently the same bird appeared again on the 13th, the 18th, the 23rd, and the 25th. (June 1950)

Kinglets in Sioux Falls (*Regulidae*)

Both Ruby-crowned and Golden-crowned kinglets were unusually numerous in Sioux Falls during September and October 1959.

I recorded my first individuals on September 17 when in an excellent concentration of passerines which invaded Woodlawn Cemetery, I counted 35 Ruby-crowns—the largest number for one day in my records.

However, I feel certain that there were many more in this wave of an estimated four to five hundred birds.

Several males flashed the red crest, perhaps in warning to members of their own species or to neighbors of other species, for the wave was fairly thickly concentrated, warblers, kinglets, flycatchers, vireos, often close together as they unhurriedly streamed through the trees, sometimes in the lower branches, infrequently in the tiptops, most often in the middle branches.

The kinglets seemed to be the liveliest members of the wave, wings flipping restlessly, greenish yellow flashes darting here and there, fluttering at a twig-end momentarily, then tumbling head-long several branches downward to another twig-end.

September 17 seems to be an early date for Sioux Falls. Larson (1925. *Wilson Bull.*, 37:75) reports September 24 as his earliest fall arrival date for this area, although Roberts (1936. Birds of Minnesota, 2:145) records September 16 as an average date for southeastern Minnesota.

On September 19, I counted ten Ruby-crowns in the same cemetery—possibly leftovers from the previous wave. On the 21st I found six but on 27th only three. On October 9, following a cold front, I noted six; on the 13th, five.

On October 22, there was another small "wave" with an incursion of Golden-crowned Kinglets. That day I counted five Ruby-crowns. My last record is October 30 when I saw a single individual.

I saw my first Golden-crowned Kinglet – a female – on October 13, shortly after the wide-spread storms of October 5 through 12.

This is earlier than Larson's October 30 date (1925. *Ibid.*) but late when compared with Roberts' September 22 average (1936. *Ibid.* 2:142).

On October 15, I counted seven, five in one American elm of which number three were females dashing with fluttering wings at each other, apparently in the excitement of a territorial squabble.

On October 22, I struck an avian jackpot—a small "wave" of Golden and Ruby-crowns. I saw four Ruby-crowns, two singing short scraps of song in American elm trees in Woodlawn Cemetery. Suddenly they were pursued by five Golden-crowns.

The Ruby-crowns flashed their red crests warningly, small scarlet spots in the dull elm, but took to their wings before the oncoming Golden-crowns.

I took one look into the neighboring trees and was certain why the Rubys fled. The branches were scattered with fluttering bits of greenish-white.

I managed to count 19 Golden-crowns in the shifting numbers but am sure there were more. I noticed that all the kinglets seemed to be responding to some kind of stimulus—perhaps invasion of feeding territory. I saw nothing more alarming.

Nevertheless, Ruby-crowns chased each other, then Golden-crowns pursued Rubys, Rubys retaliated by darting at Goldens, Goldens pestered each other, until ribbons of birds curved among the branches. Sometimes a Chickadee was caught in the excitement and flew near, only to be dive-bombed by the midget kinglets. Often when a Chickadee took off, several Golden-crowns would take wing after it, following closely but curving aside quickly when the Chickadee stopped to perch.

Though the Chickadee seemed to ignore all this twittering pigmy chit-chat, it twitched aside suddenly when a Golden-crown zoomed past its head. Between skirmishes, the kinglets fed, apparently dividing their attention equally between conifers (pine and spruce) and deciduous trees (American elm, maple and ash).

Once a Downy Woodpecker undulated by and was promptly beset by three Golden-crowns which zipped about its flight for a moment, however much they kept what seemed to be precautionary distances from the zeppelin-like Picidae.

Then, as if their over-energized spirits needed further release, they tore at each other. For a moment there was a tangle of revolving greenish blurs.

After some five minutes of activity among these trees, the kinglets suddenly drifted away. I left them. Later I counted seven more Golden-crowns in two other parts of the cemetery and one Ruby-crown—a total of 26 Goldens—more than I'd ever seen before.

All in all, it was a kinglet day in the cemetery. On the 25th I saw only two Golden-crowns. Since then I have seen them sporadically by one's and two's—seldom more.

Over a ten-year period I do not have a single winter in which they have not been present in small numbers. In contrast Larson states (1925. *Ibid.*, 75) that in 1906–1916, they were "seen occasionally in winter" and that they "wintered 1907–1908."

My records agree with Stephens-Youngworth-Felton's conclusion (1955. *Birds of Union County* 24) "a few hardy (Golden-crowned) kinglets remain all winter." (March 1960)

Migrating Shorebirds

On April 26, 1950, we (Gerry Lofgren, Miss Doris Sampson, Augustana College seniors, and I) came on four Marbled Godwits and three Western Willets in a flooded field just off Highway 16, about 12 miles west of Sioux Falls. They were feeding among other shore birds. When flushed the black-and-white wing pattern of the Willets and the rich cinnamon-brown pattern of the Godwits were clearly seen. On April 30 we (Mr. and Mrs. Chapman and I) saw six Marbled Godwits feeding in a wet grassy place in the Big Sioux Valley near Brandon, S.

Dak. With them was a Hudsonian Godwit, the dark reddish breast and the suggestion of black and white in the tail differentiating it from the Godwits. Immediately south of Wall Lake we counted 14 more Marbled Godwits, all feeding in the short grass of a dry open space, wholly unafraid. Earlier we saw three other Willets northwest of Sioux Falls; and west of Wall Lake six Dowitchers needling the shallow water of a slough edge. On May 6, we (Herman Chapman and I) saw 9 migration-tired Willets, drowsing on the edge of a roadside slough, looking as droopy as chickens with the pip. This slough is about five miles southwest of Sioux Falls. Nearby we saw another Dowitcher, and a few miles west of Wall Lake we encountered two more. (June 1950)

Migrating Warblers, Sioux Falls, South Dakota

The warbler wave passing through Sioux Falls in May seemed thinner and more erratic this year (1951) than last. Three species, the Prothonotary, the Cerulean and the Cape May were among the migrants I observed.

I had a five-minute view of the Prothonotary on May 18th. The bright yellow-orange head and breast, the area beyond the nape shading to brownish-yellow, and the bluish-light-grayish back easily identified it. Unhurriedly it passed from elm to elm, sometimes hanging poised under a half-grown leaf, wings fluttering like a Hummingbird's so that it looked like a suspended shimmer of yellow touched at the edges with the shadow of bluish-gray. From illustrations in various guides, I expected a thick-necked stoutish bird. I found it slenderer than the Yellow Warbler and much more buoyant; this individual was, at least.

The Cerulean which I saw on the 18th was resting and preening at mid-level of an elm and so afforded a good view of the airy, sky-blue back (a blue of amazing lightness yet intense), the blackish streaks on the back, the two wing bars, the white throat and breast divided by a distinct blackish line. Perhaps it is the combination of white and blue which gives this individual a freshly-washed, clean-cut appearance.

On the 15th I saw a Cape May, a female, at tree-top level of an elm. The observation was short; no more than a minute of foraging among the half-sized leaves, but the characteristic yellow mark on the neck, the faint but distinct dark streaks on the breast and the yellowish tinge in the rump, all indicated this species. It passed from limb to limb very much in the manner of the Tennessee.

I noticed a Black-throated Green Warbler on May 8th, one day earlier this year than last, and another on May 15th. Both were feeding and singing in the lower branches of a maple. I learned the song pattern, put it down in my notes and found just recently that it is a fair duplicate of the recorded performance of this species in volume two of the excellent *Bird Songs of America*.

On May 15th I recorded a Bay-breasted and on the 16th and 17th Chestnut-sided Warblers.

Other Warblers observed and recorded between May 10 and 24 were: Orange-crowned, Myrtle, Black and White, Tennessee, Blackburnian, Blackpoll, Wilson, Magnolia and Yellow. (September 1951)

Mockingbird in Minnehaha Cuonty (*Mimus polyglottos*)

Since J.S. Findley's summary of the appearances of the Mockingbird in South Dakota was printed in 1949 (*South Dakota Bird Notes* 1:43–44), there have been only occasional published notes on the species in the state. According to Stephens, Youngworth and Felton, it has not been found in Union County (1955. *Birds of Union County*). Jansen saw a single bird near Morristown, Corson County, in May 1950 (*South Dakota Bird Notes* 3:12); Weyler wrote somewhat ambiguously about. What seems to have been several individuals at Belle Fourche during 1950–1952 (*Ibid.*, 4:54, 57); and in July 1955, Nash noted three birds at Platte which he describes and about which he writes: "I am sure they were Mockingbirds as nothing else in my book resembles them" (*Ibid.*, 7:48). These three direct references represent widely scattered points in the state, near the North Dakota border, near the Wyoming line and near the Missouri River in the south-central part. This note relates to Minnehaha County near the Minnesota line.

On May 8, 1956, Sven G. Froiland and Willard Rosine of the Biology Department, Augustana College, two biology students, Joe Fenstermacher and Bob Vatne, and I were riding along a country road about 1 1/2 miles west of Palisades Park, northeast of Sioux Falls, when we came to a farm beside a small stream. Near the road grew a hedge of bushes and beyond it lay a pasture. In the hedge was perched a bird which flew and alighted in a box elder sapling. In that flight we saw the white patches on the wings, the white in the tail, the generally grayish appearance and the Brown Thrasher-size of the bird and identified it as a Mockingbird. Froiland and Rosine were familiar with the species in Colorado. I had seen it in Nebraska and Oklahoma. The five of us had an uninterrupted view for perhaps three minutes while the bird flew to the ground, apparently searching for food, and then into a nearby bush before it disappeared. We observed it through 7x35 binoculars at a distance of not more than 50 feet.

There are scattered records for Minnehaha County but none since 1949. The four observations made since 1950 in four widely separated areas of the state can hardly be regarded as anything but sporadic. The Mockingbird still seems to be a rare visitant and a rarer resident. (September 1956)

Night Herons in Park Trees (*Nycticorax nycticorax*)

Although Black-crowned Night Herons do nest in trees, we usually think of this chunky, rather long-legged bird as. a wader, standing motionless on a log half out of water or beside rushes or tall aquatic vegetation in shallow water. But on October 2, 1957, I found eight of this species perched in black walnut trees in Sioux Falls. I was walking through McKennan Park, looking for warblers, when I heard a most un-warbler-like "woc" and there among the topmost feathery branches, I saw a night heron, its wings half-lifted for flight. It settled back, however, and became motionless among the yellowing leaves. Not far away I saw a second heron and in the nearby trees, others, until in three walnut trees, I counted eight night herons. All were immatures, their striped plumage clear in the sun. Perhaps uneasy at my approach, they suddenly left, all eight mounting above the park. However, instead of leaving, they circled for perhaps a minute, then came gliding down, braking sharply above the walnut trees and settling rather awkwardly into the top branches. From their behavior, their rather droopy and tired-looking posture, the way their heads were drawn down, I guessed that apparently they were resting after completing a leg of their migration southward. This was at 8 a.m. At 11 a.m. I returned and found them still there. While I watched, they took wing. For nearly ten minutes they circled the park area, often gliding down as if to perch again, but, perhaps alarmed by the traffic in the streets surrounding the park, they always ascended again. Finally they headed south and disappeared. I don't know how often night herons perch in trees in city parks but I suspect only to rest during migration. (September 1957)

Palm Warblers at Sioux Falls (*Dendroica palmarum*)

Palm Warblers are generally uncommon during migration at Sioux Falls. Usually I am fortunate to record one or two each spring, although in my records for ten years, there are notable gaps. In fall I have only two or three observations.

Therefore it was a real event when I counted seven of this species on May 4. Considering their infrequent appearance, this was almost a "wave."

My first observation was on May 3 when I found two in McKennan Park, feeding in maple and hackberry trees, just then beginning to bloom. They often swooped to the ground or out from the tree, apparently hawing [sic] insects. The flight seemed to be much like a Chipping Sparrow's, even to the deep undulation in coming in for a landing, as the Chippy sometimes does. The song was a weak unsteadily wavering trill; not a rapid straight trill on one note like the Chipping Sparrow's song but trills on several notes, at first going up a bit and then down, with considerable variableness. The alarm note was a sharp slightly metallic "Chee-ip," which reminded me strongly of the alarm call of the Canada Warbler. I should add that in spite of its rather weak sound the song still has its element of interest.

On May 4 I saw two in McKennan, probably the same two I'd previously seen, and three in Woodlawn Cemetery. Here one was chasing the other as if two males were engaging in a battle over food territories. On May 5 the "wave" arrived with five birds feeding on the ground and in the grass at the bases of trees in McKennan and two in Woodlawn Cemetery. There was song at both places. On the 7th I saw only one in McKennan. The last record was that of the 12th when I found one singing steadily for ten minutes in Woodlawn.

Perhaps this warbler with its striking tail-bobbing habit migrates more often than we realize through eastern South Dakota, although my own records bear out the observations of Stephens, Youngworth and Felton. (1955. "Birds of Union County," *Nebraska Ornith. Union* Occ. Papers 1:28) who consider it "a rather uncommon migrant most years." (June 1960)

Peregrine Falcon Near Wall Lake (*Falco peregrinus*)
By Herbert Krause and Willard Rosine

On March 15, 1955, we were driving near Wall Lake, Minnehaha County, when we saw a crow-size falcon-shaped bird flying low over a field away from the road. The brownish back, slender body, dark bands on the tail and the pointed wings, suggested one of the Falconidae although we did not get a good view of the head or breast. The bird had been feeding on a recently killed hen pheasant. Tentatively, we identified the bird as a Peregrine Falcon or Duck Hawk.

On April 22, 1955, we came upon a hawk perched on a fence post in the same general area. We had a look at it in fairly good light. The light-colored body with whitish throat and upper breast which became washed with a bluish tinge farther down, dark, "mustaches," slate-blue head which appeared almost glossy, barred sides and under parts—all suggested the Peregrine Falcon. When it flew we saw the brownish back and the narrow compressed tail with faint dark bands which we had seen on the individual observed previously. This one, too, flew low over the field with fairly rapid wing-beats followed by a sail. We agreed that it was a Peregrine and probably the same one we had seen in March. Over and Thoms (*Birds of South Dakota*) say this species is "Frequently seen in the state, though it is not common." *South Dakota Bird Notes* lists several occurrences in recent years, as do the Christmas Bird Counts in *Audubon Field Notes*, one of which (3:126) records it for Minnehaha County in 1949. (September 1955)

Pine Grosbeak in Minnehaha County

On February 3, 1957, it was my good fortune to discover a Pine Grosbeak in Woodlawn Cemetery, Sioux Falls. This may be a first record for Minnehaha County. A female was feeding in an ash tree. The pearly gray breast, the generally grayish body, the dull yellow on head and rump (the immature males that I saw in northern Minnesota had reddish), the white wingbars, the rather heavy, darkish bill, the large (about Robin size), the longish emarginate tail–all these field marks indicated the species.

I called Mr. and Mrs. Melvin Wheeler to corroborate the points. We had good views of the bird as it leaned to pluck seeds or stretched up to pull down fruit.

On February 4, Dr. Willard Rosine, Biology Department, Augustana College, and a group of students saw two females in the same locality. Wesley Halbritter photographed them. On February 7, 10, and 17, I saw what presumably were the same individuals.

On three occasions I heard what seemed to be alarm calls, musical "taa-chee" and "ta-tee-tee-tay" notes, on the approach of an intruder–myself. Twice I found the birds high in the trees. Instead of flying out and away as I came near, they fluttered down among the branches until they were about half way down. Then they flashed out of the ash and into nearby spruces, where they disappeared among the downswept branches near the foot of the tree. The third time they were in the lower part of the ash and again flew into the conifers, alighting near the base. It may not be significant but it struck me as unusual that these birds sought the shelter of the thickest portion of the ash tree before they left its protection and then flew in the lowest branches of the conifer.

Available published literature does not reveal previous records of the Pine Grosbeak in Minnehaha County, nor perhaps in the eastern part of the State. McChesney does not list it at Ft. Sisseton (1879), though Over and Thoms' *Birds of South Dakota* (1921) refers to McChesney's report of a Pine Grosbeak in that area in 1898. I have been unable to verify this nor have I been able to find a paper written by McChesney as late as 1898 about the Ft. Sisseton area. Over and Thoms mention Mr. A.T. Colem who saw Pine Grosbeaks in Union County "in earlier years." Stephens, Youngworth and Felton (1955) do not list it for that County. It is not included in Visher's report (1912) on south-central South Dakota though Ketelle notes a male and female in 1952 at Huron (*Bird Notes*, V(1):15). Larson's *Birds of Sioux Falls and Vicinity* (1925), covering 1906–1916, does not include it for Minnehaha County. Dr. N.R. Whitney, Jr., Rapid City, writes me that a female Pine Grosbeak was killed in Watertown in December 1955, and presumably is in the Harry Behrens collection. (March 1957)

Pine Siskin at Sioux Falls (*Carduelis pinus*)

On May 9, 1953, I had the good fortune to find the young of the Pine Siskin. I heard the call of what I thought was the note of the adult Pine Siskin. But this was a hoarse, repetitiously-uttered "chay-ip" instead of a sharp "clee-ip," as Peterson terms the adult note. I found the young bird perched on the lower bare branches of a spruce, near the trunk. It continued its plaintive "chay-ip" even after I discovered it. It was more than half grown, was completely feathered with primaries developed enough to fly the distance from branch to branch. Mr. Willard Rosine, instructor of biology at Augustana College, substantiated my findings. Later we saw the adult Pine Siskin fly into a neighboring spruce and, hearing more calls, discovered a second young Pine Siskin. This one was better able to fly. We did not find the nest. Shortly after, we photographed the first young bird in habitat and out. Unfortunately the heavy rainstorm of the night of May 9 killed what I feel sure was this individual. I found it the next day under the low-swept branches of the same spruce in which it was first discovered. It is now in "deep freeze" in the biology lab at Augustana. I found no trace of the second individual.

Behrens reports nesting and rearing of young in 1941 at Rapid City, as evidence of breeding in the Black Hills area. In eastern South Dakota Larrabee reports a nest at Yankton in 1926 and Youngworth a pair nesting in the same city in 1936. No young, however, seem to be mentioned. I found one nest in Sioux Falls in April 1951, and next year in the same month discovered six nests, two with eggs. Herman Chapman and I photographed these nests and eggs. However, there was no opportunity to observe whether the hatching was successful and whether young birds were raised. The nesting individuals found this year (1953) represent what may be the first evidence that this species breeds in eastern South Dakota. Whether it breeds regularly or occasionally, only further study can determine. (September 1953)

Pine Siskin Nesting in Eastern South Dakota

The literature on the status of the Pine Siskin (*Spinus pinus*) as a breeding bird in South Dakota is meager indeed. Over and Thomas (1946. "Birds of South Dakota." Revised, *University of South Dakota Mus. Nat. Hist. Stud.* No. 1:161) list it as "a winter resident." Roberts (1936. *Birds of Minnesota.* vol. 2, p. 365) reports it as a common migrant in Minnesota but has only one record of a nest–from the northern part of the state. There are numerous sight records for South Dakota but only two published items which relate to breeding. Larrabee (1937. *Wilson Bull.*, 49:116) reported a nest in Yankton County, and Youngworth (1936. *Wilson Bull.*, 48:311) noted a pair nesting in Yankton.

Although I have checked every available item in Stephens' "An Annotated Bibliography of South Dakota Ornithology" (1945. Privately printed, Sioux City, Iowa), I have found no published records of the hatching of young of the Pine Siskin in South Dakota. Letters from Drs. W.J. Breckenridge and O.S. Pettingill, investigators in the state, who report sight and collection records but no breeding records, seem to bear this out.

The following observation therefore is probably the first record of the Pine Siskin hatching young in the state certainly in the eastern part of the state. I have been collecting data on this species at Sioux Falls, Minnehaha County, since 1948, and have sight records for all months of the year, excepting June, July and August.

Although I was certain in 1949 that this species nested in the area, it was not until May 19, 1951, that I discovered the first nest in Sioux Falls. Mr. and Mrs. Herman F. Chapman corroborated my observation. Circumstances did not permit further investigation to determine whether eggs were laid or young hatched. In April 1952, I found six nests in Woodlawn Cemetery and in McKennan Park, Sioux Falls. Two contained eggs. One nest held three eggs, the other two. Chapman and I photographed these nests and eggs. Regrettably, circumstances again made it impossible to determine whether the eggs hatched or young were reared.

On May 9, 1953, I was in Woodlawn Cemetery, listening to the call of an adult Pine Siskin, when I heard a hoarse, huskily-articulated *chay-ip*. A moment later I saw an adult Pine Siskin fly from a nearby blue spruce (*Picea pungens*), in which I found a young Pine Siskin perched on the lower bare branches, near the trunk. The young siskin continued its plaintive *chay-ip* even after I pushed the branches aside for a closer look. It was more than half grown and was completely feathered except on the sides under the wings. The bird could fly from branch to branch but not on extended flights. The yellow patch on the wing was just beginning to show, the coloring being heaviest along the shafts of the feathers. The yellow in the tail was faint but unmistakable. The breast was streaked much like the adult but tufts of down indicated its immaturity. Willard Rosine of the Biology Department, Augustana College, substantiated my observations. We photographed the bird and liberated it.

Later we saw an adult Pine Siskin fly into a neighboring spruce. Hearing more calls, we discovered a second young siskin, better able to fly. It escaped into the upper branches before we could examine or photograph it. We were unable to find a nest or nests from which the two might have come.

Unfortunately a heavy rainstorm in the night of May 9 killed what I feel sure was the individual we photographed. I found it next morning under the spruce in which I had discovered it. The specimen is now in the biology laboratory at Augustana College. I found no trace of the second individual.

Further study and observation may reveal how frequently the Pine Siskin breeds in eastern South Dakota and perhaps also something about its adaptation to an environment far removed from its usual breeding grounds in more boreal situations. (September 1954)

Prairie Falcon in Minnehaha County (*Falco mexicanus*)

Published records of the Prairie Falcon in eastern South Dakota are not very plentiful.

McChesney does not include it in his "Notes on the Birds of Fort Sisseton, Dakota Territory" (1879:71–103) which seems to cover at least a part of the northeastern area; nor does Youngworth list it in his study of the same area sixty years later (1935. "The Birds of Fort Sisseton, South Dakota," *Wilson Bull.*, 47:209–235).

Agersborg's "Birds of Southeastern Dakota" (1930. *Proc. South Dakota Acad. Sci.* 13:27) refers to it as "rare during spring migration." Visher (1915. "A List of Birds of Clay County, Southeastern South Dakota," (*Wilson Bull.*, 27(91):328) describes it as "occasional except in midsummer."

Stephens (1918. "Notes on the Birds of South Dakota with a Preliminary List for Union County," *Proc. Iowa Acad. Sci.*, 25:89) did not record it although more recently Youngworth considered it "a casual winter visitor" in Union

County (1955. Stephens, Youngworth and Felton, "The Birds of Union County, South Dakota," *Occ. Papers, Neb. Orn. Union,* 1:8).

Neither editions of Over and Thoms' *Birds of South Dakota* (1921; rev, 1946) mentions its occurrence in the east.

A recent sight record by Alfred Peterson (1953. *South Dakota Bird Notes,* V:42) notes that near Brandt, S. Dak, a Prairie Falcon harried a flock of Baird's Sandpipers without however apparently actually preying on them.

Published accounts for Minnehaha County seem to consist of Larson's single May 5, 1912, record (1925. "Birds of Sioux Falls, South Dakota," *Wilson Bull.,* 37:29).

Other occurrences there undoubtedly were but these apparently have not been published or brought to the attention of editors of *Bird Notes.*

Therefore, perhaps the following sight record may be of some interest. On January 28, 1960, I saw a hawk perched in a tree in Woodlawn Cemetery.

It appeared to be larger than crow size. With a 7x35 binocular I saw that its overall coloration was very palish with a brownish tinge shading off into grayish.

Its feet were yellow but the legs seemed short; that is, it did not seem to "stand up high" as a Cooper's or a Sharpshinned Hawk does when it perches on a limb. Instead this bird seemed more "crouched down."

What I could see of the tail seemed to have several pale bands on it. The light breast was striped.

As I approached the bird took off. The pointed wings (which eliminated both the Cooper's and the Sharp-shinned Hawks) and the dark patch where the wing and the body came together (the axillars region) confirmed my feeling that this was not an accipiter but a falcon.

Its size (crow-size or better) ruled out the smaller Pigeon and Sparrow Hawks (which are a little more than Robin-sized).

The pale lightish coloration seemed to exclude the similar-sized Duck Hawk or Peregrine Falcon which is bluish-black above, quite light below and has very prominent dark "moustaches" running down from the eye over the cheek. But the black axillars seemed to be the "clincher."

The scarcity of records probably reflects the continuing prejudice against the raptores as a group of birds.

However, an impressive array of evidence, gathered by institutional and governmental biologists alike, indicate that early reports of predations by hawks and owls probably have been highly exaggerated or based on erroneous or insufficient data, a fact which, in these days of what is sometimes called "a new enlightened look at wildlife relationships," ought to persuade even the most "die-hard" among the conservationists and sportsmen to take another look at the charge made against the raptores. (December 1959)

Preliminary Notes on the Pine Siskin in South Dakota (*Carduelis pinus*)

The literature on the status of the Pine Siskin as a breeding bird in South Dakota is meager indeed. Until comparatively recently this species was not listed for the state. Audubon on the Missouri in 1843 does not mention it, nor was it taken on Lieut. Warren's expedition into the Dakotas (1856–1857). Neither was it seen by Baird on the 1856 survey to the Pacific. Coues (1874) did not find it in South Dakota. McChesney (1879) does not include it in the Fort Sisseton listing. Agersborg (1885), whose list is the first important published record for the state by a resident, did not observe it in the southeastern area.

The earliest published mention of the Pine Siskin in South Dakota seems to be in Visher's (1908) "Birds of Western South Dakota," published in the *Auk* (1909). Visher observed "two large flocks in the pines in the Hills." Early in September 1910, he saw "a small flock" in Harding county in the extreme northwestern corner of the state. In midsummer, 1911, he noted "a large flock in the pines at Edgemont in Fall River County in southwestern South Dakota." And in 1913 he published his Sanborn county list, based on fifteen years of observation in south-central South Dakota. He writes that the Pine Siskin is a "tolerably common migrant, and occasionally common in winter," but gives no exact dates.

There have been occasional sight records since then, notably in the Black Hills region and in Clay, Union and Yankton counties in the extreme southeastern portion of the state. The Eastern border seems to have only one sight record, that of Mallory (1914) in Lincoln county. It is interesting to notice that Larson's "Birds of Sioux Falls and Vicinity" (1925), based on a ten-year study (1906–1916) in Minnehaha county, does not list a sight record of this species, although Minnehaha county lies just north of Lincoln. Over and Thoms (1946. "Birds of South Dakota," revised) report it as "a winter resident."

No mention of identification is made in any of these reports. Published records of nesting seem to be confined to Youngworth (1936) who noted a pair meeting in Yankton and Larrabee (1937) who reported a nest in Yankton county.

Although I have checked the available items in Stephens' "An Annotated Bibliography of South Dakota Ornithology" (1945), I have found no published records of the hatching and rearing to juvenile state of the young of the Pine Siskin in South Dakota. Letters from Dr. Walter J. Breckenridge of the Minnesota Museum of Natural History, University of Minnesota, and Dr. Olin S. Pettingill, Carleton College, Northfield, Minn., investigators in the state seem to bear this out. They report sight and collection but no breeding records.

The following observation therefore has to do with the nesting of the Pine Siskin on the eastern edge of South Dakota as far north as Minnehaha county. It is a first occurrence for that county and probably is a first record of juvenile Pine Siskins in the state.

I have been collecting data on this species at Sioux Falls in Minnehaha county since 1948, and have sight records for this six year period for-the months of the year excepting June, July and August. The areas of investigation were limited to McKennan Park and Woodlawn Cemetery, both of which abound in conifers, mostly blue spruce and western yellow pine, introduced as ornamental trees. I am a graveyard watcher. The dead do not disturb me though the living sometimes do.

Early in April 1948, I saw and identified flocks of small, dark, streaked, gold-finch-sized birds in Woodlawn Cemetery as the Pine Siskin. I observed the birds carefully. The curious wheeling flight and the loud songs, including the characteristically buzzy *shree*, of certain individuals, uttered on the wing, made me wonder whether this was a courtship display and whether this species nested here. During April and May I saw and noted by actual counts some 25 individuals. The numbers decreased later in April. Few were seen during early May. I am quite certain now that this is the nesting period when females are incubating and males apparently become less vocal. This may account for the scarcity of records for this period.

During 1949 I noted individuals in January, February and March, their numbers seeming to increase in early April. Again I saw the intriguing behavior of certain individuals, the wide circling flights and heard the loud incessant songs. I concluded also that this was a mating display, although I found no nests.

Not until 1951 did I discover the first nest. It was in Woodlawn on the extreme tip of a branch of a western yellow pine. It was well hidden, being partially under a cluster of cones and covered by long needles. Mr. and Mrs. Herman Chapman corroborated my observation. Circumstances however did not permit further investigation to determine whether eggs were or had been laid or young hatched. For that year, 1951, I have 63 sight records. The smallest number of individuals noted was one on January 14, the largest an estimated 40 on October 6.

In April 1952, I found six nests in Woodlawn Cemetery and two in McKennan Park. All nests were in conifers, five of them in blue spruce and three of them in yellow pines. Six were about 20 to 25 feet from the ground. Two were only about 10 or 12 feet up. Three nests were examined. One held three eggs, another two, and the third one. And in one of them was the egg of the Cowbird. Nests in pines were at the extreme ends of branches among the cones. Nests in spruce were built farther in where overhanging sprays of needles concealed them. These three nests and eggs were photographed. Regrettably circumstances again made it impossible to determine whether eggs hatched or young were raised.

Not until May 9, 1953, did I discover the young of the Pine Siskin. I was in Woodlawn again, listening to the call of the adult Pine Siskin, which is a loud, fairly sharply defined "clee-ip." I saw an adult Pine Siskin fly from a nearby blue spruce. After a little search, I found a young Pine Siskin perched on the lower bare branches of the tree, near the trunk. It continued its plaintive "chap-ip" even after I pushed the branches aside. It was more than half grown, was completely feathered except for areas on the side under the wings. The primaries were developed enough for the individual to fly from branch to branch but not for extended flight. The yellow patch in the wing was just beginning to show, the color being heaviest along the ribs of the feathers. The yellow in the tail was faint but unmistakable. The breast was streaked much like the adult, although in this individual downy tufts still indicated its immaturity. Mr. Willard Rosine, Biology Department, Augustana College, sub-stantiated my observation. We photographed the individual and finally left it in the spruce where I had found it.

Later we saw an adult siskin fly into a neighboring spruce. Hearing more calls, we investigated and found a second young of the species. This one, better able to fly, escaped into the upper branches before we could examine or photograph it. Although we searched carefully, we were unable to find a nest or nests from which the two might have come. Unfortunately a heavy rainstorm in the night of May 9 killed what I feel sure was the individual we photographed. I found it next morning under the downswept branches of the same spruce in which I had discovered it. The specimen is now among the collections of the Biology Department, Augustana College. I found no trace of the second individual. Further study and observation may reveal how frequently the Pine Siskin nests in South Dakota and also something about its adaptation to an environment far removed from what is regarded as its breeding grounds in more northern latitudes. (September 1954)

A Query on the Song of the Slate-colored Junco (*Junco hyemalis*)

I have been wondering how often the spring song of the slate-colored junco is heard in South Dakota. Perhaps my query reveals my ignorance but in defense I admit whole-heartedly that I am the lowest among the beginners in the study of bird-lore.

The usual voice of the junco as recorded by the Laboratory of Ornithology at Cornell University is "a loose quavering trill suggestive of Chipping Sparrow's song but slower and more musical," to quote Roger Tory Peterson. Thoreau calls this song a "thick, shuffling twitter…a jingle with also a shorter and drier crackling chip (or) chill chill"—the "chew, chew, chew" of John Burroughs. Chester Reed describes it as "a sweet simple trill which has a beautiful effect when given by a whole flock in unison." I have been stopped in my tracks at hearing a plum-thicket full of juncos trilling up an April morning; the effect was truly melodious. I have yet to hear them "in unison," which means, I take it, the singing of the same series of tones by all the voice parts at the same time. To hear that in a flock of juncos might be an ornithological discovery of major importance.

This "simple trill' is the one the birdwatcher is accustomed to hear. But in spring there is another song, one described by Roberts as "a much more pretentious effort very different from the simple Chippy-like trill commonly heard on the nesting grounds." I first noticed this song on April 6, 1948, in a park in Sioux Falls. It was not repeated and I was left wondering whether this was indeed different from the ordinary, or a mis-hearing on my part. In my notes for that day, I wrote, "A courting or migrational ditty," with a question mark.

On April 6 of this year, I heard it again, this time in the bushes along a road near Sioux Falls. The song was a series of runs and trills, interspersed with quavering notes and clear but short whistle-like phrases, here and there punctuated with single sharp notes which sounded like "sup, sup" and which Peterson calls a "smack" or "click." The whole strongly resembled a Lark Sparrow's performance muted or muffled, except for the "smacks" or "sups," which are absent in that bird's song. In fact, at first I thought the sounds came from an early Lark Sparrow–one that was "ventril-oquizing" his voice, as thrushes sometimes do. Later that morning I came on this migrational or courting lay, if such it be, in different places in a park. Each time it was uttered from the ground or on the lowest branches of a bush.

Next day through my window, slightly raised, I caught the song again, this time from a hedge. I lifted the sash and brought the singer up with my glasses. Two males and a female were on the ground among the winter's snow-pressed leaves. I heard distinctly the Lark Sparrow-like singing of one of the males. It resembled what Peterson says of the Lark Sparrow's voice, "buzzing and churring passages interspersed here and there." In addition to buzzes and churrs, to my ear at least, there were quavering notes and clear ones mingled with the characteristic 'sups' or 'clicks." And again the sound, while cleanly enunciated, was muffled, as if coming from a distance further than the twenty feet between my window and the hedge.

Perhaps this spring ditty is commonly heard, here and elsewhere, and like the junco's white tail-feathers, my ignorance is showing. Except for Robert's not too explicit description, however, I have not in my limited reading found a good account of the song. (June 1949)

Red Crossbills Breeding in Black Hills (*Loxia curvirostra*)

On July 4 and 5, 1958, my brothers, Julius and John, their families and I, camped in a branch of Castle Canyon south of Deerfield in the Black Hills. On July 5 we saw adult Red Crossbills feeding young. A group of about 12 adults were busily uttering their rather sharp metallic "Kip, kip" calls and bringing in food to about 25 fledglings. All were gathered in the upper branches of ponderosa (western yellow) pine. We watched the activities of this group for 20 minutes, trying accurately to distinguish the young, which were grayish with short darker gray streaks on breasts and sides, from the adult females which were olive-gray without streaks, and the males, which still showed an undertone of reddish color or revealed patches of dull red. However, at this season, in both male and female, the plumage was so well worn that the female was very dull grayish-olive, almost dried-grass colored and the male showed a fantastic mixture of red, brick-red and faded olive, the bright colors appearing in patches. Both male and female adults were involved in feeding the young. They fed material they apparently found and gathered at the end of branches where cones grew—probably plant-lice or the larvae of weevils sometimes observed in pine seeds. I had the impression that there was a great variation in the amount of "crossing" of the mandibles of the young. Some seemed to show little if any deflection, others had a very definite "slanting" of the mandibles, as if the inception of crossing had begun but wasn't as yet very well developed. (June 1958)

Red-Breasted Mergansers at Fort Randall (*Mergus serrator*)

On November 22–23, 1972, Kelly Krause and I went to the spill waters below the Fort Randall Dam. It was about four o'clock in the afternoon of November 22, and the cloudy weather made the light grayish. But we saw six birds on the water near shore. I knew by outline that they were mergansers and said so to Kelly: "I guess they are Common Mergansers." But when we got nearer and I put my glasses on them, I saw the reddish head, the crest, the gray body, the white area on the wing, and I knew we had Red-breasted Mergansers, birds I have seen only twice in my life. Then we examined the spillway waters, and there were hundreds of Red-breasted Mergansers. We went to the other shore where the light was better, and there were easily over 2,000 birds in the concentration. Along with them, for the sake of comparison perhaps, were about 350 Common Mergansers, usually staying in small groups apart from the Red-breasted. Their white bodies and blacker wings stood out in the group. When the flock of Red-breasted Mergansers finally spooked, there seemed to be an acre of white foamy water under their paddling feet as they ran along the surface in takeoff. It was a memorable sight indeed. (March 1973)

Red-Breasted Nuthatches Store Seeds (*Sitta canadensis*)

On September 12, 1954, while in Woodlawn Cemetery searching for returning warblers, I came upon five Red-breasted Nuthatches "yahnk-yahnk-yahnk-ing" their nasal calls at the top of a blue spruce where the thickly clustered cones were tan colored and ripe. They were busy pecking at the cones, and the scales flew widely. Soon some of the birds darted to the trunks of nearby American Elms where they remained for about twenty seconds, then flew back to the top of the spruce. I watched this activity for five minutes. They were carrying the spruce seeds to the elm trunks to hide them in crevices or under projecting bark. After a little prying, I found several of the brown seeds. As far as I could tell the activity went on for the two hours I was in the vicinity.

I've seen Black-capped Chickadees in winter stuff suet from a feeding table into empty seed pods of lilacs, and I caught one hiding a sunflower seed in the curl of a hanging leaf. I've seen them return for the food they had put away, but I've also found the lilac pods in spring with bits of suet still in them. I wondered whether the Nuthatches would find all the seeds they were hiding or would, like squirrels, apparently forget the hiding places before snowfall; and whether this activity meant they were preparing to remain for the winter. Perhaps it is only their custom to store spruce seeds wherever they find ripe seeds, regardless of the possibility that weather or other conditions might entice them to other areas before they retrieve their winter caches. (December 1954)

Red-Shafted Flicker in Southeast South Dakota (*Colaptes auratus*)

On October 3, 1854, I saw a male Red-shafted Flicker in Woodlawn Cemetery. It was feeding on the ground with five Yellow-shafted. The gray and brownish nape without the characteristic red crescent of the Yellow-shafted was noticeable and when it raised its head I saw the red "whiskers" of the male Red-shafted, and the red on the wing edge. When the birds were flushed, the redding flash of the Red-shafter's wing linings was in vivid contrast with the yellow of the other birds. When perched on a tree trunk, the red on the wing edge and the tail was very noticeable. Later this individual perched on a telephone wire. Mr. and Mrs. Herman Chapman and Mr. and Mrs. Scott Findley verified my observations.

Over and Thoms list the Red-shafted Flicker as a western form. Larson lists it over a period of ten years (1906–1916) as seen occasionally in summer in the Sioux Falls area. Based on reports from at least 1928, Stephens and Youngworth conclude (1947) that this species is "an uncommon winter visitor in this region." In six years of bird observation (1948–1954) in Minnehaha and adjacent counties as well as in trips along the eastern tiers of counties to the North Dakota border, I have never previously encountered this species, although I have checked hundreds of individuals. On the basis of a somewhat longer period the Findleys and Chapmans report same experience. (December 1954)

Roosting Brown Creepers (*Certhia americana*)

The nocturnal habits of many northern birds, especially those which winter in South Dakota and in those states adjacent to the Canadian Provinces, continue to intrigue investigators.

Where does the Golden-crowned Kinglet find shelter in storms as severe as that which in South Dakota saw the old year out and the new 1960 year in? Or what protection do the Snow Bunting and the Lapland Longspur, ground birds both, have against the freezing rain and sleet of a freakish storm like that which plagued South Dakota during December 26 through 29, 1959?

Or what sort of roosting place do the Common Redpoll and the Pine Siskin find when temperatures creak down to minus 20 and 30 degrees? And does the Brown Creeper actually creep under a loose piece of bark in winter to secure lodging for the night, as a woodsman once solemnly told me?

There are probably few answers to these queries, apparently because snow and deep cold compound the difficulties which confront the investigator in any study of the night-time behavior of animals. Therefore, the following observations may perhaps be of interest.

I am indebted to Dr. Dilwyn Rogers, Dept. of Biology, Augustana College, Sioux Falls, for the following information which is submitted with his approval: The weather during December—at least until Christmas time—was unusually mild with no particularly cold days and some melting periods.

On December 15, Dr. Rogers noted bird droppings in a corner of a porch on his house. However, he saw no birds and supposed that House Sparrows were the visitors. On December 16, he came out on the porch after dark. Light from the open door illuminated the area enough so that he caught sight of what seemed to be birds roosting just under the ceiling in an upper corner. He brought out a flashlight and found two Brown Creepers clinging to the rough surface of the wall. They were huddled close together as if for warmth.

At first they remained undisturbed by the flashlight, moving their heads a little as though watching this intrusion. But when Dr. Rogers turned to call his wife, both of the birds flew away. Later that evening, however, they were back in the same place, once more perched side by side.

The roosting place seemed well chosen. It was high under the ceiling in a right angle formed by a wall and a projecting frieze-like panel under the eaves of the porch. The porch itself faced south.

Here neither wind nor wet could reach the birds easily. Although they came back after the first disturbance, the birds did not return the following evening. Nor did Dr. Rogers see them again. (March 1960)

Sanderling at Grass Lake (*Calidris alba*)

That the Sanderling seems to be a fairly regular migrant in the northeastern part of the state can be seen from the entries in Alfred Peterson's excellent summaries of shorebirds in 1953–1954 in the Waubay area. (*South Dakota Bird Notes*, 5:56–67,62–62,71; 7:5–6,10). However, it apparently is a much rarer migrant in the more southerly portions of the state, if one is to judge by the scarcity of pulished accounts. This season, however, it was observed in Minnehaha County. On September 16, Willard Rosine, Biology Department, Augustana College, and I saw three individuals on the mud flats of Grass Lake where the prolonged drought has so lowered this body of water that a "beach" of mud extends at least 100 feet from the usual shoreline. The Sanderlings were feeding in soft mud, running along the ripply edge of the water, for the lake is now so shallow that even a strong northwest wind hardly stirred up what one could call waves. The plumage of the birds was in sharp contrast to the dark shore. The pure white of the underparts, the white stripe in the wings and the mottled white of the upper parts were distinctively clear, set off against the yellowish water.

On September 23, Mr. and Mrs. Herman Chapman and I found a single individual among Killdeer and a gathering of other Charadriiforms on the same shore. It was as distinctively whitish as the previous three had been.

Since Larson does not include the species in his "Birds of Sioux Falls, South Dakota and Vicinity" (1925. *Wilson Bull.*, 37:18–38) and since no previous record seems to be available, these observations may be a first record for the Sanderling in Minnehaha County. (September 1956)

Sandhill Cranes at Sioux Falls (*Grus Canadensis*)

According to Adrian Larson's "Birds of Sioux Falls, South Dakota" (1925. *Wilson Bull.*, 37:24–25), Sandhill Cranes were still "common transients" both in spring and fall migration in the Sioux Falls area as late as 1916.

Larson gives September 27 as the earliest date of fall arrival and October 22 as the latest date of fall departure. He tells of "large flocks during migration, circling and wheeling about high in the air; their loud bugle-like cries heard for miles on still days."

The region under his study included the city of Sioux Falls and the surrounding area "for a radius of about five miles," except toward the west and northwest where it extended "about twenty miles."

This would encompass Wall Lake, Grass, Beaver and Lost Lakes. Considering the agriculturalized condition of this region today with its drained sloughs and receding lakes, it seems almost incredible that Sandhill Cranes were seen as commonly in migration on the uplands surrounding the lakes and potholes in 1916 as geese are today.

In 1921 the first edition of Over and Thoms' *Birds of South Dakota*, appeared, but the authors remark only (p. 61) that the Sandhill Crane "is abundant in migration" without being specific.

However, in the second edition (1946:89) they add: "Once very common in migration over the eastern part of the state" but "of recent years the Sandhill Crane has shifted its migratory route to the west...flying over the eastern foothills of the Black Hills."

Just when this westward shift began is uncertain but presumably it occurred after 1921, and, as far as Minnehaha County is concerned, it must have been completed, if records (or lack of them) are indicative of status, sometime before 1946.

My records, begun in 1949, are not as optimistic as those of Stephens-Youngworth-Felton (1955. *Birds of Union County*, 9–10).

These authors call the Sandhill Crane "uncommon," but do have a record during the first week of November 1950, of "several flocks" seen along the Missouri River bordering on Union County. No such recent record seems to be available for Minnehaha County. In fact, one feels inclined to regard Larson's 1916 records as the latest for the area.

Therefore, it was with some excitement that I observed and recorded the appearance of three Sandhill Cranes flying over Woodlawn Cemetery, Sioux Falls, on October 9, 1959.

Wide-spread storms beginning on October 5 had brought heavy snow to western Montana; sleet, rain and heavy snow with strong winds on October 7 and 8 to a wide belt extending from Saskatoon, Sask., to Minot, Kenmare and Devils Lake, N. Dak.; a cold front with heavy winds to the Sand Lake Refuge, Columbia, S. Dak., area on October 8; and rain, lowered temperature and a crust of snow to the Sioux Falls vicinity on the 8th and 9th.

On the morning of the 9th I was walking my customary beat in the cemetery when I heard the loud "Kr-r-rooo" call–the roll and the bugle sound. I saw them high up, three birds, but not so high that my binocular could not bring down distinctly the outstretched legs and neck and the darkish-colored bodies.

These points and the call made the identification positive, in my opinion. I have seen and heard Sandhill Cranes in Upper Michigan (with Dr. O.S. Pettingill, Jr.) and on the Platte River in Nebraska, where with Dr. John Bliese and Herman and Lois Chapman I saw literally thousands of these birds, some no farther than a couple of car's lengths away from me—saw them and heard them, too.

Once heard, the call is not likely to be forgotten. It was a real thrill to see them and hear them here in the Sioux Falls sky.

Perhaps the strong northwest winds accompanying the storm of the previous days drove the birds off course and over Sioux Falls.

For those flocks which migrate through Sand Lake and Waubay Refuges in Brown and Day Counties, (and they did again this year) apparently go to the east and the west of Minnehaha County. At least it seems that no one has reported their passage since Larson.

Or, apart from the influence of the storm, is it the scarcity (or inattentiveness) of observers, or the height of their flight which permits these birds to escape detection in their migration over the Minnehaha County area? (December 1958)

Unusual Migration Waves at Sioux Falls

Two unusual bird waves, one of hawks, the other of passerines, occurred at Sioux Falls, S. Dak., during mid-September 1959. Both may have been influenced by meteorological conditions.

On the 16th a hawk flight of rather spectacular proportions drifted across the city. Up to that day the migration of all species had been thin almost to nothing.

For the five days previously, winds were southerly and temperatures rather high–in the upper 70s and lower 80s.

On the night of the 14th the wind swung to the northeast, bringing overcast skies, some precipitation, lowered temperatures and winds at 25–35 here. Rain fell to the north of us in both Dakotas.

On the 15th I noticed four Broad-winged Hawks flying low over our part of the city and later one perching–an unusual occurrence, I thought.

The 16th brought more precipitation and continued coolness. At 12:15 p.m. as I left the house, I happened to look northwestward and saw the sky dotted with dark bird forms.

I was reminded of movies of parachute drops with troops by the scores floating along on a broad front. By the time I hurriedly brought out my binocular, the birds were much closer: an unusual concentration of hawks.

A sampling number of quick observations and I realized that I was looking at one of those flocks of Broad-winged Hawks occurring in migration, which Pough describes in *Audubon Water Bird Guide* (1949:141–143) as sometimes numbering in "hundreds or thousands."

In the next forty minutes–from 12:15 to 12:55 p. m.–I managed to count and identify 112 hawks as they came somewhat leisurely from the northwest, flying or rather soaring–I saw little spiralling–against an easterly wind.

My count was 94 Broadwings, 16 Red-tails and two which I thought were Sharpshins.

How broad the flight was, I don't know. But in that portion within my view I estimated there were between 400 and 500 birds. I'm sure there were many more than that.

The flight came in three large waves with scattering numbers in between. I had the impression that at least 75 percent were Broadwings. Although most of the birds seemed to be flying fairly low–perhaps at 150–200 feet–some volplaned from considerable heights and disappeared behind the trees of McKennan Park and the cemetery to the east.

Some moved so slowly and seemed to be slanting downward that I wondered whether they were coming in for a rest. Later I learned that for some individuals this may have been true.

Though I'd often heard Herman and Lois Chapman and the J. Scott Findleys tell about the hawk numbers aloft during the Duluth, Minn., flights in mid-September, and I'd read about the drifts of hawks over Hawk Mountain in Kentucky, I was hardly prepared for the breath-taking sight of row on broken row of birds sailing to the right and the left and overhead, a passage as soundless as owls in their flight.

Fortunately, during the last part of the flight, I had the assistance of Mrs. Richard Smith, a colleague in the English Department, who came by and joined me.

At 3 p.m. that day I saw four Broadwings perched in trees near the college and five in flight. At 5 o'clock I saw three Broadwings in flight over the campus.

On the 17th I found one perched in the locust near our house, six in trees in and near McKennan Park and seven at the cemetery. Two short flights occurred that afternoon. Between 12:30 and 1 o'clock, I counted 26 Broadwings; between 1:20 and 2:45 I listed 31 hawks, of which 26 were Broadwings, two Redtails, one Sparrowhawk and two Turkey Vultures, the first I've seen in this area.

The number of perching Broadwings indicated that apparently some individuals were indeed resting or searching for food. In the next four days I saw several in trees in the twelve blocks between my apartment and the college. On the 21st, the last sight date, I saw five.

In the light of existing records for South Dakota, this wave was apparently rather extraordinary. Agersborg (1930. "Birds of Southwestern Dakota," *Proc. So. Dak. Acad. Sci.*, 13:15–33) does not mention the Broadwing in his early list (1869–1885) although his study area included parts of Minnehaha County (p. 15).

Coues (1874. *Birds of the Northwest*, 360–361) says that it was not found in the Upper Missouri region (1856–1873). McChesney, acting assistant surgeon at Fort Sisseton during the years 1875–1878, did not include it in his "Notes on the Birds of Fort Sisseton, Dakota Territory" (1879:71–103). Neither did Larson (1925. "Birds of Sioux Falls, South Dakota," *Wilson Bull.*, 37(1):18–38; 37(2):72–76) in his 1906–1916 study. Visher calls the Broadwing (1915. "A List of Birds of Clay County, Southeastern South Dakota," *Wilson Bull.*, 37 (No. 91):321–325) "a regular but uncommon migrant" (p. 328).

However, Stephens (1918. "Notes on the Birds of South Dakota, with a Preliminary List for Union County," *Proc. Iowa Acad. Sci.*, 25:85–104) does not list it.

Over and Thomas (1921. *Birds of South Dakota*, 85; 1946. *Ibid.*, rev. ed., 124) say merely that it "is only fairly common in South Dakota. The range is farther east."

Youngworth (1935. "The Birds of Fort Sisseton, South Dakota," *Wilson Bull.*, 47:209–235), reviewing McChesney's 1879 list after sixty years, calls the Broadwing "a rare summer visitor" (p. 216). And Stephens, Youngworth and Felton (1955. "Birds of Union County, South Dakota," *Occ. Papers, Neb. Orn. Union*, 1:1–35) are of the opinion that it "is an uncommon migrant" (p. 7).

My own unpublished notes for Minnehaha (1949–1959) pretty well agree with this opinion. Sight records for the period indicate that the species is generally present but never abundant, either in spring or fall, appearing in numbers from one to five or six.

It is interesting that in none of the above reports is any mention made of concentrations, at least for South Dakota, either for spring or fall migration. Therefore, the wave of September 17, 1959, appears to be most unusual.

However, the flight was small compared with the size of flocks reported in Minnesota by Roberts (1938. *Logbook of Minnesota Bird Life*). On September 14, 1924, between 6,000 and 7,000 Broadwings appeared over Mound, a suburb of Minneapolis (pp. 114–115).

The "tendency to travel together in considerable numbers," as Alexander Sprunt, Jr., describes it in *North American Birds of Prey* (1955:70), probably often results in tragic destruction, especially at the hands of human beings.

In April 1925, "immense numbers" of this species appeared in spring migration at Wheaton, Minn., many "settling in trees and flying over the buildings" of the city.

Trigger-happy gun-toters, engaged in a crow-shooting contest, left crows and turned to hawks. They brought in 1500. According to a local resident, "at least 3000" Broadwings were shot in the two-day migration over the town (Roberts, 130–131).

Fortunately, as far as I know, none was shot from the September 1959, flocks. But there may be a dire significance in the small size of this concentration–an estimated 400 to 500 compared with 6,000 to 7,000 in 1925.

The weather disturbances which probably influenced the hawk flight on September 16 may have been a factor in concentrating a wave of passerines at Sioux Falls on September 17.

The day began with northerly winds driving in light precipitation. On the way to the cemetery, I saw in a vacant lot four Nashville Warblers in a tangle of Russian thistle, and two Orange-crowns in McKennan Park.

But when I came to Woodlawn Cemetery, I ran into a swarm of birds, apparently all passerines with warblers and kinglets predominating. From 8:00 until 11:15 a.m., perhaps as many as 500 birds streamed through the trees or fluttered in the bushes.

Sometimes so many were around me that I gave up in despair and studied only those that were handiest. I saw several Warbling Vireos, one Red-eyed Vireo, a lone Brown Creeper, a dozen or so flycatchers (of which three were Wood Pewees) and a great flutter of Ruby-crowned Kinglets.

A lively curtain of movement, the wave (it was really a series of waves with thin stretches of few birds in between) drifted unhurriedly through the elms, ashes and conifers, generally in a rather straight southeasterly direction.

There was some diving and several instances of hovering at twig ends, especially among the kinglets, Nashville and Orange-crowned Warblers and Redstarts.

The Black and White Warblers were the least mobile, quietly slipping from large limb to large limb, their well-marked bodies white streaks creeping along the dark wet wood. The vireos seemed to be the rear-ward birds without being completely left behind.

But the flycatchers were either last of all or far ahead of everyone else, their habit of perching immobilely, then darting out in quick sorties and returning to perch again delaying their progress until, with a quick burst, they launched off to perch once more a dozen trees ahead to wait for the crowd to catch up.

Three were good enough to sing an incomplete song–"aa-wee" instead of "pee-aa-wee"–plaintive as in summer, giving me an additional identification mark besides the yellowish or lightish lower mandible and the wingbars. Other smaller individuals, too difficult to recognize in the field, I recorded as "flycatchers."

The warblers made the day memorable in its challenge. Could I identify these nondescript flutterers in their often drab autumn plumage? Nashvilles, Redstarts, Black and Whites–these were easy. But the difficult ones–talk about holding one's breath. I did, almost prayerfully, concentrating on backs and legs and the color of under tails.

Suddenly I found that the stray bits of information I'd noticed in these years of rather careful observation now gathered into focus. The difficulties of washed-out and puzzling fall plumages became a little less baffling. Among the many similar greenish forms I was able to distinguish between the light legs and streaked back of the Blackpoll and the dark legs, the streaked back and buffy under tail of the Bay-breasted (though fortunately, most of these individuals had the easily-recognized tinges of bay on the sides); between these two species and the plain or unstreaked back and dark legs of the Pine Warbler (when that always difficult bird confounds the difficulty by appearing with a grayish breast faintly washed with buff and practically unstreaked).

Recognition did seem easier, though some stumped me completely. I wrote them off as "warblers." But I remembered Roger Tory Peterson's sage remark: "If at the end of ten years of field work you can say you know the fall warblers you are doing very well." As it happened, this autumn was my tenth year of warbler-study. But I doubted that I was doing well.

Nevertheless in something better than the next three hours I identified and counted 17 species of warblers, numbering 170 individuals and ranking them in the following order:

Nashville	36
Orange-crowned	29
Bay-breasted	25
Black and White	24
Wilson's	15
Tennessee	10
Redstart	5
Parula	5
Chestnut-sided	3
Blackpoll	3
Canada	2
Pine	2
Black-throated Green	2
Myrtle	2
Blackburnian	1
Yellow	1
Yellowthroat	1

A dire note appears in the Myrtle numbers–I saw only two when in previous years this species was among the most abundant.

The surprise came with the five Parulas, a bird uncommon in Sioux Falls. Larson (1925. "The Birds of Sioux Falls, South Dakota, and Vicinity," *Wilson Bull.*, 27(2):72–76) does not mention it in his ten-year study (1906–1916), but Over and Thomas' revised edition of *Birds of South Dakota* (1946:179) contains the statement that it "has been seen in Yankton and Minnehaha Counties" without indicating sources or dates.

Stephens, Youngworth and Felton (1955. "The Birds of Union County," *Ibid.*, 1:27) consider it a rare migrant, citing a spring observation made by Youngworth on May 11, 1934. Published fall records seem to be unavailable. I have one unpublished occurrence, October 3, 1955.

Four of the birds in the 1959 concentration had chestnut breast bands only slightly obscured in the fall plumage. The fifth had only the faintest tinge on a rather bright yellow breast.

But the wingbars, conspicuously white, and the greenish patch on the back, faintly washed with a bluish tint, made the identification not too difficult. In fact, there is a hint of bluish about the bird even in this garb.

All in all, it was a warbler "day," one to break the dullness of an otherwise very inactive migration. (December 1959)

The Warbler Wave Along the Big Sioux River (Minnehaha County, South Dakota)

May 18, 1959, seems to be the day the Warbler Wave came to Sioux Falls, S. Dak. On the morning of that day I saw two Orange-crowned, a Bay-breasted, two Magnolias, five male and three female Tennessees, a Wilson's, a Blackpoll, two Black and Whites, four Myrtles. On the 19th I saw two male and two female Northern Yellow-throats, a Black and White, four male and female Redstarts, five male and four female Tennessees, four Chestnut-sided, two Magnolias, a male and a female Blackpoll, an Oven-bird, two Blackburnians, and one Myrtle. On May 21, my next date, I saw only a Black and White, a Wilson's and three Tennessees. (December 1959)

Wave of Passerines at Sioux Falls

A combination of atmospheric phenomena apparently halted a large wave of passerines, mostly warblers, in Sioux Falls during May 19–21, 1959. Previous to the 18th warm southerly winds had been blowing pretty steadily for several days with temperatures in the 70s and 80s. On the 18th overcast skies brought some precipitation. During the night a cold front rode in with the wind switching to the northeast. It brought a sharp electrical storm in the afternoon of the 19th with falling temperatures (high of 84 degrees on the 19th, 54 on the 20th) followed by chilly drizzle-weather. By the 21st the air current changed to the northwest with an inch of moisture falling and with temperatures in the fifties.

On the 18th in following my regularly scheduled route of observation, I encountered only the usual birds in spring migration and in no great numbers:

four yellow warblers, one blackpoll, two Wilson's, one Magnolia, one chestnut-sided, although Tennessees were present in small numbers. I counted 12. But on the morning of the 19th, with the change in weather, the influx began; or rather, the cold front was beginning to bring the northward wave to a halt and damming it up apparently in this area.

That morning early, I counted 39 Tennessees and observed Black-and-White, blackpoll, 11 yellows, a Wilson's, a mourning, as well as two Philadelphia and two warbling vireos. The next day, the 20th, was pure fun. Warblers were everywhere and in the chilly drizzle seemed to be less wary and easier to see. They were present in such numbers and species that I could not begin to keep an accurate tally. I noted 75 Tennessees, as many as 25 in one spruce tree row, but there were scores and scores more which I both heard and saw. Other warblers, however, kept fouling up my count. I observed nine blackpolls; eight Philadelphia vireos (although many more were singing), three solitary, two red-eyed, one yellow-throated and six warbling: the first time in my experience that I saw five of the six vireos one may expect to see in South Dakota and saw them on one morning.

But the uncommon warblers were the thrillers, those which I see one or two in a spring's migration. I counted four mourning warblers, including one female; eight Wilson's, ten magnolias, a Nashville singing, a Black-throated green, a chestnut-sided, a bay-breasted, a Blackburnian; and best of all, my old friend, the Canada Warbler, which I had watched for a whole summer in the wilderness of northern Michigan at the University of Michigan Biological Station. I saw eight Canadas, two being females. And they were singing, a lapse on their part, for some authorities think this species does not burst into song until it reaches the nesting ground. Added to these were a scarlet tanager, several orchard orioles, a couple of ovenbirds, a good supply of redstarts and yellow warblers, and other run of the mill species, making a rememberable birding morning.

On the 21st the Tennessees had dropped to a count of 40, though there were certainly many singing, suggesting that the wave had not diminished too much. I noted 14 magnolias, six mourning, six blackpolls, three chestnut-sided, three bay-breasted, three Canadas, one Nashville and one Connecticut warbler. Actually there were many more blackpolls but the Connecticut provided serious interference, since it was in rather nondescript and puzzling plumage. By the 22nd the numbers had dwindled almost drastically with only here and there a Tennessee lifting its sprightly song. On the evening of the 22nd the wind changed to the southeast and the next morning under a clear sky and a warm sun, I found the area as empty of warblers as if a mighty broom had swept through it. Not even a solitary Tennessee sang.

Naturally, all my counts are very rough estimates. Actually, the trees and bushes literally fluttered with restlessly moving birds. While I was counting the numbers of one species, another would arrive and disrupt my calculations. But as a sampling, the numbers may suffice. The disheartening part of the experience was that in this excellent concentration of passerines, I saw not one myrtle warbler, a bird which even at this date should be present at least in some numbers. It strikes me that is a good example of how meteorological phenomena may influence the progress of northward migration in spring or southward movement in fall. A cold front halting and grounding a concentration of birds in spring, with a subsequent lowering of temperatures, might spell disaster for the flight, as the mortality among early-arriving swallows frequently testifies. It seems to me that SDOUers might well be most alert during any season in reporting the relationship between weather and the birdlife in their area. (March–June 1959)

Wave of Yellowlegs in Eastern South Dakota (*Tringa melanoleuca*)

During the period April 23 to May 3 a wave of yellowlegs bordering on the spectacular swept over southeastern portions of South Dakota in a broad front as far west as Mitchell and Lake Andes and nearly as far east as the Minnesota border.

My first observation of the flight was made on April 23 when Jim Ely, my colleague in the English Department, and I counted 78 birds, 75 of which were seen in roadside potholes in a distance of about one-half mile. The others were sighted at scattered points. The total for the day: 78. I thought we'd hit a scolapacid jackpot but more were to come.

On the 28th in a drive of about 40 miles including Wall and Grass Lakes, we counted 157 birds, 73 of which were on the shores of one pond, a small area washing a plowed field on one side and a grassy pasture on the other. Allowing for the error of miss-identification among many birds, for there were good numbers of other shorebirds present also, we considered 90 percent of the yellowlegs to be Lessers. Several dozen were in roadways, perhaps picking up gravel or even insects.

On the 29th came the peak number. Mrs. Herman Chapman, Mrs. Melvin Wheeler and I counted 166 yellowlegs in a drive of about 45 miles via Wall Lake and Hartford with intervening roads. The birds were more widely scattered than before with groups numbering 1 to 34 instead of large concentrations.

On April 30 I went to Mitchell by bus on Highway 16, then in a private car south on Highway 218 and other roads to Lake Andes and Pickstown. There was an excellent movement of yellowlegs all the way. While admittedly a bus seat is an error-prone point of observation, I am fairly confident that my figures, however approximate, are relatively valid. The bus flushed groups of yellowlegs from roadside potholes many times. The white rump and long yellowish legs were not too difficult to identify, although counting was not always easy.

Between Sioux Falls and Mitchell, Davison County, I tallied 40 birds; between Mitchell and Stickney, Aurora County, 25; just south of Stickney a flock of approximately 75 in one flooded pasture area; from there to Armour in Douglas County, five; and between Armour and Lake Andes, Charles Mix County, four. The tally came to 150 although I'm sure there were many more. I tried to be as conservative in my approximations as possible. That there were yellow-legs in unusual numbers, however, seemed undeniable.

On the return trip, May 2, I counted 55 between Lake Andes and Mitchell and 75 between Mitchell and Sioux Falls, a "guesstimated" total of 130. On May 3, in a drive to Wall Lake and back (about 28 miles) the count was 100; on the 6th in a 40-mile drive, 23; on the 7th, ten, and on the 8th between Vermillion and Elk Point in Union and Clay counties, 17.

Greater Yellowlegs appeared in smaller numbers but were in greater abundance than is usual. The first sightings occurred on April 23 when 17 were counted in scattered potholes; on the 24th only two; on the 28th the peak number, 36; 29th, 17; May 3rd, ten; 7th, two; 8th, one. The figures indicate birds about whose identity we were reasonably sure. Doubtful individuals, those which seemed too large for Lesser, yet too small for Greater, were called yellowlegs. (September 1960)

White-Winged Crossbill (*Loxia leucoptera*)

On November 6, 1954, in Woodlawn Cemetery, I saw a bird among the cones of spruce and heard a soft, rapid "chif, chif, chif." The white wing bars, yellowish rump, crossed mandibles, and streaked olive body indicated the female White-winged Crossbill. With this female was another and a gray streaked bird which I identified as an immature. Later, a male joined the three. Willard Rosine, Biology Department, Augustana College, corroborated my observation. On November 11, I saw seven females and immatures and five males feeding with 15 Red Crossbills; and on the 20th, one male and two females. On the 21st there were three males and nine females which were also seen by Mr. and Mrs. Herman Chapman. (December 1954)

White-Winged Crossbill at Sioux Falls (*Loxia leucoptera*)

On October 5, 1957, I heard the notes of what I was sure was the White-winged Crossbill in several western yellow pines not far from McKennan Park, Sioux Falls. I had heard this species several times previously on the Hayes River, near Hudson Bay. The notes were a rapidly-uttered "shib-shib, shib-shib, shib-shib-shib," sometimes sounding almost like a soft rattle. Mingled with these notes were the sharp, clear "kip, kip" calls of the Red Crossbill. However, the birds flew before I could make a positive identification.

On October 8, I heard the notes again, this time in Woodlawn Cemetery. I found two White-winged Crossbills, males in full adult plumage. The white bars were conspicuous in the dark wings, the rump and upper tail coverts were richly light-colored wine, the head and back a slightly darker red. They were with 20 Pine Siskens, twisting out the seeds of the spruce and eating them.

On October 9, I found a male and two females where I had seen them previously. The olive or greenish-gray of the body, the yellowish rump and upper tail coverts and the white bars on the wings identified them. On October 10, I saw a single male in Woodlawn with six Red Crossbills. Red Crossbills seem customarily to utter single "kip" notes or a succession of notes precisely separated, but the White-winged appears to run them together. Whether these birds represent two groups, or one group utilizing the conifers in at least two localities in town, I haven't been able to determine. (September 1957)

Winter Singing of Cardinals (*Cardinalidae*)

Do Cardinals sing during the winter in South Dakota? Do they sing around the calendar or is there a period when they remain silent, except for call notes? My records are by no means conclusive nor is my curiosity satisfied. However, over a period of some three years (January 1949–February 7, 1952), I believe I have found that Cardinals do sing here in the wintertime but that they also begin to rest from song late in summer or early in autumn and remain so for possibly five months.

I have records of Cardinals' singing for every month of the year except June, July, November and December. June and July, the vacation months, take me away from Sioux Falls. Although I have no listings for these two months, no doubt Cardinals continue the vocal efforts they began in spring. I have records for August 1, in 1951, being as late as the 26th. September and October seem to be the uncertain months. While I have three or more records for each of the singing months, for September I have only one, and that in 1950. The day, September 7, was cold and blowy. The Cardinal, a male, sat in the lilacs outside my window, opened to a crack. The song was so softly sung that I'm sure it was inaudible forty feet away. But the "what cheer, what cheer" was distinctly articulated. Perhaps this was the "whisper song," common certainly to the Thrushes and the Robin. My impression, however, is that this ventriloquistic effort occurs more likely during the courtship than during the so-called rest period supposedly following the completion of domestic duties. My solitary October date, the 25th in 1949, is perhaps unusually late. November, December and January seem to be the silent months. I have only one record for January, and that very late—the 30th in 1952. This is also my earliest song record for the period. February seems to be the time for returning to song, as these dates may suggest: 1949, February 8th; 1950, the 4th; 1951, the 16th. Apparently these are not single attempts or isolated efforts. Once the time for song arrives, singing continues. Nor does temperature seem a determining factor, as the following records indicate. In these, temperatures were noted for only two of the three years: 1950 – February 4th, 7th, 11th; 1951 – February 16, 21 degrees, 19, 3 degrees, 21, 24 degrees; 1952 – January 30, minus 3 degrees, January 31, 40 degrees, February 1, 28 degrees, February 2–7, varying from 34 to 17 degrees.

I am wondering whether or not the records kept by SDOU members bear out my suggestion. (March 1952)

Winter Wren at Sioux Falls (*Troglodytes troglodytes*)

On September 24, 1955, John Tuthill and I identified the Winter Wren in the Country Club area along the Big Sioux River near Sioux Falls.

Over and Thoms (1946. *Birds of South Dakota*, rev. 188) consider it to be "probably only a summer resident." However, this seems somewhat doubtful. Peterson (1941. *Western Guide*, 133, and 1947. *Eastern Guide*, rev., 168) states that it "breeds in evergreen forests from Can. south to central Calif, and north Colo." and "from s. Manitoba...to Minnesota." Pough (1951. *Audubon Bird Guide*, 100) gives its range as far south as central Minnesota and Michigan. But Roberts (1936. *Birds of Minnesota*, 11:93) considers it as "breeding mainly north of the U.S.," and in Minnesota as "a summer resident in the northern evergreen forests." Available published records for South Dakota seem to agree that it is "a rare migrant" in the state.

It is not mentioned by early observers including Coues, Agersborg, McChesney, Youngworth, in the literature of South Dakota. Visher (1913. *Auk*, XXX: 573) apparently has only one spring record for Sanborn County. In Clay County he (1915. *Wilson Bull.*, XXVII:334) finds it "a rare migrant." Larson (1925. *Wilson Bull.*, XXXVII:75) calls it "transient," rarely wintering in Minnehaha County, with spring arrivals near Sioux Falls as early as May 13, 1907. He found one individual on January 11, 1908.

I could find no records of dates since then although I looked through all my available references.

Tuthill and I found this individual flitting among the roots and rocks on the shore of the Big Sioux River. We had more than a five-minute observation. The midget-size (smaller than a House Wren), the brownish back and dark brown bars on the belly, the whitish line over the eye, and many small flecks of white on the throat and breast, the stubby tail held at a pert, ridiculous upright angle—all indicated this species. It bobbed its whole body rather than its head only, appearing to bend at the knees like a Dipper. While we watched, it darted in and out of sight among the rocks and debris, moving with astonishing rapidity. We saw it pull what looked like insect larvae from the rocks and swallow them. It had a way of leaping suddenly, jack-in-the-box-like, into sight and of disappearing abruptly. About every 30 seconds it popped up and surveyed us, bobbing and crying "Kip-kip, kip-kip" with a metallic quality. Finally it hopped from rock to root and vanished.

Many more records are needed before much can be said about the status of this species in South Dakota. (December 1955)

Yellow-Bellied Sapsucker at Sioux Falls (*Sphyrapicus varius*)

On September 19, 1952, I saw what Over calls "an irregular migrant," the Yellow-bellied Sapsucker. I don't know how common or uncommon it is but this was my first sight of this species. This individual, an immature, displayed somewhat dully the characteristic long white wing-stripe. Though it had the tan-yellow belly and the brownish neck and head of the immature, the face markings of the adult were discernible. Probably it was an immature just beginning to get his adult trappings. On September 27 I saw a male, the red forehead and throat distinctive as was the "mewing" call. It was tapping the Chinese Elm outside my window but I couldn't catch the rhymthic pattern described by Peterson. This year, 1953, I saw males on April 11 and 12 and on May 5 the white-throated female, apparently resting high up in a pine tree. (September 1953)

The Yellow-Throated Warbler in Southern South Dakota (*Dendroica dominica*)

According to the AOU Check List (1957:498–499), the Yellow-throated Warbler breeds from Nebraska, northern Iowa, southern Wisconsin and southern Michigan southward. Peterson (1947. *Field Guide to the Birds*, 197, 269) mentions a Mississippi race, the Sycamore Yellow-throated Warbler (*D. d. albilora*), breeding from south Michigan and Wisconsin down the great valley. So do Griscom and Sprunt (1957. *Warblers of North America*, 156–158) who mark the range farther south, excluding both Nebraska and Iowa.

However, Musgrove's *Check List of Iowa Birds* (1949) does include this species as a rare summer resident under the name "Sycamore Warbler" without indicating breeding status. According to Sprunt (1953. Bent, *Life Histories of North American Warblers*, 358), it has been reported as far north as Sigourney, Iowa, "without indication of breeding."

For Nebraska, Pough (1951. *Audubon Bird Guides: Land Birds*, 171) localizes the breeding area in the southeast, although the Nebraska Ornithologists' Union Check List, printed in 1951, does not record it. Roberts (1936. *Birds of Minnesota*, 2 vols.) does not report it for Minnesota nor do Morrison, Breckenridge and Herz (1955. *Where to Find Birds in Minnesota*). Nor do I find it listed by Larson (1925. "Birds of Sioux Falls, South Dakota," *Wilson Bull.*, 37: 18–38; 72–76) nor by Stephens, Youngworth and Felton (1955. "Birds of Union County," *Occ. Papers, Neb. Orn. Union,* 1) for southeastern South Dakota.

I was therefore more than a little interested when I encountered this bird in Sioux Falls on April 23, 1960.

I was in McKennan Park, two blocks from home, looking for Myrtle Warblers when I heard a bird singing. The notes somehow reminded me vaguely of Grace's Warbler which I heard last summer in the Kaibab Forest near the north rim of the Grand Canyon. This, however, was intriguingly different, too. Then the bird flew toward me and alighted on a bare walnut tree no more than fifty feet away. When I focused my 7x35 wide angle binocular on it, I could hardly believe my eyes.

There on the grayish bark, alive as day, crept Peterson's portrait of the Yellow-throated Warbler. Thoughts churned in the back of my head: how did the bird get here? Who would corroborate my findings?

Between chills and fever, I noted the distinguishing points—bright yellow throat, edged on the sides with black, white line over the eye, white area back of the ear-patch and extending downward, two white wingbars, black-streaked sides, decidedly grayish upper parts.

And the song? It sounded something like "see-ta, see-ta, see-a, see-a, see, see," the first notes separate and distinct, the last portion rapid and run-together. It resembled a little some of the notes of the Myrtle Warbler as we hear it singing in migration in Sioux Falls, especially in its soft quality, although these notes were more emphatic than the Myrtle's usually are.

A good four minutes passed while I watched and the bird moved about like a Black-and-White Warbler or a Brown Creeper on the walnut limbs. There it was, but I had neither color camera nor anyone to see what I was seeing, although in this instance at least, I was sure of my identification. When it flew I noted its flight pattern—a straight away movement, rather deeply undulating; not as deeply as the American Goldfinch perhaps, but almost.

At once elated and despondent, I went home to search the records.

The next morning at about 6:30 I heard the bird singing in the Ponderosa pine next door. I remembered Sprunt's description of the song: "Sweetie, sweetie." But this bird, like the one I'd heard previously, sang the "see-ta, see-ta" song. All my searching was in vain, however; I was sure I'd never see or hear the bird again.

On Monday morning the unbelievable happened. At 5:30 there was the same song in the pine. But all I got for the pain of rushing out to see was a good view of the bird's flight—the same pattern I'd noticed two days before. I felt sure it was my bird or one of the same species.

Twice I'd seen it in pines. In the south it is sometimes associated with pinelands, I recalled. Whether fortuitous or not, I decided to follow a hunch. I went a block south where a backyard contains a rectangle of pine and spruce with hackberry, walnut and other deciduous trees.

There was my bird, singing from a hackberry limb. I re-checked the identifying points carefully. They were still the same. This time I tried to determine whether the white line over the eye was yellow anteriorly but saw nothing that resembled yellow between the eye and the bill, as in Dick's and Eckelberry's plates.

This then very probably was not the eastern but the western race of the species, the Sycamore Warbler.

Knowing that I needed further corroboration, I went to the owner of the property, Mr. J.P. Everist. He was most cooperative, using my glasses on the bird no more than 50 to 60 feet away and nodding while I ticked off the distinguishing marks of identification. Yes, he agreed with me. This bird was like the one in Peterson; he would corroborate my findings.

Feeling positively heady, now that I'd staked out my bird, I called the Department of Biology at Augustana College and Dr. Sven Froiland, the Chairman and a good bird man, to see if he would come. Yes, he would.

At 9:25 I again checked the bird; it was still singing, though why, I asked myself, should a bird stick around long enough to satisfy me and be identified by a biologist? At 9:35 Froiland arrived and with him two of his colleagues, Dr. Willard Rosine, a serious bird man in his own right, and Dr. Dilwyn Rogers, assistant professor in the department.

When we arrived at the pine grove I had three Ph. D's with me—but no bird. There wasn't a sound. Nothing.

Any bird observer knows how these things go. Ten minutes of red-faced listening and looking—not a feather.

At 9:50 some cockle-burred remarks about trusting amateurs to find elephants in hickory trees—these men were my friends. Besides they had classes to meet in the next 20 minutes. I kept a desperate eye on my timepiece. At 9:57 a bird flew into a pine overhead. I took one look.

"There she is, boys." I think I yelled. And there she – or he – was.

The men took careful note for several minutes remaining silent in the chilly official manner of scientists. Then a Myrtle Warbler charged in and chased the Yellow-throated Warbler into the next block.

Classes momentarily forgotten, we followed and had an excellent three-minute view of the bird from another angle in clear light. My colleagues then agreed; there could hardly be a mistake in the identification. All points were in agreement with Peterson's portraiture of the Yellow-throated Warbler.

Later I checked the weather and found that high temperatures and strong air currents moving northwesterly out of the south might have sent the bird straying from its normal range in the Mississippi Valley—a possible answer to why it was here at all.

Also, it was good to know that Leslie Tuck reported Sycamore Warblers in St. John's, Newfoundland, on October 24, 1953, in a spectacular flight: "as many as fifty individuals were recorded in one locality" and specimens were obtained (Griscom and Sprunt, *Ibid*, 158).

Two days later I heard the warbler singing in Woodlawn cemetery, and caught a last glimpse of it among the growing leaves of the American elm. It was a satisfying moment to remember– another bird added to my life list and possibly a new one to add to the state checklist. (September 1960)

Young of White-Breasted Nuthatch in Newton Hills
(*Sitta carolinensis*)

While there are scattered references to the White-breasted Nuthatch in the eastern half of South Dakota, the greater number of them are winter reports. Breeding records are confined to general observations such as Visher's: "Tolerably common resident" in Clay County (1915. *Wilson Bull.*, XXVII:334); Larson's: "common resident; breeds" in Minnehaha County (1925. *Wilson Bull.*, XXXVII:75); Youngworth's: "A regular resident of the region (Fort Sisseton and the Marshall County area generally)," (1935. *Wilson Bull.*, XLVII:226) and the comment by the same writer (1955. Stephens, Youngworth and Felton, *Birds of Union County*, 22) that this species is a "regular resident" in Union County. In a general statement regarding the Family Sittidae, Over and Thoms (1946. *Birds of South Dakota*, 189) note that "Nuthatches are represented in South Dakota by two species, both winter residents." This seems to vary a trifle from the description of the White-breasted Nuthatch in the same work where the writers state that this species is "common in winter, frequently remains all summer and nesting." In addition to these observations, that this nuthatch nests in the eastern area may be found in Randall's note about an individual seen near Chamberlain, S. Dak., on May 24, 1946 (1953. *South Dakota Bird Notes* V:69) and in Mallory's report of one at Canton, S. Dak., as late as July 18, 1951 (1951. *South Dakota Bird Notes,* 111:47). Randall considered it "uncommon." Adults seen as late as May and June could very well be breeding birds. Published records of nests, eggs and young, however, seem to be few. The following note therefore may be of interest.

On June 9, 1955, while we were in the Boy Scout area of Newton Hills, Lincoln County, John Tuthill and I heard the "yanhk, yanhk" of this species. In a growth of tall American Elms along a dry creek, we discovered the adults and two juveniles. The young were completely feathered and able to fly but when perched seemed to cling uncertainly to the bark and moved somewhat awkwardly. Tufts of natal down indicated their immaturity. During a fifteen-minute observation we saw them fed often, apparently by both adults. The food seemed to be worms or worm-like forms. The "yanhk" call which the adults frequently uttered was not loud and clear as one usually hears it but short and rather hoarse and guttural. The young's nasal call resembled the adult's "yanhk" but in quality was more like the thin, high-pitched "ink-yink" of the Red-breasted Nuthatch. During the time we watched, the birds, adult and young, ranged back and forth in the trees but remained in an area about fifty feet in length along the dry wash. We saw nothing that indicated a nest, although the young presumably were raised in the immediate vicinity. It might be important to learn just how often this species nests in the eastern half of the state. (December 1955)

APPENDIX

AUDUBON FIELD NOTES: THE NORTHERN GREAT PLAINS REGION

Winter Season, 1957–1958

Despite its wide range of latitude, the Region had fairly uniform weather conditions. From southern South Dakota to southeastern Saskatchewan, nearly all co-operators sang the same refrain: "relatively mild winter" at Lake Andes, S. Dak. (David McGlaughlin); "generally mild winter" in the Black Hills of South Dakota (N.R. Whitney, Jr.); "exceptionally mild winter" at Kenmare, N. Dak. (Mrs. Robert Gammell); "unusually mild and open" at Fort Peck Game Range, Lewistown, Mont. (Eugene D. Stroops); "mildest winter in years—maybe in 50 years" at Yorkton, Sask. (J. Stuart Houston). Temperatures were generally above normal, as much as 9° on the average at Moffit, N. Dak. Extremes occurred during the last half of February. A high of 70° was measured at Sioux Falls, S. Dak., on the 23rd and 68° on the 25th at Moffit, N. Dak., the highest February reading there in 84 years of record (Homer L. Bradley). Lows of –33° were recorded at Moffit, N. Dak., on February 16 and –24° at Columbia, S. Dak., during the same week. Snow cover was unusually light. However, during the last week in February, weather disturbances brought snow in a rather narrow band down through the Dakotas; ten inches fell in the Des Lacs National Wildlife Refuge area, Kenmare, N. Dak. (Edward J. Smith, Jr.). Precipitation was up in South Dakota, as much as 1.53 inches falling as rain in some eastern sections on February 27. Potholes in those portions of the state, many of them dry for a period of as long as four years, were filling again. Cover conditions were exceptionally good; access to existing food supplies was comparatively easy. The crop of spruce cones seemed heavier than usual in eastern South Dakota. Perhaps these somewhat out-of-the-ordinary features contributed to several interesting occurrences.

Grebes, Herons, Swans— In South Dakota an Eared Grebe was observed at Rapid City on December 29 (NRW) and at Huron J.W. Johnson reported a Black-crowned Night Heron on December 8. Thirteen Whistling Swans were included in the Christmas bird count at Sand Lake National Wildlife Refuge, Columbia (Howard Huenecke): late dates for all three species.

Waterfowl— Apparently because of the mild open winter, Canada Geese in small numbers lingered until December 13 at Fort Peck Game Range, Lewistown, Mont. (EDS) and until January 26 at Sand Lake Refuge (Bruce Stollberg). In mid-February about 12,000 were concentrated at Lake Andes National Wildlife Refuge, Lake Andes, at the southern edge of South Dakota (DM). Fifty Snow and Blue Geese remained at Sand Lake Refuge until January 12 (EPS). The almost balmy winter seemed to have delayed the Mallards also. About 50 were seen at Lake Wabamum, Edmonton, Alta. on February 23 (Edmonton Bird Club); none was observed at Lower Souris National Wildlife Refuge, Upham, N. Dak., (John Frye) and a decrease of about 3,000 birds from the normal wintering population of approximately 5,000 was noted at Fort Peck Game Range (EDS). However, an estimated 400,000 were gathered in mid-February at Lake Andes Refuge (DM). Solitary drake Pintails remained near Edmonton, Alta. until February 23 and at Sand Lake Refuge for the winter (E.B.C., BPS). Very unusual was the observation at Regina, Sask, of Blue-winged Teal during the Christmas count week (E.L. Fox). Eugene Stroops reported a peak population of about 250 Common Goldeneyes at Fort Peck Game Range the first week in February. Small numbers of Common Mergansers were noted in the Dakotas and Montana.

Hawks, Eagles— A somewhat bedraggled Swainson's Hawk was carefully studied at Sand Lake Refuge late in December (HH). Rough-legged Hawks were scarce in the Kenmare, N. Dak., area (Mrs. RG) and down at Fort Peck Refuge but numerous at LaCreek National Wildlife Refuge, Martin S. Dak. (NRW). Occasional Golden Eagles were observed at Slade National Wildlife Refuge, Dawson N. Dak., (Howard D. Woon) and at Des Lacs Refuge, Kenmare, N. Dak (EJS) but they were numerous at LaCreek Refuge (NRW). Several Bald Eagles were sighted in the Blunt-Highmore area of South Dakota (JWJ), they were common in the Missouri River Bottoms at Snake Creek National Wildlife Refuge, Riverdale, N. Dak., (Jerald J. Wilson) and were at an estimated peak of 21 individuals at Lake Andes Refuge, Lake Andes, S. Dak., the last week in January. Prairie Falcons appeared at Sand Lake Refuge (BPS) and Dillon Pass, Badlands National Monument, S. Dak., during the period (NRW). Notable were Pigeon Hawks at Edmonton, Alta. (A. Allan, K. Ball) and at Carlton, Sask. (JSH) on the Christmas counts.

Gallinaceous Birds— Sharp-tailed Grouse seemed to be normally abundant in North Dakota and normally scarce at reporting South Dakota stations. The Gray Partridge was in greater numbers at Waubay National Refuge, Waubay, S. Dak., than at any time since 1947 (John C. Carlsen); they were beginning to break up into pairs by March 9 at Edmonton, Alta. (E.B.C.).

Snipe, Pigeons— In the South Dakota Christmas counts John Carlsen reported a Common Snipe at Waubay Wildlife Refuge and Howard Huenecke a Mourning Dove at Sand Lake Refuge.

Owls— Great Horned Owls were about in normal numbers, some perching on television aerials in the Kenmare, N. Dak., area (Mrs. RG). Snowy Owls were scarcer than usual in the Edmonton, Alta. and Yorkton, Sask. sections (E.B.C., JSH); were rarely observed at Lower Souris Refuge, Upham, N. Dak. (JF);

but were about as usual at Kenmare, N. Dak. (Mrs. RG), and at Tewaukon Wildlife Refuge, Cayuga, N. Dak. (Kermit Dybsetter) and slightly above last year's count at Sand Lake Refuge (BPS). Homer L. Bradley reported a Short-eared Owl at Long Lake National Wildlife Refuge, Moffit, N. Dak., and Bruce Stollberg a Saw-whet Owl at Sand Lake Refuge in February.

Jays, Magpies— A Gray Jay was observed just north of Fargo, N. Dak on December 5 (O.A. Stevens). Unusual were occurrences of Black-billed Magpies north of Moorehead, Minn. on February 11 (AOS) and at Webster, S. Dak. (Herman Chilson). Three individuals of this species wintered at Slade Wildlife Refuge, Dawson, N. Dak. (HDW). Twenty-two of a flock of about 35 Piñon Jays were banded by Dr. N.R. Whitney at Rapid City, S. Dak.

Nuthatches, Thrashers— Red-breasted Nuthatches abounded in the Dakotas, especially at Rapid City, Huron, and Sioux Falls in South Dakota (NRW, JWJ, HK). Robert Randall wrote that this winter was the best in ten years at Bismarck, N. Dak., for this species. Single Brown Thrashers remained most of the winter at feeding stations at Fargo, N. Dak. and Huron, S. Dak. (OAS, JWJ). A Mountain Bluebird appeared at the Sipary Ann Game Station, Lewistown, Mont. on March 10: "the first and only observation for the period" (EDS).

Waxwings, Starlings— The Robert Gammells found a concentration of about 500 Bohemian Waxwings feeding on wolfberry and Russian olive fruit near Tolley, N. Dak on November 2. The same species was seen at Des Lacs Refuge (EJS), at Madison, Minn. on December 1 (Mrs. C.E. Peterson) and at Waubay Refuge on February 24 (JJC). Starlings appeared near Edmonton, Alta. on February 23; they seem to be decreasing as wintering birds in the Kenmare, N. Dak., area (Mrs. RG).

Blackbirds, Fringillids— Several Yellow-headed Blackbirds as well as 13 Rusty Blackbirds were included in the Christmas count at Sand Lake Refuge, Columbia, S. Dak. (HH). Evening Grosbeaks, always uncommon at Bismarck, N. Dak., appeared in very small numbers on December 29 and on several occasions in the first half of March (RR). In South Dakota two were reported at Huron and two at Sioux Falls instead of the dozens observed there in previous years (JWJ, HK). Redpolls seemed to be plentiful from Yorkton, Sask., to the Dakotas, especially at Kenmare, Lostwood and Upham in North Dakota (Mrs. RG, RRJ, JF) and in South Dakota at Huron, Sioux Falls, Columbia and Rapid City where they were in greater than normal numbers (JWJ, EPS, NRW). In North Dakota Mrs. Robert Gammell recorded four Hoary Redpolls at Kenmare on December 29. In South Dakota Red Crossbills were abundant at Rapid City (NRW) but infrequent at Huron and Sioux Falls (JWJ). They were not reported from North Dakota or points farther north. White-winged Crossbills, which had made a spectacular incursion into South Dakota in the fall months, continued to be the high point of the winter season. By contrast they were very scarce at Edmonton, Alta. where they are usually regular winter visitors (E.B.C.); they made an apparent "first" appearance at Bismarck, N. Dak between December 22 and 29 (RR) and maintained fairly large numbers in South Dakota. They arrived at Huron on November 16, reached a peak of between 50 and 60 individuals there on November 28 and began to dwindle on December 21 (JWJ). They were common in the spruce trees at Waubay Wildlife Refuge during December and early January (JCC) and were present in flocks of 10 to 25 birds on March 22 at Sioux Falls. An Oregon Junco was listed at Bismarck, N. Dak., on January 5—"rare in this area," wrote Robert Randall. Lapland Longspurs were general over the southern portion of the Region with large influxes at Snake Creek Refuge, Riverdale, N. Dak., between December 23 and January 2 where they seemed to arrive just before a cold high (JJW); at Kenmare, N. Dak., on December 29 (Mrs. RG) and at Sand Lake Refuge where they were common all winter (BPS). Alfred Peterson reported flocks regularly at Brandt, S. Dak. Snow Buntings were ordinarily abundant. However, at Tewaukon National Wildlife Refuge, Cayuga, N. Dak., Kermit Dybsetter reported that observations of this species "were very uncommon."

Spring Migration, 1958

Save for occasional exceptions, the mild dry conditions attending the winter season prevailed also throughout the migration period over the Region . Temperatures reached 91° on April 16 and fell to 20° on the 28th and 29th at Huron, S. Dak., breaking previous records there for those days (U.S. Weather Bureau, Huron, S. Dak.). It was "80° or more during 15 days in May" at Kenmare, N. Dak. (Mrs. Robert Gammell). In Saskatchewan it was warm, dry and windy at Regina; at Yorkton a "mean daily high temperature of 50° was recorded from March 31 to April 20," 60° on April 7 and 70° to 80° from the 13th–15th being the highs (Dr. Robert Nero, Dr. J. Stuart Houston).

While the southern portion of the Region appeared to have adequate moisture during the early portion of the season, rainfall during the latter part was below normal almost everywhere. April precipitation was generally below normal. May was almost bone-dry with very little rain falling in South Dakota. In North Dakota a scant .50 inches was measured at Kenmare; at Riverdale conditions were "subnormal," only a trace falling during the entire two months (Mrs. RG, Jerald J. Wilson). By the end of May, dryness in northeastern Montana was becoming a matter of grave concern; many potholes had already dried up in the Moffit and Upham areas (Baine H. Cater, Homer L. Bradley, Robert Russell); in Saskatchewan, Regina reported succinctly, "No rainfall" (RN) and Dr. J. Stuart Houston at Yorkton wrote, "70 percent of the sloughs are dry."

Influenced perhaps by these conditions, the migration appeared normal in some localities and spotty and thin in others with few sudden or dramatic buildups. In general, it was a week to two weeks later than usual. Weather shifts may have caused some abrupt deviations, such as the very early appearance of

Swainson's Thrush, Myrtle Warbler and Vesper Sparrow. It also may have influenced the goose flight into South Dakota. The first large mixed flocks of Snows. Blues, and Canadas were apparently stalled in southern Iowa by a cold front still in position on March 20. A break-through of fast-moving, northward-flowing warm air on March 21 brought the concentration apparently non-stop to the lakes and sloughs near Sioux Falls, especially Beaver Lake, where they arrived on the 22nd and 23rd. According to all reports, these flocks bypassed the usual resting grounds on the Missouri River at Yankton. A few individuals arrived at Sand Lake National Wildlife Refuge, Columbia, by March 25 but a flow of warm air from the south, breaking out on April 2, probably brought the "good migration of Snows, Blues, Canadas, and White-fronts" over the refuge on that day (Bruce Stollberg, Aaron Bagg). Stollberg reported flocks of hundreds of Harris' Sparrows at the refuge on April 29, the result perhaps of a southward-moving flow of cold air which may have concentrated the birds in that area. Following several days of southerly winds, a cold rainy period with northeasterly winds on April 5 and 6 grounded an assorted "wave" of passerines in Sioux Falls, S. Dak., where 20 Golden-crowned Kinglets (a larger-than-usual count), 21 Hermit Thrushes, a Myrtle Warbler, and nine Fox Sparrows (an unusually high count for the vicinity) were observed in a regularly checked area. None of these species was noted in a check on April 4. The Myrtle Warbler appeared a week earlier than the average of April 14, based on a nine-year record (HK). A Vesper Sparrow singing on April 7 was another early appearance. On April 20 a wave of Robins was grounded at Regina, Sask., probably because of northeasterly winds which resulted from a storm center to the south (RN, AB). While all reporting points indicated a thin warbler migration, especially a noteworthy scarcity of Myrtle Warblers, the extremely dry, low-water conditions seemed to favor the shorebird movement (Lawrence Summers, JJW, RN).

Grebes, Pelicans, and Herons— Horned and Eared Grebes were numerous in the Dakotas and northwestern Montana. A marked build-up of the Western Grebe occurred at Sand Lake Refuge, Columbia, S. Dak., on April 28 (BPS). The White Pelican seems to be down from last year's numbers. A Common Egret in flight was observed at Regina, Sask. on April 25 (RN). Bradley's comment that the American Bittern at Long Lake National Wildlife Refuge, Moffit, N. Dak., "has been dropping slowly for several years" seems to be borne out by reports from other stations in the Region, although Lowry Elliott, Milbank, S. Dak., noted "more bittern than usual" this season.

Waterfowl— Whistling Swans were observed at many points, and they doubled their number over last year at Bowdoin National Wildlife Refuge, Malta, Mont. (BHC). The goose migration was much less spectacular than usual in the Dakotas, despite large flocks at De Smet and Lake Preston, S. Dak., on April 12 (J.W. Johnson) and a band of migration on April 14 "approximately seven miles wide moving against prevailing northwest winds," reported by Jerald J. Wilson at Snake Creek National Wildlife Refuge, Riverdale, N. Dak.

Noteworthy was the bypassing of the traditional resting grounds on the Missouri River in the Yankton, S. Dak., area by nearly the entire goose flight. The duck migration was fairly regular with a heavy scaup flight reported in eastern South Dakota in late April (JJC) and exceptionally large waves of Blue-winged Teal observed the first week of May at Long Lake Refuge, Moffit, N. Dak., and in mid-May at Lake Andes National Wildlife Refuge, Lake Andes, S. Dak. (HLB, David C. McGlaughlin).

Hawks and Cranes— Although few hawks were sighted generally in the Region and a scarcity of Marsh Hawks was noteworthy in the Huron, S. Dak., vicinity (JWJ), there was a wave of Red-tails in Saskatchewan on April 13 at Spirit Lake (William Anaka) and on the 15th at Regina (RN). A heavy migration of Sparrow and Swainson's Hawks took place on the 24th and 25th at LaCreek National Wildlife Refuge, Martin, S. Dak. (Charles A. Hughlett). Four Whooping Cranes flying low over Kenmare, N. Dak., were observed on April 12 by Dr. L.E. McCulley. This seems to be the only report of this species for the season (Mrs. RG). Steady movements of the Sandhill Crane occurred in South Dakota at LaCreek Refuge on April 12; in North Dakota at Snake Creek Refuge, Riverdale, and Lostwood National Wildlife Refuge, Lostwood, on the 14th; at Long Lake Refuge, Moffit, on the 15th and at Kenmare on the 16th (CAH, JJW, RRJ, HLB, Mrs. RG). On the 15th a wave of this species appeared at Regina, Sask. (RN).

Shorebirds— In general, the moister eastern sections of the Region reported more Charadriiformes than the drier western. Semipalmated Plovers and Stilt Sandpipers were unusually plentiful at Regina (RN) . In North Dakota a flock of about 500 American Golden Plover alighted near the Tewauken Refuge and smaller numbers were sighted at Grand Forks (JCC, LS). Large flocks of shorebirds were absent from the Malta, Mont. area (BHC), but at Brandt, in eastern South Dakota, Alfred Peterson had a field day recording concentrations of sandpipers, including 91 Hudsonian Godwits and 100 Stilt Sandpipers on May 20 and 250 White-rumped Sandpipers and about 500 Dunlins on the 27th. Dr. N.R. Whitney, Jr., Rapid City, S. Dak., reports a single Whimbrel at LaCreek Refuge, Martin, S. Dak., on May 15, a new record for the state. An American Avocet was recorded at Yorkton, Sask. on the very early date of May 7 (average May 23, JSH). In South Dakota a migration of Wilson's Phalaropes took place at Sand Lake Refuge on April 29 and another on May 7 when "at least 3,000" were concentrated at Lake Andes Refuge (EPS, DC-McG). "Thousands" of Northern Phalaropes, flocks of Ruddy Turnstones and hundreds of Knots were reported from the Beaverhills Lake vicinity near Edmonton, Alta. on May 25th (Edmonton Bird Club). Black Terns peaked at Lake Andes Refuge on May 18 when about 5,000 were observed (DCMcG).

Woodpeckers, Flycatchers, and Thrushes— At Mitchell, S. Dak., a Red-bellied Woodpecker appeared on May 12 (JWJ) and a Say's Phoebe on the 2nd. The phoebe, observed for several days, may be an easternmost state record (Les

Baylor). Both birds were conspicuously out of their usual ranges. On April 25 a steady flight of Robins passed over Cranberry Portage, north of The Pas, Man., when the weather was cloudy with rain and the temperature stood at 33° (Ralph McCleary). A broad wave of Hermit Thrushes appeared in South Dakota on April 5 and 6 at Huron, Mitchell, and Sioux Falls (JWJ, Blanche Battin, HK). In North Dakota they arrived at Fargo on April 12 (J.F. Cassel, fide O.A. Stevens) and at Grand Forks on the 23rd (LS). Perhaps stormy conditions to the south influenced the occurrence of straggler Swainson's Thrushes at Columbia, S. Dak., on April 6th and at Brandt, S. Dak., on the 14th, both remarkably early dates. The main wave of Swainson's and Gray-cheeked Thrushes came May 9 at Huron and Carthage, and on May 11 at Brandt in South Dakota (JWJ, BB, Rev. and Mrs. Richard Jackson, AP), and in North Dakota at Kenmare on the 24th (Mrs. RG). A Mountain Blue-bird seen 20 miles north of Mitchell, S. Dak., on April 14 is a straggler somewhat eastward of its range (Rev. RJ).

Warblers— Although the warbler migration was very light, Tennessees, admittedly fewer than last year, were common at Sioux Fails, S. Dak., by May 10th and at Fargo, N, Dak., from the 14th to the 19th with a few at Grand Forks, N. Dak., on the 26th (HK, JFC, OAS, LS). A MacGillivray's Warbler was banded at Madison, Minn, on May 11 writes Mrs. C.E. Peterson, who first recorded this species on June 5, 1956), a first for that part of Minnesota and perhaps for the state. Both were collected and sent Dr. Breckenridge for identification. This species was also observed at Kenmare, N. Dak., on June 1 and 4, making a new record for the area (Mrs. RG). For the third year in succession Herbert Krause recorded single male Hooded Warblers at Sioux Falls, S. Dak.—apparently the first on record for eastern South Dakota and perhaps for the state.

Icterids and Fringillids— Rusty Blackbirds, normally rare at Spirit Lake, Sask. in migration were noted in flocks of "over 1,000" daily from April 13 to 17 (WA). Black-headed Grosbeaks arrived in Rapid City, S. Dak., on May 11 and 17 (Mrs. Mary Hyde, Gertrude Bachman). A Blue Grosbeak was identified twice in the Sioux Falls, S. Dak., area—an unusual occurrence if not a new record for the area (HK). Evening Grosbeaks appeared at Kenmare, N. Dak., on May 11, a rarity there (Mrs. RG). White-winged Crossbills, a dramatic feature of the winter season, were last seen at Watertown, S. Dak., on March 1 (J.O. Johnson) but were still present in small numbers at Sioux Falls on May 25 (HK). The Chestnut-collared Longspur, abundant in the Leola, S. Dak., hills (JCC), arrived in numbers in North Dakota at Tower City on April 16 (Edgar Preston) and at Grand Forks on the 19th (LS).

Nesting Season, 1958

Weather for the Region during the nesting season can be best characterized as dry and near-chilly. Except for local variations, temperatures were generally cool. In South Dakota, Huron marked up record-breaking lows for June—43° on the 24th and 39° on the 25th—and recorded the coolest July in eight years and the third coolest in 32 years (U.S. Weather Bureau, Huron; J.W. Johnson). This unseasonable coolness persisted until the latter part of July when it was succeeded by hot dry periods as far north as Yorkton, Sask. (C. Stuart Houston). Strong winds were frequent in the Columbia, S. Dak., and Riverdale, N. Dak., areas (Bruce P. Stollberg, Jerald J. Wilson). Local hailstorms, often destructive, were not unusual, though losses to nesting birds or broods were not reported. While above-normal precipitation fell in some areas, western and northern sections of the Dakotas and the Prairie Provinces remained, generally speaking, unusually dry. In South Dakota, about half the normal precipitation fell at Lake Andes National Wildlife Refuge, Lake Andes (David C. McGlaughlin). J.S. Findley wrote that Sioux Falls was inches below the average rainfall, with most sloughs dry. Almost all the potholes in the vicinity of Waubay National Wildlife Refuge, Waubay, dried up before the nesting season was well under way (John C. Carlsen). In North Dakota, rainfall was less than the average at Lostwood National Wildlife Refuge, Lostwood; low water conditions were common in the Snake Creek National Wildlife Refuge, Riverdale (George H. Gard, JJW). In Saskatchewan, Dr. C. Stuart Houston reported an extremely dry spring and summer in the Yorkton area, with surface water levels the lowest in 18 years (apologies are due to Dr. "C" Stuart Houston whose first initial is not "J", as appeared in previous reports). However, in some localities, rainfall was above normal. Lowry Elliott describes the potholes and sloughs at Milbank, S. Dak., as brimful of water. The northern portions of the prairie regions of western Minnesota received heavy downpours which brought up total precipitation. With these conditions, nesting success probably differed considerably from area to area.

Grebes, Herons— The Eared Grebe had a good year at Snake Creek Refuge in North Dakota (JJW). In South Dakota, Western Grebes were unusually successful at Sand Lake National Wildlife Refuge, Columbia, and at Huron (BPS, JWJ). White Pelicans maintained the population levels of previous years in South Dakota (JCC, JWJ) but were considerably above a three-year average at Redberry Lake, Saskatoon, Sask. (CSH). The Double-crested Cormorant, a common nester at Waubay Refuge in South Dakota and at Snake Creek Refuge in North Dakota (JCC, JJW) had the best hatch in four years at Saskatoon, Sask. (CHS). Great Blue Heron colonies at Huron, S. Dak., were smaller than usual but those at Sand Lake Refuge in the same state and those at Snake Creek Refuge in North Dakota supported about the same populations as in past years (JWJ, EPS, JWW). A single Yellow-crowned Night Heron, carefully studied by J.W. Johnson and four friends at Huron, S. Dak., on July 20, is probably the second record of this species for the state.

Geese and Ducks— In South Dakota, Canada Geese were more productive on the Waubay Refuge than in past seasons but they were less successful at Sand Lake Refuge. In North Dakota, Lostwood Refuge reported its first successful nesting of the Canada Goose; five goslings hatched on May 25th (Robert R. Johnson, GHG). Reports on puddle and diver ducks seemed to be generally unfavorable for the entire Region. In South Dakota, John C. Carlsen regarded the situation at Waubay Refuge as quite discouraging, with breeding pairs low and the success ratio of those pairs poor. Bruce Stollberg reported that general production is less than last year at Sand Lake Refuge, although some data have yet to be studied. The Blue-winged Teal, generally abundant in the state, was down in numbers in many areas, including Huron (JWJ). At Lake Andes Refuge, however, David McGlaugh-lin reported a 40 percent increase in waterfowl production. The Mallard was most abundant followed by the Blue-winged Teal, Pintail, Gadwall, Shoveler and American Widgeon. In North Dakota, waterfowl numbers appeared to be lower than last year's at Lostwood Refuge (GHG); reduced water levels greatly limited the brood production at Snake Creek Refuge (JWW). Conditions in Saskatchewan seemed to be dishearteningly unfavorable with some good sloughs near Yorkton dry for the first time in 18 years (CSH).

Upland Birds— Bobwhite, infrequently reported in South Dakota, had a second fairly good year at Lake Andes. David C. McGlaughlin wrote that this species was common in that vicinity. In South Dakota, conditions were ideal for the Ring-necked Pheasant. All state contributors agreed that hatches were good and broods abundant (JCC, EPS, DCMcG, JWJ).

Shorebirds, Gulls, Terns— Dennis Carter reported an Upland Plover in Wind Cave National Park, Custer, S. Dak., perhaps the first record there. Generally this species appeared in fewer than usual numbers at Huron, S. Dak., (JWJ) but at Snake Creek Refuge in North Dakota larger numbers of breeding pairs were observed and there appeared to be greater survival of young than has been recently noted (JJW). The Franklin's Gull was noticeably scarce in the Huron, S. Dak., area (JWJ). The Black Tern had a most advantageous year and was generally plentiful (LE, JWJ, HK).

Doves, Cuckoos, Owls— While Mourning Doves had a good season in South Dakota, they appeared to be less successful at some points in North Dakota At Snake Creek Refuge high loss resulted from predation, climatic changes and strong winds (JJW). Black-billed Cuckoos in unusual numbers were noted in South Dakota at Sioux Falls, Lake Andes, Huron and Milbank (JSF, DCMcG, JWJ, LE) but fewer were observed at Fargo, N. Dak. (O.A. Stevens). Although reports on owls were scarce, Dr. C. Stuart Houston banded 22 Great Horned Owls in ten nests at Yorkton, Sask. and Dr. N.R. Whitney, Jr., observed Short-eared Owls on the prairies bordering the eastern Black Hills area and recorded a Saw-whet Owl on July 13 near Rapid City, S. Dak.

Woodpeckers, Flycatchers— In South Dakota, Redheaded Woodpeckers were numerous in Rapid City (NRW); adults and broods of young were seen at Huron (JWJ, Blanche Battin). Black-backed Three-toed Woodpeckers were observed feeding young on July 7 and 26 at Jewel Cave National Monument, Custer, a rare breeding record for this species in South Dakota (DC, Dale Birkenholz). J.W. Johnson found the nest and young of the Eastern Phoebe at Huron, S. Dak. on June 15 and Dr. O.A. Stevens noted an Eastern Wood Pewee on August 10 at Fort Ransom in North Dakota, both observations bringing these species farther west than has been usually suspected, although the AOU Check List (Fifth Edition p. 340) includes the Black Hills of southwestern South Dakota in the range of the Eastern Phoebe. Western Flycatchers, seldom reported in South Dakota, were banded by Dr. N.R. Whitney, Jr., in three Black Hills canyon localities. Dusky Flycatchers were observed near Savoy in the same region (DC).

Jays, Wrens— Clark's Nutcracker, seldom reported from South Dakota, appeared in what can be regarded as unusually large numbers at Jewel Cave National Monument, Custer, five being sighted at late as August 5 (DC, DB, Stanley Belfore). Cañon Wrens, also very infrequently recorded in South Dakota, were both heard and seen in Hell's Canyon, Custer, on July 17 as they were at Wind Cave National Park on June 30 (DC, DB, SB).

Waxwings, Warblers— Nesting Cedar waxwings, seldom recorded in South Dakota, brooded successfully this year at Sioux Falls and at Waubay Refuge (JSF, JCC). Adult Audubon's Warblers were feeding young on July 5 near Deerfield, S. Dak., in the Black Hills (HK).

Fringillids— What may be the first nesting record of the Blue Grosbeak for northwestern South Dakota was observed at Belle Fourche National Wildlife Refuge, Belle Fourche, where three young with adults were seen on July 20 and August 4 (DC, DB). A small flock of Blue Grosbeaks, adult males and presumably females and fledglings, was seen north of Huron, S. Dak., on July 27 in a locality where this bird is rare to unknown (JWJ). The Dickcissel, Chestnut-collared Longspur and Lark Sparrow were generally at about the same level as last year. In the Black Hills at Deerfield, S. Dak. Herbert Krause counted 12 adult Red Crossbills feeding young on July 5. Young and adults were congregated in Ponderosa Pines. Lark Buntings, usually abundant in the central and western portions of South Dakota, were scarce west of Huron and remained so as far as Highmore, 70 miles westward (JWJ). Nine nests of the White-winged Junco were found in areas near Rapid City, S. Dak., and all but one were known to have fledged young successfully (NRW).

Fall Migration, 1958

Dried-up sloughs and ponds, receding water in larger lakes, and higher-than-normal temperatures were the rule in the Region from Alberta to South Dakota, despite some local rains. A well-established slough near Saskatoon, Sask., where up to 100 Whistling Swans might be seen regularly in April, "disappeared bore a fine crop of oats by August 31," wrote Dr. M. Bremner and J.F.

Roy. In South Dakota the U.S. Weather Bureau at Huron, reported the driest August since 1925 and September as the sixth month below normal precipitation (J.W. Johnson). Strong winds at Fort Peck Game Range, Lewistown, Mont. (Eugene D. Stroops) and at Tewaukon National Wildlife Refuge, Cayuga, N. Dak. (Kermit D. Dybsetter) helped to evaporate shallow waters. Temperatures were generally above normal, in North Dakota reaching 108° in August, 93° in September and 81° in October at Des Lacs National Wildlife Refuge (Homer L. Bradley). South Dakota's highs included 95° on September 8 while in October, four previous heat records were broken (JWJ). Edmonton, Alta. had a mild open fall with most of the lakes unfrozen until mid-November (Edmonton Bird Club). In Saskatchewan lakes were still open at Yorkton on November 11 (C. Stuart Houston) and at Spirit Lake on November 18 (Wm. Anaka). November brought cooler temperatures, general snow with locally heavy covers, and cold fronts in southern Saskatchewan, the Dakotas and Montana. Perhaps these meteorological vagaries explain the generally prolonged and thin migration. There were no major cold fronts until late in November and few if any dramatic build-ups or concentrations.

Loons, Herons— The first record of a Common Loon at Tewaukon Refuge, Cayuga, N. Dak., was made on November 6 (KDD). Eared and Western Grebes were relatively scarce at Des Lacs Refuge, Kenmare, N. Dak. (HLB). The White Pelican increased at this refuge, peaking at 750 on September 2 as compared with 225 in 1957 (HLB). They were about normal at Sand Lake National Wildlife Refuge, Columbia, S. Dak., but considerably below last year's numbers (Bruce P. Stollberg). Double-crested Cormorants spent the last week of October at Fort Peck Game Range, Mont. (EDS); they were down from last year's figures at Sand Lake Refuge, S. Dak. (BPS). Great Blue Herons were relatively scarce at Des Lacs Refuge, N. Dak., but in South Dakota they were plentiful at Milbank, Sand Lake Refuge, Columbia, and Sioux Falls (HLB, Lowry Elliott, BPS, J. Scott Findley). Reports indicate that Common Egrets seem to be extending their range into northeastern South Dakota, appearing at Sand Lake Refuge in mid-June, at Milbank on August 8 and October 25, when 12 were sighted (LE) and at Brandt on August 3 and September 6 (Alfred Peterson). A first record for a Green Heron, not reported for the last period, was noted at Tewaukon Refuge, N. Dak. (KDD). The American Bittern was fairly scarce in the Kenmare, N. Dak., vicinity but seemed to be increasing at Milbank, S. Dak. (HLB, LE).

Swans, Geese— Whistling Swans, arriving later than usual, were still lingering at Regina, Sask. on November 16 (Fred W. Lahrman). They were tardy by a month at Des Lacs Refuge, N. Dak., (HLB) and at Sand Lake Refuge, S. Dak., where the number of young per adult indicated a probable poor production year for the groups gathered there (BPS). In North Dakota no build-up of Canada Geese occurred at Snake Creek National Wildlife Refuge, Riverdale, where the peak was below previous years (Jerald J. Wilson) but at Tewaukon

Refuge there was a strong movement during October 21–23 and a peak on the 25th with a slight increase over the previous years (KDD). At Bowdoin National Wildlife Refuge, Malta, Mont., the goose population peaked on October 10 (Baine H. Cater). In North Dakota White-fronted Geese were up at Des Lacs Refuge (HLB) but considerably below last year's totals at Lower Souris National Wildlife Refuge, Upham (Robert R. Johnson). Bruce P. Stollberg wrote from Sand Lake Refuge, S. Dak., that a Ross' Goose was collected and positively identified there this fall.

Waterfowl– In spite of some sportsmen's optimism, listening-post figures seem to indicate that the duck migration was generally down. In the Spirit Lake, Sask. Area, William Anaka considers the local numbers of Mallards to be less than half of those in previous seasons. In North Dakota a poor migration went through Tewaukon Refuge, Cayuga, where 4,500 Mallards were totaled this fall compared with 60,000 a year ago (wrote Kermit D. Dybsetter). Homer L. Bradley states that at Des Lacs Refuge, Kenmare, Mallards were drastically reduced, a peak of 7,855 on October 30 comparing with 25,000 on October 25 last year; the Gadwall population low, Pintail, exceptionally low; Green-winged Teal were down (840 on September 19 for the peak as compared to 1,500 on October 25 in 1957); Blue-winged Teal were relatively scarce; Shovelers decreased, with a peak of 230 on September 12 compared to 1,500 on October 25 last year. In South Dakota, the Mallard was the most numerous species at Waubay National Wildlife Refuge, Waubay, followed by Lesser Scaup and Pintail (John C. Carlsen). The peak of the duck migration at Sand Lake Refuge, Columbia, took place on November 16–22 (EPS). Divers were hard to find at Milbank (LE). Major waterfowl movements occurred at Lake Andes National Wildlife Refuge, Lake Andes, on October 5–6 and November 15 (David C. McGlauchlin). In Montana the peak population of divers was considerably lower than for several seasons past at Bowdoin Refuge, Malta (BHC). Fort Peck Game Range found a noticeable decrease in most species of ducks (EDS).

Hawks– Unusual numbers of Sharp-shinned and Cooper's Hawks were spotted at Tewaukon Refuge, N. Dak., this fall (KDD). In South Dakota many hawks were aloft in the Milbank vicinity (LE) while at Waubay Refuge several (Krider's) Red-tails and up to 15 Rough-legs were recorded (JJC). However, in the Sioux Falls area, hawks were practically nonexistent (JSF, Herbert Krause). A small flight of Swainson's Hawks was sighted at Lower Souris Refuge, N. Dak., on September 9 (RRJ). Winter populations of Golden Eagles were building up at Fort Peck Game Range during mid-October (EDS). In an aerial survey on the Missouri River near Lake Andes, S. Dak., 11 Bald Eagles were counted on November 4 (DCMcG). Sparrow Hawk concentrations were noticed at Edmonton, Alta. on August 29 (EEC) and at Regina, Sask. on September 1 (FWL). At Bowdoin Refuge, Mont. six Peregrine Falcons were observed on September 4 (BHC).

Gallinaceous Birds— Single Prairie Chickens were seen at Tower City, N. Dak., the first in a couple of years (Edgar Preston), and at Sand Lake Refuge, S. Dak. (Elmer Podell, *fide* BPS).

Cranes— In Saskatchewan two adult and two young Whooping Cranes were observed in the Ceepee-Langham district, October 3–21, and at Buffalo Pound on October 15 (FWL). Two adults and two young were watched many times along the North Saskatchewan River northwest of Saskatoon during early October, probably forced to the river by dried-up remote interior sloughs (RMB, JFR). Some 7,000 Sandhill Cranes were seen at Regina, Sask. on August 15 (FWL); flocks remained at Saskatoon during the first three weeks of September (RMB, JFR); and at Spirit Lake until September 11 (WA). In North Dakota they were seen at Upham as early as August 13 and as late as the last of September (RRJ); at Kenmare from September 12 to October 12; at Snake Creek Refuge, Riverdale, in a mass movement on October 7 (JJW). In Montana small flocks swept over Malta on October 3 and October 11 (BHC) and at Fort Peck Game Range on October 20–23, a week late (EDS). In South Dakota they were over Rapid City on September 27 and 28 (R.N. Whitney, Jr.) and at Sand Lake Refuge on November 5 and 6, "the best migration in quite a few years," concluded Bruce P. Stollberg. A straggler was sighted in a cornfield near Sioux Falls on December 5 (Barney Ordal, *fide* HK).

Shorebirds— Shorebirds in varying numbers were found wherever receding lakes and sloughs left suitable mud flats. Sernipalmated Plovers were numerous at Edmonton, Alta. on August 2 (EBC). Alfred Peterson observed 14 American Golden Plover at Brandt, S. Dak., on September 28 and 1 on November l, the only reports of this species for the period. However, Black-bellied Plover were in evidence at Yorkton, Sask. on September 28 (CSH) and were still present at Regina on November 1 (FWL). In South Dakota three were observed at Milbank on November 14 just before a snowstorm (LE), and several at Brandt on September 2 and October 13 (AP). Common Snipe apparently are increasing. In South Dakota there were distinct movements at Sand Lake Refuge on October 10 (BPS) and at Brandt on September 28 and October 8 (AP); they were abundant at Milbank (LE) and were reported near Huron—two on September 28 where they have not been seen recently (JWJ). But at Snake Creek Refuge, N. Dak., they were direly reduced—only two birds seen during the fall, on September 20, compared with a high of 100 in 1956 (JJW).

Gulls and Terns— On October 7, a Bonaparte's Gull was carefully studied by Alfred Peterson near Brandt, S. Dak. —an uncommon appearance. Near Billings, Mont., seven Caspian Terns were reported at Rattlesnake Lake (Mrs. Phillip Hendricks).

Owls through Woodpeckers— Snowy Owls were first noted on October 21, then occasionally, at Lower Souris Refuge, N. Dak. (RRJ). At Brandt, S. Dak., two adult and four young Burrowing Owls were recorded—a species almost rare in eastern South Dakota (AP). Chimney Swifts were last sighted on August 21 at Fargo, N. Dak., although they were still wheeling over Sioux Falls, S. Dak., as late as September 17 (HK). Black-backed Three-toed Woodpeckers, still decidedly uncommon in South Dakota, were identified in Jewel Cave National Monument in the southern Black Hills by Dennis Carter who saw females on August 15 and 28. Another individual was seen on August 24 at Hill City (NRW, Jr.). A Northern Three-toed Woodpecker was collected in the northern Black Hills and examined by Dr. N.R. Whitney, Jr., on August 20.

Flycatchers, Magpies, Nuthatches— An excellent movement of Empidonax flycatchers came through Kenmare, N. Dak., during August 19–24, while an Olive-sided Flycatcher, a bird seldom seen in the area, was recorded on August 22 (Mrs. RG). Judging by reports, Black-billed Magpies seem to be extending their range eastward. They were seen at Tower City, N. Dak., where until last year they apparently had never been observed (EP). In South Dakota a flock of 19 was seen at Sand Lake Refuge on October 20—an unusually large number for the area—and at Waubay Refuge flocks comprising up to 30 individuals were counted regularly (BPS, JCC). They were also fairly common in the Huron area (JWJ). Pigmy Nuthatches, seldom seen in South Dakota, were carefully studied and identified at Jewel Cave Monument on August 24 (DC).

Mockers, Thrushes— A Mockingbird was observed daily in Parshall, N. Dak., between November 4–11 (Mr. and Mrs. R. Nordby, Dr. and Mrs. R. Gammell). An unusual appearance was a Townsend's Solitaire seen at close range at Iroquois, S. Dak., on September 14 (JWJ). A Brown Thrasher remained at Billings, Mont., until September 11 (Mrs. PH). Nine Gray-cheeked Thrushes were banded at Yorkton, Sask. on September 18—"A big wave for them" (CSH). In eastern South Dakota more than the usual number of Eastern Bluebirds—actually becoming an uncommon bird in the state—were present from September to mid-October at Waubay Refuge and at Milbank (JJC, LE).

Warblers— The warbler migration reached a height at Saskatoon, Sask. during August 20–24, following a heavy rainstorm—in an area where "warblers are a rarity at any time" (RMB, JFR). In Edmonton, Alta. the peak was attained during September 14–20 (EEC); at Kenmare, N. Dak., large waves were recorded on August 19–20, September 10–12, 18 (Mrs. RG). In South Dakota marked warbler advances arrived at Sand Lake Refuge during August 5–11 but at Huron and Sioux Falls the migration was rather thin as to numbers if fairly satisfactory as to number of species (BPS, JWJ, JSF, HK). Nashville Warblers were banded at Brookings, S. Dak., on September 10 (Mrs. David Holden). For the third year in succession, male Black-throated Blue Warblers were identified at Sioux Falls, this year on September 15 (HK). A male was seen at Brookings on November 4—a late date indeed (Oreena Cooper). Myrtle Warblers, almost rare in last spring's migration, were abundant at Edmonton, Alta. during September 14–16, scarce at Saskatoon and few at Yorkton, Sask. between September 9 and 24; they were inconspicuous at Spirit Lake until October 12; they came in good waves at Kenmare, N. Dak., during September 9–11, although not in the usually expected numbers. In South Dakota they were better than usual at Winner, below normal at Huron and Brandt and straggling along thinly at Sioux Falls until with dramatic suddenness they leaped from four on September 3 to 71 on September 4, then declined rapidly (BBC, RMB, JFR, CSH, WA, Mrs. RG, Harold Wager, JWJ, Blanche Battin, AP, JSF, HK). Black-throated Green Warblers, seldom seen in Kenmare, N. Dak., were identified there on September 18 and October 20 (Mrs. RG). Blackburnian and Bay-breasted Warblers were spotted at Sioux Falls on September 9 and 10 (HK). Canada Warblers, extremely rare in the Kenmare, N. Dak., area, were the highlight of the warbler migration there, as many as five at one time being seen during waves on August 19 and 20. They were seen occasionally in Sioux Falls, S. Dak., during September 5–11 (Mrs. RG, HK). The Wilson's Warbler is not listed for the Black Hills area but single birds at Jewel Cave Monument were sighted between August 20–30 and on September 1 (DC). On September 21 an unusual concentration of better than 1,000 Brown-headed Cowbirds was found in a pasture near Sioux Falls, S. Dak. (Mr. and Mrs. H.F. Chapman HK).

Fringillids— Two broods of the Blue Grosbeak apparently were raised at Huron, S. Dak., this season in an area where they are not considered residents; adults and young were seen between August 18 and 31 (JWJ). Evening Grosbeaks were sighted at Huron on October 19 and at Sioux Falls on September 25 (JWJ, HK), but there were no reports of White-winged Crossbills, this season. In Montana total populations of Lark Buntings were lower than usual at Fort Peck Game Range (EDS). Tree Sparrows "poured" into Edmonton, Alta. on September 19 (EEC), came in large numbers into Regina, Sask. (FWL) but were rare at Yorkton (CSH). Clay-colored Sparrows appeared in large numbers at Regina on September 1 (FWL); at Kenmare, N. Dak., in a main movement on September 7 (Mrs. RG); and in small numbers in South Dakota at Huron between September 27 and October 3 (JWJ). At Sioux Falls, where they and the Chipping Sparrow are usually very abundant, they were exceptional by their conspicuous absence (HK). Fox Sparrows, the "first in fourteen years at Yorkton, Sask.," were banded there on September 24 and October 11 (CSH); considered uncommon at Kenmare, N. Dak., they were observed there on October 6 and 7. They appeared at Sioux Falls, S. Dak., on October 16 (Mrs. RG, HK). White-crowned Sparrows were noticeably decreased at Spirit Lake, Sask., Wash., were seen in small numbers at Kenmare, N. Dak., (Mrs. RG) and in South Dakota, were notable for their scarceness at Huron (JWJ) and rare at Sioux Falls.

Winter Season, 1958–1959

Except for local variations, the Region had dry weather for the period, few if any severe snowstorms and especially in the northern areas, colder than normal temperatures during January and the first weeks of February. The winter was generally "open" with below precipitation almost everywhere, although snow was light to average at Billings, Mont. (Mrs. Philip Hendricks) and the heaviest in ten years at Medora, N. Dak., a notable exception (Arthur Bennett). In South Dakota the season was one of the driest in 70 years of record, according to W.T. Hodge, state climatologist. The most noteworthy events were the irruption of Bohemian Waxwings throughout the Region and the continued presence in unusual numbers of the Black-billed Magpies in the eastern portions.

Swans, Geese, Ducks— During Montana's annual midwinter census, 324 Trumpeter Swans were counted as compared with 216 in 1958 (Montana Fish and Game Dept.). Approximately 200 of the 13,000 Canada Geese wintering at Red Lake, near Chamberlain, S. Dak., were killed, apparently by botulism: victims, perhaps, of a by-product of drought and receding waters. A new high in waterfowl numbers was recorded on the Fort Randall Reservoir near Lake Andes, S. Dak., when more than a million and a half Mallards were counted on December 1 (David McGlaughlin). In South Dakota a Wood Duck at Lake Andes, a Ring-necked Duck at LaCreek National Wildlife Refuge, Martin, and a Hooded Merganser at Rapid City were seen on Christmas Counts (DMcG, Charles Hughlett, Dr. N.R. Whitney, Jr.).

Hawks, Eagles— A second winter record of Pigeon Hawks was obtained for the Yorkton, Sask., area on December 24 and 26 (Dr. Stuart Houston). In Montana Bald Eagles were up in the midwinter census (Mont. FGD); 65 were observed with 35 Golden Eagles on a February aerial survey over the Missouri River between Vermillion and Pickstown, S. Dak. (DMcG).

Gallinaceous Birds— Ruffed Grouse wintered well at Edmonton, Alta. and at Saskatoon and Yorkton, Sask. with larger numbers than usual (Edmonton Bird Club, Dr. Ronald Bremner, SH). The declining Prairie Chicken was noticed several times at Tower City, N. Dak., and once at Sand Lake National Wildlife Refuge, Columbia, S. Dak. (Edgar Preston, Bruce C. Stollberg). The Sharp-tailed Grouse and Gray Partridge, surviving the winter, were more numerous than for some years at Edmonton, Alta. and in good supply at Saskatoon and Yorkton, Sask., (EEC, RB, SH). In North Dakota they were fairly conspicuous at Des Lacs National Wildlife Refuge, Kenmare; suffered little kill-off at Lostwood National Wildlife Refuge, Lostwood, and were up in numbers from the last few years at Arrowwood National Wildlife Refuge, Kensal, where Sharp-tailed Grouse were observed dancing on one of the established grounds on December 31 (Homer Bradley, George Gard, John Frye). A few Gray Partridges were sighted at Sand Lake Refuge, Columbia, S. Dak. (BCS).

Coot, Snipe— In South Dakota four American Coot wintered at Lake Andes Refuge where 35 were seen on the Christmas Count (DMcG); from one to three Common Snipe were observed all winter at a disposal plant at Huron (J.W. Johnson).

Owls— Six species of owls were recorded. Eleven Great Horned Owls were included in the Christmas Count at Sand Lake Refuge (BCS). Snowy Owls were fairly common at Edmonton, Alta. (EEC), but rare or sporadic at Regina, Saskatoon, Spirit Lake and Yorkton, Sask. (Saskatchewan Museum of Natural History, RB, Wm. Anaka, SH). In North Dakota they were common on Lower Souris National Wildlife Refuge, Upham, but scarce elsewhere, only one being seen at Grand Forks on the Christmas Count; one at Tewaukon Refuge, Cayuga, and one on January 31 at Snake Creek National Wildlife Refuge, Coleharbor; and at Arrowwood Wildlife Refuge, Kensal, the smallest number in many years were recorded (LeRoy W. Sowl, Lawrence Summers, Kenneth Dybsetter, Jerald Wilson, JF). None was observed at Bowdoin National Wildlife Refuge, Malta, Mont. (Baine Cater). In South Dakota they were very scarce everywhere. Two Burrowing Owls, most uncommon in winter, were identified on the Christmas Count at Rapid City (Roland Gray, *fide* NRW). Long-eared and Short-eared Owls seemed to be in usual numbers but at LaCreek Wildlife Refuge, 13 were listed on the Christmas Count (CH). Noteworthy was the appearance during February at Theodore Roosevelt National Park, Medora, N. Dak., of a Boreal Owl which ate mice that had been killed and put on a post by a ranchhand. Several times that owl was fed hamburger (AB).

Woodpeckers, Jays, Magpies— The Red-shafted Flicker appeared in smaller numbers than usual at Billings, Mont. (Mrs. PH); its presence at Huron, S. Dak., was unusual (JWJ). In South Dakota the four Red-bellied Woodpeckers identified along the Big Sioux River near Brookings seem to be somewhat north of their usual range; three also were seen on the Christmas Count at Sioux Falls (Mrs. David Holden, Willard Rosine). After an absence from the Spirit Lake area during the preceding two winters, the Gray Jay reappeared late in October and remained through the winter (WA), Black-billed Magpies were widely scattered. They were at an all-time high at Yorkton, Sask. (SH); in North Dakota there were many reports at Fargo; at Tewaukon Refuge, Cayuga, two were noticed, the first since 1956 (O.A. Stevens, KD); in South Dakota they were in considerably higher numbers than normal at Sand Lake Refuge; they appeared in smaller numbers at Waubay National Wildlife Refuge, Waubay, and on the Christmas Count at Sioux Falls, where they are extremely uncommon (BCS, John Carlsen, WR, HK).

Nuthatches, Thrushes— The White-breasted Nuthatch, rare in Alberta, was seen on numerous occasions in Edmonton. "There are but few authentic records and no specimens," wrote Robert Lister for E.B.C. At a disposal plant at Huron, S. Dak., as many as 110 Robins were feeding on earthworms which warm water brought up through the sludge; and a Townsend's Solitaire wintered there, an unusual occurrence (JWJ).

Waxwings— The Bohemian Waxwing irruption was as spectacular this winter as the White-winged Crossbill's was last season. They appeared at Edmonton,

Alta., in large numbers during November and December, feeding on Mountain Ash, and were still present in March (E.B.C.). In Saskatchewan flocks seemed larger than usual at Saskatoon but smaller at Regina (RB, S.M.N.H.). In North Dakota large concentrations at Kenmare fed daily on Russian Olive berries in early December; they appeared in November at Fargo and in December at Grand Forks but not until February at Dickinson; they appeared at Lower Souris Wildlife Refuge, Upham, remaining until the last week in February, and at Arrowwood Wildlife Refuge, Kensal, in flocks of 50 throughout the period (Mrs. Robert Gammell, OAS, LS, D.M. Noetzel, *fide* OAS, LWS, JF). In Montana they were observed at Bowdoin Wildlife Refuge (BC) and in Billings flocks were common from December 8 to March 23, some of the birds being so tame "they took currants from the hand," wrote Mrs. Philip Hendricks. In South Dakota they were listed on the Christmas Count at Waubay; they came in flocks of up to a hundred or more at Milbank, where they fed on frozen crab apples; were present at Brookings and Rapid City in some numbers; were on the Christmas Count in Yankton and remained in Sioux Falls until at least March 18, where their principal food seemed to be mulberries (JC, Lowry Elliott, JWJ, Mrs. DH, NRW, Willis Hall, J. Scott Findley, HK).

Blackbirds, Grosbeaks, Crossbills— Rusty Blackbirds appeared much out of their usual winter range, one being listed on the Christmas Count at Regina (S.M.N.H.) and another at Kenmare, N. Dak. (Mrs. RG). More Evening Grosbeaks were seen at Yorkton, Sask., than have been seen there for many years (SH) ; they were in fair numbers at Edmonton, Alta., and in small numbers at Spirit Lake, Sask. (EEC, WA). Nine were banded out of flocks numbering as high as 30 at Kenmare, N. Dak. (Mrs. RG). Pine Grosbeaks were scarce at most reporting stations. White-winged Crossbills, infrequently observed at Spirit Lake, Sask., where there are no natural evergreens, were noted on March 20.

Pine Siskins, Goldfinches, Redpolls— Conspicuously unreported elsewhere, two Pine Siskins were included on the Christmas Count at Huron and half a dozen appeared at Brandt in South Dakota (JWJ, Alfred Peterson). American Goldfinches, not reported from other stations, appeared at seven localities in South Dakota, where 82 appeared on the Christmas Count at Madison and as many as 200 were observed at Milbank (Dennis Doerr, LE). Redpolls were noteworthily absent in most areas; they were not nearly as common as usual at Edmonton, Alta., and had decreased in numbers from the previous year at Spirit Lake, Sask. (EEC, WA). In North Dakota they were present in large flocks at Arrowwood Wildlife Refuge, Kensal (JF), but apparently were scarce elsewhere. They were reported as rare at Huron (JWJ) and in small numbers if at all present in other South Dakota areas. Hoary Redpolls were observed at Lower Souris Wildlife Refuge, Upham, N. Dak on March 13 (LWS).

Sparrows, Longspurs, Buntings— Several Song Sparrows remained for the winter in the Region. In South Dakota they were seen at Rapid City, Lake Andes

Wildlife Refuge and Sioux Falls (NRW, DMcG, WS). One was included in the Christmas Count at Regina, Sask. (EEC). Tree Sparrows were in usual numbers except at Snake Creek Wildlife Refuge, Coleharbor, N. Dak., where upwards of 2,000 were noted, March 21–29 (JW). Two Harris' Sparrows remained most of the winter at Brookings, S. Dak. (Mrs. DH). Lapland Longspurs, not exceptionally plentiful elsewhere, were observed in larger numbers than during the past two winters at Tewaukon Refuge, Cayuga, N. Dak. (KD). Snow Buntings, in small supply generally, were concentrated in several areas in North Dakota, especially at Tewaukon Refuge, Cayuga, where more were seen than in the past two winters (KD); at Arrowwood Wildlife Refuge, Kensal, N. Dak., where they were commonly observed (JF); and at Tower City where on February 15 some 250,000 birds were seen in a stubble field. When they were flushed, "the noise of the flight could be heard in the car with doors closed," wrote Edgar Preston.

Spring Migration, 1959

Spring in the Region was characterized by a dry April, little spring run-off, water areas shrinking or disappearing, and a few abnormally warm days followed by longer periods of cooler weather. May, too, was generally dry with rain coming in any quantity only during the last weeks. The U.S. Weather Bureau at Huron, S. Dak., reported the driest April since 1952 and the seventh driest on record (J.W. Johnson). In Saskatchewan late snow storms at Spirit Lake on May 6 and 12, with strong, prolonged cold winds but comparatively little snow, apparently affected flycatchers, swallows and thrushes (William Anaka). In Montana, April precipitation was 50 percent of normal and May 75 percent at Fort Peck Game Range (Philip Lehenbauer). But at Malta and Billings, April temperatures were near normal and moisture above average, though May brought cooler weather and less moisture (Mrs. Philip Hendricks, Baine Cater). In North Dakota hailstones, golf-ball size, struck at Tewaukon National Wildlife Refuge, Cayuga, on May 4, killing an estimated 100 Blue and Snow Geese (Kermit Dybsetter). Another storm damaged nesting species at Snake Creek National Wildlife Refuge, Coleharbor, on May 24 (Jerold Wilson).

Grebes, Pelican, Herons— The largest number of Western Grebes in the past four years appeared at Tewaukon Refuge the last week in April (KD). In Montana, White Pelicans at Bowdoin National Wildlife Refuge, Malta, were up about 52 percent over previous years (BC) but definitely down from last year at Fort Peck Game Range (PL). Gratifyingly enough the Great Blue Heron reportedly increased at Bowdoin Refuge (BC); large evening movements during May appeared near Fort Peck Game Range with numbers up (PL). The Snowy Egret appearing at Medicine Lake National Wildlife Refuge, Medicine Lake, Mont., on May 23 and reported by Elmo Adams, apparently was considerably north of its general range (AOU Check List, 1957:48). Though not a "first" for South Dakota, the Yellow-crowned Night Heron found dead at DeSmet approximately May 12 was at least 150 miles (crow-flight) north of its first occurrence in the state (JW).

Swans, Geese, Ducks— Whistling Swans were more common than usual at Spirit Lake, Sask., April 19 to 29 (WA). About 300 were seen on lakes near Alice, N. Dak., on April 2 (Edgar Preston) but at Bowdoin Refuge in Montana their numbers were lower than last year's (BC). The goose migration appeared about normal. An estimated 350,000 Blue-Snows were concentrated at DeSmet, S. Dak., on March 27 (FWS Report, Central Fly way; HK). However, geese seem to be avoiding the traditional resting grounds along the Missouri River between Yankton and Vermilion, S. Dak., possibly because of impoundment disturbances. "Fewer geese than last year used the Sand Lake National Wildlife Refuge, at Columbia, S. Dak., this spring," writes James Monnie. They were particularly low in numbers at Regina, Sask., as compared to recent years (F.W. Lahrman). However, they peaked at the highest population recorded to date at Tewaukon Refuge, Cayuga, N. Dak. (KD), north and east of Sand Lake. Waterfowl populations were down about 50 percent from 1958 at Sand Lake Refuge (JM). Ducks of all species increased in numbers the first ten days of April at Bowdoin Refuge, Malta. Exceptions were Lesser Scaup and Common Goldeneye, both down (BC). Over-all use was above last year's at Fort Peck Game Range, but Mallard, American Widgeon and Lesser Scaup decreased (PL). Elsewhere, however, the general duck migration was singularly unspectacular. In South Dakota Pintails were definitely below normal at Brandt and Huron but there was a substantial movement on March 19 at Sand Lake Refuge (Alfred Peterson, Mrs. H.M. Pierce, JM). Green-winged Teal were in great "abundance" at Brookings, S. Dak., (Mrs. David Holden) but reported as usual elsewhere. The Wood Duck seen during the last half of May at Saskatoon, Sask., was the first for the area (Frank Ray).

Hawks, Cranes— A minor flight of Cooper's Hawks occurred on April 19 at Spirit Lake, Sask. (WA). A Krider's Hawk was identified at Waubay National Wildlife Refuge, Waubay, S. Dak., on May 3 (John Carlsen). The sighting of Whooping Cranes on April 25 was the highlight of the season at Lower Souris National Wildlife Refuge, Upham, N. Dak. (Lloyd Halverson, *fide* LeRoy Sowl). Two Sandhill Cranes, uncommon in the Billings, Mont., area, were reported at Rattlesnake Lake on April 29 (Mrs. PH).

Shorebirds— Admittedly becoming scarce in South Dakota, Long-billed Curlews were seen on April 12 north of Rapid City in the same locality where several were noted on April 13, 1958 (Richard Hurd). Sixteen Stilt Sandpipers were carefully identified by Dennis Carter on May 16 along Lewis and Clark Lake near Yankton, S. Dak. Seventy-one American Avocets in an area of less than 1/4 acre at Arrowwood National Wildlife Refuge, Kensal, N. Dak., on April 28—"quite a sight," writes John Frye. Forty-five were counted in the Webster-Waubay area in South Dakota on May 2 and 3 (Herman Chilson, HK). Other concentrations were reported at Snake Creek Refuge, Coleharbor, N.

Dak., on May 6 (JW). A Black-necked Stilt, carefully observed by a dozen experienced hands at Huron, S. Dak., on May 23, marks a second record for the state (JWJ, Blanche Battin, Mrs. HMP, *et al.*). Three Northern Phalaropes noted at Brandt, S. Dak., on May 25, provide further evidence that this species probably migrates regularly if unreportedly through the eastern portion of the state (AP).

Owls, Woodpeckers— Dr. Stuart Houston and two colleagues at Regina, Sask., banded 66 nestling owls—presumably Great Horns—by May 27. "A good year for owls," the Doctor writes. The Red-bellied Woodpecker collected at Regina on May 23, marks a first Saskatchewan record (FWL).

Wrens, Thrushes, Pipits, Waxwings— A Cañon Wren singing in the Hot Springs, S. Dak., vicinity on March 22, was an uncommon occurrence (N.R. Whitney, Jr.). Swainson's Thrush reached peak numbers at Saskatoon, Sask., May 11 to 18 (FR); the woods along the Yellowstone River at Billings, Mont., seemed "alive" with them on May 23, reports Mrs. Philip Hendricks. Five Water Pipits were observed at Brandt, S. Dak., on May 2 (AP). A wave of Cedar Waxwings, described as in "hundreds," invaded the Webster, S. Dak., area on May 31 (HC).

Warblers— Generally, another sorry warbler season, except for a sudden irruption in Sioux Falls and Brookings, S. Dak., where after several days of southerly winds, a cold front with an electrical storm followed by cold drizzly rain and low temperatures drove in from the north on May 19 and apparently "grounded" hundreds of warblers and vireos. Canada Warblers, Mourning, Bay-breasted, Chestnut-sided, Magnolias, all scarce spring migrants in the Sioux Falls area, were remarkably numerous on May 20 and 21. As many as ten Canadas and 15 Mourning Warblers were counted—a substantial "wave" for the area. Tennessee and Blackpolls appeared by the scores (HK). A similar but apparently smaller wave, including several Connecticut Warblers, struck Brookings on the 20th (Mrs. DH). Tennessee Warblers were common in Fargo, N. Dak., during May 22 to 29 (O.A. Stevens). An Orange-crowned Warbler, uncommon in Billings, Mont., was observed feeding on May 20 and 21 (Mrs. PH). Myrtle Warblers, generally numerous and early, were few and late. They were singularly absent in the invasions at Sioux Falls and Brookings. The 12 recorded at Madison, S. Dak., between May 6 and 15 is the highest reported number for the period (Ruth Habeger). In North Dakota they were seen at Medora in the Badlands on May 1 and several were still present at Belfield in Stark County on May 25 (Arthur Henderson, Mrs. Richard Swenson). In South Dakota, Connecticut Warblers were banded at Winner, Milbank and at Brookings on May 28, indicating perhaps that this species migrates through the state more regularly than is suspected (Harold Wager, Mrs. DH, Lowry Elliott). The MacGillivray's Warbler banded by Lowry Elliott at Milbank, S. Dak., in the northeastern part of the state, is probably a new record for the eastern part of South Dakota. A Yellow-breasted Chat, noted at Tewaukon

Refuge, Cayuga, N. Dak., on May 29, is a first for the refuge (KD). Male Hooded Warblers have been noted previously in the Sioux Falls, S. Dak., area (*Audubon Field Notes* 12(4):364); but the female Hooded Warbler was apparently observed and identified for the first time there on May 6 (HK). Three Wilson's Warblers seen at Upham, N. Dak., on May 23 were "firsts" for the Lower Souris Refuge (LS).

Fringillids— Rather uncommon was the appearance of two Lazuli Buntings at Huron, S. Dak., on May 16 (BB). In South Dakota White-crowned Sparrows were reported as more common than usual at Huron but fewer at Sioux Falls while the White-throated Sparrow was much scarcer than usual in both areas (JWJ, HK).

Nesting Season, 1959

Warm, sometimes hot, dry weather, shrinking water areas, reduced and destroyed habitat and lowered reproduction rates—these were some of the gloomy elements in the Region for the period. In the Prairie Provinces, half the average usual rainfall occurred in the Saskatoon, Sask. area (Ronald Bremner); the few remaining pot holes and sloughs were drying up in the Spirit Lake, Sask. vicinity (William Anaka). In North Dakota precipitation was 28 percent below normal for May through July at Kenmare and many semi permanent pot holes were going fast at Dawson (Homer Bradley, Bob Timmerman). In South Dakota, portions of Lakes Whitewood and Preston near DeSmet are under plow—lakes which on March 27, 1959, held an estimated 350,000 "resting" migrant geese (HK). Sioux Falls marked up the driest July since 1890 (Sioux Falls Weather Bureau). The fellow traveler of drought is fire. With acres of vegetation in pot holes and marshes bone dry, the temptation to burn with its attendant runaway fires is a dire factor in further reducing habitat. William Anaka writes that 60 percent of the marsh and 15 percent of the woodland areas in the Spirit Lake district were burned out, mostly by property owners. Much burning was done in late April and May after nesting had commenced, he adds. Scattered rains did fall. Heartening to read was Elmo Adams' report for the Medicine Lake, Mont., neighborhood: "Water conditions have been much better than last year. Our waterfowl population is the best in the last four years." In Saskatchewan the nesting season seemed to be "considerably delayed in the south, owing to low water levels and unseasonable weather, but earlier in the north," writes Dr. Robert Nero, Regina. Small birds had a good year at Milbank, S. Dak.; they were well fed and supported fewer parasites, Lowry Elliott found in his banding activities. Perhaps because of hot and windy weather, birds that normally nest twice brooded only once this year, he notes.

Pelicans, Herons, Egrets, Bitterns— The White Pelican increased from 500 to 800 at LaCreek National Wildlife Refuge, Martin, S. Dak., this year (Art Hughlett). A Great Blue Heron sighted near Rapid City, S. Dak., on July 12 was perhaps an uncommon occurrence (N.R. Whitney, Jr.). Snowy Egrets were identified at Rush Lake near Webster, S. Dak., on July 26 and 28 (Herman Chilson). Little Blue Herons reported in South Dakota near Huron on June 14 (J.W. Johnson) and near Webster on August 8 (HC) were considerably north of their range, although the AOU Check List (1957:45) lists casual postnesting wanderers in North Dakota. The American Bittern, common as late as 1956 in the Spirit Lake, Sask. area, declined markedly in 1958 and seemed to be totally absent this year (WA).

Waterfowl— In Saskatchewan all species had a very poor nesting season in the Spirit Lake district with the number of breeding pairs low and the success ratio lower yet: probably ten percent of the production of two years ago (WA). In early August a serious die-off of ducks and other waterfowl occurred at Old Wives Lake near Regina. Some 3,000 ducks and waterfowl were picked up dead (RN). In North Dakota only one fifth of last year's number of early broods was observed at Slade National Wildlife Refuge, Dawson. Blue-winged Teal dropped most, Mallard held up best (BT). At Des Lacs National Wildlife Refuge, Kenmare, production was expected to be far below last year's: the breeding pair count was 1,022 as compared with 1,464 in 1958; diving ducks were scarce; only two broods of Canvasbacks were noted (HB). At Lostwood National Wildlife Refuge, Lostwood, 2,166 breeding pairs were counted this year, 4,600 in 1958 (George Card). At Lower Souris National Wildlife Refuge, Upham, overall production was down (LeRoy Sowl). In South Dakota only about ten percent of normal nesting success was expected locally at Milbank (LE). At Lake Andes National Wildlife Refuge, Lake Andes, 32 broods were counted in July as compared with 78 last year. Production was thought to be down between 25 percent and 35 percent on the refuges (David McGlaughlin). Though the nesting population was higher than last year at LaCreek Refuge, Martin, the brood population was down, especially in Redheads, Pintail, Gadwall and American Widgeon (AH). But in Montana at Medicine Lake National Wildlife Refuge, Medicine Lake, there was water and food and an increase in Ruddies, Redheads and Canvasbacks (EA).

Hawks, Grouse— The Red-tailed Hawk seemed to have a good year in scattered areas. They increased at Spirit Lake, Sask., with nine young banded in six nests (WA); a large number of nests were noted in the sandhills near Upham, N. Dak. (LS); they were the most conspicuous hawk in the Black Hills (NW). At Huron, S. Dak. three young Swainson's Hawks were banded on July 5 (JWJ). Seven Ferruginous Hawk nests were found near Regina, Sask.; one nest containing three young (which were banded July 6) was located at Billings, Mont. (RN, Mrs. Philip Hendricks). In the Regina, Sask. region, five Golden Eagles' nests, 15 Prairie Falcon nests and seven Pigeon Hawks' nests were discovered (RN). A Ruffed Grouse, whose nest was singed by fire on May 16—one of many runaway fires—at Spirit Lake, Sask., continued brooding the infertile eggs until August 7—"almost 12 weeks," writes William Anaka. Sharp-tails suffered serious reduction in some North Dakota areas: 41

percent loss of male birds counted on the spring dancing grounds at Des Lacs Refuge, Kenmare; a drastic 75 percent loss of males at Lostwood Refuge, Lostwood, while breeding populations were greatly reduced at Lower Souris Refuge, Upham (HB, GG, LS). But the numbers in the canyon country near LaCreek Refuge, Martin, S. Dak., seemed to be higher than last year's (AH). At Lavina, Mont., a Gray Partridge nest was found to contain 15 partridge eggs and five Ring-necked Pheasant eggs—perhaps a most unusual occurrence (Louis Moos, fide Mrs. PH).

Shorebirds— Although common in the area in previous years, including last season, Soras seem to have vanished from the marshes in the Spirit Lake, Sask. vicinity (WA). A Piping Plover nest with four eggs was found near Yankton, S. Dak., and two individuals were caught and banded on May 17 (J. Scott Findley, Carl Johnson). American Woodcock are almost non-existent in South Dakota but William Youngworth flushed one on June 13 in the extreme southeast corner of Union County (*South Dakota Bird Notes* 1959:63); and one was identified in a residential area in Sioux Falls (John Tuthill, fide HK). Another scolopacid very scarce in the state is the Long-billed Curlew. At LaCreek Refuge, Martin, however, they nested locally and could be seen in flocks of 50 to 100 during the last week in July and into August (AH). Brood success among American Avocets at Long Lake Refuge, Moffit, N. Dak., apparently was high. Some 3,000 birds were concentrated there early in August (E.V. Pierce). Near Regina, Sask. a colony of Ring-billed Gulls nesting on land, left high and dry by receding waters, were later seen with eggs and young and a farmer working the land in a circle about them (RN).

Cuckoos, Owls, Nighthawks— Black-billed Cuckoos apparently had a high rate of hatching success at Spirit Lake, Sask.—33 young fledged from five nests; and they had increased at Tower, N. Dak., also (WA, Edgar Preston). A Snowy Owl, seen at Langdon, Cavalier County, N. Dak., on August 2, was said to have been there for some three or four weeks (Einar Sigeirsson, *fide* O.A. Stevens). Burrowing Owls, uncommon in eastern South Dakota, brooded successfully at Brandt (Alfred Peterson). Common Night-hawks probably took a terrific nesting loss in the Rapid City neighborhood, writes Dr. N.R. Whitney, Jr.

Woodpeckers, Flycatchers— Dr. Whitney identified the Northern Three-toed Woodpecker on July 12 at Rochford in the Black Hills. The male Vermilion Flycatcher, studied at close range and observed twice in late June by John Bauman, manager at Sullys Hill Game Preserve, Fort Totten, N. Dak., was certainly far north of his range. "However, a male Vermilion Flycatcher can hardly be mistaken at close range," writes Mr. Bauman. An unrecorded occurrence of this species, undoubtedly the first for the state, was observed and described by L.M. Baylor and two colleagues at Mitchell, S. Dak., on May 24, 1958.

Jays, Wrens, Thrashers— Piñon Jays, common in the western part of the state, are unusual at Huron, S. Dak. (JWJ). The Rock Wren nest containing five young, found in a cutbank near Kenmare, N. Dak., is a new nesting record for the area (Mrs. Robert Gammell). Few observations of Sage Thrashers have been recorded for North Dakota. On June 12, 13 and 14, two were seen in a coulee on the Des Lacs Refuge, Kenmare (Mrs. RG).

*Thrushes, Meadowlarks, Lark Buntings, Sparrows—*The nesting populations of Robins at Huron, S. Dak., was apparently reduced by ten percent from last year's number, according to J.W. Johnson. Mountain Bluebirds definitely increased in the Saskatoon, Sask. vicinity; the five young discovered near Kenmare, N. Dak., in late June constitute the first-known nesting record for that area (RN, Olive Bodmer, *fide* Mrs. RG). In South Dakota both Eastern and Western Meadowlarks nested at LaCreek Refuge, Martin, and were heard regularly at Huron and at Lake Andes Refuge (AH, JWJ, DMcL). Lark Buntings were exceptionally plentiful west of Lake Andes (DMcL); and in North Dakota, at Kenmare, it was a "Lark Bunting" year—the best since the early forties. And Grasshopper Sparrows—"I have never seen such numbers," writes Mrs. Robert Gammell. She also noted a few McCown's Longspurs, the first observations since the "dust bowl" years.

Fall Migration, 1959

The gist of the Region's weather for the period—summer's drought became autumn's wet and cold with a fairly early freeze-up and a shorter-than-usual migration. With some exceptions, the northern portion was wet and cool in September, and cold and snowy in October and November. The southern portion had both wet and dry areas in September, and temperatures somewhat below normal. It was cold with some snow in October; several areas, however, were left windy and dry. A number of record-breaking below-zero dips were noted for early November, although warming trends occurred intermittently. By the first week in November most water areas were frozen—November 4 at both Spirit Lake, Sask. and Martin, S. Dak.—substantially halting migration (Wm. Anaka, Charles Hughlett). Several disturbances high-lighted the weather pattern. A turbulence on September 14 switched winds from southerly to northeasterly in eastern South Dakota, bringing lowered temperatures, high winds and precipitation to the Sioux Falls neighborhood between the 15th and 18th. This may have brought about the unusually large hawk wave that drifted over Sioux Falls on September 16. From 12:15 to 12:55 p.m., 95 Broad-wings, 16 Red-tails and two Turkey Vultures were counted out of the hundreds in the concentration. At least 75 percent seemed to be Broad-wings. On the 17th, probably because of the same disturbance, a wave of passerines, mostly warblers, struck Sioux Falls. In a three-hour period, 17 species of warblers were identified (HK). The Orange-crown-Myrtle wave, which passed through Saskatoon, Sask. on the 13th, may have been influenced by the same turbulence; "many hundreds" of these birds were seen (Ronald Bremner, Frank Roy). Wide-spread storms between October five and 12 left seven inches of snow at Calgary, Alta. and Spirit Lake, Sask.; ten inches at Kenmare, N. Dak.; 12 inches at Malta, Mont.; and strong winds in South Dakota with a cold front at Columbia. In North Dakota passerine species were lost at Slade National Wildlife Refuge, Dawson; shorebirds and songbirds were storm-bound at Sullys Hill Game Preserve, Fort Totten, with some perishing. In the Kenmare vicinity, farmers commented on finding dead meadowlarks; and quite a few dead Myrtle Warblers and Slate-colored Juncos were found in town. Horned Larks and Lapland Longspurs, attracted to bare roadways, were killed in traffic (Robert Timmerman, John Bauman, Mrs. Robert Gammell). Probably greater destruction occurred than is known.

In general a dreary migration was the rule with few notable concentrations: in Saskatchewan a warbler wave at Regina on September 22 and in the Mortlach-Caron area, September 21 (Fred Lahrman, Frank Brazier); and a wave of fringillids at Saskatoon between September 28 and 30 (RB, FR). The scarcity of birds was pronounced at Billings, Mont., Fargo, N. Dak., and Huron and Sioux Fails, S. Dak., with some reporters expressing the fear that the widespread use of insecticides and weed-killers may be more definitely in the picture than is realized (Mrs. Philip Hendricks, O.A. Stevens, J.W. Johnson, HK). The high totals of some waterfowl species at certain points may indicate, not necessarily greater numbers, but merely, with wetlands mainly dry, that birds crowded into the few remaining water places.

In the opinion of Dr. N.R. Whitney, Jr. the fire that blackened the forested hills about Deadwood, S. Dak., on September 8, spectacular though it was, probably had little effect upon the birdlife of the area. The more spectacular "crash" among South Dakota's Ring-necked Pheasants, wherein allegedly one third to one half of the population "disappeared" just before the hunting season, is still a controversial subject. Disease, insecticides and weed-killers, changes in land use, even foxes and alleged contributory ineptitude of high game officials—all were convenient "villains" charged with responsibility for the "crime." The "mystery," frequently highly polemical, is still unsolved. Wildlife authorities in Saskatchewan permitted the shooting of Sandhill Cranes ("with no bag limit") in the "poor crop area" north of Last Mountain Lake where, farmers report, the birds concentrated so heavily they damaged crops. On October 17, the Saskatchewan Natural History Society passed a resolution, strongly urging the authorities to ensure protection of the cranes (*Blue Jay* 17:140–142). On September 22, 33 birds of 13 species were found dead at the Moose Jaw TV tower near Caron, Sask.—Myrtle and Orange-crowned Warblers heading the list (Robbert Nero, FL in *Blue Jay* 17: 142–143).

Loons, Herons, Bitterns— The Arctic Loons identified at Regina, Sask. on October 11 and 12 constitute the third record for the Province (FL; FB in Blue Jay 17:154–155). In South Dakota Great Blue Herons peaked at about 100 in August at Sand Lake National Wildlife Refuge, Columbia (Jerry J. Blackard). Snowy Egrets and Little Blue Herons, previously reported (AFN 13:437) in the Waubay, S. Dak., area, remained there, the egret until September 2, the herons until October 6 (Herman Chilson, John Carlson). American Bitterns were scarce again this fall at Des Lacs National Wildlife Refuge, Kenmare, N. Dak., but were about twice as numerous as last season at LaCreek National Wildlife Refuge, Martin, S. Dak. (Homer Bradley, CH).

Swans— Whistling Swans were up at some points. In North Dakota a peak of 279 on October 30 at Des Lacs Refuge, Kenmare, compared with 73 on November seven last year; 400 to 450 at Tewaukon Refuge, Cayuga, this year compared with about 40 in 1958; and at Lostwood National Wildlife Refuge, Lostwood, numbers were about the same as last season's average (HB, James Monnie, George Gard). In South Dakota they peaked at 200 at Sand Lake Refuge, Columbia, with many young birds, suggesting good production this year; and the 250 in the Waubay Lake area around October 22 was a substantial increase over the usual population (JJB, JC). But at Bowdoin National Wildlife Refuge, Malta, Mont. they were slightly down (Baine Cater).

Geese— In general, overall waterfowl populations were down at most points. In North Dakota there was a 62 percent decrease in duck use and a 53 percent decline in goose use on the Garrison Reservoir and at Snake Creek National Wildlife Refuge, Coleharbor; the population was as much as 25 percent below normal at Arrowwood National Wildlife Refuge, Kensal. However, at some points it was near normal. The goose migration at Fort Totten was better than average (David McGlachlin, John Frye, JB). In South Dakota, Canada Geese peaked at 500 on October 12 at Sand Lake Refuge, Columbia, compared with 1,200 in 1958. The total passing through Bowdoin Refuge, Malta, Mont., was as high as in other years, but the refuge peak was 1553 — 33 percent below last year's peak (JJB, BC). "Little" Canadas created much interest at Tewaukon Refuge, Cayuga, N. Dak., where they reached 3500 birds as compared with 1,500 in 1958, and at Sand Lake Refuge, Columbia, S. Dak., where the total of 17,990 by October 12 was three times last year's peak figure of some 5,000 birds (JM, JJB). White-fronts decreased by 95 percent in the Snake Creek-Garrison Reservoir area, Coleharbor, N. Dak., but were near normal at Sand Lake Refuge, the 600 by October 12 being about 100 birds fewer than last year's top number (DMcL, JJB). Snow Geese were down in the Coleharbor, N. Dak., area and at Sand Lake Refuge, Columbia, S. Dak., where the peak of 24,000 birds on November 1 was 37 percent below the 1,958 peak of 38,500 (DMcL, JJB). Blue Geese seemed to be even scarcer: 2,500 on November 1 at Sand Lake Refuge, Columbia, S. Dak., as compared with 7,000 in 1958. Three Ross' Geese seen on October 21 at Bowdoin Refuge, Malta, Mont., were firsts for the refuge (JJB, BC). The brant caught during banding operations at Sand Lake Refuge, Columbia, S. Dak., on October 18 and still waiting specific identification is the first for the refuge—perhaps for the area (JJB).

Ducks— Most reports indicate a sad slump in the duck migration, particularly in Mallards and divers. In North Dakota the Mallard total at Des Lacs Refuge,

Kenmare, was 6,370 on August 28—the peak—compared with 7,855 last year and 25,000 in 1957. There was a 62 percent decrease in duck use on the Garrison Reservoir-Snake Creek Refuge, Coleharbor, N. Dak., area. At Tewaukon Refuge, Cayuga, the peak duck population of 10,000 in mid-October was down from 14,000 in 1958 and 60,000 in 1956. Last year's peak at Lostwood Refuge, Lostwood, was 6,510—nearly twice as many as this year's peak of 2,880 birds. At Slade Refuge, Dawson, total duck days use was less than one third of the total in 1958 (HB, DMcG, JM, GG, Robert Timmerman). In South Dakota the duck peak of 53,475 at Sand Lake Refuge, Columbia, occurred between October 11 and 18—about 24 percent of last year's peak number. At Waubay Refuge, the peak was 50 percent below the 1958 total. However, in Montana the peak population of 59,670 on September 23 at Bowdoin Refuge, Malta was up slightly over the 58,000 of last year (JJB, JC, BC). Local Mallards were low in the Spirit Lake, Sask., area because of a poor hatch. Population totals of Mallards were below those of previous years at Des Lacs Refuge, Kenmare, N. Dak.—a peak of 6370 on August 28 as compared with 7,858 last year and 25,000 in 1957 (WA, HB). In South Dakota they were drastically reduced at Waubay though they were less so at LaCreek Refuge, Martin—25,000 this year, 30,000 last year (JC, CH). American Widgeon showed surprising strength at several points: nearly 35,000 on an inlet at Devils Lake, N. Dak., on October 10 (JB). In South Dakota they peaked at 7,955 on Waubay Refuge, Waubay, where last year there were only a few thousand; and at LaCreek Refuge, Martin, there were three times as many as in 1958 (JC, CH). Blue-winged Teal gained at Lostwood Refuge, Lostwood, N. Dak., by 290 birds—350 in 1958, 640 in 1959; but at LaCreek Refuge, Martin, S. Dak., they dropped some 50 percent of the total recorded in 1958 (GG, CH). During migration scaup increased by ten percent to 20 percent over last year in the Spirit Lake, Sask. district; they were down slightly at Lostwood Refuge, Lostwood, N. Dak.—2,340 this year, 2,500 in 1958: they were in a drastic slump at Waubay Refuge, Waubay, S. Dak., where usually they are the most abundant species (WA, GG, JC). Wood Ducks were observed at Arrowwood Refuge, Kensal, N. Dak.—the first since the refuge was established in 1935 (JF). At Le Duc, Alta., II.W. Burns reported six nests of Buffalohead occupied this year (*fide* Anthony Erskine). Surf Scoters were observed at two points: at Conrich near Calgary, Alta., on October 24 and at Regina, Sask., on October 11; the White-winged Scoter recorded at Des Lacs Refuge, Kenmare, N. Dak., on October 16, 29, and 30 is an irregular visitor (Cedric Hitchon, FL, FB in *Blue Jay* 17:142–143; HB). Two Hooded Mergansers appeared at Regina, Sask., on October 11, and seven on October 12; a female was seen at Rapid City, S. Dak., on November 15 and a male on November 26—all uncommon records (FL, FB, NW).

Eagles, Pheasants, Cranes— A slight increase in Golden Eagles was reported at various stations . Eight birds at Sand Lake Refuge, Columbia, S. Dak., took care of many geese and ducks crippled by hunters' shot (JJB). The Ring-necked Pheasant, generally down, sustained an apparent "crash" in South Dakota, reducing the population by an alleged one third to one half. In Alberta, Whooping Cranes were reported at Mud Lake near Rocky Mountain House on October 10 and 11 and near Lethbridge on October 13 (H.B. Grigsby, *fide* E.D. Beacham). In Saskatchewan, records were rather unsatisfactory. A pair was seen at Richard on October 7 but none was reported from Saskatoon, the first absence there in several years (*Blue Jay* 17:148–149, RB).

Shorebirds— Semipalmated Plover, uncommon in the Spirit Lake, Sask. district, were observed on September 16 (WA). Common Snipe, sporadically seen in the Huron vicinity, appeared in two flocks of about 40 each on September 4 at Lake Henry (Blanche Battin). The flock of Long-billed Curlews, numbering nearly 100 reported previously (AFN 13:438), remained in the Martin, S. Dak neighborhood well into the migration period (CH). Dowitchers gathered in tidy numbers at Des Lacs Refuge, Kenmare. N. Dak., totaling 450 on September 17, but in South Dakota they concentrated to an amazing 70,000 peak during the second week in August at Sand Lake Refuge, Columbia; some 300 were sighted on October 22 at Lake Mary (HB, JJB, Alfred Peterson). Seventy-plus Stilt Sandpipers, seen at Conrich, Alta., are uncommon to rare in that district (EDB, CH); 500 were counted near Lake Norden, S. Dak., on September 19 (AP). Avocets, relatively scarce at Des Lacs Refuge, Kenmare, N. Dak., totaled 500 the first three weeks in August at Sand Lake Refuge, Columbia, S. Dak. (HB, JJB). At Spirit Lake, Wm. Anaka reported a Northern Phalarope on September 6, uncommon there; on the same day, a Forster's Tern and on September 3, 1920 Bonaparte's Gulls, a first record in the district for both tern and gull.

Owls— By September the energetic Dr. Stuart Houston had banded 70 Great Horned Owls (67 in 30 nests plus three on the wing), all found between Yorkton and Saltcoats, Sask. (*not* at Regina, as reported in AFN 13:381—HK). He also banded 12 Long-eared Owls in four nests. A Boreal Owl was observed in a Saskatoon, Sask., garden after the storm of October 9 and 10 (RB). A Sawwhet Owl with a damaged wing throve on strips of beef kidney and recovered enough to become a "welcome visitor at several schoolrooms" at Billings, Mont., writes Mrs. Philip Hendricks.

Nighthawks, Swifts, Swallows— About a hundred Common Nighthawks, observed flying over forests at Hills City in the Black Hills, S. Dak., on August 16, apparently were migrating (NW). Chimney Swifts were heading south by September 24 at Milbank, S. Dak. (Lowry Elliott). Swallows declined markedly, especially Tree Swallows, which were noticeably missing this fall at Spirit Lake, Sask., where thousands usually are seen in late August; hundreds were traveling on August 25 at Milbank but none was reported from Huron and Sioux Falls in South Dakota (WM, JWJ, HK). Purple Martin were comparable with 1958 and 1957 numbers at Huron, but those numbers were down two thirds or more from those of 1956, indicating a rather slow recovery (JWJ).

Corvids— Two Clark's Nutcrackers, rare away from the mountains in Alberta, were seen at Morley on September 12 (Kay Hodges) and October 25 (Dick Decker).

Mockingbirds, Thrushes— In North Dakota four Mockingbirds, identified at Des Lacs Refuge on August 23, were uncommon in that area (Mrs. RG). At Fargo, Dr. O.A. Stevens banded 20 Swainson's Thrushes between August 26 and October 4, a heartening record when other stations report them scarce or absent. More Eastern Bluebirds than usual migrated through the Milbank and Waubay, S. Dak., areas (LE, JC). Townsend's Solitaires appeared at points where usually they are uncommon: at Calgary, Alta. on September 30 (KH); at Regina, Sask. on October 2 (FL, FB) and at Huron, S. Dak., from November 9 to 14 (JWJ).

Kinglets, Waxwings, Shrikes— Ruby-crowned Kinglets were the second most numerous species of the passerine wave that passed through Sioux Falls, S. Dak., on September 17; a total of 35 were counted in a three-hour period (HK). Bohemian Waxwings were reported as far south as Watertown, S. Dak., by November 17; there they fed on frozen crab-apples (L. Moriarty). In South Dakota Northern Shrikes were identified at Waubay Refuge, Waubay on November 20 and at Rapid City (JC, NW).

Warblers— It was a dreary warbler migration except for occasional concentrations. "Clouds of warblers" arrived at Regina, Sask. on September 22: Myrtles, Yellow-throats, Tennessees, and Orange-crowns (FL, FB). A wave at Mortlach and Caron, 60 miles west of Regina, September 21, produced Myrtles, Yellow Warblers, Blackpolls and Palms (mostly Palms) (FL). Among the 17 species identified in the Sioux Falls, S. Dak., wave of September 17, Nashvilles were most numerous, followed by Orange-crowns, Bay-breasted, Black-and-white, and Wilson's. Twelve other species included Chest-nut-sided, Pine, Blackburnian and Canada, but only two Myrtles. The surprise came with five Parulas, an uncommon species here (HK). August was a banner month for Tennessee Warblers in the Nipawin, Sask. district where between the 1st and the 25th, Maurice Street banded 551 individuals (*Blue Jay* 17: 156). In South Dakota the first report for the Black-throated Blue Warbler at Sand Lake Refuge, Columbia, was recorded on October 12; a male was observed at Sioux Falls on October 19—noteworthy appearances (JC, HK). Despite the Saskatchewan "waves," the Myrtle remained the scarcest of the warbler species in the reports. In North Dakota one was observed at Snake Creek Refuge, Coleharbor, on October 10; there was a "five-minute wave" at Kenmare on September 21; two were banded at Fargo on September 24, the only appearance there (DMcL, Mrs. RG, OAS). In South Dakota they were scarce at Webster, Huron and Sioux Falls (HC, JWJ, HK, J.S. Findley). The Bay-breasted Warbler identified at Huron, S. Dak., on October 9 was probably the first for the area (JWJ). In addition to the Mortlach and Caron, Sask. wave, Palm Warblers occurred also at Spirit Lake, where an increase was noted (WA). In South Dakota Canada Warblers were unusually plentiful at Huron; a male was banded at Winner on September 1 — an infrequent occurrence; few records of this species apparently exist for the middle of the state (JWJ, Harold Wager).

Fringillids— At Saskatoon, Sask., a "deluge of fringillids" appeared from September 28 through 30 — "in the greatest numbers ever recorded" by Dr. Ronald Bremner and Frank Roy. Among the species were Slate-colored Juncos, Tree Sparrows, Harris', White-throated, Lincoln's and Fox Sparrows — the only large incursion reported for the period. But at Spirit Lake, Sask., fringillids of approximately the same species were about 50 percent of normal (WA). The Rose-breasted Grosbeak found dead at Waubay Refuge, Waubay, S. Dak., on September 2 was the first record in many years, and the Purple Finch identified there on November 7 was the first for the refuge (JC). At Watertown, S. Dak., two Pine Grosbeaks were noted on November 14, and 16 on November 17 (LM). Common Redpolls, apparently scarce elsewhere, were unusually abundant at Roosevelt National Memorial Park, Medora, N. Dak. (Arthur Henderson). Harris' Sparrows were notably scarce in nearly all reports. The one seen at Calgary, Alta. (rare there) between October 1 and 4, was the first observed since 1955 (Vera Morrisson). White-crowned and White-throated Sparrows were generally not plentiful, though a marked wave of White-throats was noted at Fargo, N. Dak., on September 23 (OAS). Dr. and Mrs. Robert Gammell banded 93 Chestnut-collared Longspurs on August 18 and 62 on August 30, the peak numbers this fall.

Corrigendum— Sixteen Stilt Sandpipers were seen at Lake Andes, S. Dak., May 17, not at Lewis and Clark Lake, May 16 (AFN 13:381); Black-billed Magpies, not Black-billed Cuckoos nested successfully at Spirit Lake, Sask. (AFN 13:438).

Winter Season, 1959–1960

The most dramatic aspects of the period were the general scarcity of birds, a spectacular invasion of Boreal and Short-eared Owls and what seemed to be a reversal of weather patterns. December was mild nearly everywhere, going into the records as the warmest in 75 years in the Calgary, Alta. Region (E.D. Beacham); the third warmest on record at Winnipeg, Man. (Harold Hosford); abnormally mild at Cayuga, N. Dak. (U.S. Weather Bureau, J.W, Johnson). January and February were cooler but March was frosty with winter temperatures: 20° below normal the first two weeks at Calgary (EDB); the coldest month of the winter at Spirit Lake, Sask. (Wm. Anaka); the coldest March on record at Huron, S. Dak. (JWJ). Snowfall was light at Edmonton and Calgary (Robert Lister, EDB); twice the amount compared with last winter fell at Spirit Lake, Sask. (WA); 86 percent of normal at Kenmare, N. Dak. (Homer Bradley); near record falls on January 2 and March 9–11 at Sioux Falls, S. Dak. (HK). Perhaps the weather did little to influence birdlife but it brought forth such comments as these from South Dakota—"fewest birds in 16 years of observation" at Huron

(JWJ); "notable scarcity of juncos. Tree Sparrows and American Goldfinches" at Brookings (Mrs. David Holden); "very scarce both as to numbers and species" at Milbank (Lowry Elliott); from North Dakota—"wintering birdlife quite scarce" Lostwood (George Gard); "very few birds this winter" at Coleharbor (David McGlauchlin); "practically nothing to report" at Fargo (O.A. Stevens); from Saskatchewan—"most migrant species absent or noted infrequently" at Spirit Lake (WA); "winter birds scarce or absent" at Saskatoon (Ronald Bremner); from Alberta—"very few summer residents or migrants remained, compared with previous years" at Calgary (EDB). At Calgary and Edmonton, thanks to rainy fall weather, much grain, both swathed and unswathed was left in the fields with a possible resulting rise in the mouse population and an increase in the so-called birds of prey; for instance, the Short-eared Owl flocks in the Edmonton-Calgary Regions (RL, EDB) . However, because of light snowcover, the anticipated eruption of short-tailed meadow voles did not occur, reported Robert Lister. Most remarkable was Dr. Stuart Houston's vivid record of the Boreal Owl invasion in an area mainly at Melville and south and east of Yorkton and Melville, Sask. Some birds were caught by hand or with butterfly or fish nets in barns and outbuildings and in bushes. "Quite a high percentage perished–presumed starved," writes Dr. Houston. "Those that were doing well had learned to enter barns and granaries and feed on House Sparrows, an item of prey that is absent in their native boreal woods."

Grebes, Waterfowl— During the period two Western Grebes were recorded at Lake Wabamun at Edmonton (Edmonton Bird Club). The 2000 Mallards that wintered at Calgary were less than half of last year's population of 5000 birds (EDB). South Dakota's wintering ducks, inventoried in January at nearly 78,000, dropped dismally from the half million tally of January 1959 and drastically from the 1957 count of over a million (*Argus Leader*, Sioux Falls, January 24, 1960). In Montana the seasonal population of nearly 75,000 ducks and geese was slightly down from last year's numbers (U.S. Fish & Wildlife, Mrs. Philip Hendricks). The Brant caught during banding operations at Sand Lake National Wildlife Refuge, Columbia, S. Dak., on October 18, 1959 was an (American) Brant—apparently a first for the refuge (Jerry Blackard).

Hawks— All or most species were scarce, uncommon or entirely absent in most localities except in areas in southeastern Alberta. Goshawks, never common in Saskatchewan, were unusually few this winter (SH). The Rough-legged Hawks sighted both east and west of Calgary and Conrich, Alta. were the first winter records since 1956 (Cedric Hitchon, W.E. McKay). Five Bald Eagles, four adults and one immature, wintering at Calgary, were seen on December 12 (Dick Dekker) as well as on January 4, February 14 and March 13 (EDB). For the third consecutive year gray-phased Gyrfalcons were seen at Calgary; the first on January (DD); the last on January 24 was observed attacking and driving off both a Rough-legged Hawk and a Prairie Falcon (EDB). Both prairie Falcon and Pigeon Hawks entered at Calgary (EDB, CH, John Clarke, Kay

Hodges). A Prairie Falcon was carefully identified at Sioux Falls, S. Dak., on January 28 (HK in *South Dakota Bird Notes* 11:76–77). The Sparrow Hawk observed over downtown Winnipeg, Man. on March 2 was a rather uncommon occurrence (HH).

Gallinaceous Birds — In Saskatchewan Ruffed Grouse remained unchanged from last year and in good numbers at Spirit Lake, as did Sharp-tailed Grouse (WA). Gray Partridge wintered well and plentifully at Calgary, probably because of unswathed grain in the fields (EDB). Eleven Sharp-tails were seen feeding on unthreshed grain near Winnipeg on March 11 (HH). But in North Dakota only one or two were noted at Des Lacs National Wildlife Refuge headquarters where up to 24 birds fed regularly last year (HB); they were about the same as last autumn at Snake Creek National Wildlife Refuge, Coleharbor (DMcG). Gray Partridges were on the upswing at Tower City, N. Dak., where 30 Prairie Chickens also were counted (Ed Preston). North Dakota Ring-necked Pheasants enjoyed a good season at Tower City, were locally abundant in normal numbers at Arrowwood National Wildlife Refuge, Kensal, with a cock:hen ratio of one to five (John Frye) but dropped over 50 percent at Tewaukon National Wildlife Refuge, Cayuga (JM). In southeastern Alberta they apparently rode out the winter pretty well: 80 were counted between Calgary and Carseland on January 24 (EDB). But in South Dakota, to worsen the pheasant "crash" that occurred previous to the fall hunting season, Ring-necks were found dead and dying of starvation in mid-March. Losses were said to be five percent statewide but ranged up to 60 percent in several maximum distress areas, which covered some 6,300 square miles and included Brown, Beadle, McCook and Hanson Counties. Six additional counties tallied significant to minor depletions (*Argus Leader*, Sioux Falls, March 7, 18, 23). In the Clark vicinity (Clark County) road kills were heavy; many almost weightless and flightless birds, seeking food on the highway shoulders were apparently sucked under the passing wheels of vehicles. Of the thousands of birds lining the highway between DeSmet and Clark (a distance of perhaps 45 miles in Kingsbury and Clark Counties) the greatest number were hens — an indication of an abnormal sex ratio prevalent in some sections of the state (*Ibid*, March 14).

Owls — Apparently this was an "owl" year, nine species being reported. A gray-phased Screech Owl captured alive at Cardston on December 31 was the fourth record for Alberta and the first for the southern section of the Province (R. Salt, *fide* EDB). Snowy Owls were observed occasionally at Edmonton (EDB); 12 were seen at Shepard (EDB, JC, CH) and one at Drumheller in Alberta (Ian Halladay). They were absent from the Spirit Lake district (WA) and seen only twice near Winnipeg — on December 2 and March 20 (HH). In North Dakota they were scarce at Des Lacs Refuge, Kenmare, although several were noted between December 3 and January 10 (HB) and three were under observation at Kenmare during the period (Mrs. RG). They were below normal at Arrowwood Refuge, Kensal (JF) and noted only once, in November, at Tower City (EP). In South Dakota a sight record on February 29 was made at Sand Lake Refuge, Columbia (JB). In Alberta a Hawk-Owl appeared at Turner Valley on February 6 and at Rocky Mountain House on February 7 (EDB); a Pygmy Owl was seen at Caroline, west of Red Deer, on February 7 (EDB, CH, DD, WEMcK). A Barred Owl, captured at High Hill northeast of Kelvington on December 27, and banded and released on January 2, was the first banding record for Saskatchewan of a species placed on the Saskatchewan list only last June (SH). A Great Gray Owl intrigued visitors in a Winnipeg park for a day in December (HH). In Alberta, Short-eared Owls in flocks of 20 to 30 were reported 20 miles north of Edmonton on two occasions in December, attracted perhaps by increased mouse populations in swathed grain in the fields (RL, EBC). They were fairly common at Conrich, Alta. six being seen on January 10 (EDB). Dr. Stuart Houston reported a spectacular invasion of Boreal Owls south and east of Yorkton and Melville, near Melville, and northwest and northeast of Yorkton at Margo and Aaran, Sask. in a wide area where none had been recorded previously. Between December 19 and April 4 he banded 24 Boreal Owls and retrieved nine as specimens—an astonishing achievement. Picking these birds up put a terrific number of miles on his car; "one Saturday I drove 400 miles, and several times I went on a 150-mile drive after finishing hospital rounds at 10 or 11 p.m.," writes the doctor. "This included bucking some pretty fancy drifts on country roads." One Boreal Owl, seen frequently at Kenmare, N. Dak., was later found dead and brought in (Mrs. RG). A Saw-whet Owl was banded at Waldron and another at Hazelcliffe, Sask. (SH) and two were banded at Kenmare (Mrs. RG). The injured Saw-whet Owl found in Billings, Mont., last October (*Audubon Field Notes* 14:49) "is still hale and hearty," writes Mrs. Philip Hendricks.

Flickers, Woodpeckers— The Yellow-shafted Flickers observed in Winnipeg in December were the first winter records for the area (HH). Woodpeckers were conspicuously absent at Piedmont in the Black Hills (Mr. & Mrs. Elva Barrows, *fide* N.R. Whitney, Jr.) although eight to ten Lewis' Woodpeckers wintered in Spring Creek bottoms (NRW). Downy and Hairy Woodpeckers were in normal numbers at Columbia, S. Dak. (JB) and elsewhere generally but were not seen at Belfield, N. Dak. (Mrs. Richard Swenson).

Chickadees, Nuthatches, Wrens— Black-capped Chickadees, down at Sioux Falls, S. Dak. (HK), were not to be found at Belfield, N. Dak. (Mrs. RS). Though few Red-breasted Nuthatches were seen at Brookings and none in Rapid City (Mrs. DH, NRW) there was an influx at Billings, Mont. (Mrs. PH). The one observed about 60 miles northeast of Winnipeg on March 6 was a rare winter visitor in the area (HH). Unknown at Edmonton until a few years ago, the White-breasted Nuthatch is apparently increasing in the district or "the greater numbers of observers are turning up more records," writes Robert Lister. On March 23, at Billings, two Cañon Wrens in song were observed—a relatively rare bird in Montana, despite its regular appearance in some sections (Mrs. PH).

Waxwings, Shrikes, Grackles, Blackbirds— In South Dakota, Bohemian Waxwings were seldom noted or were seen only in sporadic flocks at Rapid City, Milbank, Waubay and Huron (NRW, LE, John C. Carlsen, JWJ). In North Dakota they were absent at Fargo (OAS); none were seen at Kensal for the first time in several years (JF); and at Kenmare, writes Mrs. Robert Gammell, "this is the first winter Bohemian Waxwings failed to show up in our yard." At Billings, Mont. small groups appeared where ordinarily hundreds are seen (Mrs. PH). In Saskatchewan they were infrequent at Spirit Lake and Saskatoon (WA, RB), but in Alberta they appeared at Edmonton in large numbers in late December (EDC) and at Calgary flocks upwards of 300 birds were present at times (EDB). Northern Shrikes were very scarce to uncommon at Calgary and Edmonton (EDB, JC, CH, EEC). At Kenmare, N. Dak., one remained for the winter and three others were reported present (Mrs. RG); at Webster, S. Dak., one was seen on February 6 (Herman Chilson). An unusual occurrence was the sighting of two Common Grackles on the Christmas count at Billings (Mrs. PH). Up to six Rusty Blackbirds were seen daily in a feed lot south of Kenmare, N. Dak. (Mrs. RG).

Grosbeaks, Finches, Redpolls, Pine Siskins, Crossbills— Both Evening and Pine Grosbeak numbers seemed to be less than normal in the Region (HH, NRW, EDB, EEC). Pine Grosbeaks were few and far between at Saskatoon, Sask. (RB). It was a good Purple Finch season at Brookings, S. Dak., where 29 were tallied on the Christmas count (Mrs. DH). In Alberta, Hoary Redpolls appeared in much larger numbers than usual at Edmonton (EEC); a few were seen at Calgary on December 5 and 27 (KH). At Kenmare, N. Dak., they were noted in a coulee on the Upper Souris Refuge (Mrs. RG). Common Redpolls had a good season at Winnipeg (HH); they were the most "plethoric" bird seen at Saskatoon, Sask. (RB) and fairly common at Calgary and Edmonton but less so than last year (EDB, EEC); excellent flocks appeared in South Dakota at Rapid City, Brookings (where some appeared at feeders) and Waubay Wildlife Refuge (NRW, Mrs. DH, JCC) but they were below normal at Huron and Milbank (JWJ, Blanche Battin, LE); also in North Dakota at Kenmare and in Saskatchewan at Spirit Lake (Mrs. RG, WA). Pine Siskins and Red Crossbills were infrequent at Rapid City, Waubay and Sioux Falls in South Dakota (NRW, JCC, HK). The five Red Crossbills seen in Billings, Mont., and the 30 on the University Campus at Edmonton, Alta. were unusual occurrences; this species is rare to uncommon in both localities (Mrs. PH, RL, EEC).

Sparrows, Longspurs, Buntings— Tree Sparrows were noteworthily scarce; scattered groups were seen at Billings where usually large flocks congregate; they were almost absent at Rapid City and not to be found at Huron where dozens were observed last year (Mrs. PH, NRW, JWJ, BB); two or three were seen from March 21 to 29 at Snake Creek Refuge, Coleharbor, N. Dak., compared with 2000 reported last year during the same period (DMcG). A White-crowned Sparrow on the Christmas count was a rare sight at Billings (Mrs. PH). Lapland Longspurs were not observed at Tower City, N. Dak. (EP), but were in good numbers in South Dakota at Brookings (Mrs. DH), at Brandt where 60 presumably of this species were seen on December 9 (Alfred Peterson) and at Sioux Falls where a flock of 500 plus was observed as late as March 27 (HK). Snow Buntings were apparently scarcer than usual at Milbank and Columbia but were fairly plentiful at Waubay in South Dakota (LE, JB, JCC); they were numerous in North Dakota at Lostwood and Kenmare (George Gard, Mrs. RG) and abundant in Saskatchewan at Spirit Lake where they were the only common migrant species (WA) and at Saskatoon where on February 28, near Dinsmore, Frank Roy recorded up to 10,000 birds in a flock (RB). In Alberta large flocks were seen all winter at Edmonton and concentrations up to 1,000 birds at Calgary (EBC, CH).

Nesting Season, 1960

June was generally cool and moist in the Region but July was a sizzler—the second driest on record at Winnipeg, Man. with rainfall less than three-quarters of an inch (Harold Hosford); the seventh driest in Sioux Falls, S. Dak since 1890 (U.S. Weather Bureau, HK); the driest in 60 years in Saskatchewan and the fifth hottest (Dr. C. Stuart Houston) with one-fourth inch of precipitation at Saskatoon (Dr. Ronald Bremner) very dry at Billings, Mont., with maximum temperatures at 105° (Mrs. Philip Hendricks). From June 28 to July 29, Spirit Lake, Sask. recorded no precipitation (Wm. Anaka). Water conditions, generally good in May and June, deteriorated in July in most localities with unfortunate results for many species, such as the Black Terns at Kenmare. N. Dak., which abandoned their nests in wet meadows when the water dried up (Mrs. Robert Gammell). At Waubay National Wildlife Refuge an abundance of pothole inhabitats in June encouraged nesting, but drought in July probably curtailed reproduction (John Carlsen). Despite extravagant optimism in certain quarters, the waterfowl picture at the moment is far from clear. Late hatches (resulting from unseasonable snows), receding lake levels, continuing dry weather, dried-up sloughs in many areas and heavy aquatic cover making the counting of broods difficult—these factors make a clear-cut description difficult if not impossible. The pheasant situation in South Dakota, though promising improvement, is by no means completely rosy. Bird-banding activity increases; its hazards were graphically illustrated when Louis Moos banded California Gulls at Aarod Lake, Conrad, Mont., where one excited gull knocked his hat off and another drew blood at the back of his head (Mrs. PH). The untiring Dr. Stuart Houston of Yorkton (more recently of Saskatoon), Sask., continues his astonishing owl banding work—over 300 owls in "just over six months." Thanks and felicitations to Mrs. Robert Gammell who added the preparation of the Spring Summary to her busy schedule.

Grebes, Pelicans, Cormorants— Few Eared Grebes nested at Des Lacs National Wildlife Refuge, Kenmare, N. Dak., this season (Homer Bradley). No Western Grebes were seen on July 4 at Rush Lake, Waubay, S. Dak., where in previous years they were abundant nesters (J.S. Findley, Alfred Peterson); this year, driven out by receding water levels, they apparently spent the summer in nearby lakes although no nesting activity was observed (JC). However, for the first time since 1956, they nested at Oakwood Lakes near Brookings (Mrs. David Holden). In North Dakota they brought off young for the first time since 1946 at Des Lacs Refuge, producing 50 broods (HB); at Snake Creek National Wildlife Refuge, Coleharbor, an immature, seen on August 8, was apparently "the first nesting record for the refuge," reported David Mc-Gla-chlin. In Saskatchewan, a nest with four eggs, found in Wascana Marsh, was a first breeding record for the Regina district (Frank Brazier). The four White Pelicans seen at Belle Fourche Reservoir in S. Dak., on July 22 constituted a first record in the area (Charles Hughlett). On June 14, Rooky Island in South Waubay Lake, Day County, S. Dak., held 1,050 nests of Double-crested Cormorants with 480 living young (JC).

Egrets, Herons, Bitterns— The highlight of the summer at Snake Creek Refuge was the observation on July 22 of a Snowy Egret—a probable first for the Region (DMcG). An estimated 1,000 nests of Black-crowned Night Herons were found at Lower Souris National Wildlife Refuge, Upham, N. Dak., on June 14; there were young in many nests by the 29th (Robert Johnson); but in South Dakota not a heron was sighted in the colony usually nesting in the Waubay Region (JSF). The American Bittern, hardly plentiful anywhere, had a good year at Milbank, S. Dak. (Lowry Elliott).

Canada Geese— In North Dakota the Canada Geese that hatched on June 5 at Snake Creek Refuge, though brought off by captive birds, were first broods for the refuge and a step toward establishing a goose flock in the area (DMcG). And the 73 Canada Goose nests, the highest number in the history of Lower Souris Refuge, had a hatching success of 85 percent or better, with first broods off on May 12 (RJ). In South Dakota the hatch at Waubay Refuge definitely exceeded last year's: 45 nesting pair were found in Day County of which 20 were on the refuge; on July 6, 1987 honkers were rounded up and banded.

Waterfowl— Waterfowl production in the southern third of Saskatchewan "does not look good," wrote Dr. Stuart Houston on August 2. Although still considerably below the numbers of previous years, nesting success of ducks was above that in 1959 at Spirit Lake (WA). In North Dakota, breeding pair counts at Des Lacs Refuge disclosed 1,062 pairs this year as compared with 1,022 pairs in 1959 and 1,464 in 1958; but to-date production promised to be better than last year (HB); at Slade National Wildlife Refuge, Dawson, nesting success was good and brood sizes above average (Robert Timmerman); at Lower Souris Refuge, though breeding pairs went down from 1959, preliminary brood counts indicated a better production than last year (RJ). In

South Dakota brood success was better than average at Waubay Refuge (JC) and elsewhere in the eastern pothole section of the state. Mallards apparently were declining. In North Dakota the chronology brood counts at Des Lacs Refuge, begun the last week in June, indicated that 43 percent of the duck production for 1959 consisted of Mallards, as compared with 13 percent for I960 — a drastic reduction (HB); nesting and production were low this season at Snake Creek and Lower Souris Refuges where breeding pair counts were down from 1959 (DMcG, RJ). Gadwalls were up in North Dakota at Des Lacs Refuge where they made up 51 percent of the population as compared with 32 percent in 1959 — a marked increase (HB). At Snake Creek Refuge they were especially numerous; but at Lower Souris Refuge breeding pairs were reduced from 1959 (DMcG, RJ). However, they were apparently doing well at Saskatoon, Sask. (CSH). Green-winged Teal, rare nesters in South Dakota, produced young at Waubay Refuge (JC). In South Dakota Wood Ducks were noted uncommonly at Waubay Refuge (JC); a female was seen in mid-June at Oakwood Lakes near Brookings (Mrs. DH). Redheads and Canvasbacks showed a serious decline in the Yorkton, Sask. area (CSH); not one Redhead was known positively to nest in the Wascana Marsh at Regina although adults were seen there all summer (FB). In North Dakota no Redhead broods were found at Des Lacs Refuge (HB). In South Dakota, pairs were abundant in spring at Waubay Refuge and several areas produced good hatches (JC), but farther south few broods were seen (Lloyd Oldenburg). Canvasbacks showed a slight improvement at Des Lacs, N. Dak.: six broods this year, two last year (HB); at Waubay Refuge, S. Dak., only two broods were sighted this summer (JC). Des Las Refuge held not a single scaup brood this season (HB). A Harlequin Duck, found on a slough in the Conrich, Alta. region on June 28 by I. Halliday and Cedric Hitchen, was of unusual interest. "I know of no similar record," wrote Hitchen.

Hawks— The nest of a Cooper's Hawk with three small young, found west of Calgary on June 24 and photographed by Miss K. Hodges, was of more than ordinary interest for the area (CH). In Saskatchewan Red-tailed Hawks equaled 1959 in the number of nests and fledged young at Spirit Lake (WA) and returned to an expected average of two young per nest in the Yorkton area, where 46 young were banded in 22 nests (CSH). Fewer than usual, however, nested in the sandhills at Upham, N. Dak. (RJ). In North Dakota two young Golden Eagles were observed in Theodore Roosevelt National Park at Medora on July 22 (Arthur Henderson); and a nest with two eggs, found in the badlands at Watford City, hatched on May 1 (Mrs. RG). In Saskatchewan two young, found on the South Saskatchewan River south of Lucky Lake, were banded on June 24 (CSH). The young of the Prairie and Peregrine Falcon in several nests at Red Deer and Calgary were banded in June and July by W.E. McKay; in one instance, the adult Prairie Falcons had been shot and the young were found starved (D. Dekker, WEMcK).

Pheasants— In North Dakota Ring-necked Pheasants were down on Lower Souris Refuge (RJ); at Des Lacs Refuge a brood of six was observed in August—the first in two years at the refuge (HB). In South Dakota spring surveys this year indicated a 56 percent decline in the pheasant population as compared with the 1959 surveys. As examples, last spring Clark County had 1.65 birds per mile; this spring, .79. Last season Campbell County had 1.05 and Edmunds County 1.97 but only .50 and .85 respectively this season (*Argus Leader*, Sioux Falls, July 17). Despite considerable variation, by mid-August the hatch in some localities apparently was as good as last year's, higher in others and decidedly lower in several areas. In Brookings County an estimated 20 percent of the hens were chickless (*Ibid.*, August 14).

Rails, Shorebirds— A Virginia Rail, quite scarce in the Coleharbor, N. Dak., area, was seen flying over a pothole between Lostwood and Des Lacs Refuges on August 4 (Merrill Hammond, *fide* DMcG); and one was seen in Wascana Marsh, Regina, Sask., where last year an adult with three young established a breeding record (FB). At Scenic, S. Dak., 22 Long-billed Curlews were seen feeding in a short-grass field on July 28 (Dr. N.R. Whitney, Jr.). Several Piping Plover nests were observed in South Waubay Lake on June 14—an unusual occurrence for this area (JC). American Avocets, so far observed only south of Regina, Sask., this year were seen north of the city (FB). The most abundant shorebird at Snake Creek Refuge, Coleharbor, N. Dak., this year was Wilson's Phalarope, numbering 200 to 300 birds (DMcG). A surprising fall arrival date for Northern Phalarope was recorded at Spirit Lake, Sask.—a flock of 60 July 31 (WA).

Gulls, Terns— Forster's Terns, nesting with Common Terns on a gravel island in Wascana Marsh were photographed with chicks and eggs on June 20 to establish a first breeding record for the Regina Sask. district (FB, Elmer Fox). The Regina region's first Caspian Tern observation was recorded on June 20 (Reg Fox, EF, FB). Black Terns in considerably greater numbers than usual were observed at Brown's and Rattlesnake Lakes, near Billings, Mont., in June and July (Mrs. PH).

Doves, Cuckoos— Mourning Doves were down from last year at Des Lacs Refuge, N. Dak., but nesting success seemed to be promising (HB). In South Dakota they were down locally from a half to a quarter of last year's number—a loss laid partly to promiscuous poison spraying (J.W. Johnson). At Watertown 50 percent of this season's hatch was lost to Blue Jay predation, in the opinion of Dr. L.J. Moriarity. But they were abundant in the Sioux Falls area (HK). Yellow-billed Cuckoos in greater than ordinary numbers appeared in eastern South Dakota. At Waubay Refuge they were more common than the Black-billed; at Pickerel Lake near Waubay one flew into a picture window on July 23 (Herman Chilson) and at Sioux Falls three hit windows and were collected as specimens (HK).

Owls— In Saskatchewan 150 Great Horned Owls were banded in 66 nests in the Dubuc, MacNutt, Salt-coats, Invermay and Langenburg areas (CSH)—something of an all-time record for the season. In the Dunleath, Willowbrook, Salt-coats and Stornaway areas, west, southeast and northeast of Yorkton, Sask., 74 Long-eared Owls were banded in 19 nests (CSH). Last season's unharvested grain fields in the Prairie Provinces, encouraging a large rodent population, apparently attracted Short-eared Owls to several localities. They became resident in the Spirit Lake district and were frequently seen hunting at dusk (WA). An evening's drive of eight miles on August 8 at Conrich, Alta. yielded 29 Short-ears, mostly immatures, sitting on fence posts (CH). In 20 nests, 68 young were banded in the general Yorkton district, including Theodore, Saltcoats, Hazelcliffe and Stornaway (west, southeast and northeast). Nests in unthreshed swaths in stubbles found between May 4 and 13 represented the first nesting dates for the Yorkton district (CSH).

Kingfishers, Goatsuckers, Woodpeckers— A pair of Belted Kingfishers, nesting at Regina, Sask., was a first breeding record; the nest was vandalized and the five young died (FB). Poorwills, usually present in some numbers in Rapid City, S. Dak., were not observed nor heard during the period (NRW, Jr.). The Red-headed Woodpecker, noted south of Regina, Sask. on June 11, has been recorded in the area on only three previous occasions (FB). On May 30 a party had a good view of three Black-backed Three-toed Woodpeckers at Jewel Cave in South Dakota (NRW, Jr.).

Flycatchers, Swallows, Wrens— The male Scissor-tailed Flycatcher seen south of Kenmare, N. Dak., on July 12 by the Gammells and the Rytters, Russell, Darrel and Viggo, was probably a state record (Mrs. RG). The 12 nests of the Purple Martin observed at Brookings, S. Dak., produced 45 young; 16 adults were banded (Mrs. DH). Since the first breeding of purple Martins at Regina in 1958, martin houses have been erected and the species is doing very well (FB). Long-billed Marsh Wrens were especially numerous at Waubay Refuge and had a successful year at Milbank in South Dakota (JC, LE); apparently they were back at Wascana Marsh, Regina, Sask. after an absence of some years when a road and a bridge went through their territory (FB). The second known breeding record of the Rock Wren was established at Kenmare, N. Dak., on August 4 (Mrs. RG); and a singing Rock Wren heard on July 3, at Pilot Butte, Sask. was noteworthy (RF, EF, FB).

Catbirds, Thrushes, Warblers— Catbirds had a good year at Winnipeg, Man. (HH); in South Dakota, they increased somewhat at Milbank (LE); but at Sioux Falls only eight were observed in spring migration and no nestings were reported (HK); none was seen at Brookings nor reported for the area (Mrs. DH). In Brookings Robins were down by about one half (Mrs. DH); at Huron there were only five percent to ten percent as many this year as last. "It takes six mist nets to get as many birds now as we did last year with one," wrote J.W. Johnson; they were scarce at Milbank (LE) but broods were good at Sioux Falls (HK). Yellow Warblers were reduced below the number of 1959 at Kenmare, N. Dak. (Mrs. RG). The Blackpoll Warbler, a scarce bird in the Calgary, Alta. district, was seen at Inglewood on May 24 (KH). A pair of Yellow-breasted Chats with a single bob-tailed young was observed at Bredin, Sask. on July 21—an unusual if not a rare occurrence (FB). Male and female American Redstarts were banded at Sturgis, S. Dak., on July 26 and 30 (Harold Wagar).

Blackbirds, Fringillids— The Bobolink, last seen at Calgary in 1958, nested there and in the Madden area this season, nests, eggs, and young being found (CH, KH). A pair of adult Orchard Orioles, observed in Kenmare, N. Dak., in June and July with immatures seen later in the month, apparently indicated breeding—a first record for this area (Mrs. RG). In South Dakota Cassin's Finches were noted at Jewel Cave on May 30 and at Nemo on July 10 (Dennis Carter, NRW, Jr.). American Goldfinches were scarce at Sioux Falls; and at Pickerel Lake, near Waubay; the first and last individual was seen on June 19 (HK, HC). Something like an irruption of Lark Buntings took place at Snake Creek Refuge, N. Dak., with between 10,000 and 15,000 birds on the refuge. "They were nesting everywhere," wrote David McGlachlin. Individuals were seen as far east as Carrington in east-central North Dakota (Mrs. RG); they nested at Watertown, S. Dak., an uncommon occurrence so far east in South Dakota (LJM). For the first time in ten years they nested within the city limits of Regina; "the countryside was flooded with them," reported Frank Brazier. They showed a sudden increase in the Maple Creek-Swift Current, Sask. area (Steve Mann, CSH). The nest and egg of the Field Sparrow discovered at Tuxedo on June 30 was a first nesting record for Manitoba and only "the third or fourth record" for the Province (HH). Swamp Sparrows, reported infrequently from eastern South Dakota, were heard singing in Minnehaha and Lake Counties on July 10 and 25 and August 1, although nests were not found (HK). While Kenmare reported a drastic reduction of Clay-colored Sparrows, they were quite common at Snake Creek Refuge, N. Dak., and the most abundant native breeder at Regina, Sask. (Mrs. RG, DMcG, FB). A new colony of Chestnut-collared Longspurs at Saskatoon provided the most northerly breeding record in Saskatchewan (RB).

Fall Migration, 1960

Most of the Region experienced real "butterfly" weather for the period with Common Sulphurs (*Colias philodice*) on the wing at Sioux Falls, S. Dak., on November 13. Warm and dry conditions were reported at almost every station. August and September set near record-breaking highs in southern Saskatchewan and southeastern Alberta (J.B. Gollop) and in South Dakota (Weather Bureau, Huron, J.W. Johnson). October and November were relatively mild and dry with sharp dips and snowstorms during October 18–19 in some localities. While precipitation was scarce in many areas, including portions of the Prairie Provinces, none was recorded in October and little in November for the Kenmare, N. Dak., region (Homer Bradley). However, eastern South Dakota received above normal and the Edmonton region excessive amounts of moisture (JBG, Weather Bureau, Sioux Falls). Nevertheless, water levels for much of the Region remained low or fell to little or nothing. Generally, the migration was gradual, often thin and late and never spectacular with no unusual waves or build-ups. The late fall and dry weather apparently resulted in the easiest and fastest harvest on record in the Regina region and thus averted if it did not solve the Sandhill Crane problem northwest of Regina, Sask. (JBG). The noteworthy concentration of geese in southern Saskatchewan was more "a case of halving the habitat (excessive flooding of the Athabasca Delta) rather than doubling the goose population," writes J.B. Gollop, Canadian Wildlife Service. Incredible as it seems, heavy burning of potholes and roadside ditches over most of North Dakota and northeastern South Dakota destroyed much of the lush nesting cover produced this year (USF&W Summary, October 21 and November 14).

Loons, Grebes, Herons, Egrets— A Common Loon, for which apparently no previous record is extant for the Rapid City, S. Dak., vicinity, was observed on November 13 (N.R. Whitney, Jr., Richard Hurd). Several Pacific Loons, extremely rare in the Edmonton, Alta. region and recorded on only three previous occasions in the Province, were identified at Losegun Lake on September 20 (Robert Lister). The Red-necked Grebe, identified on the School of Mines campus, Rapid City, and banded on November 9, was a first for the region (NRW). In North Dakota Western Grebes peaked at 345 at Des Lacs National Refuge, Kenmare, on September 15, as compared with 30 on September 4, 1959 (HB); at Tewaukon National Refuge, Cayuga, 150 were counted where only 40 were seen last year (James Monnie); at Rapid City the two birds found on the college campus on October 17 were uncommon occurrences (Harry Behrens, *fide* NRW). Great Blue Herons, relatively scarce these several past years at Des Lacs Refuge, Kenmare, were in greater abundance than in any previous fall migration at Huron, S. Dak. (HB, Mrs. H.M. Pierce). A Green Heron, seldom reported in fall migration in South Dakota, was noted at Clear Lake on September 17 (Alfred Peterson). An immature Black-crowned Night Heron was seen on August 20 at Namaka Lake in the Strathmore area (Cedric Hichon) where the first Alberta specimen was collected in August 1958. Although a colony was discovered at Beaverhills Lake near Edmonton, no nests were found in the Strathmore area (E.D. Beacham). At LaCreek National Refuge, Martin, S. Dak., this species was about half as numerous as in 1959 when 400 were totaled in late summer (C.A. Hughlett). A single American Bittern, seldom observed at Des Lacs National Refuge, Kenmare, N. Dak., was noted on September 22; and only one was seen at Brandt, S. Dak., this fall, September 19 (HB, AP). A Common Egret was observed at Milbank, S. Dak., late in August (Lowry Elliott).

Swans, Geese— In North Dakota Whistling Swans were up 50 percent from 1959 at Arrowwood Refuge, Kensal (John Frye), and peaked at 513 on October 29 at Des Lacs Refuge, Kenmare, compared to 279 on October 30, 1959, and 73 in 1958; they totaled 275 at Tewaukon Refuge, Cayuga, much lower than last year's 400–460 birds but much above the previously reported high of 40 birds for the area (HB, JM); they were down at Bowdoin National Refuge, Malta, Mont. (Baine Cater); in Saskatchewan they peaked at 2,900 at the north end of Last Mountain Lake on November 3 (Alex Dzubin); at Spirit Lake a flock of 35 appeared on November 8 — a late date (William Anaka). Canada Geese were reduced 75 percent from the 1959 total at Arrowwood Refuge, Kensal, N. Dak.; they peaked 112 on November 3 at Des Lacs Refuge, Kenmare, compared with 250 on October 30, 1959; they were more common than in previous years at Spirit Lake, Sask., and slightly up at Bowdoin Refuge, Malta, Mont., though fewer than in other years (JF, HB, WA, BC). At Tewaukon Refuge, Cayuga, N. Dak., the "small races" increased to 4,500 this fall as compared with 3,500 in 1959 and 1,500 in 1958 (JM). All species of geese including Canada were at least twice as abundant this year as last year in the Kindersley district (JBG). White-fronted Geese turned up at Last Mountain Lake in larger numbers than local people could recall for seven years (JBG); although a regular but uncommon migrant at Waubay National Refuge, Waubay, S. Dak., they totaled 1,100 birds on October 10 (J. Carlsen). At Bowdoin Refuge, Malta, Mont., however, only a few appeared (BC). Snow Geese numbered 29,500 on October 17 in the Kindersley, Sask. district but at Tewaukon Refuge, Cayuga, N. Dak., where flocks of 8000 to 10,000 Snow and Blue Geese have been tallied in previous years, a peak of only 3700 was attained this fall (AD, JM). Fifteen Blue Geese, uncommon in the Malta, Mont., area, appeared at Bowdoin Refuge this fall (BC). Of particular interest in the estimated 1,000 Snows at Beaverhills Lake near Edmonton, Alta. were the numerous juveniles (RL). A single Blue Goose, for which there are few Alberta records, appeared at Sullivan Lake in the Hanna district on September 25 (CH, Ian Halliday, EDB). The 3,500 plus or minus Ross' Geese, present in the Kindersley district of southern Saskatchewan from September 6 to October 29, were probably half the population of this species (AD, *fide* JBG).

Waterfowl— While there were no unusual observations or spectacular "waves," there were apparent increases in some species in localized areas. All species were up at Lostwood Refuge, Lostwood, N. Dak., with a peak population of 18,600 birds from October 2 to 8 compared with last year's 2,800 (Donald White). At Tewaukon Refuge, Cayuga, the peak of 15,000 birds was only slightly above the number for the past two years (JM). But in South Dakota the total at Waubay Refuge, Waubay, was more than twice last year's number of 14,500 (J. Carlsen). In Montana the peak of 66,025 at Bowdoin Refuge, Malta, was up ten percent over last year's count (BC). In Saskatchewan, Mallard totals were lower than in 1959 in the Spirit Lake district, even with an apparently successful hatch (William Anaka); at Des Lacs Refuge in North Dakota the peak of 19,600 on October 15 was much higher than the 6,370 peak on August 28 in 1959 but below the total of 25,000 in 1957 (HB); they were up at LaCreek National Refuge, Martin, S. Dak., peaking at 34,500 birds compared with 25,000 last year (CAH). Gadwalls increased at Des Lacs Refuge, Kenmare, totaling 4,315 on September 15, as compared with 1,360 on October 9 last year and 1,000 in 1957 (HB). In North Dakota large flocks of Green-winged Teal appeared at Arrowwood Refuge, Kensal, during September 15 to 26 (JF); they were in greater numbers than usual at Slade National Refuge, Dawson (Robert Timmerman) and at Lostwood Refuge, Lostwood (DN). In South Dakota an unusual concentration of some 500 birds appeared in a flooded cornfield on September 9 near Madison in Lake County (HK, Herman F. and Lois Chapman). At Des Lacs Refuge, Kenmare, N. Dak., American Widgeon climbed remarkably—8,575 on September 15 for a peak as compared to 1,200 on September 17, 1959, 900 in 1958 and 800 in 1957 (HB); but they dropped from 4,000 in 1959 to 1100 this year at LaCreek Refuge, Martin, S. Dak. (CAH). A single Wood Duck on August 29 was the first seen at Slide Refuge, Dawson, N. Dak. (RT). Redheads showed up in the largest concentration since 1955 at Arrowwood Refuge, Kensal (JF); they rose to a peak of 2,115 on October 13 at Des Lacs Refuge, Kenmare, as compared with 1,225 last season, but were far below the 6,050 total in 1958 (HB); they doubled last year's population of 476 at LaCreek Refuge, Martin, S. Dak. (CAH). The 43 Ring-necked Ducks noted during the last half of September were the first of this species seen at Slade Refuge, Dawson, writes Robert Timmerman; no Ring-necks were reported from LaCreek Refuge, Martin, S. Dak., last year, but over 1,100 this year (CAH). Canvasbacks in the largest concentrations since 1955 were seen at Arrowwood Refuge this season (JF); they peaked at 5,300 on September 13, as compared with 1,065 last year and 4,070 in 1958 at Des Lacs Refuge in North Dakota (HB); and they were up from 860 in 1959 to 1,275 this year at LaCreek Refuge in South Dakota (CAH). A single Oldsquaw, rare in southern Alberta, was observed at Conrich on November 4 and 5 (EDB, CH, IH). Two White-winged Scoters, uncommon visitors at Des Lacs Refuge, were recorded on October 13; this species appeared in good numbers on Isogun Lake, 120 miles northwest of Edmonton, Alta. on September 10. With them in large numbers were Surf Scoters for which fall records in Alberta are comparatively rare (RL). In Saskatchewan the Hooded Merganser observed at Spirit Lake on November 6 and the female of this species at Regina on November 8 are infrequent visitors (WA, Frank Brazier).

Hawks— The Cooper's Hawks recorded at Calgary, Alta. on October 9 and at LaCreek Refuge, Martin, S Dak., on September 8 were rather rare observations (EDB, CAH). A fairly large migration of Red-tailed Hawks passed through the Edmonton district during October 8 and 9 (RL); they were numerous in the Brandt and Martin, S. Dak., localities (AP, CAH). Harlan's and Krider's Red-tails on November 16 were both firsts for LaCreek Refuge, Martin, where a Red-shouldered Hawk on October 9 was also a rarity (CAH). Two

Krider's in northeastern South Dakota were noteworthy appearances (AP). A notable concentration of an estimated 100 Swainson's Hawks gathered in the Regina district during the first two weeks in September (FB). More Rough-legged Hawks than usual were sighted at Milbank and Sioux Falls, S. Dak., this season (LE, J.S. Findley, HK); ten were counted near Regina, Sask. on October 20 (FB). Black Gyrfalcons were noteworthy in Alberta, one seen badgering duck decoys on Whitford Lake, near Edmonton on October 15 (RL) and one pursuing a pheasant at Cassils in the Calgary district on November 19 (John Waychik, *fide* EDB). Pigeon Hawks, infrequent in eastern South Dakota, were observed, one in a Sioux Falls park harrying a group of flickers on September 18, and one near Brandt disturbing a flock of longspurs on November 13 (HK, AP).

Cranes— An adult Whooping Crane was identified at Ilo National Refuge, Dunn Center, N. Dak., on October 10 (HB). Two flocks of Sandhill Cranes were sighted near Huron, S. Dak., on October 23, the first report for the species in many years (Marion Ritchey, *fide* J.W. Johnson); an estimated 10,000 passed over Malta, Mont. late in September and early October, a larger number than for some time (BC).

Shorebirds— In South Dakota nine American Golden Plover were discovered at Webster on October 21 (Herman Chilson) and 25 near Castlewood on October 24 (AP). Forty-three Black-bellied Plover were observed at Des Lacs Refuge. Kenmare, on September 15 and four at Spirit Lake, Sask. from October 18 to 26, where they are infrequent and irregular fall migrants (AP, WA). Forty Stilt Sandpipers were counted at Lake Albert near Brandt, S. Dak., on October 27 (AP). An extraordinary shorebird record for the Calgary area was a Western Sandpiper on August 21 at Sullivan Lake where the bird was observed at length with a 20x spotting scope and 12x50 binoculars. The only known Alberta record was made in May 1955 and the species is still on the hypothetical list for the Province (CH, IH, *fide* EDB). An unusually large flock of Marbled Godwits, 150 plus, was observed at North Waubay Lake, Day County, on July 9, probably composed mostly of non-breeding birds (LE). Four Sanderlings were recorded at Kenmare, N. Dak., on August 4 (Mrs. Robert Gammell). A remarkable gathering of some 2,000 Wilson's Phalaropes was at Des Lacs Refuge in late July and early August (HB). The 40 Northern Phalaropes reported on July 31 at Spirit Lake, Sask. apparently made up the flock noted there on August 2 and 7 (WA).

Jaegers, Gulls— Noteworthy were the two sight records near Calgary, Alta. of Parasitic Jaegers, one seen at Morley on September 24 attacking a Red-tailed Hawk (DD, CH, *fide* EDB) and one at Sullivan Lake on August 19 (DD). Six Short-billed Gulls were identified among Franklin's and Ring-billed Gulls on the Bow River near Calgary on August 24 and closely observed on several occasions during the following ten days of their stay (IH, *fide* EDB). Three Bonaparte's Gulls, scarce migrants in southern Alberta, were identified at

Keho Lake near Lethbridge on October 24 (EDB); the same species, observed for the first time in 1959 in the Spirit Lake, Sask. district, was noted daily from September 4 to 26 (WA).

Owls, Nighthawks, Swifts— "The best owl record to date" was a Hawk-Owl seen at Waiparous Creek in the Calgary district on November 13 (DD). Late dates for Common Nighthawks appeared to be September 20 for Winnipeg, Man. (Harold Hosford); September 11 for Saskatoon, Sask. (JBG); September 4 for Rapid City, S. Dak. (NRW) and September 10 for Billings, Mont. (Mrs. Philip Hendricks). A flock of 20 White-throated Swifts feeding over Canyon Lake near Rapid City on August 30 seemed to be late (NRW).

Woodpeckers, Swallows, Jays— A Red-shafted Flicker, reported only once in ten years for the area, was seen on September 30 at Sioux Falls, S. Dak. (HK). A Black-backed Three-toed Woodpecker, infrequent anywhere in South Dakota, was noted on December 3 near Sturgis (Harold Wager). Fifty Cliff Swallows were seen entering and leaving old nests plastered on a coulee wall near Billings, Mont., on November 20—perhaps an unusual occurrence and a late date (Mrs. PH). A Gray Jay, seen on November 6 at Huron, S. Dak., was considerably out of its normal range (George Jonkels, *fide* JWJ).

Thrashers, Thrushes, Kinglets— A Sage Thrasher, identified at Park Headquarters on September 24, was a most uncommon occurrence for the South Dakota Badlands Monument (John Palmer, *fide* NRW). Eastern Bluebirds apparently continue to be scarce. Only one pair was observed in the Winnipeg area where formerly as many as eight pairs have been seen (HH). Flocks upward of 100 Mountain Bluebirds were observed between Cockrane, Alta. and the first ranges of the Rockies on September 15 and 16 (IH). Golden-crowned Kinglets, scarce at Milbank in South Dakota, were numerous at Sioux Falls, 16 being counted on October 10 (LE, HK). Ruby-crowned Kinglets were unusually plentiful at Sioux Falls where some were banded (JSF) and where a flock of 40 was noted on September 24 and one of 30 on October 11 (HK).

Waxwings, Starlings— Bohemian Waxwings appeared at Belfield, N. Dak., on October 24 and at Milbank, S. Dak., on December 3, when 20 fed on Mountain Ash berries (Mrs. Richard Swenson, LE). In Alberta Starlings gathered in huge flocks at Edmonton up to November 13 (RL) and in Calgary until late in October (EDB, J. Clarke); at Bowdoin Refuge in Malta their numbers were 50 percent greater than last year (BC).

Warblers— A Golden-winged Warbler, identified on September 6, was a rare sight in Winnipeg, Man. (HH). Orange-crowned Warblers, not uncommon at Milbank (LE), were abundant at Sioux Falls, as many as 51 being counted in a two-hour period on September 23; a late date was October 18 (HK), although one was still lingering in Calgary, Alta. on October 7 (J. Clarke). Four Parula Warblers, not often reported in fall migration in South Dakota, appeared in Sioux Falls on September 20 (HK). A Black-throated Blue Warbler, found dead on October 26, was a first specimen record for the Regina district and a third occurrence for Saskatchewan (FR, R.W. Nero in *Blue Jay*, 18:156). Myrtle Warblers stayed as late as September 24 in Saskatoon, Sask. (JBG). In South Dakota they were scarce at Milbank (LE); one was banded on September 28 and two on October 5 at Sturgis where in the Audubon's Warbler's range they are seldom reported (HW); a "wave" of this species passed through Webster on September 27 (HC); and in Sioux Falls where they have been scarce these last two seasons, flocks totaled 38 on October 6 and 69 on October 8 (HK). Though MacGillivray's Warbler, out of its range in eastern South Dakota, is a rare occurrence east of the Missouri River, one was found dead in Watertown on August 15 (J. Moriarty, Herman Chapman, HK), one was banded and photographed on September 4 in Sioux Falls (JSF) and another one was identified on September 8 (HK).

Fringillids— A late date for the Rose-breasted Grosbeak near Sioux Falls occurred on November 13 (Charles Rogge, Max Pierce, *fide* HK). Common Rosy Finches were reported as numerous in the Priddis district in southern Alberta on October 16 (Alfred Schultze). Evening Grosbeaks in small numbers appeared at Kenmare, N. Dak., on October 17 (Mrs. RG), and at Calgary, Alta. on October 19 (J. Clarke); in South Dakota they were noted at Sturgis on October 22 (HW), at Huron on October 21 and November 17, at LaCreek Refuge, Martin, on December 4; and at Rapid City flocks were conspicuous (NRW). The Purple Finch, killed in flight against a window at Rapid City in November, was a probable first record for the area; several flocks were reported during that month (NRW). A flock of 11 Pine Grosbeaks on November 26 at Calgary was worthy of mention (EDB). In South Dakota they appeared at Sioux Falls on October 29 and November 13, the second occurrence in ten years (HK); at Huron, where they are rare, they were seen from November 2 to 24 (Mrs. HMP); at Brookings on November 3 (Mrs. David Holden); and at Waubay Refuge on November 23 when a dead bird was found and where several were seen a few days later (J. Carlsen). Red Crossbills broke out in many places: at Calgary on October 2 (J. Clarke) and October 19 (EDB); at Kenmare, Foxholm, Upham, and Mandan in North Dakota between September 11 and December 4 (Mrs. RG); in South Dakota at Milbank on October 6 (LE), at Huron during October 16–23 (JWJ); at Brookings on October 6 (Mrs. DH); at Webster on October 7 (HC); in Sioux Falls from September 15 to December 15 (HK); and at Waubay Refuge, Waubay, on October 7 where they were the first for the refuge and the area (J. Carlsen, HC), although reported previously elsewhere in the state. White-winged Crossbills, last observed in the Calgary district during 1958–1959, were distributed in small numbers there on November 13 and at Bowness on November 6 (EBD, J. Clarke). In South Dakota 25 White-wings were found in spruce trees at Watertown on November 11 (JM) and several at Huron on November 16 (Mrs. HMP). Nelson's Sharptailed Sparrow, infrequently encountered in South Dakota in fall migration, was closely studied on October 20 near Sioux Falls (HK, Dilwyn Rogers). A

Fox Sparrow, very rare in any season at Huron, was identified on October 26 (JWJ, Mrs. HMP); and one was seen at Sioux Falls on October 23 (HK). Bird-bander Lowry Elliott, Milbank, S. Dak, trapped a late Clay-colored Sparrow on December 7. A Lincoln's Sparrow was banded on October 12 at Sturgis, S. Dak.—a species not often reported from western South Dakota (HW). Tremendous flocks of Lapland Longspurs appeared at Kenmare, N. Dak., where Dr. and Mrs, Robert Gammell reported they banded 2250 individuals between October 7 and 23. Nine Smith's Longspurs were banded at Kenmare in late September and early October.

NOTES

Cover: The cover painting by Sioux Falls artist Mark Anderson was the winning entry in the 2005–2006 Federal Duck Stamp Contest, the image of a pair of Hooded Mergansers taking first place over 223 other entries. Established in 1934, the Federal Duck Stamp program has played an important role in preserving wetlands and wildlife habitats, two of Herbert Krause's greatest concerns as an ornithologist. Mark Anderson is a self-taught wildlife artist who began painting in 1980 and today can claim 15 stamp wins to his credit.

"Song Tomorrow": Krause was a close observer of the natural world well before he became a dedicated ornithologist. "Song Tomorrow," included in the master's thesis he submitted at the University of Iowa in 1935, appeared in the published collection *Neighbor Boy* in 1939.

"The Ornithology of the Major Long Expedition": In this essay for the *Minnesota Naturalist* for September 1956, and its companion piece the following year about the mammals observed on the expedition, Krause continued to deepen and broaden his interest in natural history.

"Song Sparrows": Sometime in the spring of 1945 Krause began his study of ornithology. In this short piece and three others published in the *Fergus Falls Daily Journal* on October 19, November 12 and 26, and December 1, 1947, he presents short observations about bird life in his characteristically pictorial prose.

"Birding in the Sioux Falls Area": In Pettingill's *A Guide to Bird Finding West of the Mississippi* (New York, Oxford University Press, 1953) this piece is titled simply "Sioux Falls." Krause's copy of the book is inscribed: "To you, Herbert Krause, who creates exciting incidents and living, breathing people out of words–with my everlasting admiration and deep appreciation. [signed] Olin Sewall Pettingill, Jr."

"The Black Hills of South Dakota": Professor O.S. Pettingill Jr., of the Cornell Bird Laboratories was so impressed by Krause's ornithological knowledge and "his smooth-flowing descriptive style and meaty anecdotes" that he invited the novelist to contribute to his book on American birds. This chapter appeared in *The Bird Watcher's America* in 1965.

"Geese Along the Missouri": This chapter about migrating flocks of geese from Pettingill's *Bird Watcher's America* (1965) appears in the section titled "Migration Spectacles." Krause's pictorial writing captures well "the whirl and surge of this contagious movement," "one of the continent's great spectacles."

"Trailing Lewis and Clark": In this guest column, also written for Pettingill, Krause lays out an historical and ornithological tour from Elk Point to Chamberlain. The piece appeared in *Audubon Magazine*, March–April 1966.

"Distribution of the Cardinal in South Dakota": Dr. Sven G. Froiland, Krause's co-author, joined the faculty at Augustana in 1946, taught biology, and served as chairman of that department and of the Natural Science Division. He succeeded Krause as executive director of the Center for Western Studies, retiring in 1987.

"Nesting of a Pair of Canada Warblers": Published first in *The Living Bird* in 1965, the piece was accompanied by a full-color photo, "Male Canada Warbler at the Nest," taken in northern Michigan by Betty Darling Cottrille. Krause identified the article as coming from the "Department of Biology, Augustana College, Sioux Falls, South Dakota." His department was in fact English and he also carried the designation "Writer-in-Residence"at the college.

"A Census of the Breeding Bird Populations in an Aspen Plot": Prepared for a course in Advanced Ornithology at the University of Michigan Biological Studies, this piece is published here for the first time.

"The McCown's Longspur, A Life History": Printed first in Arthur Cleveland Bent's *Life Histories* Series, the study was issued separately in 1968 by MDB Publishing House, in Manila, the Philippines, where Krause was a visiting Rockefeller Professor of English at the University of the Philippines. He dedicated the little book to "Herman and Lois Chapman, Pioneers in South Dakota bird study, who first introduced me to the art of recognizing identification marks in the field." He acknowledged "all who responded to my letters of inquiry about birds in particular regions, especially Canadian friends and contributors." He acknowledged specifically Dr. C. Stuart Houston of Saskatoon, Dr. Timothy Myers of Calgary, Robert E. Stewart of Jamestown, Dr. Olin Sewall Pettingill, Jr., Director, the Laboratory of Ornithology, Cornell University, "for the kind of spacious awareness which defies words," and to Dr. Oliver L. Austin, Jr., Florida State Museum, "without whose understanding, encouragement, and patience this project would never have got off the ground in the first place." Krause added that the article "has been slightly revised and augmented since its first appearance."

"Nesting Sites of the Birds of the Audubon Center of Greenwich, Connecticut": Written in the summer of 1964 at the Audubon Camp of Connecticut, this article appears in print here for the first time. The compilation is remarkable for the range of nesting sites that Krause has identified for the 179 species of birds selected. The Hooded Merganser, for example, listed among the "cavity nesters" and pictured on the cover of this book, is to be found nesting in "cavity of any type in forested watery places though site may sometimes be some distance from water."

"The Bald Eagle": Between 1961 and 1969, while he was lecturing abroad and carrying out research projects for the Rockefeller Foundation and the National Endowment for the Humanities, Krause produced little creative work. He began a book on the bald eagle but left it unfinished because new legislation was beginning to ameliorate the environmental effects of DDT and other toxins. This essay, rescued from the rough notes of an address to a PEO group, is as timely in its opposition to pesticides as it was when it was delivered in 1964.

"Adventure Lit Their Star": Behind this review of Kenneth Allsop's popular book lies an unusual editorial misadventure: Krause's piece appeared in *The Wilson Bulletin* for 17 June 1966 in a form twice the present length. In *The Wilson Bulletin* version a page of unrelated matter from another review had been unintentionally inserted beginning in the middle of the third sentence between the words "secluded" and "spots." The intruder has been eliminated in the present printing and now the review appears as Krause originally wrote it.

"President's Page–Purpose of SDOU, June 1957": The SDOU Board of Directors prevailed upon Herbert Krause to fulfill the office of president for the term June 1964 through June 1965 so that he would be the president when SDOU hosted the combined annual meetings of the Wilson Ornithological Society and the Cooper Ornithological Society in June 1965 at Sylvan Lake Lodge. In response to the invitation by Olin Sewell Pettingill, Herbert Krause was the featured speaker at the banquet culminating the historic gathering of two major ornithological organizations at the Black Hills. Krause wrote eight editorials during his two terms as president of the South Dakota Ornithologists' Union, all of them encouraging members in their work of gathering and disseminating information about state birds. Their work, he asserted in the first editorial, "was an important contribution not only to the natural history of South Dakota but also to the conservation of natural resources of the state." At the end of this group of pieces, from 1957 to 1958 and 1964 to 1965, is included a guest editorial to the membership, printed in the March, June 1959 issue, in which Krause urges greater cooperation with other agencies that are involved in the work of conservation and offers a series of recommendations for the further work of the Union, closing with six optimistic words: "The next decade rings with promise."

Section VI, Chapter 3–Forty-two of the forty-four articles printed here appeared in the pages of *South Dakota Bird Notes*, the publication of the South Dakota Ornithologists' Union. The forty-third is "The Black-throated Blue Warbler in South Dakota," published in the South Dakota Academy of Science *Proceedings* in 1958. The forty-fourth is "Pine Siskin Nesting in Eastern South Dakota," published in *The Wilson Bulletin* for September 1954. The articles are arranged in alphabetical order, each of them for the most part relating to a single species.

BIBLIOGRAPHY OF TITLES

by Herbert Krause

"Audubon Warblers Breeding in the Black Hills." *South Dakota Bird Notes* X (2) (June 1958) 28.

"Autumn Plumage." *Fergus Falls* (Minnesota) *Daily Journal*, CXXIX (148) (November 12, 1947).

"The Bald Eagle." Manuscript, (1964).

"Bewick's Wren at Sioux Falls." *South Dakota Bird Notes* III (1) (March 1951) 13.

"Birding in the Sioux Falls, South Dakota, Area" in *A Guide to Bird Finding West of the Mississippi* by Olin Sewall Pettingill, Jr. New York: Oxford University Press, 1953 pp. 491–92.

"The Black Hills of South Dakota" in *The Birdwatcher's America* by Olin Sewall Pettingill, Jr. New York: McGraw Hill, 1965, pp. 143–51; also in *Audubon Magazine*, LXVII (3) (May–June 1965) 140, 142–145.

"Black-Crowned Night Heron Comes to Town." *South Dakota Bird Notes* X (1) (March 1958) 81.

"Black-Throated Blue Warbler in South Dakota." South Dakota Academy of Science, *Proceedings* XXXVII (1958) 107.

"Blue-Winged Warbler." *South Dakota Bird Notes* VI (2) (June 1954) 33.

"Bohemian Waxwings in Sioux Falls." *South Dakota Bird Notes* VII (1) (March 1955) 14.

"Broad-winged Hawks in Eastern South Dakota." Co-author H.F. Chapman. *South Dakota Bird Notes* V (3) (September 1953) 46–47.

"A Census of Breeding Bird Populations in an Aspen Plot" (Burt Township, Cheboygan County, Michigan). Report for Advanced Ornithology (Zoology 209), University of Michigan Biological Station (July 25, 1957).

"Common Grackles on College Campus." *South Dakota Bird Notes* XII (4) (December 1960) 87–88.

"Defensive Flocking." Co-author H.F. Chapman. *South Dakota Bird Notes* III (4) (December 1951) 60–61.

"Distribution of the Cardinal in South Dakota." Co-author Sven G. Froiland. *The Wilson Bull.*, LXVIII (2) (June 1956) 111–117.

"Don't Laugh at the Bird Watcher." *Fergus Falls* [Minnesota] *Daily Journal*, CXXX (13) (December 1, 1947).

"Geese Along the Missouri" in *The Birdwatcher's America* by Olin Sewall Pettingill, Jr. New York: McGraw Hill, 1965, pp. 365–370.

"Gyrfalcon." *South Dakota Bird Notes* VII (3) (September 1955) 48.

"H.F. Chapman." *South Dakota Bird Notes* XIII (3) (September 1961) 60–63.

"Hermit Thrushes at Sioux Falls." South *Dakota Bird Notes* V (3) (September 1953) 43.

"Hudsonian Godwits in Minnehaha County." *South Dakota Bird Notes* IX (3) (September 1957) 45.

"Juncos!" *South Dakota Bird Notes* II (2) (June 1950) 28.

"Kinglets in Sioux Falls." *South Dakota Bird Notes* XII (1) (March 1960) 14–15.

"The McCown's Longspur" in *Life Histories of North American Cardinals, Grosbeaks, Buntings, Towhee, Finches, Sparrows, and Allies; Order Passeriformes of the Family Fringillidae* by Arthur Cleveland Bent and collaborators. Washington, D.C., Smithsonian Institution Press, 1968, pp. 1564–1597; reprinted as a separate pamphlet by MDB Publishing House, Manila, 1968.

"Mighty Hunters are Still Seen on the Ottertail." *Fergus Falls* [Minnesota] *Daily Journal*, CXXX (10) (November 26, 1947) 11.

"Migrating Shorebirds." *South Dakota Bird Notes* II (2) (June 1950) 27.

"Migrating Warblers." *South Dakota Bird Notes* III (3) (September 1951) 42–43.

"Mockingbird in Minnehaha County." *South Dakota Bird Notes* VIII (3) (September 1956) 51–52.

"Nesting of a Pair of Canada Warblers." *The Living Bird*, IV (June 1965) 5–11.

"Nesting Sites of the Birds of the Audubon Center of Greenwich, Connecticut" (Typescript). Greenwich, Connecticut (1964?).

"Night Herons in Park Trees." *South Dakota Bird Notes* IX (3) (September 1957) 48.

"Northern Great Plains Region [Winter Season December 1, 1957–March 31, 1958]." *Audubon Field Notes* 12 (3) (June 1958) 287–289.

"Northern Great Plains Region [Spring Migration April 1–May 31, 1958]." *Audubon Field Notes* 12 (4) (August 1958) 362–364.

"Northern Great Plains Region [Nesting Season June 1–August 15, 1958]." *Audubon Field Notes* 12 (5) (October 1958) 421–423.

"Northern Great Plains Region [Fall Migration August 16–November 30, 1958]." *Audubon Field Notes* 13 (1) (February 1959) 41–43.

"Northern Great Plains Region [Winter Season December 1, 1958–March 31, 1959]." *Audubon Field Notes* 13 (3) (June 1959) 303–304.

"Northern Great Plains Region [Spring Migration April 1–May 31, 1959]." *Audubon Field Notes* 13 (4) (August 1959) 380–381.

"Northern Great Plains Region [Nesting Season June 1–August 15, 1959]." *Audubon Field Notes* 13 (5) (October 1959) 437–439.

"Northern Great Plains Region [Fall Migration August 16–November 30, 1959]." *Audubon Field Notes* 14 (1) (February 1960) 47–50.

"Northern Great Plains Region [Winter Season December 1, 1959–March 31, 1960]." *Audubon Field Notes* 14 (3) (June 1960) 318–320.

"Northern Great Plains Region [Nesting Season June 1–August 15, 1960]." *Audubon Field Notes* 14 (5) (October 1960) 456–459.

"Northern Great Plains Region [Fall Migration August 16–November 30, 1960]." *Audubon Field Notes* 15 (1) (February 1961) 51–54.

"Ornithology in South Dakota before Audubon." South Dakota Academy of Science, *Proceedings*, XXXV (1956) 198–201.

"The Ornithology of the Great Plains." *South Dakota Bird Notes* XVI (1) (March 1964) 12–21.

"Ornithology of the Major Long Expedition, 1823." *Minnesota Naturalist* VII (3) (September 1956) 39–42.

"Palm Warblers at Sioux Falls." *South Dakota Bird Notes* XII (2) (June 1960) 36.

"Peregrine Falcon Near Wall Lake." Co-author Willard Rosine. *South Dakota Bird Notes* VII (3) (September 1955) 45–46.

"Pine Grosbeak in Minnehaha County." *South Dakota Bird Notes* IX (1) (March 1957) 9–10.

"Pine Siskin at Sioux Falls." *South Dakota Bird Notes* V (3) (September 1953) 41.

"Pine Siskin Nesting in Eastern South Dakota." *The Wilson Bull.* LXVI (3) (September 1954) 221–222.

"Prairie Falcon in Minnehaha County." *South Dakota Bird Notes* XI (4) (December 1959) 76–77.

"Preliminary Notes on the Pine Siskin in South Dakota." *South Dakota Bird Notes* VI (3) (September 1954) 41–42, 48.

"President's Page [Accuracy in Birding Observations]." *South Dakota Bird Notes* X (1) (March 1958) 71.

"President's Page [The AOU Check List]." *South Dakota Bird Notes* IX (4) (December 1957) 51.

"President's Page [The Check List of South Dakota Birds]." *South Dakota Bird Notes* IX (3) (September 1957) 35.

"President's Page [Farm Island]." *South Dakota Bird Notes* XVI (3) (September 1964) 59, 68.

"President's Page [Pesticide and Pheasants]." *South Dakota Bird Notes* XVI (4) (December 1964) 83.

"President's Page [Pesticide Menace]." *South Dakota Bird Notes* XVII (1) (March 1965) 3.

"President's Page [Purpose of SDOU]." *South Dakota Bird Notes* IX (2) (June 1957) 19.

"President's Page [SDOU Membership Duties]." *South Dakota Bird Notes* XVI (2) (June 1964) 35.

Progress Report on "An Annotated Bibliography of South Dakota Ornithology, 1794–1954." South Dakota Academy of Sciences *Proceedings* XXXV (1956) 202.

"Query on the Song of the Slate-colored Junco." *South Dakota Bird Notes* I (1) (July 1949) 10–11.

"Red-Breasted Mergansers at Fort Randall." *South Dakota Bird Notes* XXV (1) (March 1973) 11.

"Red-Breasted Nuthatches Store Seeds." *South Dakota Bird Notes* VI (4) (December 1954) 67.

"Red Crossbills Breeding in Black Hills." *South Dakota Bird Notes* X (2) (June, 1959) 32.

"Red-Shafted Flicker in Southeast South Dakota." *South Dakota Bird Notes* VI (4) (December 1954) 68–69.

"Review - Adventure Lit Their Star, by Kenneth Allsop." *The Wilson Bull.* LXXVIII (2) (June 17, 1966) 246–248.

"Review - Bird Guide: Land Birds East of the Rockies by Chester Reed." *South Dakota Bird Notes* VI (4) (December 1954) 59.

"Review - Thoreau on Birds, edited by Helen Cruickshank." *The Wilson Bull.* LXXVII (3) (September 30, 1965) 308–310.

"Roosting Brown Creepers." *South Dakota Bird Notes* XII (1) (March 1960) 16–17.

"Sanderling at Grass Lake." *South Dakota Bird Notes* VIII (3) (September 1956) 50.

"Sandhill Cranes at Sioux Falls." *South Dakota Bird Notes* XI (4) (December 1959) 68–69.

"SDOU…Tomorrow." *South Dakota Bird Notes* XI (1 & 2) (March–June 1959) 6.

"Song Sparrows." *Fergus Falls* [Minnesota] *Daily Journal*, CXXIX (128) (October 18, 1947) 5.

"Trailing Lewis and Clark" in Bird Finding, with Olin Sewall Pettingill, Jr. *Audubon Magazine*, 68 (2) (March–April 1966), 78–80.

"Unusual Migration Waves at Sioux Falls." *South Dakota Bird Notes* XI (4) (December 1959) 72–75, 79.

"The Warbler Wave Along the Big Sioux River: (Minnehaha County, South Dakota)." *South Dakota Bird Notes* II (2) (June 1950) 29.

"Wave of Passerines at Sioux Falls." *South Dakota Bird Notes* XI (1 & 2) (March–June 1959) 36.

"Wave of Yellowlegs in Eastern South Dakota" *South Dakota Bird Notes* XII (3) (September 1960) 58–59.

"White-Winged Crossbill." *South Dakota Bird Notes* VI (4) (December 1954) 65.

"White-Winged Crossbill at Sioux Falls." *South Dakota Bird Notes* IX (3) (September 1957) 42.

"Winter Singing of Cardinals." *South Dakota Bird Notes* IV (1) (March 1952) 13.

"Winter Wren at Sioux Falls." *South Dakota Bird Notes* VII (4) (December 1955) 58–59.

"Yellow-Bellied Sapsucker at Sioux Falls." *South Dakota Bird Notes* V (3) (September 1953) 43.

"Yellow-Throated Warbler in Southeastern South Dakota" *South Dakota Bird Notes* XII (3) (September 1960) 48–49.

"Young of White-Breasted Nuthatch in Newton Hills." *South Dakota Bird Notes* VII (4) (December 1955) 61–62.

INDEX TO COMMON NAMES OF BIRDS